INSPIRE / PLAN / DISCOVER / EXPERIENCE

LONDON

LONDON

CONTENTS

DISCOVER 6

EXPERIENCE 66

NEED TO KNOW 332

Left: The skyscraping Shard in Southwark
Previous: The bustling streets of Piccadilly Circus

DISCOVER

An aerial view of London

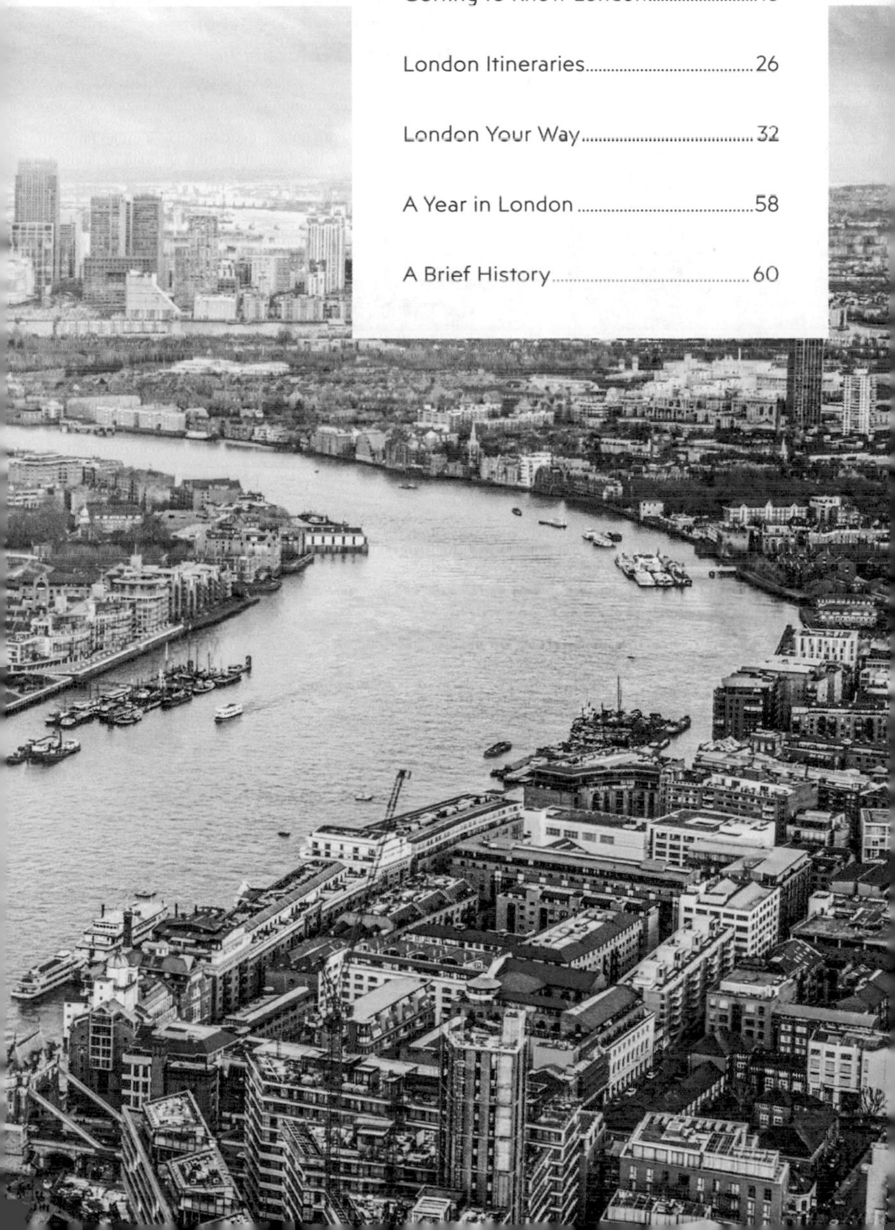

WELCOME TO LONDON

Built on pomp and ceremony, London has become a cosmopolitan capital. This diverse city has it all: amazing art and ground-breaking music, royal palaces and historic pubs, futuristic skyscrapers and picturesque parks. Whatever your dream trip to London includes, this DK Eyewitness Travel Guide is the perfect companion.

1 Enjoying the view on Hampstead Heath

2 A typical London pub

3 Admiring art at the National Gallery

4 Royal Festival Hall on the South Bank

Steeped in history, from the imposing fortress of the Tower of London to graceful Buckingham Palace, it's easy to tread in the footsteps of kings and queens in London. The city is a cultural colossus, brimming with free museums and art galleries, from the National Gallery, with its late-medieval masterpieces, to the Tate Modern's cutting-edge performance works. London also boasts a vibrant music scene and the world's busiest theatre district, the West End. A paradise for foodies, you can sample street food from around the world, as well as dine in an enticing array of Michelin-starred restaurants. Countless wonderful green spaces punctuate the city's heart, including eight royal parks, and swathes of bucolic bliss such as Hampstead Heath are never too far away.

The city's charms extend beyond its centre. Head to places such as Brixton or Richmond to experience the diverse personalities of London's urban villages. Alternatively, escape the crowds at Kew Gardens or the Queen Elizabeth Olympic Park, ambling along the winding trails and landscaped flowerbeds.

With so many different things to discover and experience, London can seem overwhelming. We've broken the city down into easily navigable chapters, with detailed itineraries, expert local knowledge and colourful, comprehensive maps to help you plan the perfect visit. Whether you're staying for a weekend, a week or longer, this Eyewitness guide will ensure that you see the very best London has to offer. Enjoy the book, and enjoy London.

REASONS TO LOVE
LONDON

It's a world in a city. It's a buzzing metropolis. It has a story to tell on every corner. Ask any Londoner and you'll hear a different reason why they love their city. Here, we pick some of our favourites.

1 PRICELESS MUSEUMS AND GALLERIES

Take a turn through Ancient Egypt or meet a roaring dinosaur at one of London's unbeatable museums – and all without spending a penny.

WALKING THE THAMES PATH 2

With 45 km of riverside walkways between Richmond in the west and the Thames Barrier in the east, there is no better way to see the sights.

3 MARKETS

Will it be the tasty treats of Borough (p211) or the kaleido-scopic flowers of Columbia Road (p200)? Browse, haggle and pick up goodies at any one of London's many markets.

POMP AND CEREMONY 4

Time your trip with the Opening of Parliament, the Lord Mayor's Show or the extravagant Trooping the Colour to see London's traditions at their finest.

INCREDIBLE ARCHITECTURE 5

There are architectural treats all over the city. Discover staggering skyscrapers, Brutalist art centres and even a majestic Hindu temple.

NOTTING HILL CARNIVAL 6

Europe's largest street festival is an exuberant celebration of Afro-Caribbean culture that turns Notting Hill into one enormous party (p270).

THE SOUTH BANK 7
Hugging a curve of the River Thames, the South Bank is filled with accessible-to-all institutions of theatre, film, art and music, and buzzing bars perfect for a sundowner.

PARKS AND GARDENS 8
In a city that hums with traffic and noise, it may be a surprise to find green spaces at every turn – so many in fact that London is petitioning for National Park City status.

9 THEATRELAND
From Shakespeare to Pinter, London has always enjoyed a wonderful theatrical tradition, no more so than in the heart of the West End. Book a show for a first-class evening out *(p129)*.

10 GLOBAL RESTAURANT SCENE

Thanks to its multicultural population, London has an enviable array of culinary experiences to tantalise the tastebuds of any foodie.

HOUSES OF PARLIAMENT 11

The Mother of Parliaments, housed in the Gothic Palace of Westminster, is a city icon (p76). Explore the moody interior and discover centuries of turbulent and fascinating history.

A CITY OF PUBS 12

One of Britain's enduring institutions, the pub is ubiquitous on London's streets. And the choice is staggering – from traditional affairs to plucky craft beer breweries.

EXPLORE
LONDON

This guide divides London into 17 colour-coded sightseeing areas, as shown on the map below. Find out more about each area on the following pages. For areas beyond the main city centre see p310.

CAMDEN

London Zoo

Regent's Park

REGENT'S PARK AND MARYLEBONE
p274

MARYLEBONE

PADDINGTON

KENSINGTON, HOLLAND PARK AND NOTTING HILL
p260

NOTTING HILL

MAYFAIR

MAYFAIR AND ST JAMES'S
p86

HOLLAND PARK

Kensington Gardens

Hyde Park

Green Park

Holland Park

Kensington Palace

Buckingham Palace

SOUTH KENSINGTON AND KNIGHTSBRIDGE
p240

KNIGHTSBRIDGE

KENSINGTON

Science Museum

Natural History Museum

Victoria and Albert Museum

CHELSEA AND BATTERSEA
p230

SOUTH KENSINGTON

Ranelagh Gardens

CHELSEA

River Thames

Battersea Park

BATTERSEA

GREAT BRITAIN

Edinburgh

North Sea

Belfast

GREAT BRITAIN

IRELAND

NETHERLANDS

Birmingham

Cardiff

LONDON

BELGIUM

Atlantic Ocean

FRANCE

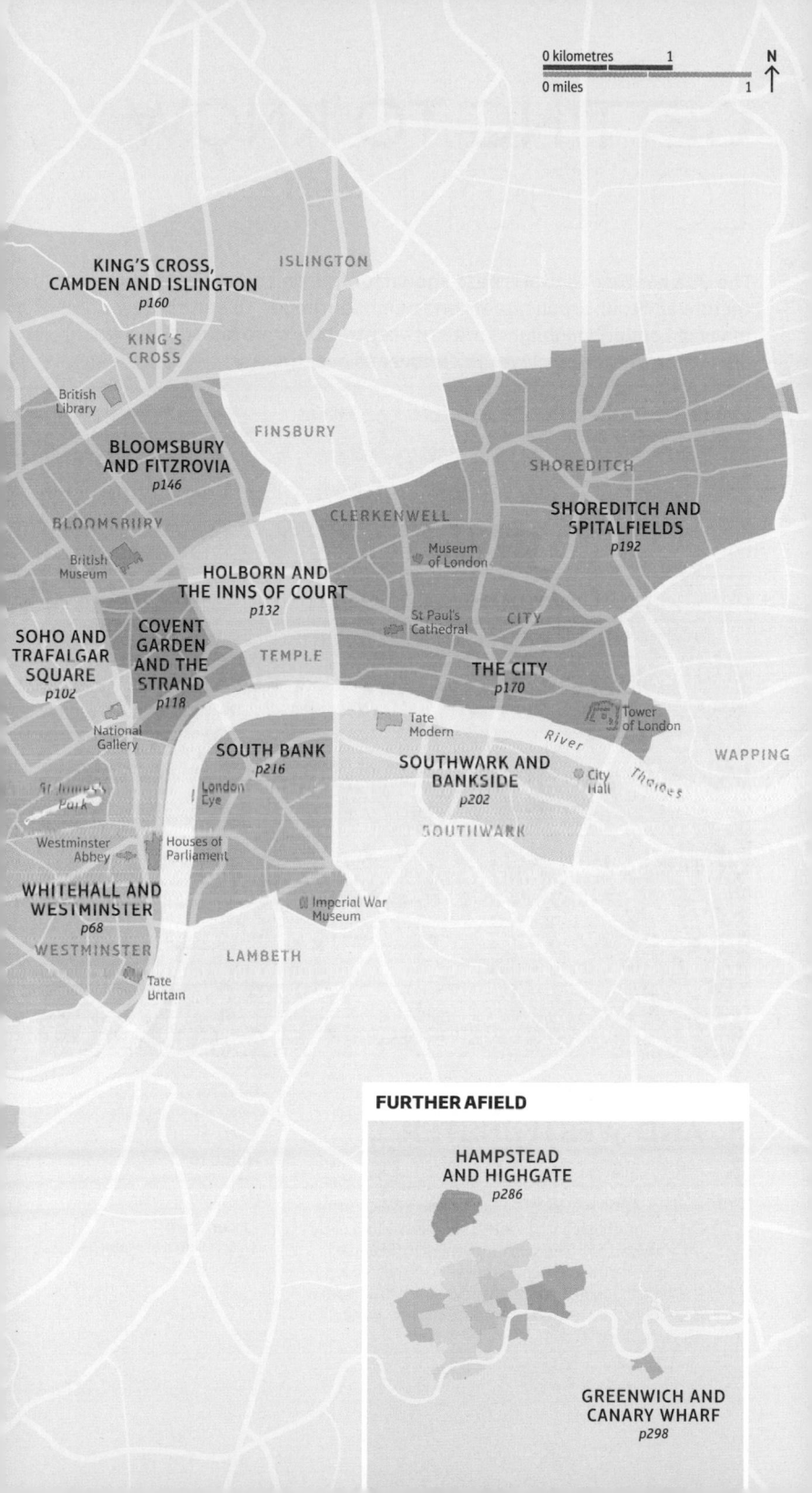

0 kilometres 1
0 miles 1

N

GETTING TO KNOW
LONDON

The UK's bustling capital is best-known for its iconic sights, regal architecture and cool, urban streets and neighbourhoods. Unsurprisingly, many of London's highlights are in its centre but, more unusually, there are visitor-friendly enclaves to discover all over the city.

WHITEHALL AND WESTMINSTER

PAGE 68

The seat of government for a millennium, Westminster is synonymous with two of the most stunning buildings in London: the Houses of Parliament and Westminster Abbey. The area is packed with a curious mixture of civil servants and sightseers, many of them making their way up and down Whitehall, the grand street linking Parliament Square and Trafalgar Square. You'll find few locals here, with its traditional pubs mostly the haunts of government workers.

Best for
Sightseeing and iconic London landmarks

Home to
Westminster Abbey, Houses of Parliament, Tate Britain

Experience
A tour of the tombs of royalty at Westminster Abbey

PAGE 86

MAYFAIR AND ST JAMES'S

Home to some of London's most wealthy individuals (the word Mayfair screams "money"), neither of these elite areas are exclusively for the rich, with some good, affordable restaurants, welcoming pubs and delightful gardens dotted around. Cut through by brash, traffic-clogged Piccadilly, the streets of St James's are often surprisingly quiet, given this is the heart of London. There are historical buildings aplenty but, really, this is the place to shop for designer fashion and mingle with the moneyed.

Best for
Designer fashion and high-end men's tailoring

Home to
Buckingham Palace, Royal Academy of Arts

Experience
A shopping spree on Mayfair's Bond Street

PAGE 102

SOHO AND TRAFALGAR SQUARE

Trafalgar Square can lay strong claim to being the epicentre of touristic London, a well-placed launching pad for much of what the city has to offer. Nearby is the liveliest part of the West End, with clumsily commercialized Leicester Square, lantern-strewn Chinatown and cool, unconventional Soho, the main LGBT+ district of London. Many of Soho's streets are replete with excellent independent restaurants, bars and theatres, making it the perfect spot for an evening out.

Best for
Eating out and a buzzing, lively atmosphere

Home to
National Gallery, National Portrait Gallery, Chinatown

Experience
A night of theatre in the West End.

$\rightarrow$

PAGE 118

COVENT GARDEN AND THE STRAND

The distinctive Covent Garden is always crowded, attracting visitors and locals in equally large numbers. A dense mix of markets, independent shops and restaurants side-by-side with fashion chain stores and street performers looking for applause, there's usually a spirited family-friendly atmosphere. Running along its southern border is The Strand, a busy road largely worth visiting for Somerset House only, with its excellent art gallery, cafés and restaurants, and large elegant courtyard and riverside views.

Best for
The buzz on Covent Garden Piazza

Home to
Covent Garden Piazza and Central Market, Somerset House

Experience
The brightly painted warehouses of Neal's Yard

PAGE 132

HOLBORN AND THE INNS OF COURT

This is one of the calmest areas of central London. The traditional home of the legal profession, the relative absence of shops and restaurants means there are almost as many lawyers as visitors. The Inns of Court themselves are subdued havens of tranquillity, a maze of alleyways and gardens overlooked by city residents. Add to this the excellent small museums and the lovely Lincoln's Inn Fields, and you have a great place to escape the chaos and crowds.

Best for
Hidden and quiet corners in the heart of London

Home to
Inns of Court, Sir John Soane's Museum

Experience
A picnic in the green squares of the Inns of Court

PAGE 146

BLOOMSBURY AND FITZROVIA

Though not exactly avant-garde, these relatively gentle districts are a little bit more laid back than a lot of the city. Fitzrovia is akin to Soho but turned down a few notches, and parts of it are densely packed with an enjoyable mix of restaurants. Bloomsbury is the student quarter, home to several university campuses, lots of independent bookshops and large garden squares. Its most famous location, by far, is the British Museum, but elsewhere it is characterized by a pleasing sense of detachment.

Best for
A laid back, campus atmosphere and a strong literary heritage

Home to
British Museum

Experience
Some of the world's greatest treasures at the British Museum

PAGE 160

KING'S CROSS, CAMDEN AND ISLINGTON

Imaginatively converted from a downbeat industrial landscape into a collection of culinary, commercial and artsy hotspots, King's Cross has undergone staggering transformation in recent years. Not entirely finished, it's still gaining reputation – the same of which cannot be said of neighbouring Camden, with its infamous alternative locale keeping the place thriving day and night. Adding yet more to the mix is well-heeled Islington, a more bourgeois district full of gastro pubs.

Best for
Canal walks and a wide range of shopping and dining options

Home to
Camden Market, St Pancras Station, British Library

Experience
Off-beat fashion and food at Camden Market

$\rightarrow$

PAGE 170

THE CITY

The towering skyscrapers of the City make up London's traditional financial district, where corporates in suits scurry around during the week, making it a bustling place at lunchtimes, but an eerily deserted one during the weekend. Also the historical heart of the city, with traces of the Roman occupation in places, the sights are dispersed over a relatively wide area but there are plenty of them, including London's highest concentration of medieval and early modern churches, crowned by the most famous church of all, St Paul's Cathedral.

Best for
Getting up close to London's staggering history

Home to
St Paul's Cathedral, Tower of London, Barbican Centre

Experience
The gore and glory of the centuries-old Tower of London

PAGE 192

SHOREDITCH AND SPITALFIELDS

These districts have attracted and spawned a once cutting-edge, much caricatured and now simply trendy local population. Though gentrification has firmly set in there is still an alluring energy here, particularly in lively Shoreditch. It's not entirely hipster-centric though, with Brick Lane home to a large Bangladeshi community, and markets like Old Spitalfields and Columbia Road continuing traditions that stretch way beyond the latest incarnation of the neighbourhood.

Best for
Feasting on street food and people-watching

Home to
Columbia Road Flower Market, Brick Lane

Experience
The hustle and bustle of some of London's top markets

SOUTHWARK AND BANKSIDE

Over the river from The City, Bankside, in the borough of Southwark, contains some of the most popular tourist attractions on the Thames. Tate Modern and Shakespeare's Globe along with waterside restaurants, pubs and Borough Market keep this stretch of the Thames Path happily congested most days. The recently developed area emanating out from London Bridge station has plenty of new places to eat, a few of them in Europe's tallest building, the Shard.

Best for
Urban river walks and riverside sightseeing

Home to
Tate Modern, Shakespeare's Globe

Experience
Striking and strange modern art at the Tate Modern

SOUTH BANK

At night this is the liveliest part of the river but it is cultural institutions rather than nightclubs that draw in the after-dark crowds. The Southbank Centre's concert halls and galleries alongside the National Theatre and British Film Institute form a Brutalist architectural line-up along the river. Any gaps are filled mostly with mediocre chain restaurants, though bookstalls, a skate park and food market provide a more homespun angle. Always busy in the daytime too, the South Bank's views from the embankment – and from atop the London Eye – have cemented it as one of London's must-visit areas.

Best for
A sundowner and an evening's entertainment

Home to
Southbank Centre, Imperial War Museum, London Eye

Experience
A stroll along the Thames Path

→

PAGE 230

CHELSEA AND BATTERSEA

Sitting on opposite sides of the Thames are wealthy Chelsea and energetic Battersea. Flashy sedans and 4WD vehicles, known locally as Chelsea tractors, ply Chelsea's main shopping street, King's Road, where upmarket fashion boutiques sit next door to more humdrum high-street stores. Away from King's Road the area is largely residential, though there are some decent pubs, worthwhile museums and gardens. The glorious park, trendy shops and varied restaurants of Battersea are a welcome retreat from the touristy sights of central London.

Best for
Upmarket shopping and riverside parks and gardens

Home to
Saatchi Gallery, Battersea Park

Experience
A spot of shopping along the King's Road.

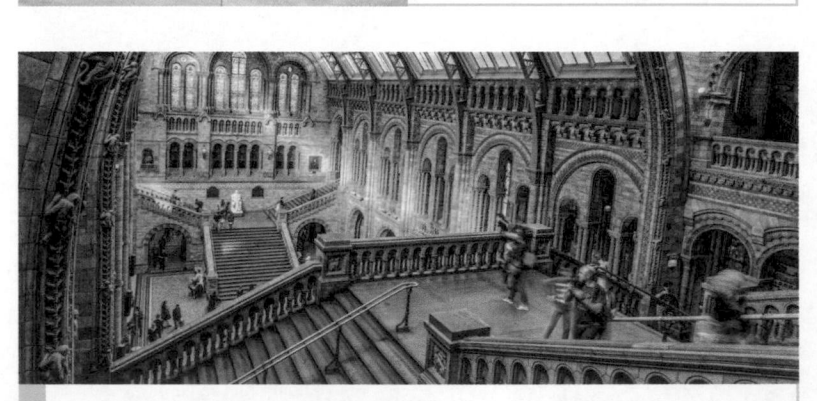

PAGE 240

SOUTH KENSINGTON AND KNIGHTSBRIDGE

London's museum quarter, South Kensington is home to three of the largest and best museums in the city, exhibiting stunning natural history, science and decorative arts collections. In keeping with the spirit of learning that pervades here, the wide streets house several important royal colleges and societies. In contrast, Knightsbridge, just up the road, oozes ostentatious wealth and is the location of one of the city's most iconic department stores, Harrods.

Best for
World-class free museums

Home to
Victoria and Albert Museum, Natural History Museum, Science Museum

Experience
The weird and wonderful skeletons and species inside the Natural History Museum

PAGE 260

KENSINGTON, HOLLAND PARK AND NOTTING HILL

From well-to-do High Street Kensington, the neighbourhoods to the north drift uphill through expensive townhouses, some original little museums and Holland Park. Partially wooded and beautifully landscaped, the park reflects its upmarket location with its pricey restaurant and café, and outdoor operas. At the top is Notting Hill, more touristy than High Street Kensington, in part because of the eponymous film, but also because of its market on Portobello Road.

Best for
Markets, parks and beautiful neighbourhoods

Home to
Design Museum

Experience
Browsing for bargains on Portobello Road

PAGE 274

REGENT'S PARK AND MARYLEBONE

The residents of Marylebone are generally less aristocratic than their Mayfair counterparts but this is still a genteel area with one of London's more high-brow high streets. There is a distinct change in tone on the main road between here and Regent's Park to the north, where the massive queues for Madame Tussauds are accompanied by non-stop traffic. This all melts pleasantly away in the attractive park itself, with its canalside location providing universal appeal.

Best for
Georgian architecture, open-air theatre

Home to
London Zoo

Experience
The splendid shelves of the marvellous Daunt Books

$\rightarrow$

PAGE 286

HAMPSTEAD AND HIGHGATE

Separated by the rolling fields and woodlands of Hampstead Heath and the atmospheric Highgate Cemetery, two of the biggest draws for visitors, the "villages" of Hampstead and Highgate have maintained much of their quaintness and independence, despite London's rapid urban expansion. The jumbled streets graced with boutique shops and upscale restaurants that make up the old villages are great for a stroll in a part of the city where the pace is noticeably slower.

Best for
London villages and vast swathes of heathland

Home to
Hampstead Heath, Highgate Cemetery

Experience
A dip in the chilling Hampstead bathing ponds

PAGE 298

GREENWICH AND CANARY WHARF

Separated by a U-bend in the river, but joined by a foot tunnel underneath it, Greenwich and Canary Wharf are as different as it gets. Built around the old docks in the 1980s, the business district of Canary Wharf lacks soul but is full of hidden history and dockside walking routes, the sum of which makes it unlike anywhere else in the city. In contrast, Greenwich has history seeping from its pores, populated as it is by a swathe of heavily visited royal and historical buildings and museums, an ancient park and handsome town centre.

Best for
Maritime London

Home to
National Maritime Museum, Cutty Sark, Greenwich Park, Royal Observatory

Experience
The home of Greenwich Mean Time atop Greenwich Park

BEYOND THE CENTRE

Though it has a distinct city centre, London's sprawling capital reaches far beyond the banks of the Thames. In pockets punctuated by independent shops, cafés, museums and more, you'll find the locals: urban families and young professionals, multinational and multicultural, all fiercely protective of their backyard, and with good reason. There are some big-name attractions out here – royal palaces, stately homes and film studios to name a few – but a trip beyond the centre is really a thrilling opportunity to get to know the locals behind this multifaceted city.

Best for
Local life and getting off the beaten path

Home to
Hampton Court, Kew Gardens, Warner Bros. Studio Tour: The Making of Harry Potter

Experience
The sights, sounds and smells of energetic Brixton

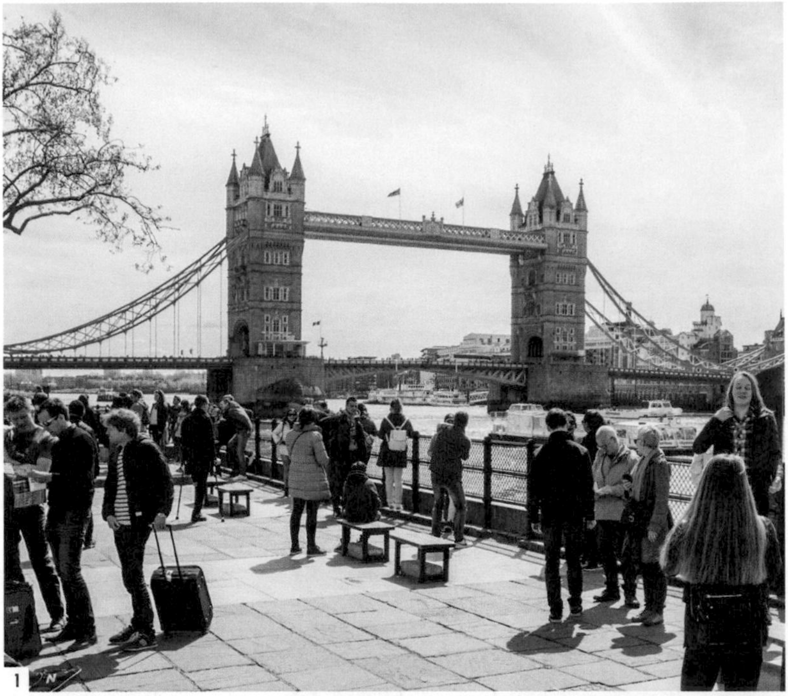
1

2

3

4

←

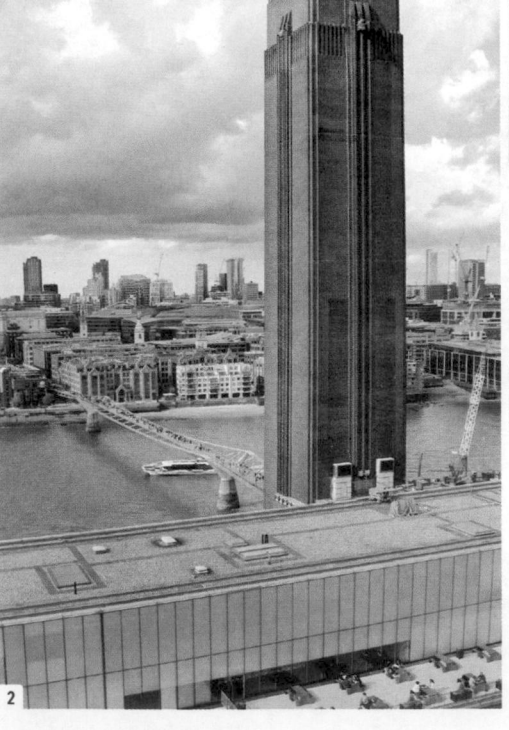

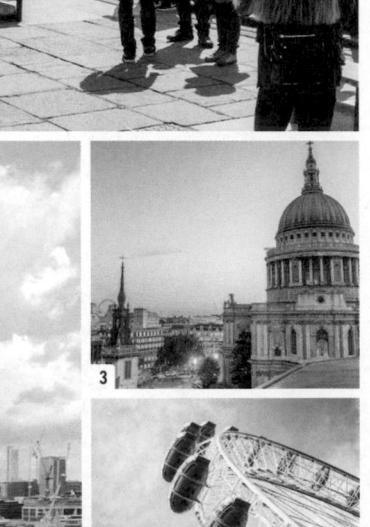

1 Looking towards iconic Tower Bridge

2 Tate Modern, housed in a former power station

3 St Paul's Cathedral

4 The London Eye

With so much to see and do in London it can be difficult knowing where to start. Here we suggest a few itineraries to help you get the most out of your visit.

24 HOURS

Morning

By following the river you can fit an awful lot into one day without having to travel too far or rely on public transport. Begin at Butler's Wharf; located close to Tower Bridge (p186)and lined with decent river-facing restaurants, it's a great spot for breakfast. From there, walk across the world-famous bridge to the Tower of London (p178) and immerse yourself for a few hours in a thousand years of royal history and scandal. Ready for lunch? Follow the river to London Bridge and cross back over to the southbank where you can pick up tasty street food or a gourmet picnic from Borough Market (p211).

Afternoon

Wander through the streets of Southwark past the Golden Hinde and through Clink Street. Soon you'll reach Shakespeare's Globe (p208) and the Tate Modern (p206). Stop at the Millennium Bridge to enjoy a picture-perfect view of St Paul's Cathedral (p174) before heading into the gigantic old power station to admire – or puzzle over – modern art. Check out the views from the top floor of the Blavatnik Building before having a coffee in the gallery's cafe (the view from here isn't bad either). Sated, continue along the Thames Path, around a bend in the river, to the South Bank (p216). Pause to watch skateboarders and browse the popular second-hand book stall under Waterloo Bridge before joining the queues for the London Eye (p226), which is is open until at least 8pm on most days of the year.

Evening

It's a half-hour walk back along the river to Southwark (p202). Have a spot of dinner at one of the many restaurants in the area – Roast, within Borough Market, is a good choice (p212) – before ending the day with a pint at London's last galleried pub, the 17th-century George Inn (p211).

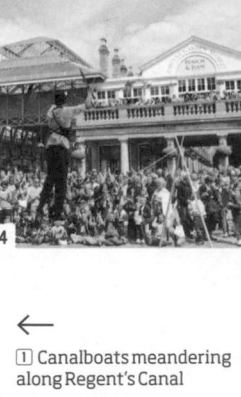

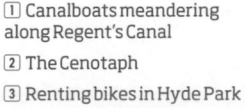

←

1 Canalboats meandering along Regent's Canal

2 The Cenotaph

3 Renting bikes in Hyde Park

4 A street performer in Covent Garden

2 DAYS

Day 1

Morning Have breakfast in Art Deco style at the St Pancras Grand, right inside St Pancras station. It's a short stroll to the innovatively resurrected King's Cross quarter (p160), where you can wander the city's newest independent hub and relax in Camley Street Natural Park (p165). From here, follow the winding Regent's Canal path to infamous Camden Market (p168) for quirky, offbeat shopping and a casual lunch.

Afternoon From Camden Town Tube station take the Northern Line down to Embankment – from there it's just a 600m-walk along the north bank of the river to the Houses of Parliament (p76), one of the great wonders of London, and only another 300m to the architecturally and historically awe-inspiring Westminster Abbey (p72).

Evening Make your way up Whitehall, past 10 Downing Street (p81) and the Cenotaph (p81), towards Trafalgar Square (p114). Once at the square stroll up through always-bustling Chinatown (p112) to the edge of Soho, the West End's most vibrant and eclectic restaurant district. Get a taste of one of London's current culinary crazes by dining on the delectable Peruvian tapas at Casita Andina (p115). It's just a few hundred metres from here to Ronnie Scott's, the city's most famous archetypal jazz club.

Day 2

Morning Have a traditional English breakfast at the atmospheric Café in the Crypt (p115), below St Martin-in-the-Fields church just off Trafalgar Square. Afterwards, cross the road to the National Gallery (p106) and explore one of the world's greatest art collections. Pick up something delicious for lunch from one of the many cafés in nearby Soho.

Afternoon From here you could head directly up the tree-lined Mall to Buckingham Palace (p90) but take the more meandering route through beautifully landscaped St James's Park, past the pelicans on the lake and over the blue bridge, a great spot for photos of the palace. In August visit the grandiose State Rooms in the palace itself; otherwise admire the precious art collection at the Queen's Gallery or the ornate carriages at the Royal Mews. From the palace, at the other end of Constitution Hill, pick up bikes and see out the daylight hours cycling around the expansive Hyde Park (p257).

Evening Park the bikes at the docking station in Knightsbridge and hop on the Piccadilly Line to the always bustling Covent Garden (p122). Enjoy the street performers at the atmospheric piazza and then settle into dinner accompanied by opera singers at Sarastro on Drury Lane, in the heart of Theatreland. See out the evening with a drink – and great views – on the riverside terrace of Somerset House (p124).

7 DAYS

Day 1

Morning Start at the Shard – there's no better vantage point from which to survey the city (p212). Down at street level, stroll along the cobbled alleys of Southwark and pick up lunch at Borough Market (p211).

Afternoon Head west along the Thames Path, popping into the cavernous Tate Modern (p206) to see what's new in the world of modern art.

Evening Finish up at the Southbank Centre (p220) for a spin on the London Eye and, afterwards, dinner and drinks.

Day 2

Morning Choose from three of the city's top museums: the Natural History Museum (p248), the Science Museum (p250) or the Victoria and Albert (p244). Any one could occupy you for a day but as they're free split your time across two or perhaps all three.

Afternoon Have a picnic in nearby Hyde Park (p257) before returning to another of the museums for the afternoon.

Evening If you've pre-booked tickets, enjoy a performance at the refined Royal Albert Hall (p252).

Day 3

Morning Head east to The City and explore the history of the capital at the Museum of London (p183).

Afternoon Have lunch at the historic Leadenhall Market (p188). After, take the Docklands Light Railway to Greenwich (p298) to discover centuries of maritime history.

Evening Walk to the top of Greenwich Park to enjoy sunset views.

Day 4

Morning Take the Tube north to enjoy the alternative vibe at Camden Market (p168). Browse the stalls until lunchtime – there's plenty here to feast on.

Afternoon Head to the characterful villages of Highgate and Hampstead. Walk between the two via the heath (p290) and Highgate Cemetery (p292).

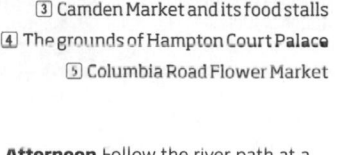

1 Leadenhall Market
2 The Southbank Centre in the sunshine
3 Camden Market and its food stalls
4 The grounds of Hampton Court Palace
5 Columbia Road Flower Market

Evening Have a relaxed dinner at one of Hampstead's excellent pubs such as the Holly Bush (p295).

Day 5

Morning Travel south to Dulwich Picture Gallery (p325) in upper-crust Dulwich Village, taking in the gorgeous park (p325) over the road.

Afternoon Catch a train at West Dulwich station for livelier Brixton. Do the full circuit of the Brixton Village and Market Row arcades (p328), a foodie's haven, before settling down for a late lunch.

Evening Stick about in Brixton for a spot of live music at one of its venues, catch a film at the Ritzy cinema, or simply chill out in Pop Brixton, a complex of shipping containers packed with street food start-ups and bars.

Day 6

Morning After a hard week's sightseeing, catch the train from London Waterloo to Kew Bridge, from which it's a short walk to the glorious gardens of Kew (p318).

Afternoon Follow the river path at a relaxed pace to the attractive riverside town of Richmond (p329). Have lunch on the go or, better yet, take a picnic to the expansive Richmond Park.

Evening Keep close to the Thames and enjoy a riverside dinner as the evening draws in.

Day 7

Morning Sunday morning is the only time Columbia Road Market (p200) operates and it's well worth a visit, whether or not you want to buy flowers. Here you'll catch sight of the sellers or "barrow boys" flaunting their impressive displays of flowers and foliage.

Afternoon Check out what's on at the Barbican (p182) or Rich Mix (p200), both of which have an ever-changing roster of film screenings, exhibitions and talks.

Evening Spend the evening in super-cool Shoreditch. There are plenty of trendy places to eat, drink and relax in, not least on Brick Lane (p197), the curry capital of London.

TOP 5 DIVERSE DISTRICTS

Brick Lane
AKA the "curry capital of Europe" and home to a large Bangladeshi community.

Ealing
The unofficial Polish capital of Britain – over 6 percent of people here speak Polish.

Stockwell
Nicknamed "Little Portugal", there are over 27,000 Portuguese in the local area.

Stamford Hill
London's largest community of ultra-Orthodox Jews live here.

Southall
Home to the biggest Punjabi population outside of India.

Did You Know?

One in three people who live in London were born in another part of the world.

LONDON IS
A WORLD CITY

Sit on the Tube and listen. You'll hear conversations in Polish, Chinese, Yoruba and 300 other languages besides. These are the voices of London, one of the most wonderfully multicultural cities in the world. Wherever you go, you'll find slices of life from every continent begging to be explored.

Places of Worship

Lighting up neighbourhoods from east to west are spectacular places of worship, many of them open to the public and each one a crash-course in understanding the cultural traditions they serve. From the largest Hindu temple in Europe (p322) to the towering mosque in Regent's Park (p279), these architectural anomalies spice up the urban landscape wherever they stand.

→

BAPS Shri Swaminarayan Mandir, an incredible Hindu temple in Neasden

Festivals

Aside from the popular Chinese New Year and Notting Hill Carnival, there are plenty of festivals that showcase London's locals. St Patrick's Day in March is widely celebrated with all-out revelry, as is Australia Day in January, less raucous in numbers only. Plaza Latina in August unites the Latin American communities for parades and merriment, and the fireworks of Diwali in the autumn sparkle over the city's skies. Whenever you visit, there's sure to be something to celebrate.

←

Entertainers contribute to the party atmosphere at the Notting Hill Carnival

↑ Vibrant Chinatown, the original home of London's Chinese population

Welcome to the Neighbourhood

West Indian barbershops to the south, Turkish grocers to the north, London's diversity is palpable whichever way you turn. Head to the East End to find the traditional heart of immigrant London, where so many have settled and dispersed into the cultural soup that is London.

A snapshot of ↑ modern London, in Brixton Market

Ceremonies and Traditions

A number of centuries-old royal ceremonies and traditions continue today, despite the sometimes baffling outfits and proceedings. Most famous is the Changing the Guard, which takes place daily at Buckingham Palace and Horse Guards Parade on Whitehall. Once a year, in June, the far more elaborate military parade Trooping the Colour is staged to celebrate the Queen's birthday. Find out how to book tickets at www.householddivision.org.uk.

→

Queen Elizabeth II waving to the crowd during the military parade Trooping the Colour

LONDON FOR
ROYALTY

London has been the royal capital of the UK for almost a thousand years and most of the royal family, including the Queen, live in the city. Over the centuries, successive monarchs have done much to shape the character of the city, from the landscaping of royal parks to the landmarks they left behind.

The Legacy of Victoria and Albert

We have much to thank Queen Victoria and her husband Prince Albert for. The Christmas tree, housing projects for the poor and the superb museums in South Kensington are just some of the things accredited to the forward-thinking pair. Give them a nod at the Queen Victoria Memorial outside Buckingham Palace and the Albert Memorial in Hyde Park.

←

The stunning Natural History Museum, a legacy of Prince Albert

↑ Trooping the Colour, a parade to celebrate the Queen's birthday

Tower of London

At times a royal palace, at others a prison and place of execution for fallen monarchs or rejected courtiers, the story of the Tower of London *(p178)* is to some extent the story of the English monarchy itself. Built by William the Conqueror in the late eleventh century, this was where Anne Boleyn awaited her fate after falling out of Henry VIII's favour and was later beheaded. Curiously, for 600 years it was also home to the royal menagerie, a collection of exotic wild animals, including lions and an elephant, gifted to the monarchy. It is now one of London's most popular attractions.

> **INSIDER TIP**
> **Sneak Preview**
>
> You can catch members of the Household Cavalry leaving the barracks on the south side of Hyde Park at 10:28 on weekdays and 9:28 on Sundays on their way to the Changing the Guard at Horse Guards Parade.

↑ The stark image of the Tower of London

Royal Palaces

Go behind the scenes of royal households to discover how the upper echelons of power have lived over the centuries. Hampton Court *(p314)* is arguably the most impressive with its long and rich history, while Kew Palace *(p318)*, surrounded by its beautiful gardens, is relatively modest by royal standards. Pop by the famous Buckingham Palace *(p90)*, the official London residence of the monarch since 1837, to say hello to the Queen – if the Royal Standard flag is flying, she's at home.

←

Visitors exploring the interior of Hampton Court Palace

Royal Parks

During a day of sightseeing take a detour to the former stomping grounds of kings and queens. Boat on the lake at the vast Hyde Park *(p257)*, wander landscaped gardens at Kensington *(p256)* or take in the view of Buckingham Palace in St James's Park *(p95)*. Venture a little further out and spend the day exploring the rural landscapes of Richmond Park *(p328)*. A hike up the hill in Greenwick Park *(p303)* provides sweeping views over the city of London, the perfect end to any day.

→

Relaxing by the lakeside in the vast Hyde Park

LONDON FOR
GREEN SPACES

With its 8 million trees and 3,000 parks, London is one of the greenest capitals in Europe. There's even a campaign to grant it National Park City status. Take a break from the city hubbub and venture to any one of these green spaces.

An English City Garden

The English have an unabashed love affair with their gardens. The green-fingered should make their way to the gorgeous scenic gardens that surround manor houses like Chiswick House *(p331)* and Syon House *(p329)*. If it's respite you're after, any of the public garden squares throughout the city will do, particularly those in Bloomsbury *(p154)*. The breathtaking Kew Gardens *(p318)* crowns them all and is a must for any budding gardener.

←

The exquisite Kew Gardens, a veritable haven for the green-fingered

47
—
Percentage of green space in Greater London, most of which is open to the public.

Back to Nature

There are more than 40 nature reserves and pockets of woodland across London, some of them not so far away from the centre. Go bird-spotting at Walthamstow Wetlands, hunt for creepy crawlies at Camley Street Natural Park *(p165)* or walk through woodland at the ancient Highgate Wood.

→ Sifting for creepy crawlies at the Camley Street Natural Park

A Walk on the Wild Side

Linking a lot of the city's green spaces together, along rivers, canals, old train tracks and park paths, is the Capital Ring, a painstakingly plotted 126 km circular walking route. Sign-posted throughout the route, it's worth downloading a map for one of the 15 sections from the TfL website (tfl.gov.uk).

→ A couple of couples on the Capital Ring trail

Football in London

The capital city of the country that invented the game has more professional football clubs and large football stadiums than any other on the planet. Premier League games are usually booked up well in advance, mostly with corporate guests and season ticket holders. Your best hope of watching some action is to try to book in a cup match, particularly a League Cup game, when tickets are not only more widely available but a bit cheaper too.

→

Arsenal players and fans celebrate a goal

LONDON FOR
SPORTS FANS

Britain is a nation of sports fans and its capital is no exception. London, the only city to have hosted the Olympic Games three times, puts on a dazzling range of sporting events and tournaments, from football to boxing and everything in-between.

An Olympic Legacy

Head to the Queen Elizabeth Olympic Park *(p312)* and relive the magic of the 2012 London Olympics. There are frequent events here ranging from the hotly contested Athletics World Cup to all-star basketball championships, plus a range of first-class facilities, fit for any budding Olympian.

→

The Queen Elizabeth Olympic Park, with the ArcelorMittal Orbit

Sports Museums and Stadium Tours

London's sporting heritage is unparalleled, with legendary areas dotted all over. Given their long histories they all have stories to tell and a tour is the best way to hear them. Walk through the player's tunnel at Wembley, go behind the scenes at the home of rugby in Twickenham or explore the courts of Wimbledon. The oldest sporting museums in the world, the MCC Museum at Lord's cricket ground, is a must-visit for fans.

←

England's national stadium, Wembley

The Sporting Calendar

The Six Nations Rugby tournament kickstarts the year, with some games held at Twickenham. The hotly contested Boat Race brings in spring, followed swiftly by the London Marathon and people's favourite the FA Cup Final. Expect strawberries and sunburn in summer, as crowds watch Wimbledon and cricket test matches. After the frenzy of the transfer window, the Premier League kicks off in mid-August. Rugby Union Internationals and the ATP World Tour Finals round off the year.

→

Pounding the pavements for the London Marathon *(above)* and enjoying a game of tennis *(inset)*

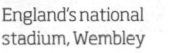

The simply gorgeous
Albert Bridge, ↑
illuminated at night

LONDON
ON THE RIVER

Like many cities, London grew up around its river. The Romans used it as a line of defence, the Victorians established it as the world's largest port and the city today claims it as a cultural hotspot. Take to the water to see London landmarks from a different angle.

Follow the Thames Path

Twisting and turning along the river through London and out into the nearby countryside is the Thames Path. With few breaks in its 80 km (50 mile) length, rarely do you lose sight of the river. The path runs from Hampton Court in the west to Crayford Ness in the east, and it's recommended to tackle small sections at a time. The best stretch for sightseeing is between Tower Bridge and Westminster Bridge but there are some pretty sections, dotted with pubs and full of greenery, between Hammersmith Bridge and Kew Bridge in the west.

→

A section of
the Thames Path,
running past City Hall

Spanning the River

For centuries, right up until 1750, London Bridge was the only bridge across the Thames in London. Now there are more than 30 – and tunnels too. Instantly recognizable is Tower Bridge (p186), with its twin towers and famous drawbridge. A favourite for many Londoners is the attractive 19th-century Albert Bridge, near Battersea Park (p238), spectacular at night when it is illuminated by thousands of lights. The somewhat eerie Greenwich Foot Tunnel links the Isle of Dogs, the home of Canary Wharf (p307), and Greenwich – it's an unusual way to get from one bank to the other. Snap great shots or take in the view of the riverscape from the Golden Jubilee Bridges, each flanking Hungerford Bridge.

← A legend of London, the turreted Tower Bridge

EAT

Dine at one of these top riverside locations.

Skylon

Cool, refined restaurant on the first floor of the Royal Festival Hall.

🏛 Southbank Centre
🌐 skylon-restaurant.co.uk

€€€

Sea Containers

Tuck into a bottomless breakfast or Sunday roast on the marvellous riverside terrace.

🏛 20 Upper Ground SE1
🌐 seacontainers restaurant.com

€€€

A Thames Clipper coasting the river ↑

From the Water

Board the Thames Clipper rather than a sightseeing boat to cruise the river and see the sights for a fraction of the price. There are four main routes, all of them covering the busiest section of the river between the London Eye and London Bridge. There are boats roughly every 15 minutes at peak times.

LONDON
ON TAP

Londoners, like most Brits, come together in pubs. They eat and drink in them, they chat and dance in them, and they watch comedy and sport in them. And whether you're on the river, in a park or on a busy street, no matter the neighbourhood, there will be a pub just round the corner.

Brewing a Beer

The father of London breweries is Fuller's, established in 1845. Unlike most big-hitters, it has weathered the competition created by the craft breweries that have emerged since the 2000s. London's taste for hoppy IPAs shows no sign of dissipating, and there are more than a hundred microbreweries and brewpubs across the city. Tackle the Bermondsey Beer Mile on a Saturday to try some of the best.

Some of the London-
brewed ales on offer
at a local pub

A Traditional Public House

The title of "oldest pub in London" is claimed by quite a number of pubs. Though very few pub interiors are more than 200 years old, there have been pubs and inns in the city for over a millennium and there are certainly a select few establishments whose current building dates to the 16th century. Look out for timber-framed interiors and compartments separated by frosted glass screens – the classic tells of a Victorian-era pub.

← The Victorian Market Porter pub set in Southwark

DRINK

Hoop and Grapes
This 17th-century pub is one of the oldest still standing in London.
⌂ 47 Aldgate High Street ⊜ Aldgate East ⦿ nicholsonspubs.co.uk

Ye Olde Cheshire Cheese
Rebuilt in 1667, this retains many original 17th-century features.
⌂ 145 Fleet Street ⊜ Blackfriars ☏ 020 7353 6170

↑ A pint of London Pride, brewed by London stalwart, Fuller's

Pub Lunch

Since the 1990s, there has been a gastropub explosion in London. Though many pubs have stuck to traditional pub grub, some can compete with top restaurants for quality. Among those most renowned for their food are the Anchor & Hope in Waterloo, The Harwood Arms in Fulham and The Marksman in Hackney.

↑ Serving up an impressive Sunday roast dinner at a London gastropub

Independent Cinemas

Intimate art house venues, Golden Age auditoriums and trendy establishments with bars and restaurants attached are just some of the places you can watch big screen films around the city. The historic Regent Street Cinema, the Electric Cinema on Portobello Road, with its diner and leather armchairs, and the Art Deco Phoenix in East Finchley, which opened in 1912, are among the most memorable. Look out, too, for a branch of the excellent cinema chains Picturehouse, Curzon and Everyman.

> 💬 INSIDER TIP
> **Summer Cinema Tickets**
>
> Tickets for summer screenings go on sale months in advance and often sell out. The best site to check for multiple venues is thelunacinema.com. Screenings are rarely cancelled so don't expect refunds if it rains, and bring an umbrella.

The plush setting of ↑
the Electric Cinema
on Portobello Road

LONDON FOR
FILM BUFFS

From the grimy, sinister streets of Victorian London to the romantic home of middle-class bumblers and eccentrics, the capital has been the backdrop to countless movies over the decades. Here, we round up the best of London's film scene.

Big Screen Scenes

Finding the streets of London familiar? It's no surprise, given the city's role in film. Hugh Grant wooed Julia Roberts in *Notting Hill* and Cillian Murphy faced a post-apocalyptic Westminster in *28 Days Later*. James Bond fans will recognize landmarks at every turn, particularly after Bond's high-speed chase down the Thames. And let's not forget a certain boy wizard, who boarded the train to Hogwarts at King's Cross Station (look out for the staged Platform 9¾, see p165).

←

Film fans on their way to
Hogwarts at Platform 9¾

British Film Institute

The British Film Institute (BFI) aims to promote and preserve film-making in the UK. It's headquartered at its BFI Southbank building, equipped with a four-screen cinema, film shop and a publicly accessible film archive. The BFI organizes the London Film Festival, which runs for just less than a fortnight every October at cinemas around the city.

←

The film shop at the British Film Institute

Summer Cinema

Every summer, dates are set for outdoor cinema seasons. Among the big names is the central courtyard at Somerset House. Rooftops are a favourite, with screenings at the Bussey Building in Peckham and the Queen of Hoxton pub in Shoreditch, among others. Look out for Luna Cinema, which has a jampacked summer schedule at over a dozen parks and gardens as well as royal palaces.

→

Settling down to watch an open-air film screening at Somerset House

Classical, Opera and Ballet

The classical music calendar in London is dominated every year by The Proms, eight weeks of summer concerts climaxing at the Royal Albert Hall. There is plenty going on for the rest of the year – check out programmes at the Royal Festival Hall, the Barbican and Wigmore Hall. These venues host opera, too, but for that and ballet head to the sumptuous London Coliseum and the Royal Opera House.

→
The enthusiastically attended Last Night of the Proms

> **INSIDER TIP**
> **Getting Tickets**
>
> Head to the TKTS booth on Leicester Square for on-the-day last-minute and discounted tickets for first-rate West End productions.

LONDON FOR
LIVE SHOWS

"When a man is tired of London, he is tired of life," Samuel Johnson famously declared and that is as true in the 21st century as it was in the late 1700s. With an overwhelming choice of live entertainment, from a thriving comedy circuit to world-class theatre, visitors to London really are spoilt for choice.

Take Me to Church

There is much more to church music than stuffy choirs and organ recitals. Free lunchtime concerts are common and St Martin-in-the-Fields *(p114)* has weekday concerts. It also stages regular jazz concerts at its Café in the Crypt. St John's on Smith Square, in Westminster, has ticketed concerts almost every afternoon or evening. Frequently named the city's best live music venue, Union Chapel in Islington is an extra special place to hear world and contemporary music.

→
A performance at the atmospheric Union Chapel

Pub Performances

Some of the future greats of British music started their careers gigging on the London pub circuit, and legendary venues like the Hope & Anchor in Islington and the Dublin Castle in Camden still host regular live performances. London's pubs also play a major role on the comedy circuit, at pubs like The Bedford in Balham and the Camden Head.

←

A band playing at the Dublin Castle in Camden

A City of Theatre

The West End is the city's answer to Broadway and commercial theatre, much of it of a very high standard, is in rude health. The city's indepenent theatre is thriving, too. The National Theatre and the Barbican provide audience-pulling platforms for first-time directors and experimental productions, injecting an extra dose of creativity into London's theatre scene.

→

The long-running Les Misérables in the West End

A Fashion Mecca

When it comes to style, London is a city where anything goes. Iconic designers to seek out include Vivienne Westwood and Alexander McQueen, a graduate of Central Saint Martins, the London art and design school renowned for churning out superstar designers. Check out the edgy and the experimental at London Fashion Week, which takes place in February and September.

←

A Vivienne Westwood show presenting her unique collection

LONDON IN
FASHION

London is Europe's undisputed heavyweight champion of shopping. Perhaps best known for its luxurious department stores, the city's thriving markets also provide much to delight in. In these festivals of independent retail, the walk through is as at least as much fun as the eventual purchase.

Hit the High Street

Oxford Street is a bustling 2 km- (1 mile-) long parade of over 300 shops and stores. Find here the staples of the British wardrobe, with flagship stores for perennial favourites John Lewis, Marks & Spencer and Topshop. On adjoining Regent Street are famous national and international names, such as Hackett, Barbour and Ted Baker.

→

The ever-popular Oxford Street

Embrace Your Independents

On every corner there are chances to find something unique, whether high-end goods or vintage bargains. For the best suits in the city, head for the unbeatable tradition of Savile Row and Jermyn Street. Independent boutiques abound in Notting Hill and Hampstead, while for vintage and alternative fashion you can't do much better than Brick Lane and Camden.

← An independent clothing store in trendy Notting Hill

↑ Cutting-edge tailoring at a London boutique

TOP 5 LONDON MARKETS

Camden Lock Market
A canalside market, best for alternative fashion.

Portobello Road
A long road lined with antiques-loaded stalls.

Old Spitalfields Market
A covered market with themed days, like vinyl.

Columbia Road Market
Cut flowers, plants, and seedlings at great prices on Sunday mornings.

Petticoat Lane Market
Historic street market, with great leather goods.

↑ The interior of luxury department store, Liberty

World-Class Department Stores

You can shop till you drop in London's top department stores – and certainly your jaw will drop when you see some of the prices. The sheer extravagance of Harrods is absolutely worth braving the crowds for, as is the historic Liberty, housed in a Tudor revival building. Selfridges, second only to Harrods in size, has built a reputation not just for the staggering breadth and quality of its stock, but for its artistic and innovative window displays.

LONDON
ON THE ROOF

London is in the midst of a tall building boom, and as fast as the towers shoot up, so the trend for socializing up high thrives. Popping up on London's rooftops are open-air cinemas, adventure playgrounds for adults and buzzing bars – and all with superlative views of the cityscape.

Sky-High Jinks

Take to the rooftops for an evening of summer entertainment. Roof East in Stratford is a riotous activity playground with mini golf, batting cages and lawn bowls surrounded by the obligatory street food pop-ups. Rooftop Film Club shows classic movies from a height, supplying their audience with wireless headphones and rows of deckchairs to settle back in. Choose from one of three venues and book your ticket in advance.

$\longrightarrow$

A screening of *Saturday Night Fever* at Peckham Rooftop Film Club

Rooftop Gardens

Some of the most delightful rooftops are those with gardens, a number of which are open to the public. Book (free of charge) to see the terraced palms and ferns of the Sky Garden *(p187)*, or walk through the landscaped flowerbed of the Crossrail Place Roof Garden in Canary Wharf. The greenery of the Queen Elizabeth Hall Roof Garden may be modest but its riverside location in one of London's most dynamic cultural districts more than makes up for it.

←

The Sky Garden's panoramic views and the Crossrail Place Roof Garden *(inset)*

EAT

SUSHISAMBA London
An inventive menu, served 38 floors up.
⌂ 110 Bishopsgate, EC2
Ⓦ sushisamba.com

£ £ £

Oxo Tower Restaurant
Thameside location and a modern British menu.
⌂ Barge House St, SE1
Ⓦ harveynichols.com

£ £ £

Madison
In-your-face views of St Paul's from the terrace.
⌂ One New Change, EC4
Ⓦ madisonlondon.net

£ £ £

Take in the View

The Shard *(p212)*, western Europe's tallest building, provides miles of eye-busting views from its 72nd-floor viewing platform. The price of a ticket is high, too, but you can opt for one of the bars on a slightly lower floor, where the view is the cost of a cocktail. Even closer to earth are some of the city's more long-lived buildings; the viewing galleries of St Paul's and Westminster cathedrals present captivating vistas along with a satisfying sense of history.

↑
The lights and landmarks of London, as seen from the Shard

EAT

Rainforest Café
Its jungle decorations will delight little ones.

🏠 20 Shaftesbury Ave
🌐 therainforest cafe.co.uk

£ £ £

Giraffe World Kitchen
Lively, with a menu to satisfy all tastes.

🏠 Southbank Centre
🌐 giraffe.net

£ £ £

Diana Memorial Playground in Kensington Gardens ↑

LONDON FOR
FAMILIES

You won't struggle to find places geared up for kids in this city, with its innovative museums, abundance of expansive parks and family-friendly restaurants. Although some attractions are a little pricey, there's a huge range of free and low-cost activities to be found.

Rainy-Day Activities

Given the unpredictable British climate, it's lucky that some of the most entertaining experiences for kids are indoors. The standout is the Science Museum *(p250)*, a veritable world of wonder that pairs well with a trip to the Natural History Museum *(p248)*. A far less wholesome experience is to be had at the London Dungeon *(p228)*, where gory moments in the city's history are brought to life. The similarly macabre Clink Prison Museum *(p212)* will delight fiendish teenagers.

←

Coming face-to-face with the specimens at the Natural History Museum

Let Off Steam

The hundreds of parks in London – both large and small – provide, at the very least, a space for kids to run around. In the city centre, head for St James's Park *(p95)*, Holland Park *(p266)*, Regent's Park *(p279)* and Kensington Gardens *(p256)*, all of which have playgrounds. As well as climbing frames, a swing set and slide, Hyde Park also has a lido and boating lake *(p257)*. Don't miss Coram's Fields in Bloomsbury, a park designed solely for children and young people, with adventure play areas, a city farm and a paddling pool.

> 💬 INSIDER TIP
> **Kids Go Free**
>
> Under-11s can travel for free on public transport when they're accompanied by an adult and can gain admission to most attractions for a reduced price. At many sights, entry is free for under-5s.

Urban Safari

Inexpensive or free, London's city farms are great places for families on a budget. One of the biggest is Mudchute Park and Farm, near Canary Wharf (www.mudchute.org), home to over 100 animals. For more exotic creatures, head to the children's zoo at Battersea Park *(p238)*, which counts monkeys, snakes and emus among its residents, while for the biggest beasts make a beeline for London Zoo *(p278)*.

$\rightarrow$

Feeding the donkeys at Mudchute Park and Farm

Acting Up

From traditional puppet shows to cutting-edge plays, there are plenty of theatres for children. The marionette shows at the Puppet Theatre Barge in Little Venice *(p270)* and Richmond offer a unique, floating setting, while the Unicorn Theatre in London Bridge puts on around 20 kids' shows a year (www.unicorntheatre.com).

$\leftarrow$

A performance at the Puppet Theatre Barge

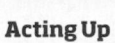

Dickensian London

Inspired by the city and its people, Charles Dickens is inextricably linked to London. Read *The Pickwick Papers* and *Oliver Twist* to get you in the mood, then tour the streets he made famous with Charles Dickens Walks and Tours *(dickenslondontours. co.uk)*. To get to know the man himself, visit his Bloomsbury house, now the Charles Dickens Museum *(p155)*.

←

Victorian interior of the Charles Dickens Museum

LONDON FOR
BOOKWORMS

If you're a lover of books you'll be a lover of London. Writers and readers alike have much to celebrate in the city, with the world's largest library and Europe's largest bookshop, a thriving independent bookshop scene and a literary heritage stretching back centuries.

Recommended Reads

Dickens classics aside, there are plenty of London-set novels to devour. George Orwell's *Keep The Aspidistra Flying* is a portrayal of city poverty. There's a strong sense of place in Zadie Smith's *White Teeth* and Sam Selvon's *The Lonely Londoners*, both examinations of the immigrant experience. John Lanchester's *Capital* explores the dynamics on a London street around the 2008 financial crisis.

→

Browsing at the Foyles store at Charing Cross

Take a Tour

A Bloomsbury tour is a must for bibliophiles. Walk in the footsteps of the Bloomsbury Group (p154) in and around Russell Square and Gordon Square. Look out for towering Senate House (p158), the inspiration behind George Orwell's Ministry of Truth in his prescient 1984, then make a beeline for the British Library, home to riches from the literary world (p164).

→

Researchers at the British Library, and the imposing Senate House (inset)

Did You Know?

The British Library receives a copy of every publication produced in the UK and holds over 150 million separate items.

SHOP

Foyles

This renowned store is the largest independent bookseller in London, with a history dating back to 1903 when brothers William and Gilbert began the venture by selling the textbooks they didn't need. The five-story flagship store on Charing Cross Road includes a jazz music concession, an excellent foreign language books section and over 6 km (4 miles) of shelving.

⌂ 107 Charing Cross Rd
🌐 foyles.co.uk

LONDON FOR
FOODIES

You can sample food from hundreds of countries in every imaginable setting and on any budget in London. Shining with Michelin-starred restaurants, the city is also in the midst of a sparks-flying street food explosion. Here, we explore some of its must-eats.

Festival Seasoning

For more food stalls than you can wave a bread stick at, time your visit to coincide with one of the city's summer food festivals. In May, KERB Does Alchemy at the Southbank Centre celebrates South Asian cuisine. In June, bag a ticket for Taste of London, a fine-dining jamboree in Regent's Park (london.tastefestivals.com). Looser and livelier are the several StrEATlife festivals held between May and August at Alexandra Palace *(p322)*. The vibe is more like a music festival here, with DJs and bands providing a soundtrack for grazing while gazing out over London.

Trying out nibbles at the Taste of London festival

Eat the Street

There are plenty of restaurants jumping on the street food bandwagon but genuine on-the-hoof eats – sold from market stalls, shipping containers, trucks and more – are popping up wherever there are crowds of people. The best-known option – although on the pricey side – is Borough Market *(p211)*. The Southbank Centre Food Market *(p222)* is also slap-bang in the middle of the tourist circuit and sells breads and cheeses, as well as a mix of British and international dishes. For a more authentic street experience, head to Street Feast Dalston (streetfeast.com), KERB Camden Market (kerbfood.com) or Maltby Street Market (www.maltby.st).

←

Street stall at Borough Market selling freshly baked breads

TOP 5 LONDON FOOD HUBS

Brixton Village and Market Row
Old market arcades now heaving with cafés and restaurants *(p328)*.

Flat Iron Square
Food counters in a set of railways arches *(p212)*.

The Prince
A polished street food hub with alfresco dining (theprincelondon.com).

Feast Canteen
A reinvented canteen-food court hybrid (feastcanteen.co.uk).

Bang Bang Oriental
A specialist Asian cuisine food hall (bangbangoriental.com).

↑ Le Gavroche, and a dish from the Connaught Restaurant *(inset)*

Fine Dining

With over 70 Michelin-starred restaurants, the fine dining scene is booming. Most of the extravagant eateries are found in the West End, the City, Kensington and Knightsbridge. They tend to be formal affairs, but there are hipper exceptions, such as industrial chic tapas place Barrafina *(p115)* and Cantonese master Hakkasan (hakkasan.com). Most of these places build their reputation on their chefs, like Michel Roux of Le Gavroche (www.le-gavroche.co.uk) and Gordon Ramsay, whose eponymous restaurant is one of only three in the city with three Michelin stars (www.gordonramsayrestaurants.com).

A YEAR IN
LONDON

JANUARY

London Art Fair *(mid-Jan)*. Top-notch modern and contemporary art show.

△ **Chinese New Year** *(late-Jan or early-Feb)*. Chinatown celebrates the new year with a parade, performances and plenty of food.

FEBRUARY

△ **Six Nations** *(early Feb)*. This Rugby Union tournament takes place in Ireland, France, Scotland, Wales, Italy and England's Twickenham, a short train ride from London.

MAY

FA Cup Final *(mid-May)*. The annual conclusion of the oldest cup tournament in world football is held at Wembley Stadium.

△ **Chelsea Flower Show** *(late-May)*. A five-day horticultural show at the Royal Hospital Chelsea.

Test-match Cricket *(late-May)*. The cricket season kicks off; catch it at Lord's or the Oval.

JUNE

△ **Trooping the Colour** *(mid-June)*. A show of extravagant military pageantry for the Queen's Birthday Parade

Wimbledon Lawn Tennis Championships *(late-Jun to early-Jul)*. The only Grand Slam tournament played on grass.

Royal Academy of Arts Summer Exhibition *(Jun–Aug)*. Hundreds of works are exhibited in one of the most popular art events of the year.

SEPTEMBER

Totally Thames *(all month)*. A month-long festival featuring events along and on the river.

△ **Open House Weekend** *(mid- or late-Sep)*. Citywide iconic and little-known buildings open their doors to the public free of charge for one weekend only.

OCTOBER

△ **London Film Festival** *(mid- to late-Sep)*. Some 300 British and international films are screened at cinemas large and small around the city.

MARCH

△ **The Boat Race** *(late-Mar or early-Apr)*. The Oxford and Cambridge University rowing crews take to the river in this annual race that runs from Putney Bridge to Chiswick Bridge.

APRIL

△ **London Marathon** *(mid-Apr)*. Thousands pound the city's streets, from Blackheath to The Mall, as they tackle the gruelling 26.2-mile (42.2-km) course.

Queen's Birthday gun salute *(21 Apr)*. A 41-gun salute at Hyde Park and 62-gun salute at the Tower of London herald the Queen's birthday.

JULY

△ **Pride in London** *(early Jul)*. The culmination of London's Pride Festival, thousands parade through the streets of London to celebrate the LGBT+ community.

Lovebox Festival *(mid-Jul)*. One of the largest contemporary dance and black music festivals in London.

The Proms *(late Jul to mid-Sep)*. An eight-week festival of classical and orchestral music, concluding with the over-the-top, uproarious Last Night of the Proms.

Buckingham Palace State Rooms open to the public *(late Jul to end-Aug)*.

AUGUST

△ **Notting Hill Carnival** *(last weekend of Aug)*. Europe's largest street festival is a riotous celebration of Afro-Caribbean music and culture.

Film4 Summer Screen at Somerset House *(2 wks in Aug)*. Open-air cinema screenings in Somerset House's fountain court.

NOVEMBER

Lord Mayor's Show *(2nd Sat)*. A procession of bands, floats and military detachments accompany the Lord Mayor in his gold state coach as it makes its way through the City.

Remembrance Sunday *(2nd Sun)*. A ceremony giving thanks to those who died fighting in any conflict from World War I onwards. The Cenotaph is the focus of London's main ceremony.

△ **London Jazz Festival** *(mid-Nov)*. Big names, local acts and the broadest possible definition of jazz characterize this eclectic festival.

DECEMBER

Hyde Park Winter Wonderland *(throughout)*. Festive markets, fairground rides and a huge outdoor ice rink attract crowds to London's largest inner-city park.

△ **New Year's Eve Fireworks** *(31 Dec)*. A spectacular display of fireworks lighting up the Houses of Parliament, the London Eye and the South Bank.

A BRIEF
HISTORY

Founded by the Romans, London changed hands many times in its first thousand years. Devastated by fire, plague and war during the subsequent one thousand years, the city rebuilt itself every time to become a centre of world trade and the largest metropolis on the planet.

Roman London

The first permanent settlement on land within what is now London was established after the first Roman invasion of Britain in 55 BC, though it was not cemented until almost a century later, following another, greater invasion of 43 AD. The Romans bridged the river and built their administrative headquarters, Londinium, on the north bank, the present site of the City of London. The Roman occupation lasted some 350 years but following its withdrawal in the early fifth century during the decline of the Roman Empire, the city lay more or less abandoned.

1 A map of London from 1570 ↑

2 Work begins on Westminster Abbey

3 The Battle of 1066

4 Thousands were killed by the Black Death of 1348

Timeline of events

55 BC
Julius Caesar invades Britain

50 AD
Londinium founded

AD 61
Londinium is sacked by the Iceni, British Celts led by their queen Boudicca

200
Romans build a wall around the city

410
Romans withdraw from Britain

Saxons and Vikings

Saxon and Viking invaders fought over the city over the following centuries, during which time its importance fell below that of others like Winchester and Canterbury. It wasn't until 1016 that it recovered its status as the capital under King Canute. Edward the Confessor, one of the last Anglo-Saxon kings of England, moved the base for royal government to the City of Westminster, a distinction that remains to this day. Edward also founded Westminster Abbey where, following the subsequent Norman invasion, William the Conqueror was crowned, in 1066.

Norman and Medieval London

William allowed the City of London a degree of independence, reliant as he and his successors were on the City's backing, with all its wealth, for the maintenance of power. City tradesmen set up their own institutions and guilds and the first City of London mayor was appointed in 1189. By the early 14th century London enjoyed a period of relative prosperity, though much of the population, thought to be around 80,000 by this time, lived in poverty. This number was cut in half by the arrival of the bubonic plague, known as the Black Death, in 1348.

WHERE TO SEE MEDIEVAL LONDON

The Museum of London (p183) contains medieval artifacts while the Tate Britain (p78) and National Gallery (p106) both display paintings of the time. Manuscripts, including the Domesday Book, are found at the British Library (p164). A 14th-century rose window is all that remains of Winchester Palace near the Clink (p212).

872
The Danes occupy London

1066
Edward the Confessor buried, and William the Conqueror crowned on Christmas Day

1209
Old London Bridge completed

1348
The Black Death kills half of the London population

1381
Peasants' Revolt defeated

1

2

Tudor London

The Tudors' reign began in 1485 with Henry VII. They established peace throughout England, allowing art and commerce to flourish. Under Elizabeth I, explorers opened up the New World, installing London as the world's foremost trade market. It was also during Elizabeth's reign that the foundations of England's great theatrical and literary traditions were firmly laid. The Globe Theatre was erected in 1576 and premiered many of Shakespeare's plays.

Religious Strife and Civil War

Just two years after Elizabeth I's death Catholic conspirators, led by Guy Fawkes, attempted to assassinate King James I by blowing him up in the Houses of Parliament. An anti-Catholic backlash followed and religious conflict, married to a power struggle between Parliament and the monarch, led to Civil War in 1642. London, a Parliamentarian stronghold, became a key battleground. Parliamentarian victory in 1649 established an English Commonwealth dominated by Puritans under Oliver Cromwell. Their rule was, however, short lived and the monarchy was restored under Charles II in 1660.

↑ Charles I beheaded by the Parliamentarians, led by Oliver Cromwell

Timeline of events

1585
Shakespeare arrives in London

1642
Civil War begins and Charles I decamps from London

1649
Charles I beheaded at Whitehall, Commonwealth established

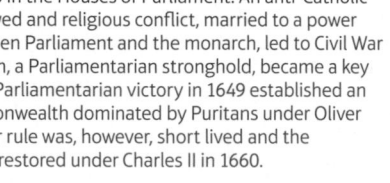

1665
The Great Plague kills 100,000

1660
Monarchy restored under Charles II

Devastation and Reconstruction

On 2 September 1666 a fire broke out at a bakery in Pudding Lane, near London Bridge. It raged for five days, destroying much of the City of London. The post-fire reconstruction formed the basis of the modern-day City of London. As settlements spread beyond the original walled city, the City of London was soon stretching as far as the previously separate City of Westminster.

Expansion

The foundation of the Bank of England in 1694 spurred growth and transformed London into a global financial powerhouse. By the middle of the 18th century London was the largest city in Europe and within a hundred years had become the most populous and wealthiest in the world. The prospect of jobs and money lured millions of the dispossessed from the countryside and from abroad. They crowded into insanitary dwellings, many just east of the City, where docks provided employment. From the 1820s the fields and villages that ringed the city, places like Brompton, Islington and Battersea, filled rapidly with terraced housing for the growing numbers of people.

1 Queen Elizabeth I, who oversaw great change in the city ↑

2 Guy Fawkes, plotting King James I's downfall

2 The Great Fire of London, 1666

Did You Know?

After the Great Fire, Sir Christopher Wren designed 51 new churches for the city, plus St Paul's Cathedral.

1710

Christopher Wren's St Paul's cathedral is completed

1666

The Great Fire of London devastates the City

1801

The first census records a London population of over one million

1802

West India Dock is built, the beginning of a major expansion of London docklands

1826

London University established

1

2

Victorian London

Much of London today is Victorian. In this golden age of British engineering, many of the city's iconic buildings and structures – the modern Houses of Parliament, Tower Bridge, St Pancras station, the Royal Albert Hall and the London Underground – were built. In 1855 the Metropolitan Board of Works was created, the beginnings of a form of local government. Its chief engineer, Joseph Bazalgette, designed a ground-breaking underground sewer system which did much to alleviate the filth and stink in the streets and the river, reducing the outbreaks of cholera that had accompanied urban expansion. By the end of the 19th century, 4.5 million people lived in inner London and another 4 million in its immediate vicinity.

World Wars and Post-War Reconstruction

During World War I, Zeppelin airships bombed the city, but the damage and number of casualties was nothing as compared to the devastation wreaked during World War II. Much of London, particularly central areas, was flattened, first by the bombing during the Blitz of 1940–41 and then towards the end of the war by V-1 and V-2 rockets, early forms of cruise missiles. The

↑ Winston Churchill, prime minister during World War II

Timeline of events

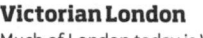

1836
First London rail terminus opens at London Bridge

1837
Queen Victoria makes Buckingham Palace her London residence

1858
Smelliness of the Thames forces parliament into recess

1851
The Great Exhibition is held in Hyde Park

1863
World's first underground railway opens between Paddington and Farringdon

substantial rebuilding that followed the war coincided with the decline of the docks and other Victorian industries. Enormous, imposing housing estates sprung up around the city, some of which remain to this day. Still around too are the Brutalist buildings of the Southbank Centre, developed on the banks of the Thames for the 1951 Festival of Britain, a celebration of British technology and culture. Mass immigration from the former colonies of Britain's rapidly disappearing empire, and from the Indian subcontinent and the West Indies in particular, contributed to the city's ever diverse population.

London Today

The city saw in the new millennium with a swathe of grand building projects the London Eye, Tate Modern and the ill-fated Millennium Dome – and cranes continue to dominate the skyline in a city that never seems finished. Indeed, regeneration reverberates around the city as it grapples to combat a housing crisis and toxic pollution levels. Despite a number of terror attacks and frequent, albeit moderate, clashes, especially in light of so-called gentrification, the enduring spirit of the city's inhabitants and sense of community prevails.

1 The Great Exhibition of 1851

2 Sleeping in a Tube station during World War II

3 The Festival of London

4 Millennium celebrations

Did You Know?

The Millennium Dome cost over £700 million to construct.

1908
London hosts the Olympic Games

2000
Ken Livingstone becomes London's first directly elected mayor

2005
Major terrorist attack takes place on London's transport system

1951
Festival of Britain held on the South Bank

2012
London hosts the Olympic Games for the third time

EXPERIENCE

Looking towards St Paul's Cathedral

WHITEHALL AND WESTMINSTER

Whitehall and Westminster have been at the centre of political and religious power in England for a thousand years. King Canute, who ruled at the beginning of the 11th century, was the first monarch to have a palace on what was then an island in the swampy meeting point of the Thames and its vanished tributary, the Tyburn. Canute built his palace beside the church that, some 50 years later, Edward the Confessor would enlarge into England's greatest abbey, giving the area its name (a minster is an abbey church). Over the following centuries the offices of state were established in the vicinity, many of them in Whitehall. This grand street took its name from the Palace of Whitehall that once stood there, established by Henry VIII in the early 16th century as a home of the royal court. The palace burnt down in 1698 but Whitehall remained at the heart of government, its buildings now occupied by the Ministry of Defence, the Foreign Office, Cabinet Office and several other prestigious government departments.

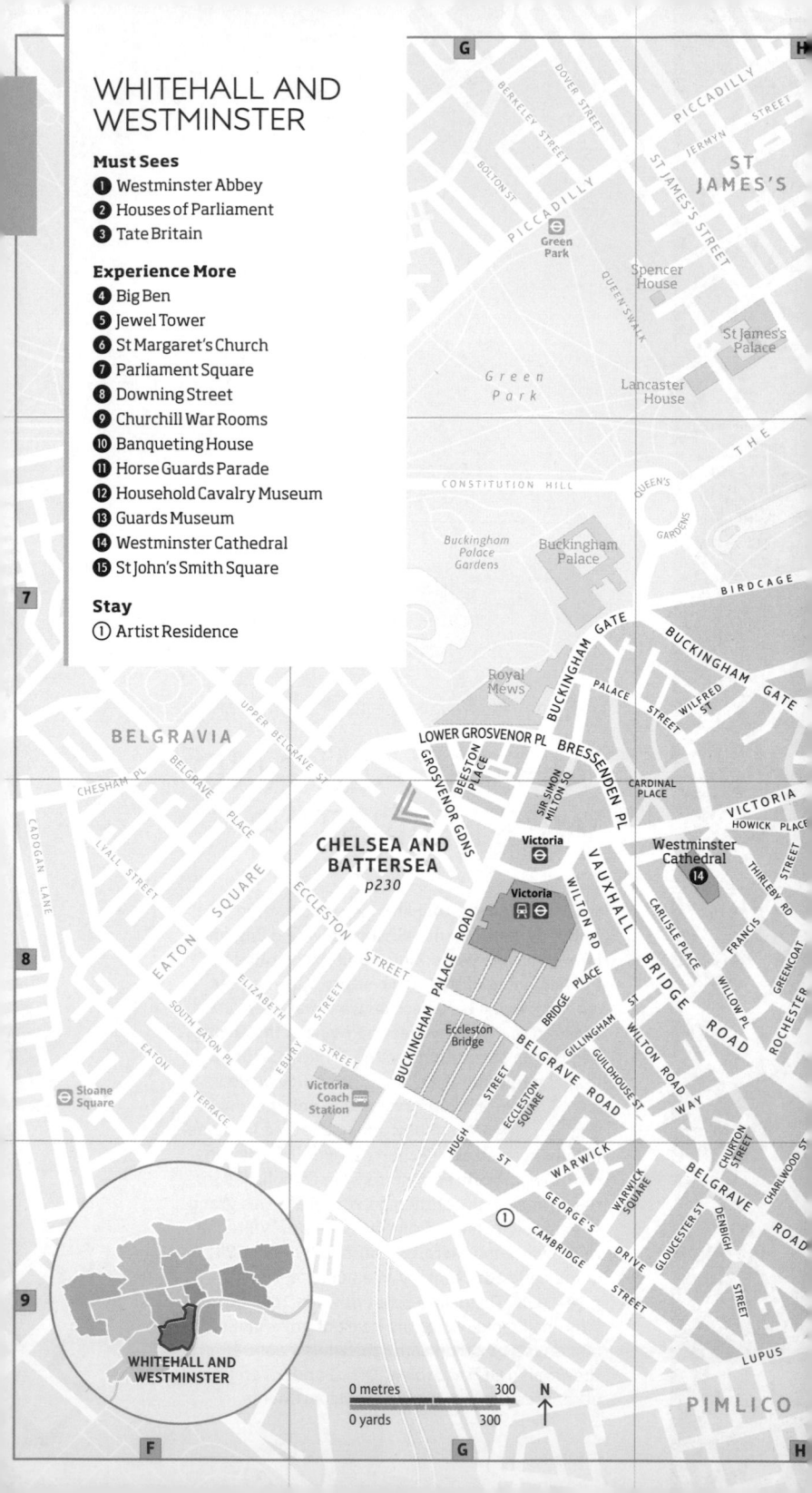

WHITEHALL AND WESTMINSTER

Must Sees
1. Westminster Abbey
2. Houses of Parliament
3. Tate Britain

Experience More
4. Big Ben
5. Jewel Tower
6. St Margaret's Church
7. Parliament Square
8. Downing Street
9. Churchill War Rooms
10. Banqueting House
11. Horse Guards Parade
12. Household Cavalry Museum
13. Guards Museum
14. Westminster Cathedral
15. St John's Smith Square

Stay
1. Artist Residence

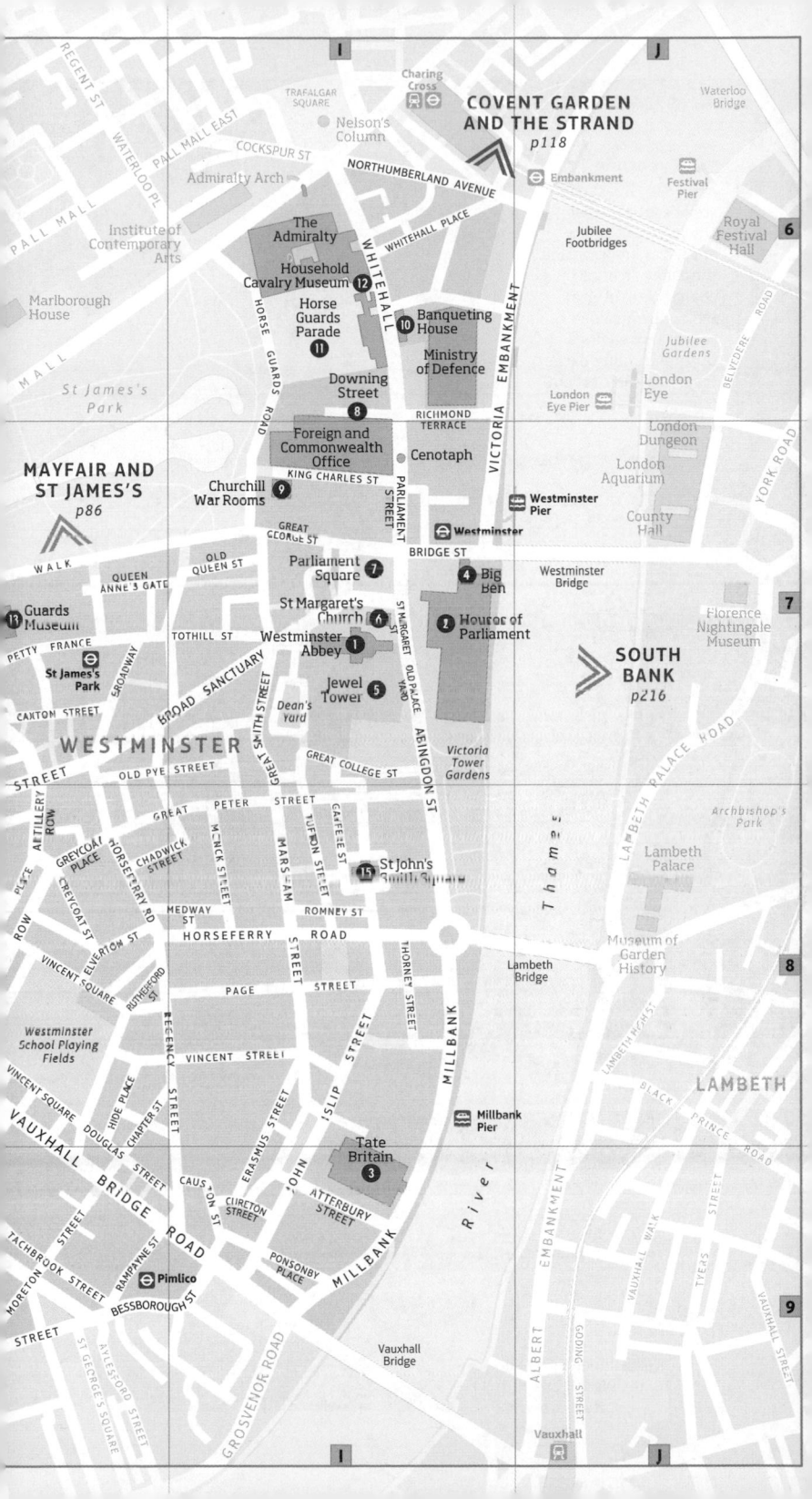

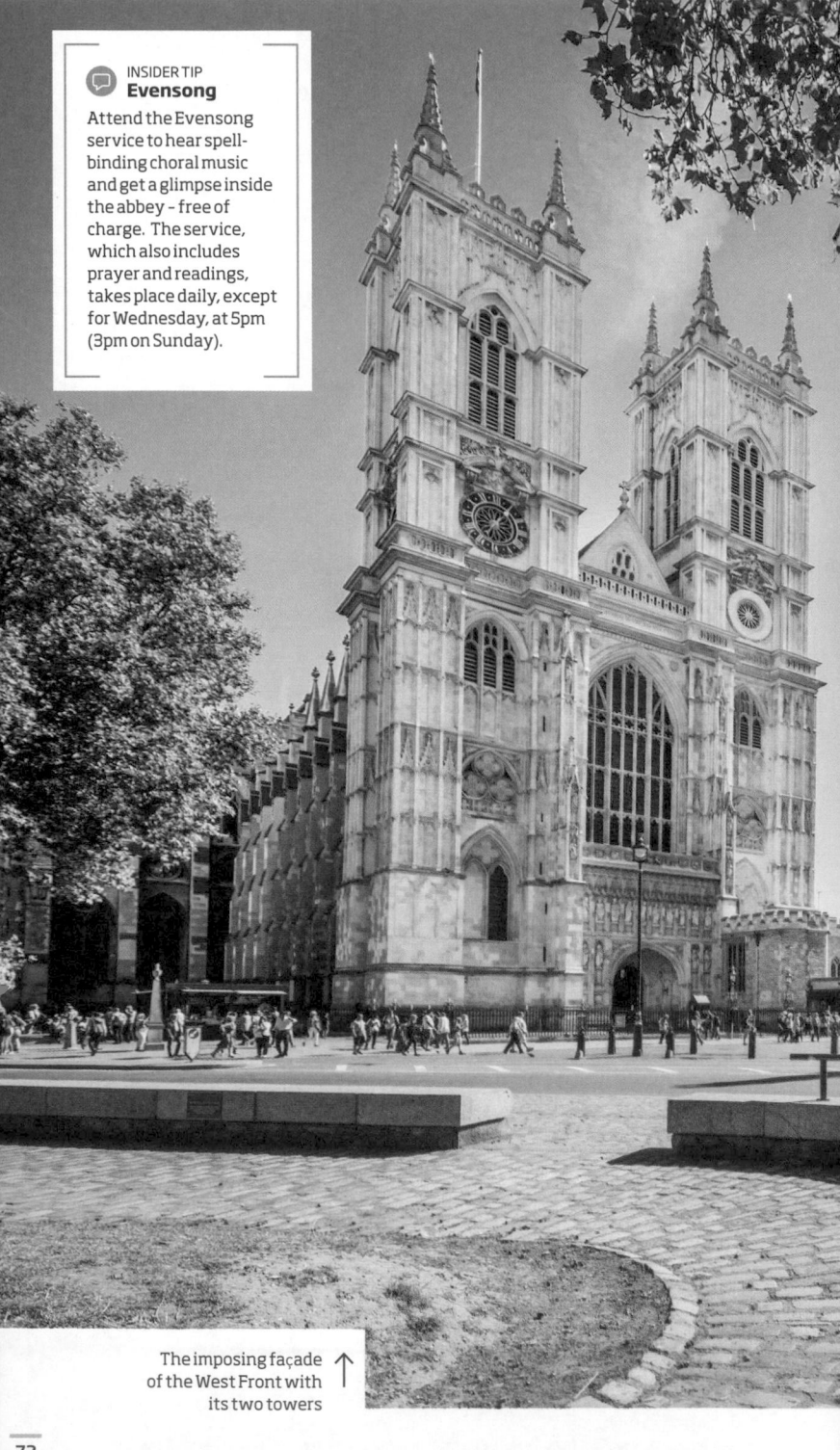

💬 INSIDER TIP
Evensong

Attend the Evensong service to hear spell-binding choral music and get a glimpse inside the abbey - free of charge. The service, which also includes prayer and readings, takes place daily, except for Wednesday, at 5pm (3pm on Sunday).

The imposing façade of the West Front with its two towers ↑

WESTMINSTER ABBEY

📍 I7 📍 Broad Sanctuary SW1 📍 St James's Park, Westminster
📍 Victoria, Waterloo 📍 Check website for specific parts of the
church 🌐 westminster-abbey.org

The final resting place of 17 of Britain's monarchs and numerous political and cultural icons, the glorious Gothic Westminster Abbey is the stunning setting for coronations, royal marriages and Christian worship.

Within the abbey walls are some of the best examples of medieval architecture in London and one of the most impressive collections of tombs and monuments in the world. Half national church, half national museum, the abbey is part of British national consciousness. Many of the leading lights from British history are buried or memorialized here, including poets and politicians, writers and scientists.

History of the Abbey

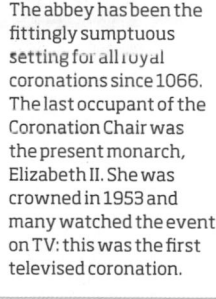

The first abbey church was established as early as the 10th century, by St Dunstan and a group of Benedictine monks. The present structure dates largely from the 13th century; the new French-influenced design was begun in 1245 at the behest of Henry III. It survived Henry VIII's 16th century onslaught on Britain's monastic buildings due to its unique role as the royal coronation church.

←

Statue of Richard I, known as Richard the Lionheart, facing the rear of Westminster Abbey

---

CORONATION

The abbey has been the fittingly sumptuous setting for all royal coronations since 1066. The last occupant of the Coronation Chair was the present monarch, Elizabeth II. She was crowned in 1953 and many watched the event on TV: this was the first televised coronation.

Inside the Abbey

The abbey's interior presents an exceptionally diverse array of architectural and sculptural styles, from the austere French Gothic of the nave, through the stunning complexity of Henry VII's Tudor chapel, to the riotous invention of the later 18th-century monuments. The latest addition is the 2018 Weston Tower, which provides access to the triforium and its Queen's Diamond Jubilee Galleries, packed with historical treasures.

The West Front towers were designed by Nicholas Hawksmoor.

① Monument to William Shakespeare in Poets' Corner.

② Executed by Queen Elizabeth I, the body of Mary Queen of Scots was brought to rest in Henry VII's Lady Chapel by her son James I in 1612.

③ The Westminster Abbey choir sing from their stalls in the quire every day. The original quire stalls were medieval but the ones you see now date from 1848.

Timeline

1050
△ New Benedictine abbey church begun by Edward the Confessor

1245
New church begun to the designs of Henry of Reyns

1269
△ Body of Edward the Confessor is moved to a new shrine in the abbey

1540
△ Monastery dissolved on the orders of King Henry VIII

74

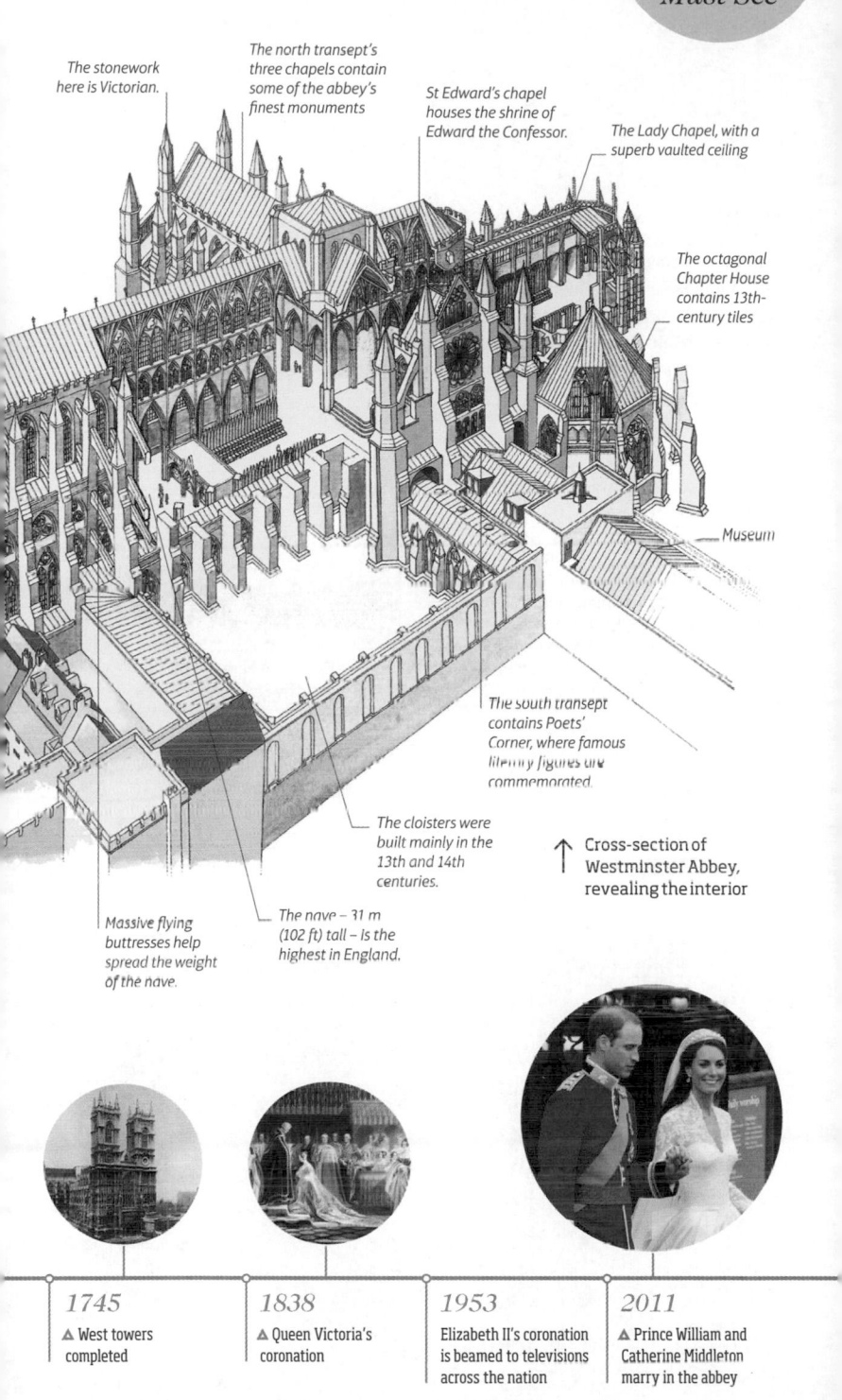

The stonework here is Victorian.

The north transept's three chapels contain some of the abbey's finest monuments

St Edward's chapel houses the shrine of Edward the Confessor.

The Lady Chapel, with a superb vaulted ceiling

The octagonal Chapter House contains 13th-century tiles

Museum

The south transept contains Poets' Corner, where famous literary figures are commemorated.

The cloisters were built mainly in the 13th and 14th centuries.

↑ Cross-section of Westminster Abbey, revealing the interior

Massive flying buttresses help spread the weight of the nave.

The nave – 31 m (102 ft) tall – is the highest in England.

1745
△ West towers completed

1838
△ Queen Victoria's coronation

1953
Elizabeth II's coronation is beamed to televisions across the nation

2011
△ Prince William and Catherine Middleton marry in the abbey

2 ⬙ 🚇 🛍

HOUSES OF PARLIAMENT

📍I7 🏠London SW1 🚇Westminster 🚆Victoria 🚢Westminster Pier
🕐For details on visiting and to buy tickets, check website 🔒Recesses: Easter,
Whitsun, summer (late Jul–early Sep), conference (mid-Sep–mid-Oct), mid-Nov,
Christmas 🌐parliament.uk/visit

At the heart of political power in England is the Palace of Westminster. Built in mock-Gothic style it lies beside the Thames near Westminster Bridge and makes an impressive sight, especially with the distinctive Elizabeth Tower.

For over 500 years the Palace of Westminster has been the seat of the two Houses of Parliament, called the Lords and the Commons. The Commons is made up of elected Members of Parliament (MPs) of different political parties; the party – or coalition of parties – with the most MPs forms the Government, and its leader becomes prime minister. MPs from other parties make up the Opposition. Commons debates are impartially chaired by an MP designated as Speaker. The Government formulates legislation which must be agreed to in both Houses before it becomes law.

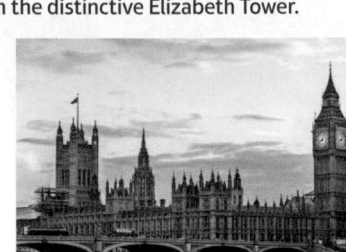

↑ The Houses of Parliament, designed by Sir Charles Barry

→ The mock-Gothic masterpiece of the Palace of Westminster

Government and Opposition parties face each other across the Common Chamber.

The vast bell named Big Ben was hung in 1858 and chimes on the hour.

Entrance to Westminster Hall

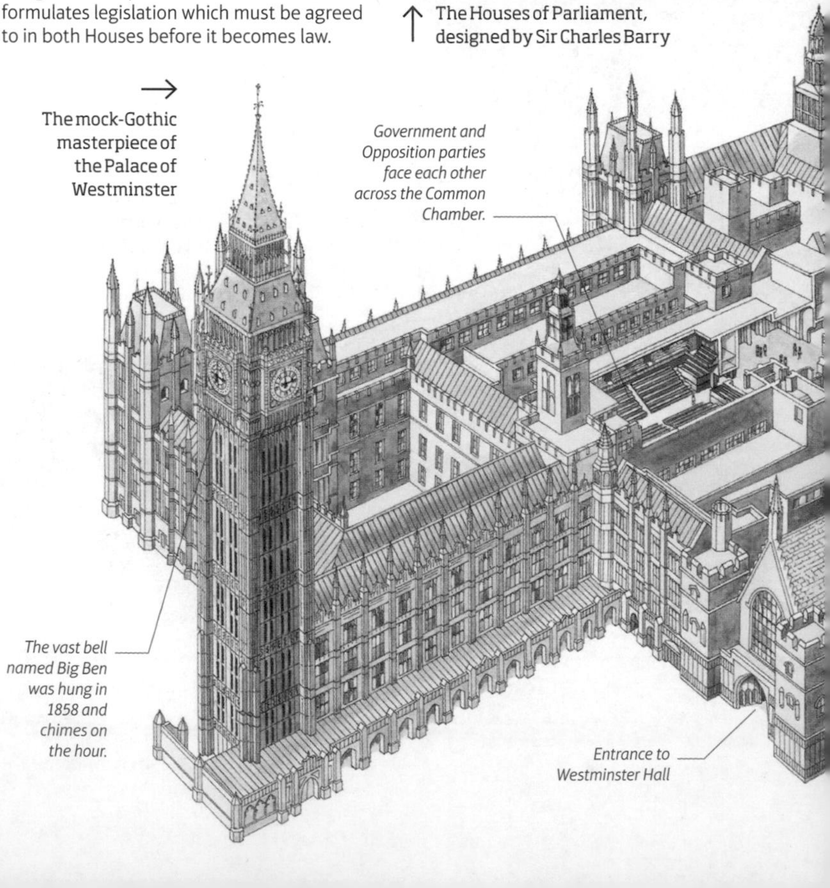

1605
▽ Guy Fawkes and others try to blow up the king and Houses of Parliament

1941
▽ Chamber of House of Commons destroyed by World War II bomb

1042
△ Work starts on first palace for Edward the Confessor

1834
△ Palace destroyed by fire; only Westminster Hall and the Jewel Tower survive

People who come to meet their MP wait under a ceiling of rich mosaics in the central lobby.

The Lords Chamber is upholstered in red.

Peers' entrance

This is one of the surviving parts of the original Palace of Westminster, dating from 1097.

↑ The green-upholstered seats of the Common Chamber, where the government sits

TATE BRITAIN

THE NATIONAL
COLLECTION OF
BRITISH ART

The stately façade ↑
of Tate Britain, home
of British art

3 🜄 🍴 🖥 🛍

TATE BRITAIN

📍I9 🚇Millbank SW1 🚇Pimlico 🚆Victoria, Vauxhall 🚢4 Millbank Pier, every 40 mins 🕐10am–6pm daily (til 10pm first Fri, usually every other month) 🚫24–26 Dec 🌐tate.org.uk

The nation's largest collection of British art, spanning the 16th to the 21st centuries, is held in a fabulous Neo-Classical building facing the river. The works include sculpture and modern installation pieces, plus a separate wing given over to the moody paintings of British artist J M W Turner.

The gallery exhibits a broad range of British art, from Tudor portraits and 18th-century landscapes to a large sculpture collection and modern art. Displays change frequently and the gallery's broad definition of British art stretches to work by non-British artists who spent time in the country, such as Canaletto and James Whistler. The gallery opened in 1897, founded on the private collection of the sugar merchant Henry Tate and works from the older National Gallery. The Tate includes seven rooms added to display the paintings of J M W Turner, one of Britain's most revered artists. The Turner Bequest, as it is known, was left to the nation by Turner on his death in 1851. It is displayed in its own wing, called the Clore Gallery, and consists of some 300 oil paintings, 300 sketchbooks, and about 20,000 watercolours and drawings, . Major temporary exhibitions here always draw huge crowds

↑ Turner's *Peace – Burial at Sea* (1842), a tribute to his friend and rival David Wilkie

↑ Inside the gallery, where art graces every corner

TURNER PRIZE

Every other year, Tate Britain exhibits the shortlisted works for the prestigious and often controversial Turner Prize, which was established in 1904. Representing all visual arts, four contemporary artists are shortlisted annually on the basis of their work during the preceding year, before a judging panel picks the winner. Among the most sensational of the boundary-testing winners have been Damien Hirst's *Mother and Child, Divided* (1995) and the ceramics of Grayson Perry *(right)*.

EXPERIENCE MORE

4
Big Ben

📍 I7 🏛 Bridge St
SW1 🚇 Westminster
🌐 parliament.uk/bigben

Big Ben is not the name of
the world-famous four-faced
clock in the 96 m (315 ft)
tower that rises above the
Houses of Parliament, but of
the resonant 13.7-tonne bell
inside the tower on which the
hours are struck. It is thought
to be named after the Chief
Commissioner of Works Sir
Benjamin Hall. Cast at Whitechapel in 1858, it was the
second giant bell made for
the clock, the first having
become cracked during a test
ringing. The clock is the largest in Britain, its four dials 7 m
(23 ft) in diameter and the
minute hand 4.2 m (14 ft)
long, made in hollow copper
for lightness. The tower itself
was renamed the Elizabeth
Tower in 2012 in honour of
Queen Elizabeth II in her
Diamond Jubilee year.

A symbol the world over,
Big Ben has kept exact time
for the nation more or less
continuously since it was first
set in motion in May 1859.

Now, however, it stands silent,
closed for essential building
works until 2021 – tours are
suspended for the duration.

5
Jewel Tower

📍 I7 🏛 Abingdon St SW1
🚇 Westminster 🕐 Apr-
Sep: 10am–6pm daily; Oct:
10am–5pm daily; Nov-
Mar: 10am–4pm Sat & Sun
🚫 Jan 1, 24–26 & 31 Dec
🌐 english-heritage.org.uk

This and Westminster Hall
(p70) are the only remaining
vestiges of the old Palace of
Westminster. The tower was
built in 1365 as a stronghold
for Edward III's treasure and
today houses a fascinating
exhibition, "Parliament Past
and Present", which relates
the history of Parliament. The
display on the upper floor is
devoted to the history of the
tower itself.

The tower served as the
Weights and Measures office
from 1869 until 1938 and
another small display relates
to that era. Alongside are the
remains of the moat and a
medieval quay.

6
St Margaret's Church

📍 I7 🏛 Parliament Sq SW1
🚇 Westminster 🕐 9:30am-
3:30pm Mon-Fri, 9:30am-
1:30pm Sat, 2:30-4:30pm
Sun 🌐 westminster-abbey.
org/st-margarets-church

This late-15th-century church
has long been a favoured
venue for political and society
weddings, such as Winston
and Clementine Churchill's.
Although much restored, the
church retains some Tudor

→
Telephones in the Map Room of the Churchill War Rooms

features, notably a stained-glass window commemorating the marriage of King Henry VIII and his first wife, Catherine of Aragon.

7 Parliament Square

◎ I7 ⚑ SW1 🚇 Westminster

Laid out in 1868 to provide a more open aspect for the new Houses of Parliament, the square today is hemmed in by heavy traffic. Statues of statesmen are dominated by Winston Churchill, glowering at the House of Commons. On the north side, Abraham Lincoln stands in front of the mock-Gothic Middlesex Guildhall. Millicent Fawcett – a campaigner for women's suffrage – is the only female represented in the square.

8 Downing Street

◎ I6 ⚑ SW1 🚇 Westminster ⚠ To the public

Sir George Downing (1623–84) spent part of his youth in the American colonies. He was the second person to graduate from the nascent Harvard College, before returning to

←
The Elizabeth Tower, seen from Albert Embankment

fight for the Parliamentarians in the English Civil War. In 1680, he bought land near Whitehall Palace and built a street of houses. Four of these survive, though they are much altered. King George II gave No 10 to Sir Robert Walpole in 1732. Since then it has been the official residence of the British prime minister.

9 🚴🚇Ⓜ📧🏛 Churchill War Rooms

◎ I7 ⚑ Clive Steps, King Charles St SW1 🚇 Westminster, St James's Park 🕐 9:30am 6pm daily (last adm: 5pm) 🚫 24–26 Dec, 1 Jan 🌐 iwm.org.uk

This intriguing slice of 20th-century history is a warren of rooms below the Government Office building, where the War Cabinet met during World War II, when German bombs were falling on London. The War Rooms include living quarters for key ministers and military leaders and a Cabinet Room, where strategic decisions were taken. They are laid out as they were when the war ended, complete with Churchill's desk, communications equipment and maps for plotting military strategy. The Churchill Museum is a multimedia exhibit recording Churchill's life and career, and the display "Undercover: Life in Churchill's Bunker" features personal stories, objects and interviews with those who worked in the War Rooms. Tours must be booked ahead.

THE CENOTAPH

On Remembrance Sunday every year - the Sunday nearest 11 November - ceremonies held around the UK honour those who have lost their lives serving in conflicts since World War I. The Cenotaph, a monument on Whitehall completed in 1920 by Sir Edwin Lutyens, is the focal point of London's remembrance service, when members of the royal family and other dignitaries place wreaths of red poppies at its base.

Henry VIII's jousting
grounds, now Horse
Guards Parade ↑

10 🅐 🅑

Banqueting House

📍 I6 🏛 Whitehall SW1
🚇 Embankment, Charing
Cross, Westminster
🕐 10am–5pm daily (last
adm: 4:15pm) 🚫 Public hols,
22 Dec–1 Jan 🌐 hrp.org.uk

This delightful building is of
great architectural importance.
It was the first in central
London to embody the
Classical Palladian style that
designer Inigo Jones brought
back from his travels in Italy.
Completed in 1622, its
disciplined stone façade
marked a startling change
from the Elizabethans' fussy
turrets and unrestrained
external decoration.

Rubens's ceiling paintings,
a complex allegory on the
exaltation of James I, were
commissioned by his son,
Charles I, in 1630. This blatant
glorification of royalty was
despised by Oliver Cromwell
and the Parliamentarians,
who executed King Charles I
on a scaffold outside
Banqueting House in 1649.
Eleven years later, the English
monarchy was restored with
the coronation of Charles II.

The building is used today
for official functions, and may
close early when these are
scheduled: check the website
for details.

11

Horse Guards Parade

📍 I6 🏛 Whitehall SW1
🚇 Westminster, Charing
Cross, Embankment

This is where the Trooping the
Colour ceremony (p58) takes
place each year, but you can
see royal pageantry in action
daily: Changing the Life Guard
takes place at 10am (11am
on Sunday), and there's a
guard inspection at 4pm.

This was Henry VIII's tiltyard
(tournament ground); nearby
is a trace of the "real tennis"
court where the king is said to
have played the precursor of
modern lawn tennis. The
elegant buildings, completed
in 1755, were designed by
William Kent. On the opposite
side, the ivy-covered Citadel is
a bomb-proof structure built in
1940 beside the Admiralty.
During World War II, it was
used as a communications
headquarters by the Navy.

QUEEN ANNE'S GATE

Not far from St James's Park Tube station is Queen Anne's
Gate, a well-preserved street lined with spacious
terraced houses, many of which are Grade I-listed.
Most date from 1704 and are notable for the ornate
canopies over each front door. At the east end of the
street are houses built some 70 years later, some
sporting blue plaques that record former residents,
such as Lord Palmerston, a prime minister during the
Victorian era. It is rumoured that the British Secret
Service, MI5, was formerly based in this unlikely spot.

working stables, and kids (big and small) can try on uniforms.

---

13 ⟨⟩ ⟨⟩ ⟨⟩

Guards Museum

📍H7 🏠 Birdcage Walk SW1 🚇 St James's Park ⏰ 10am–4pm daily (last adm: 3:30pm) 🚫 Mid-Dec–end Jan & for ceremonies 🌐 theguardsmuseum.com

Entered from Birdcage Walk, this museum is under the parade ground of Wellington Barracks, headquarters of the five Foot Guards regiments. A must for military buffs, the museum illustrates battles in which the Guards have taken part, from the English Civil War (1642–8) to the present. Weapons and colourful uniforms are on display, as are some fascinating models.

---

14 ⟨⟩

Westminster Cathedral

📍H8 🏠 Victoria Street SW1 🚇 Victoria ⏰ 7am–7pm Mon–Fri, 8am–7pm Sat & Sun 🌐 westminstercathedral.org.uk

One of London's rare Byzantine buildings, this cathedral was designed by John Francis Bentley for the Catholic diocese and completed in 1903. Its 87-m- (285-ft-) high red-brick bell tower, with horizontal stripes of white stone, has a superb viewing gallery at the top (there is a charge to take the lift). The rich interior decoration, with marble of varying colours and intricate mosaics, makes the domes above the nave seem incongruous. They were left bare because the project ran out of money. Eric Gill's dramatic reliefs of the 14 Stations of the Cross, created during World War I, adorn the piers of the nave. Service times are on the website. The organ is superb; there are often free recitals on Sundays at 4:45pm.

---

15 ⟨⟩

St John's Smith Square

📍J8 🏠 Smith Sq SW1 🚇 Westminster ⏰ For concerts only 🌐 sjss.org.uk

A masterpiece of English Baroque architecture, Thomas Archer's plump church looks as if it is trying to burst from the confines of the square. Today principally a concert hall, it has an accident-prone history: completed in 1728, it was burned down in 1742, struck by lightning in 1773 and destroyed by a World War II bomb in 1941. There is a basement restaurant, open on weekdays for lunch and on concert evenings.

---

12 ⟨⟩ ⟨⟩

Household Cavalry Museum

📍I6 🏠 Horse Guards, Whitehall SW1 🚇 Charing Cross, Westminster, Embankment ⏰ Apr–Oct: 10am–6pm daily; Nov–Mar: 10am–5pm daily 🚫 Good Fri, 20 Jul, 24–26 Dec; occasionally for ceremonies 🌐 householdcavalrymuseum.co.uk

A collection of artifacts and interactive displays cover the history of the senior regiments based at Horse Guards, from their role in the 1815 Battle of Waterloo to their service in Afghanistan in the early 21st century. Visitors can see the

The Life Guards, part of the royal Household Cavalry ↑

A SHORT WALK
WHITEHALL AND WESTMINSTER

Distance 2 km (1.25 miles) **Nearest Tube**
St James's Park **Time** 20 minutes

London has comparatively little monumental
architecture, but a stroll through the historic
seat of both the government and the established
church uncovers broad, stately avenues designed to
overawe with pomp. On weekdays the streets are
crowded with members of the civil service, while at
weekends they teem mainly with tourists, visiting
some of London's most famous sights.

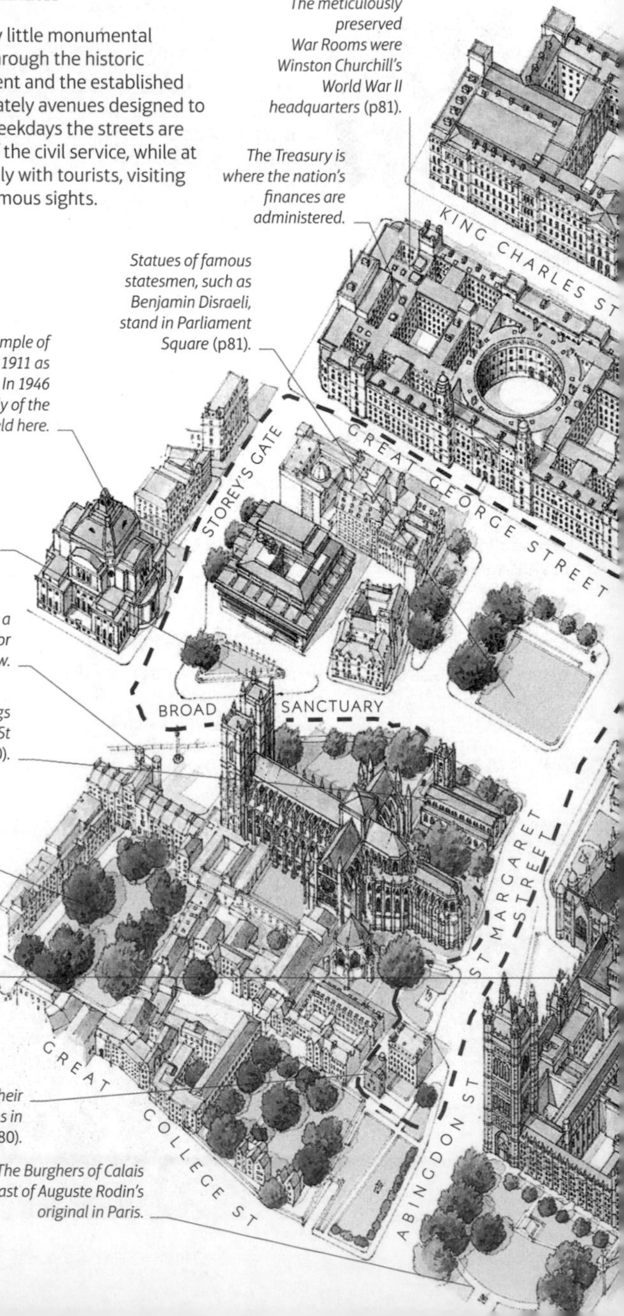

The meticulously
preserved
War Rooms were
Winston Churchill's
World War II
headquarters (p81).

The Treasury is
where the nation's
finances are
administered.

Statues of famous
statesmen, such as
Benjamin Disraeli,
stand in Parliament
Square (p81).

Central Hall is a florid example of
the Beaux Arts style, built in 1911 as
a Methodist meeting hall. In 1946
the first General Assembly of the
United Nations was held here.

Westminster Abbey
is London's most
important church (p72).

The Sanctuary was a
medieval safe place for
those escaping the law.

Society weddings
often take place in St
Margaret's Church (p80).

Westminster School
was founded in
Dean's Yard in 1540.

Richard I's Statue, by
Carlo Marochetti (1860),
depicts the 12th-century
Coeur de Lion (Lionheart).

Kings once stored their
most valuable possessions in
the Jewel Tower (p80).

The Burghers of Calais
is a cast of Auguste Rodin's
original in Paris.

KING CHARLES ST

GREAT GEORGE STREET

STOREY'S GATE

BROAD SANCTUARY

ST MARGARET STREET

GREAT COLLEGE ST

ABINGDON ST

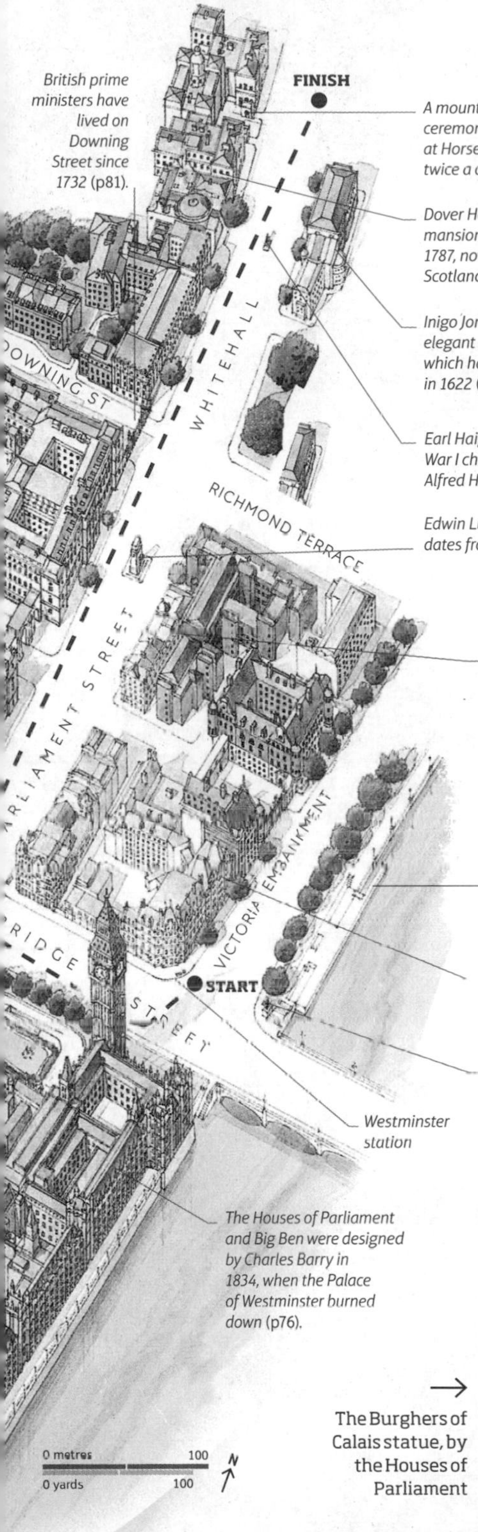

FINISH ●

British prime ministers have lived on Downing Street since 1732 (p81).

A mounted guard is ceremonially changed at Horse Guards Parade twice a day (p82).

Dover House, a stately mansion dating from 1787, now houses the Scotland Office.

Inigo Jones designed the elegant Banqueting House, which has a Rubens ceiling, in 1622 (p82).

Earl Haig, the British World War I chief, was sculpted by Alfred Hardiman in 1936.

Edwin Lutyens's Cenotaph dates from 1920 (p81).

Richmond House is William Whitfield's prize-winning 1980s building for the Department of Health.

DOWNING ST

WHITEHALL

RICHMOND TERRACE

PARLIAMENT STREET

VICTORIA EMBANKMENT

BRIDGE

STREET

Westminster Pier is a starting point for riverboat excursions.

Portcullis House provides offices for Members of Parliament.

Boudicca, the British queen who resisted the Romans, was portrayed by Thomas Thornycroft in the 1850s.

● **START**

Westminster station

The Houses of Parliament and Big Ben were designed by Charles Barry in 1834, when the Palace of Westminster burned down (p76).

0 metres		100
0 yards		100

N ↑

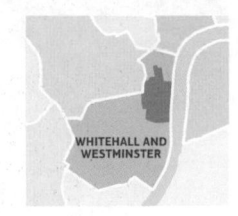

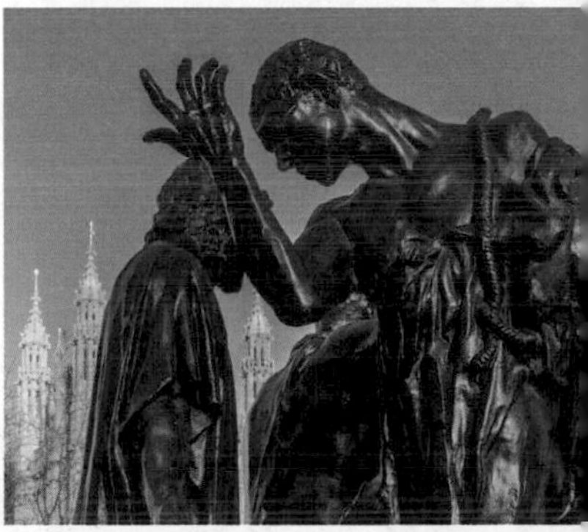

→
The Burghers of Calais statue, by the Houses of Parliament

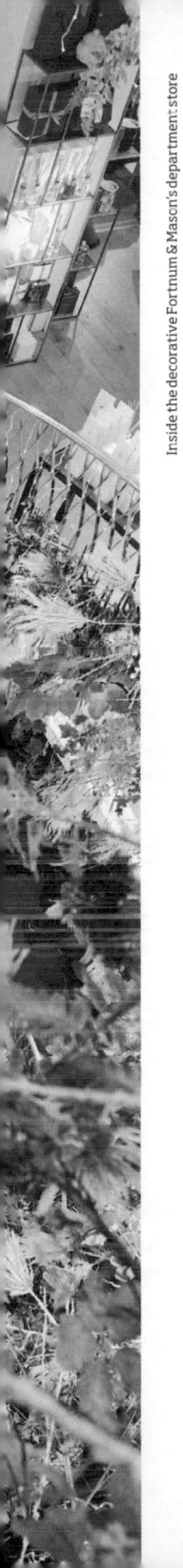

MAYFAIR AND ST JAMES'S

The exclusivity of these most gentrified of London districts, with their royal connections, stretches back centuries. St James's Palace was the first royal residence to be constructed on this patch of land, built in the 1530s by Henry VIII who also laid out the hunting grounds that would become St James's Park. During the 17th century several large mansions were added as aristocrats sought proximity to the royal court. Mayfair did not emerge as a tangible district until the late 17th century when the annual May Fair, held around present-day Shepherd Market, was moved here. The fair was abolished in 1764, having earned a reputation for debauchery and rowdiness that did not sit well with the wealthy residents moving to the area as the city expanded westwards. Three great squares were built and Mayfair became the property of a small number of landed estates, the most significant of which, the Grosvenor Estate, remains in the hands of the Grosvenor family to this day.

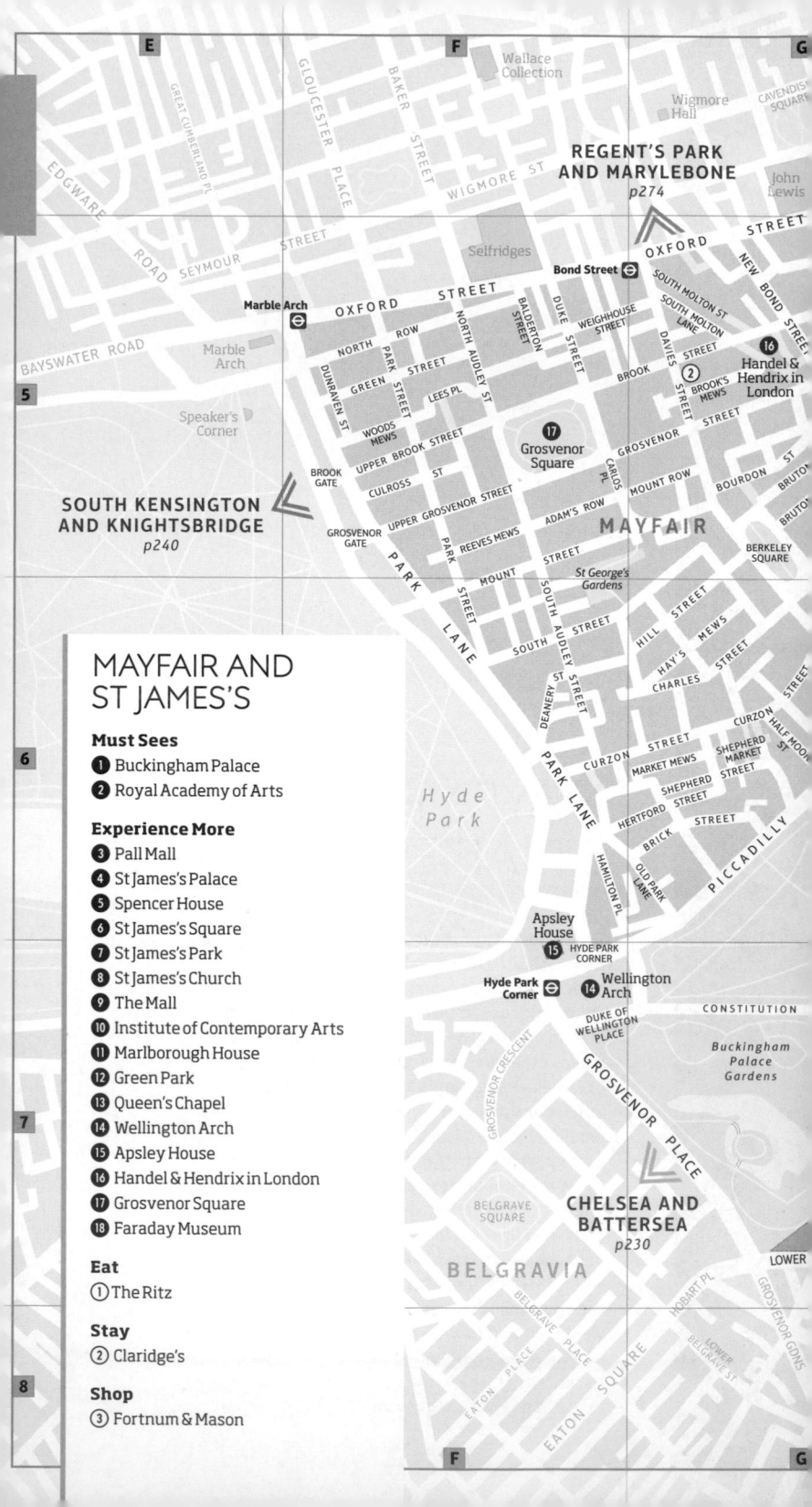

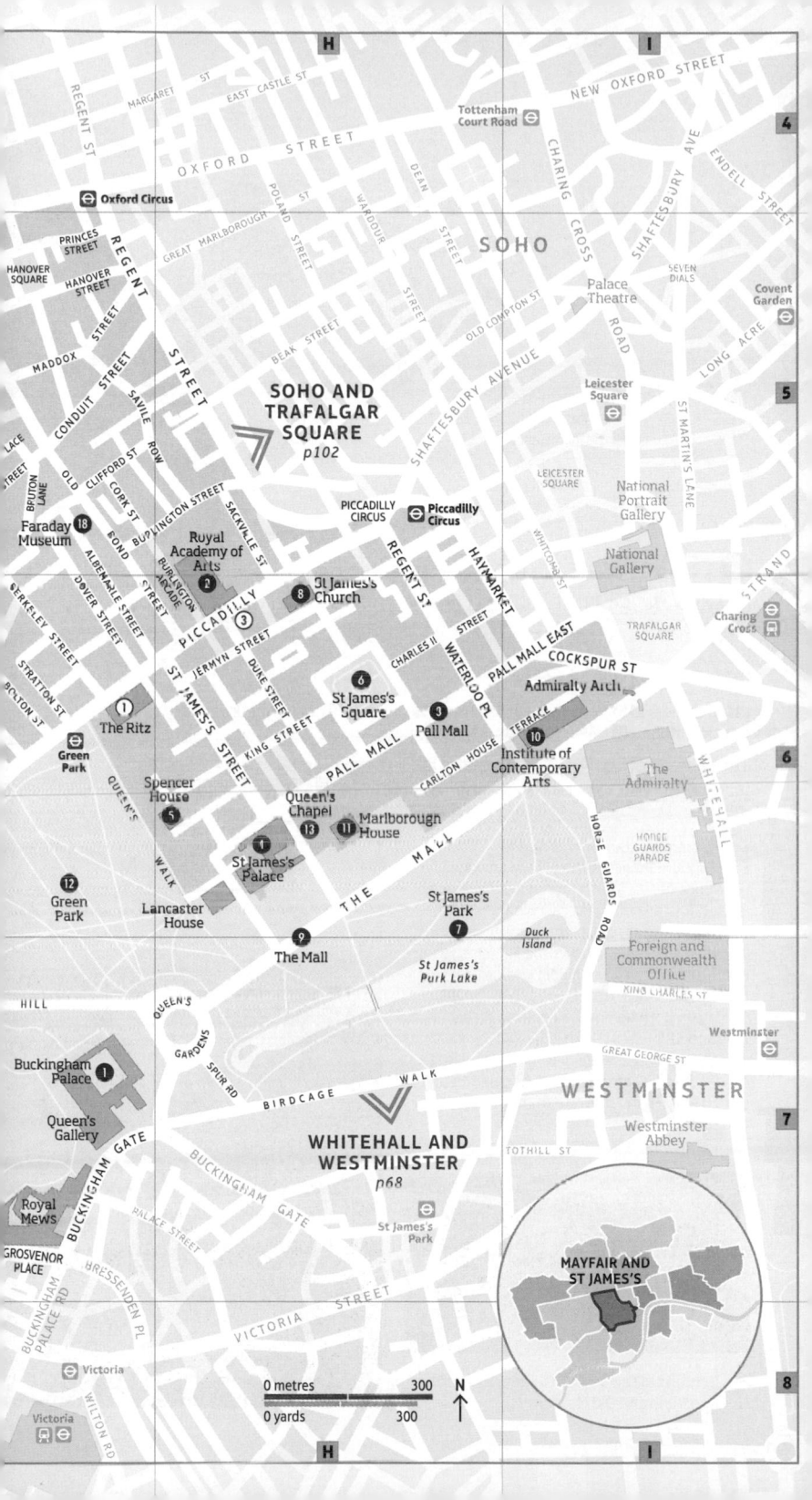

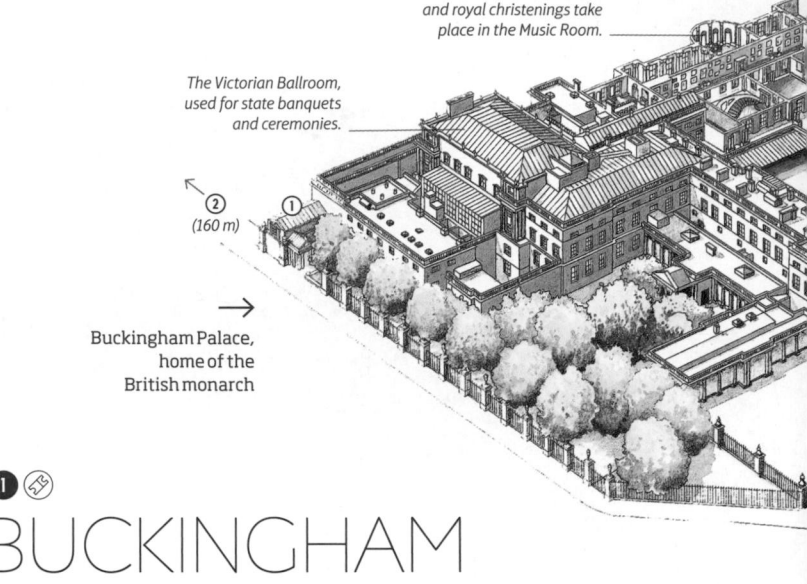

State guests are presented and royal christenings take place in the Music Room.

The Victorian Ballroom, used for state banquets and ceremonies.

② (160 m) ①

→

Buckingham Palace, home of the British monarch

❶ 🎨

BUCKINGHAM PALACE

📍G7 🏠SW1 🚇St James's Park, Victoria 🚆Victoria 🕐Opening times vary, check website 🌐royalcollection.org.uk

The Queen's official London residence is one of the capital's best recognized landmarks. Visit to get a behind-the-scenes look at how the royals live.

Both administrative offices and family home, Buckingham Palace is the official London residence of the British monarchy. The palace is used for ceremonial occasions for visiting heads of state as well as the weekly meeting between the Queen and Prime Minister. John Nash converted the original Buckingham House into a palace for George IV (reigned 1820–30). Both he and his brother, William IV (reigned 1830–37), died before work was completed, and Queen Victoria was the first monarch to live at the palace. She added a fourth wing to incorporate more bedrooms and guest rooms.

↑ Exhibits in the Queen's Gallery include fine porcelain and Old Masters

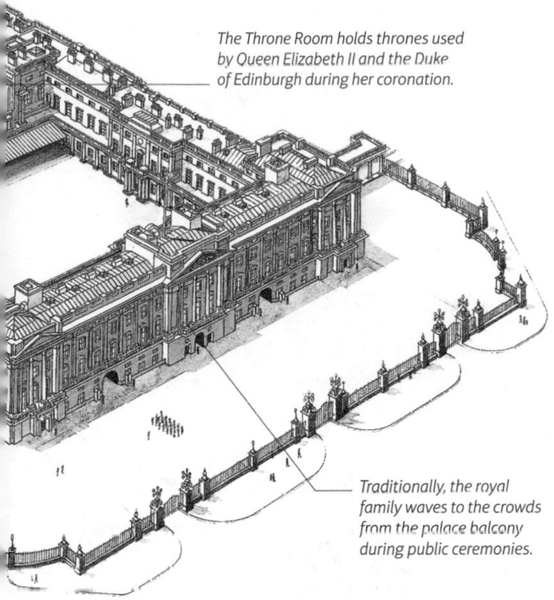

The Throne Room holds thrones used by Queen Elizabeth II and the Duke of Edinburgh during her coronation.

Traditionally, the royal family waves to the crowds from the palace balcony during public ceremonies.

→ Soldiers take part in the Trooping the Colour ceremony

↑ Dusk falls over the East façade, which was added to the Palace in 1913

The Queen's Gallery

📍G7 🚇St James's Park, Victoria 🕐10am-5:30pm daily (Aug & Sep: 9:30am-5:30pm; last adm: 4:15pm) 🚫Between exhibitions, check website

The royal family posesses one of the finest and most valuable art collections in the world, including works by Johannes Vermeer and Leonardo da Vinci. The Queen's Gallery hosts a rolling programme of the Royal Collection's most impressive masterpieces, with temporary exhibitions featuring fine art, porcelain, jewels, furniture and manuscripts.

Royal Mews

📍G7 🚇St James's Park, Victoria 🕐Apr-Oct: 10am-5pm daily; Nov, Feb-Mar: 10am-4pm Mon-Sat 🚫Subject to closure at short notice, check website; Dec-Jan

Head to the Royal Mews to discover plenty of royal pomp. Stables and coach houses, designed by Nash in 1825, accommodate the horses and coaches used by the royal family on state occasions. The Mews' extensive collection of coaches, motorcars and carriages include the Irish state coach, bought by Queen Victoria for the State Opening of Parliament; the open-topped 1902 royal landau, used to give the best view of newlywed royal couples; and the glass coach, also used for royal weddings. The newest coach is the Diamond Jubilee State Coach, built in 2012. The star exhibit is the Gold State Coach: built for George III in 1761, with panels by Giovanni Cipriani, it has been used at every coronation since 1821.

ROYAL ACADEMY OF ARTS

H6 **Burlington House, Piccadilly W1** **Piccadilly Circus, Green Park**
10am–6pm daily (til 10pm Fri) **Good Fri, 24–26 Dec** **royalacademy.org.uk**

Though it holds one of the nation's great art collections, the Royal Academy of Arts is most renowned for its blockbuster temporary exhibitions, as well as its popular annual Summer Exhibition.

Celebrating its 250th anniversary in 2018, the Royal Academy of Arts (RA) is one of Britain's oldest art institutions and holds one of its most prestigious collections of British art. It has always been led by its elected and appointed Royal Academicians, artists themselves, whose works make up the bulk of the permanent collection and who help to deliver the Royal Academy Schools' programme. The collection is displayed across two Italianate buildings, palatial Burlington House and Burlington Gardens. The two are now linked by a bridge, built to mark the anniversary. Several new galleries including The Vaults and the Collection Gallery were opened for the occasion too.

↑ The exterior of the Royal Academy of Arts

→ Considering works on display during the annual Summer Exhibition

1 Sir Joshua Reynolds attempted to rival Dutch master Rembrandt with this self-portrait painted in c 1780.

2 The only marble sculpture by Michelangelo in Britain is his *Taddei Tondo*; carved in 1504–5, it depicts the Virgin and Child with the Infant St John.

3 The Collection Gallery features Giampetrino's 16th-century copy of Leonardo da Vinci's *The Last Supper*.

Did You Know?

As well as a gallery, the RA is an independent fine art school – it was Britain's first, founded in 1769.

THE SUMMER EXHIBITION

The highlight of the RA calendar and among the most talked-about events in British art is the Summer Exhibition, held annually since 1769. Anyone can submit their work, for a fee, to be considered for the show, making it a potentially career-changing event for unknown artists, though established artists exhibit too. Over a thousand entries are selected, ranging from painting, printmaking and sculpture to photography, film and architecture, and displayed to the public, for an admission charge, between June and August in the main galleries of Burlington House. Most of the works displayed are for sale.

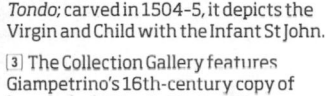

EXPERIENCE MORE

3

Pall Mall

📍 H6 🏠 SW1 🚇 Charing Cross, Piccadilly Circus, Green Park

This dignified street is named for the game of palle-maille – a cross between croquet and golf – which was played here in the 17th century. For close to 200 years, Pall Mall has been at the heart of London's clubland. Here, exclusive gentlemen's clubs were formed for members of the elite.

The clubhouses now amount to a textbook of the most fashionable architects of their era. At the east end, on the left is the colonnaded entrance to No 116, Nash's United Services Club (1827). This was the favourite club of the Duke of Wellington and now houses the Institute of Directors. Facing it, on the other side of Waterloo Place, is the Athenaeum (No 107), designed three years later by Decimus Burton, and long the powerhouse of the British establishment. Next door are two clubs by Sir Charles Barry, architect of the Houses of Parliament (p76): the Travellers' at No 106 and the Reform at No 104. The clubs' stately interiors are well-preserved but only members and their guests are admitted.

4

St James's Palace

📍 H6 🏠 Pall Mall SW1 🚇 Green Park 🕐 To the public 🌐 royal.uk

Built by Henry VIII in the late 1530s on the site of a former leper hospital, this palace was a primary royal residence only briefly, mainly during the reign of Elizabeth I and in the late 17th and early 18th centuries. In 1952, Queen Elizabeth II made her first speech as monarch here, and foreign ambassadors are still officially accredited to the Court of St James's. Its northern gatehouse, seen from St James's Street, is one of London's great Tudor landmarks. The palace remains a royal residence for, among others, The Princess Royal and Princess Alexandra, and its State Apartments are used during official State visits.

5 ♿ Ⓜ

Spencer House

📍 H6 🏠 27 St James's Pl SW1 🚇 Green Park 🕐 Sep-Jul: 10am-5:30pm Sun (last adm: 4:30pm) 🌐 spencerhouse.co.uk

This Palladian palace, built in 1766 for the first Earl Spencer,

an ancestor of the late Diana Princess of Wales, has been completely restored to its 18th-century splendour (thanks to an £18 million renovation project). It contains some wonderful paintings and contemporary furniture. The house is open to the public on Sundays, for guided tours only.

6

St James's Square

📍 H6 🏠 SW1 🚇 Green Park, Piccadilly Circus

London's squares, quadrangles of elegant homes surrounding gated gardens, are among the city's most attractive features. St James's, one of London's earliest, was laid out in the 1670s and lined by exclusive houses for those whose business made it vital for them to live near St James's Palace. Many buildings date from the 18th and 19th centuries and have had many illustrious residents. During World War II, generals Eisenhower and de Gaulle both had headquarters here.

Today, No 10 on the north side, Chatham House (1736), is home to the Royal Institute for International Affairs. In the northwest corner, at No 14, is

←

The elegant Spencer House, on the edge of Green Park

→ The royal St James's Park, famed for its floral displays

the **London Library** (1896), a private lending library founded in 1841 by historian Thomas Carlyle (p234) and others. It offers guided tours at 6pm on some weekdays (check the website). The lovely gardens in the middle contain an equestrian statue of William III, here since 1808.

London Library
🌐 londonlibrary.co.uk

St James's Park

📍 H6 🏠 SW1 🚇 St James's Park 🕐 5am-midnight daily 🌐 royalparks.org.uk

In summer, office workers sunbathe between the dazzling flowerbeds of the

↑ Stained glass at the Wren-designed St James's Church

capital's most ornamental park. In winter, the sunbathers are replaced with overcoated civil servants discuss affairs of state as they stroll by the lake, eyed by its resident ducks, geese and pelicans (which are fed at 2:30pm daily).

Originally a marsh, the park was drained by Henry VIII and incorporated into his hunting grounds. On his return from exile in France, Charles II had it remodelled in the more continental style as pedestrian pleasure gardens, with an aviary along its southern edge (hence Birdcage Walk, the name of the street running alongside the park, where the aviary once was).

It is a hugely popular place to escape the city's hustle and bustle, with an appealing view of Whitehall rooftops and Buckingham Palace, a restaurant open daily and an attractive lake.

St James's Church

📍 H6 🏠 197 Piccadilly W1 🚇 Piccadilly Circus 🕐 8am-7pm daily 🌐 sjp.org.uk

Among the many churches Christopher Wren designed, this is said to be one of his favourites. It has been altered

SHOP

Fortnum & Mason
The finest foods, wrapped in teal, and sales floors are the hallmarks of Fortnum & Mason. Established in 1707, this is one of the city's most renowned and extravagant stores.

📍 H6 🏠 181 Piccadilly W1 🌐 fortnumand mason.com

over the years and was half-wrecked by a bomb in 1940, but it maintains its essential features from 1684 – the tall, arched windows and a thin spire (a 1966 replica of the original). The ornate screen behind the altar is one of the finest works of the 17th-century master carver Grinling Gibbons. Artist and poet William Blake and prime minister Pitt the Elder were both baptized here.

The church hosts concerts, talks and events, and houses a popular café. The outer courtyard hosts a food market on Monday and Tuesday, an antiques market on Tuesday and a crafts market from Wednesday to Saturday.

↑ Tourists throng the Mall en route to Buckingham Palace

⑨ The Mall

📍H6 🏠SW1 🚇Charing Cross, Piccadilly Circus, Green Park

This broad triumphal approach to Buckingham Palace was created by Aston Webb when he redesigned the front of the palace and the Victoria Monument in 1911. It follows the course of the old path at the edge of St James's Park, laid out in the reign of Charles II, when it became London's most fashionable promenade. Down both sides of the Mall the national flags of foreign heads of state fly during their official visits. The annual London Marathon (p59) finishes on the Mall, amid a mass of crowds who cheer as enthusiastically for the weary stragglers at the end as they do for the elated runners at the front.

⑩  Institute of Contemporary Arts

📍I6 🏠The Mall SW1 🚇Charing Cross, Piccadilly Circus ⏰11am–11pm Tue–Sun; exhibition space closes 6pm (9pm Thu) 🚫1 Jan, 24–26 & 31 Dec, public hols 🌐ica.art

The Institute of Contemporary Arts (ICA) was established in 1947 to offer British artists some of the facilities available to artists at the Museum of Modern Art in New York. Originally on Dover Street, it has been situated in John Nash's Classically designed Carlton House Terrace (1833) since 1968. With its entrance on The Mall, this extensive warren contains exhibition spaces, a cinema, auditorium, bookshop, art gallery, bar and restaurant. It also hosts concerts, theatre and dance performances, and lectures. A modest fee applies to non-members, providing all-day access to most exhibitions and events.

⑪ Marlborough House

📍H6 🏠Pall Mall SW1 🚇St James's Park, Green Park ⏰Only for pre-booked group tours 🌐thecommonwealth.org/marlborough-house

Marlborough House was designed by Christopher Wren for the Duchess of Marlborough and completed

in 1711. It was substantially enlarged in the 19th century and used by members of the royal family. From 1863 until he became Edward VII in 1901, it was the home of the Prince and Princess of Wales and the social centre of London. The building now houses the Commonwealth Secretariat.

12
Green Park

G6 **SW1** **Green Park, Hyde Park Corner** **royalparks.org.uk**

Once part of Henry VIII's hunting grounds, this was, like St James's Park, adapted for public use by Charles II in the 1660s and is a natural, undulating landscape of grass and trees (with a fine spring show of daffodils). It was a favourite site for duels during the 18th century: in 1771 the poet Alfieri was wounded here by his mistress's husband, Viscount Ligonier, but then rushed back to the Haymarket Theatre in time to catch the last act of a play. Today the park is a popular place to take a breather from the city.

13
Queen's Chapel

H6 **Marlborough Rd SW1** **Green Park** **royal.gov.uk**

This chapel by architect Inigo Jones was built for Charles I's French wife, Henrietta Maria, in 1627. Originally intended to be part of St James's Palace, it was the first Classical church in England. George III married Charlotte of Mecklenburg-Strelitz here in 1761. Grinling Gibbons and Wren contributed to the interior. The chapel is only open for Sunday services from Easter to the end of July, at 8:30 and 11:15am.

SHOPPING ARCADES

On and around Piccadilly are four arch-fronted shopping arcades built in the 19th and early 20th centuries. These elegant covered walkways were the luxury shopping malls of their day, and are still home to the same kinds of top-drawer retailers. The first one to open, in 1819, was the Burlington Arcade, setting the template for the other three: the Royal, Princes and Piccadilly Arcades.

← Relaxing in the shade in picturesque Green Park

Wellington Arch

⊙F7 ⊖Hyde Park Corner SW1 ⊜Hyde Park Corner ⌚Apr–Sep: 10am–6pm daily; Oct: 10am–5pm daily; Nov–Mar: 10am–4pm daily ⊠1 Jan, Good Fri, 24–26 & 31 Dec ⊚english-heritage.org.uk

After nearly a century of debate about what to do with the patch of land in front of Apsley House, Wellington Arch, designed by Decimus Burton, was erected in 1828 (it was moved to its current position in the 1880s). The sculpture by Adrian Jones of Nike, winged goddess of Victory, was added in 1912. Before it was installed Jones seated three people for dinner in the body of one of the horses.

Exhibitions are held in the inner rooms of the arch. A viewing platform beneath the sculpture has great views over the royal parks and the gardens of Buckingham Palace.

AUCTION HOUSES

Venerable Sotheby's, Bonhams and Christie's head the list of auction houses dotted around Mayfair and St James's. All three were founded in the 18th century and have overseen the sale of many of the most treasured and expensive antiques and works of art on the planet. In 1836 Bonhams sold a collection of furniture from Buckingham Palace; Van Gogh's *Sunflowers* sold at Christie's in 1987 for £24.75 million; and in 2006 Sotheby's New Bond Street auction rooms sold a First Folio of Shakespeare's plays for £2.5 million.

Apsley House

⊙F7 ⊖Hyde Park Corner W1 ⊜Hyde Park Corner ⌚Apr–Oct: 11am–5pm Wed–Sun; Nov–Mar: 10am–4pm Sat & Sun ⊠1 Jan, 24–26 & 31 Dec ⊚english-heritage.org.uk

Apsley House, or Number One London, as it is also known, at the southeast corner of Hyde Park, was completed by Robert Adam for Baron Apsley in 1778. Fifty years later it was enlarged and altered by the architect Benjamin Dean Wyatt to provide a grand home for the Duke of Wellington. His dual career as soldier and politician brought him victory against his archenemy Napoleon at Waterloo (1815) and two terms as prime minister (1828–30 and 1834). Against sumptuous silk hangings and gilt decoration is the duke's art collection: works by Goya, Velázquez, Titian and Rubens hang alongside displays of porcelain, silver and furniture. Ironically, the duke's memorabilia is dominated by Canova's colossal statue of Napoleon.

16
Handel & Hendrix in London

G5 **25 Brook St W1** **Bond Street** **11am-6pm Mon-Sat** **handelhendrix.org**

A pair of Georgian houses on Brook Street have a couple of notable, very different, musical connections. The composer George Frideric Handel lived at No 25 from 1723 until his death in 1759, and his rooms have been restored to the early Georgian appearance they would have had during the composer's time, with portraits and musical instruments on display. The museum hosts changing exhibitions and regular recitals in an intimate performance space. In 1968, Jimi Hendrix moved into the

↑ A bust of Handel at the Handel & Hendrix in London museum

attic apartment next door. These rooms were used for a time as offices by the museum, but have now also been lovingly restored to resemble Hendrix's former apartment, complete with 1960s decor.

17
Grosvenor Square

F5 **W1** **Bond Street**

Mayfair has long been home to some of the grandest addresses in London, most notably in a series of prestigious squares, originally laid out in the early 18th century and still retaining many Georgian buildings. Grosvenor Square is the

largest, and has had connections with the USA since John Adams – the second US President – lived at No 9 between 1785 and 1789. The west side is dominated by what was the US Embassy until 2017, when embassy staff moved to new headquarters south of the River Thames. The Brutalist building, with its stone grid façade, was designed by US architect Eero Saarinen. A statue of Franklin D Roosevelt – the 32nd US President – stands at the centre of the square.

18
Faraday Museum

G5 **The Royal Institution, 21 Albemarle St W1** **Green Park** **8am-6pm Mon-Fri** **24 Dec-3 Jan** **rigb.org**

Michael Faraday was a 19th-century pioneer of the uses of electricity. Part of the Royal Institution, a body dedicated to scientific study, the museum includes a re-creation of Faraday's laboratory and some of his scientific apparatus, as well as exhibits on the work of other great scientists.

← Londoners enjoying the sun in Grosvenor Square; a portico *(inset)* provides shade

A SHORT WALK

AROUND
ST JAMES'S

Distance 2.5 km (1.5 miles) **Nearest Tube**
Green Park **Time** 25 minutes

After Henry VIII built St James's Palace in the 1530s,
the area around it became the centre of fashionable
London, and it has remained so ever since. Its historic
streets, squares and arcades attract a truly
international – and extremely wealthy – set.
A walk through the district will take you past the
flagship stores of exclusive global brands and
classic British names that have served royalty
and aristocracy for centuries, as well as the Royal
Academy and many independent art galleries.

*The Albany mansion has
been one of London's
smartest addresses
since it opened in 1803.*

*Sir Joshua Reynolds founded
the Royal Academy of Arts in 1768.
Now it mounts large popular
exhibitions (p92).*

*Uniformed beadles
discourage unruly behaviour
in the Burlington Arcade, a
19th-century mall (p97).*

*Fortnum & Mason
was founded in 1707 by
one of Queen Anne's
footmen (p95).*

*Named after César Ritz,
and opened in 1906,
the Ritz Hotel still lives
up to his name.*

*An ancestor of Princess
Diana built Spencer
House in 1766 (p94).*

*Clarence House was
designed by John Nash
for William IV, and is
now Prince Charles's
London home.*

Did You Know?

Hatchards on Picadilly
is London's oldest
bookshop, opened
in 1797.

0 metres   100
0 yards   100

N ↑

START

Piccadilly derives its name from the ruffs, or "pickadills", worn by 17th-century dandies.

Piccadilly station

Jermyn Street is one of London's most elegant streets, lined with shops for style-conscious men.

FINISH

The crowds and dazzling neon lights make Piccadilly Circus the West End's focal point.

The organ in Christopher Wren's favourite church, St James's Church, was brought here from Whitehall Palace in 1691 (p95).

Pall Mall's famous clubs provide a haven for businessmen (and a few women) (p94).

William III's statue dominates St James's Square (p94).

King Street is lined with art galleries.

The Tudor St James's Palace is still the Royal Court's official headquarters (p94).

↑ St James's Square, with the statue of William III at its centre

SOHO AND TRAFALGAR SQUARE

Before Soho was built upon the land had been used as royal hunting grounds. First developed in the late 17th century by wealthy landowners, its aristocratic residents, in contrast to those in neighbouring Mayfair, soon moved on and their influence on the character of the area went with them. Instead, the area became synonymous with bohemians and immigrants. French Huguenots, Jews, Greeks, Italians, Maltese and Chinese all came to Soho in significant numbers between the end of the 17th and the mid-20th centuries. Artists, writers and musicians flocked here too, as did gangsters and prostitutes, and the area retained an edgy, alternative air until the late 1980s. In contrast, Trafalgar Square, with its grandiose buildings and its proximity to Whitehall has always had closer ties to the establishment, though it has also long been a place of protest. For centuries the site of the royal stables (or mews), the square itself is a 19th century construct, given its name in 1830.

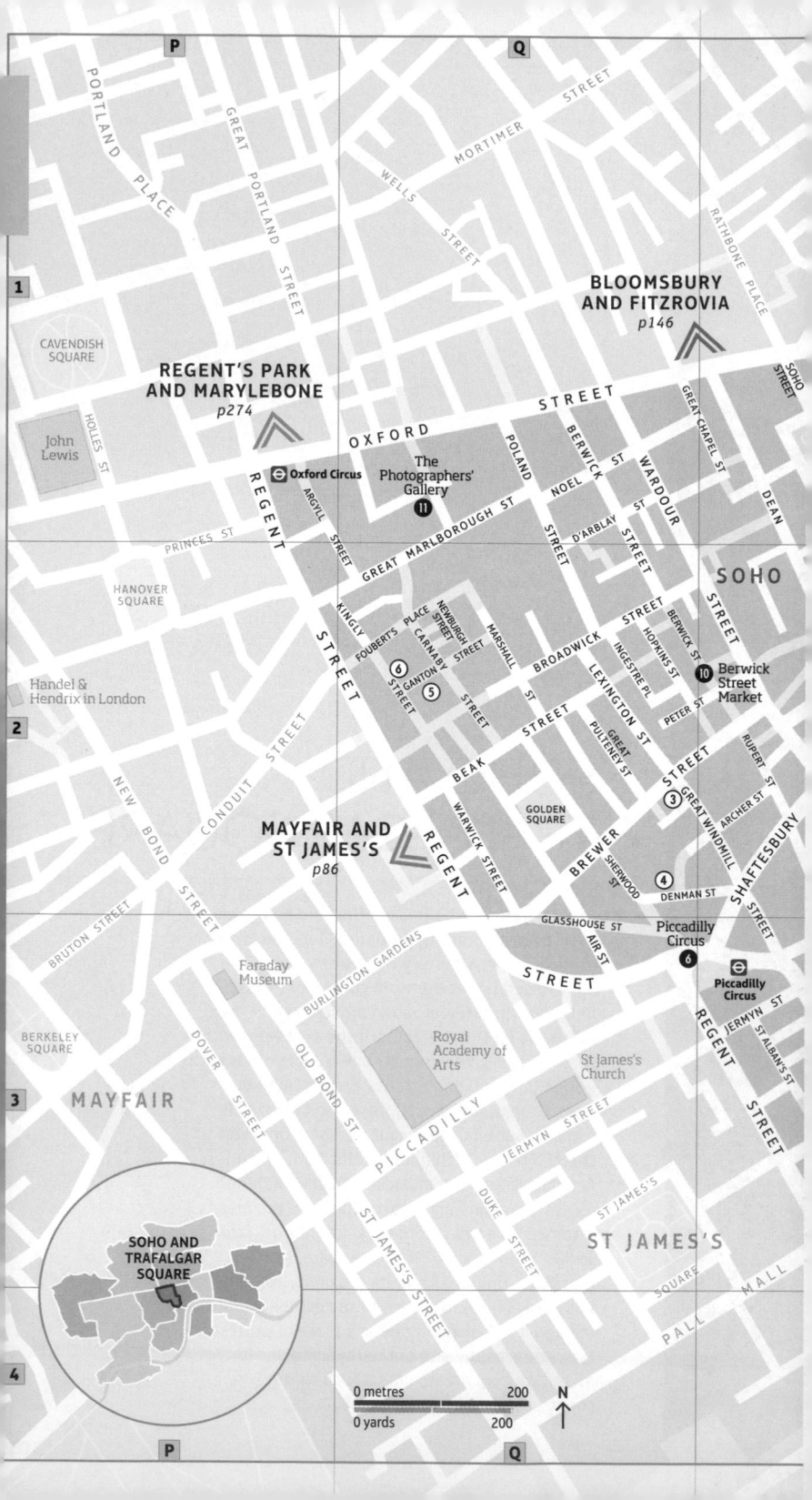

P

Q

PORTLAND PLACE

GREAT PORTLAND STREET

MORTIMER STREET

WELLS STREET

RATHBONE PLACE

1

CAVENDISH SQUARE

REGENT'S PARK AND MARYLEBONE
p274

John Lewis

HOLLES ST

OXFORD STREET

BLOOMSBURY AND FITZROVIA
p146

SOHO STREET

GREAT CHAPEL ST

DEAN STREET

Oxford Circus

The Photographers' Gallery
11

REGENT STREET

ARGYLL STREET

GREAT MARLBOROUGH ST

POLAND STREET

NOEL STREET

BERWICK STREET

D'ARBLAY STREET

WARDOUR STREET

SOHO

PRINCES ST

HANOVER SQUARE

Handel & Hendrix in London

KINGLY STREET

FOUBERT'S PLACE

NEWBURGH STREET

CARNABY STREET

GANTON STREET

MARSHALL STREET

BROADWICK STREET

INGESTRE PL

LEXINGTON STREET

HOPKINS ST

BERWICK STREET

PETER ST

10
Berwick Street Market

2

CONDUIT STREET

REGENT STREET

BEAK STREET

WARWICK STREET

GREAT PULTENEY ST

GOLDEN SQUARE

BREWER STREET

SHERWOOD ST

GREAT WINDMILL STREET

3

RUPERT ST

ARCHER ST

SHAFTESBURY AVENUE

MAYFAIR AND ST JAMES'S
p86

NEW BOND STREET

4
DENMAN ST

GLASSHOUSE ST

AIR ST

Piccadilly Circus
6

Piccadilly Circus

BRUTON STREET

Faraday Museum

BURLINGTON GARDENS

STREET

REGENT STREET

JERMYN ST

ST ALBAN'S ST

BERKELEY SQUARE

DOVER STREET

OLD BOND STREET

Royal Academy of Arts

St James's Church

3

MAYFAIR

PICCADILLY

JERMYN STREET

DUKE STREET

ST JAMES'S

ST JAMES'S STREET

ST JAMES'S SQUARE

PALL MALL

SOHO AND TRAFALGAR SQUARE

4

0 metres   200

0 yards   200

N ↑

P

Q

SOHO AND TRAFALGAR SQUARE

Must Sees
1. National Gallery
2. National Portrait Gallery
3. Chinatown

Experience More
4. Trafalgar Square
5. St Martin-in-the-Fields
6. Piccadilly Circus
7. Leicester Square
8. Charing Cross Road
9. Shaftesbury Avenue
10. Berwick Street Market
11. The Photographers' Gallery

Eat
1. Café in the Crypt
2. Barrafina
3. Casita Andina
4. Kricket
5. Pastaio

Drink
6. Ain't Nothin' But

1

NATIONAL GALLERY

S3 Trafalgar Square WC2 Charing Cross, Leicester Sq,
Piccadilly Circus Charing Cross 10am-6pm daily (til 9pm Fri)
24-26 Dec, 1 Jan nationalgallery.org.uk

Erected in the heart of the West End in order to be accessible by all, the National Gallery houses some of the most famous paintings in the world, by masters such as Rubens, Velázquez, Monet and Van Gogh.

The National Gallery has flourished since its inception. In 1824 the House of Commons was persuaded to buy 38 major paintings, including works by Raphael and Rubens, and these became the start of a national collection. Today the gallery has more than 2,300 paintings produced in the Western European painting tradition. The main gallery building, designed in Greek Revival style by William Wilkins, was built between 1833 and 1838. It was subsequently enlarged and the dome added in 1876. To its left lies the Sainsbury Wing, financed by the grocery family and completed in 1991.

The Collection

The National Gallery's paintings are mostly kept on permanent display. The collection spans late-medieval times to the early 20th century, covering Renaissance Italy and the French Impressionists. There are works by artists such as Botticelli, Leonardo, Monet and Goya, and highlights include Van Eyck's *Arnolfini Portrait*, Velázquez's *Rokeby Venus*, Raphael's *The Madonna of the Pinks* and Van Gogh's *Sunflowers*.

$\rightarrow$
The National Gallery, overlooking Trafalgar Square

$\leftarrow$
Groups of visitors studying works by the masters in the airy galleries

GALLERY GUIDE

Most of the collection is housed on one floor divided into four wings. The paintings hang chronologically, with the earliest works (1250-1500) in the Sainsbury Wing. The North, West and East Wings cover 1500-1600, 1600-1700 and 1700-1900. Lesser paintings from all periods are on the lower floor.

Did You Know?

Close examination of the *Madonna of the Veil* showed it was a 19th-century fake, and not by Botticelli.

↑ Pausing for thought in front of some of the gallery's masterpieces

↑ Dating from 1437, Piero della Francesca's *The Baptism of Christ*

Early Renaissance (1250–1500): Italian and Northern European Painting

Three lustrous panels from the *Maestà*, Duccio's great altarpiece in Siena cathedral and his outstanding *Madonna* are among the earliest paintings here. The fine *Wilton Diptych* portraying England's Richard II maybe by a French artist. It displays the

---

TOP 5 PAINTINGS NOT TO MISS

Seek out these impressive paintings.

Sunflowers
Vincent Van Gogh
Room 43

The Hay Wain
John Constable
Room 34

Bathers at Asnières
Georges Seurat
Room 43

The Fighting Temeraire
J M W Turner
Room 43

The Rokeby Venus
Diego Velázquez
Room 30

---

lyrical elegance of the International Gothic style. Italian masters of this style include Pisanello and Gentile da Fabriano, whose *Madonna* often hangs beside another, by Masaccio – both from the 1420s. Also shown are works by Masaccio's pupil, Fra Filippo Lippi, Botticelli and Uccello. Umbrian paintings include Piero della Francesca's *Nativity* and *Baptism*, and there is a fine collection of Mantegna, Bellini and other works from the Venetian and Ferrarese schools. Antonello da Messina's *St Jerome in his Study* has been mistaken for a Van Eyck; it is not hard to see why, when you compare it with Van Eyck's *Arnolfini Portrait*. Netherlandish pictures, including some by Rogier van der Weyden and his followers, are in the Sainsbury Wing.

High Renaissance (1500–1600): Italian, Netherlandish and German Painting

Sebastiano del Piombo's *The Raising of Lazarus* was painted, with Michelangelo's help, to rival Raphael's *Transfiguration*, which hangs in the Vatican in Rome. These and other well-known names of the High (or Late) Renaissance are very well represented. Exquisite Raphaels include the famous *Madonna of the Pinks*, only identified in the 1990s and

---

💬 INSIDER TIP
Get a Guide

If you are short of time there is a one-hour guided tour that takes place twice daily at 11:30am and 2:30pm. It takes in the gallery's most iconic works.

bought by the gallery for £22 million in 2004. Look out for Leonardo da Vinci's charcoal cartoon of the *Virgin and Child*, and his second version of the *Virgin of the Rocks*. There are also tender and amusing works by Piero di Cosimo, and several Titians, including *Bacchus and Ariadne* – which the public found too garish when it was cleaned in the 1840s. The Netherlandish and German collections include *The Ambassadors*, a fine double portrait by Holbein; and Altdorfer's superb *Christ Taking Leave of his Mother*. There is also a Hieronymus Bosch of *Christ Mocked* (sometimes known as *The Crowning with Thorns*) and an excellent Bruegel, *The Adoration of the Kings*.

Dutch, Italian, French and Spanish Painting (1600–1700)

The superb Dutch collection gives almost two rooms to Rembrandt. There are also

↑ Turner's *Dido Building Carthage*, found next to Claude's *Seaport with the Embarkation of the Queen of Sheba*

Examining Canaletto's famous work, *The Stonemason's Yard*

works by Vermeer, Van Dyck (among them his equestrian portrait of King Charles I) and Rubens (including the popular *Chapeau de Paille*). From Italy, Carracci and Caravaggio are strongly represented, and Salvator Rosa has a glowering portrait entitled *Philosophy*. French works include a grand portrait of Cardinal Richelieu by Philippe de Champaigne. Claude's seascape *Seaport with the Embarkation of the Queen of Sheba* hangs beside Turner's rival painting *Dido Building Carthage*. The Spanish collection has works by Murillo, Velázquez and Zurbarán.

Venetian, French and English Painting (1700–1800)

One of the gallery's most famous 18th-century works is Canaletto's *The Stonemason's Yard*. Other Venetians here are Longhi and Tiepolo. The French collection includes Rococo masters Chardin, Watteau and Boucher. Gainsborough's early work *Mr and Mrs Andrews* and *The Morning Walk* are popular; his rival, Sir Joshua Reynolds, is represented by several of his portraits. Hogarth's satirical *Marriage à-la-mode* series is another highlight.

English, French and German Painting (1800–1900)

The great age of 19th-century landscape painting is amply represented here, with fine works by Constable and Turner, including Constable's *The Hay Wain* and Turner's *The Fighting Temeraire*, as well as works by the French artists Corot and Daubigny. Of Romantic art, there are Géricault's vivid works, *Horse Frightened by Lightning* and *A Shipwreck*, which possibly prefigures his *The Raft of the Medusa*. In contrast, the society portrait of *Madame Moltessier* by Ingres, though Romantic, is restrained and Classical. Impressionists and other French avant-garde artists are well represented. Among the highlights are *The Water-Lily Pond* by Monet, Renoir's *At the Theatre*, Van Gogh's *Sunflowers*, and Rousseau's *Surprised!* In Seurat's *Bathers at Asnières* he did not originally use his pointillist technique, but only later reworked areas of the picture using dots of colour.

→ One of the highlights of the collection, Van Gogh's *Sunflowers*

NATIONAL PORTRAIT GALLERY

📍S3 🏠2 St Martin's Place WC2 🚇Leicester Sq, Charing Cross 🚊Charing Cross
🕐10am-6pm Sat-Wed (til 9pm Thu & Fri) 🚫24-26 Dec 🌐npg.org.uk

Somewhat unfairly in the shadow of the National Gallery next door, the National Portrait Gallery, with over 210,000 separate works spanning six centuries, holds the world's greatest collection of portraits.

💬 INSIDER TIP
Lunchtime Learning

A great way to dig a bit deeper into aspects of the collection, whether themes, backstories or the pictures themselves, is to attend one of the gallery's Lunchtime Lectures (£3). They take place on Thursdays, are delivered by staff or by visiting speakers and last approximately one hour. Buy tickets online or in person.

The gallery tells the story of Britain since the 16th century through the portraits of a wide cast of the nation's main characters, giving faces to the names familiar from history books. Founded in 1856, the gallery's first acquisition was one of the most famous depictions of William Shakespeare, known as the "Chandos portrait", after its former owner the Duke of Chandos. That portrait still hangs in the gallery today along with pictures of kings, queens, musicians, artists, thinkers, heroes and villains from every period since Shakespeare's day. Another of the gallery's oldest works is a Hans Holbein cartoon of Henry VIII, while there are Victorian portraits of key figures such as Charles Darwin, Charles Dickens and the Brontë Sisters.

Examining the portraits of key figures in Britain's long and varied history ↑

Entrance to the National Portrait Gallery on St Martin's Place ←

GALLERY GUIDE

The main collection runs chronologically from the early Tudors in the first room on the second floor down to the contemporary portraits on the ground floor, most of which change regularly. Much of the space on the ground floor is taken up with temporary exhibitions. Arranged initially by royal dynasties, progressing along the timeline brings up themes that overlap with time periods so that, for example, the Romantics are given their own room in the late 18th to early 19th century section.

A visitor enjoying the "Fabiola" exhibition by Francis Alÿs at the National Portrait Gallery →

CHINATOWN

Q R2 A Gerrard St and around W1 ⓔ Leicester Sq, Piccadilly Circus W chinatown.co.uk

Though much smaller than its equivalents in New York City and San Francisco, London's Chinatown packs a punch. There are restaurants aplenty and a constant buzz that attracts countless locals and visitors.

Chinatown occupies the small network of pedestrianized streets north of Leicester Square, and revolves around the main drag, Gerrard Street. Historically the Chinese community in London, who total more than 120,000, came predominantly from Hong Kong, and were concentrated initially in Limehouse, in the East End. The current base in Soho was established in the 1960s, though the Chinese population is now widely dispersed across the city. Today, Chinatown is an intense little precinct marked by ornamental archways and, more often than not, strewn with paper lanterns. It is packed overwhelmingly with authentic restaurants and Chinese supermarkets, with bakeries and bubble tea shops, and herbal medicine, acupuncture and massage centres filling the gaps.

CHINESE NEW YEAR

Based on lunar cycles, Chinese New Year falls between 21 January and 20 February. It is raucously celebrated in Chinatown in a sea of red paper lanterns, to the noise of firecrackers and the smell of Chinese street food. Though celebrations last for a fortnight, the main event usually falls on a Sunday when a parade makes its way through Chinatown. Shaftesbury Avenue is closed to traffic and stages are erected there and in Trafalgar Square for dance and martial arts shows.

Gerrard Street, at the heart of Chinatown, during ↑ Chinese New Year

1 Ornate Chinese arches stand over the area of Chinatown in Soho.

2 There are many authentic places to try a variety of Chinese cuisines from all over China.

3 Traditional Chinese goods are on sale in the shops around Chinatown.

Did You Know?

Wong Kei, a restaurant at 41–43 Wardour St, has a reputation for the rudest waiting staff in London.

EAT

Shu Xiangge
Specialists in traditional Sichuan hot pots, with 80 different ingredients to add to their fragrant, communal broths. The authentic interior has a hand-painted mural.

🏠 10 Gerrard St W1

£ £ £

XU
Atmospheric Taiwanese restaurant which re-creates the look of a 1930s Taipei social club, with wood panelling, hand-painted murals and a tea room on the ground floor. The food is modern, a fusion of Taiwanese and Cantonese cuisine.

🏠 30 Rupert St W1
🌐 xulondon.com

£ £ £

EXPERIENCE MORE

❹
Trafalgar Square

📍 S3 🅰 WC2 🚇 Charing Cross

London's main venue for rallies and outdoor public meetings was conceived by John Nash and was mostly constructed during the 1830s. The 50-m (165-ft) column commemorates Admiral Lord Nelson, Britain's most famous sea lord, who died heroically at the Battle of Trafalgar in 1805. It dates from 1842; 14 stonemasons held a dinner on its flat top before the statue of Nelson was finally installed. Edwin Landseer's four lions guard its base. The north side of the square is now taken up by the National Gallery (p106), with Canada House on the west side and South Africa House on the east. Three plinths support statues of the great and the good; funds ran out before the fourth plinth, on the northwest corner, could be filled. It now hosts one of London's most idiosyncratic art displays, as artworks are commissioned specially for it, and change each year.

---

❺ 📷 🛍
St Martin-in-the-Fields

📍 S3 🅰 Trafalgar Sq WC2 🚇 Charing Cross 🕐 8:30am–6pm Mon–Fri, 9am–6pm Sat & Sun 🌐 stmartin-in-the-fields.org

There has been a church on this site since the 13th century. Famous people buried here include Charles II's mistress Nell Gwyn, and the painters William Hogarth and Joshua Reynolds. The present church was designed by James Gibbs and completed in 1726. In architectural terms it was one of the most influential ever built; it was much copied in the US, where it became a model for the Colonial style of church architecture. An unusual feature of the interior is the royal box at gallery level to the left of the altar.

From 1914 until 1927, the crypt was used as a shelter for homeless soldiers and others; during World War II it was an air-raid shelter. It is still today well-known for its work on behalf of the homeless and vulnerable. The crypt also contains a café, a religious bookshop and the London Brass Rubbing Centre, which is open daily. Lunchtime and evening concerts are held in the church and jazz evenings in the café. All are welcome at the daily services; check the website for times; as they vary.

---

❻ 🍴 📷 🛍
Piccadilly Circus

📍 Q3 🅰 W1 🚇 Piccadilly Circus

For years people have been drawn to gather beneath Piccadilly Circus's centrepiece, the statue of Eros, originally intended as an angel of mercy but renamed in the public imagination after the Greek god of love. Poised delicately

← Looking across Trafalgar Square to St-Martin-in-the-Fields

↑ The bustling pavements of Piccadilly Circus, overseen by the statue of Eros

with his bow, Eros has become almost a trademark of the capital. It was erected in 1892 as a memorial to the Earl of Shaftesbury, the Victorian philanthropist. Part of Nash's master plan for Regent Street, Piccadilly Circus has been considerably altered over the years and consists for the most part of shops selling souvenirs for visitors and high-street chains. It has London's gaudiest array of neon advertising signs, marking the entrance to the city's lively entertainment district with its cinemas, theatres, nightclubs, restaurants and pubs.

7 (🍴) (🖥) (🛍)

Leicester Square

R2 **WC2** **⊖ Leicester Sq, Piccadilly Circus**

It is hard to imagine that this, the perpetually animated heart of the West End entertainment district, was once a fashionable place to live. Laid out in 1670 south of Leicester House, a long-gone royal residence, the square's occupants included the scientist Sir Isaac Newton and the

artists Joshua Reynolds and William Hogarth.

In Victorian times, several popular music halls were established here, including the Empire (today the cinema on the same site perpetuates the name) and the Alhambra, replaced in 1937 by the Art Deco Odeon. The TKTS booth, sat in the square, is a must-visit for cut-price theatre tickets. There is also a statue of Charlie Chaplin, which was unveiled in 1981. The statue of William Shakespeare dates from 1874.

Often crowded with visitors, the area around the Tube station here can be very congested at times; the streets of Soho and China-town to the north (p112) can be a better bet for a meal or drink.

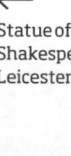

←

Statue of William Shakespeare in Leicester Square

(p112)

EAT

Café in the Crypt

Popular, good-value canteen with simple food under the arches of a church crypt.

S3 **A St Martin-in-the-Fields, Trafalgar Sq WC2** **W stmartin-in-the-fields.org**

£££

Barrafina

Ultracool Spanish joint with industrial modern decor.

R2 **A Dean St W1** **W barrafina.co.uk**

£££

Casita Andina

Stylish Peruvian restaurant: try ceviche, octopus or dumplings.

Q2 **A 31 Great Windmill St W1** **W andinalondon.com**

£££

Kricket

Gourmet Indian food served in tapas-style portions.

Q2 **A 12 Denman St W1** **W kricket.co.uk**

£££

Pastaio

Trendy pasta specialist with communal seating.

Q2 **A 19 Ganton St W1** **W pastaio.london**

£££

Shaftesbury Avenue, home to London's theatre district ↑

8 (🍴) (🖥) (🛍)

Charing Cross Road

📍S2 🚇WC2 🚊Leicester Sq

Once London's favourite street with book lovers, with a clutch of shops able to supply just about any recent volume, many of Charing Cross Road's independent bookshops have been forced to shut due to rising rents. Several smaller, second-hand bookshops remain, however, including Quinto & Francis Edwards, which specializes in antiquarian books, and a handful in nearby Cecil Court. At the junction with New Oxford Street rises the 1960s Centrepoint tower. This junction is one of the key

sites for the huge Crossrail underground rail project, so expect traffic disruption.

---

9 (🍴) (🖥) (🛍)

Shaftesbury Avenue

📍R2 🚇W1 🚊Piccadilly Circus, Leicester Sq

The main artery of London's theatreland, Shaftesbury Avenue has six theatres and three cinemas, all but one on its north side. It is also packed with restaurants, bars and clubs, making it a go-to destination of an evening. This street was cut through an area of terrible slums between 1877 and 1886 in order to improve communications across the city's busy West End; it follows the route of a much earlier highway. It is named after the Earl of Shaftesbury (1801–85), whose attempts to improve housing conditions had helped some of the local poor. The earl is also commemorated by the Eros statue in Piccadilly Circus (p114). The Lyric Theatre, designed by C J Phipps, has been open for almost as long as the avenue.

10 (🍴) (🖥) (🛍)

Berwick Street Market

📍R2 🚇W1 🚊Piccadilly Circus 🕗8am–6pm Mon-Sat 🌐thisissoho.co.uk/the-market

There has been a market here since the late 18th century. It was a Berwick Street trader, Jack Smith, who introduced

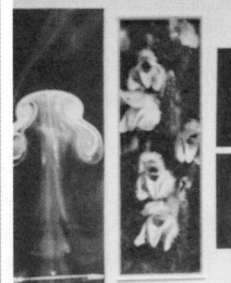

DRINK

Ain't Nothin' But
Popularly referred to simply as the Blues Bar, this London stalwart squeezes an always-enthusiastic crowd into its dimly lit single room, rarely failing to get the party cookin'.

📍Q2 🚇20 Kingly St W1 🌐aintnothinbut.co.uk

→

Installation images from Deutsche Börse Photography Foundation Prize 2018 at the Photographers' Gallery

grapefruit to London in 1890. Today this is the West End's best street market (although the traders could be under threat with development taking place on the west side of Berwick Street). Today you'll find sizzling street food alongside the fresh produce and flowers. There are also some interesting shops and a growing number of cafés and restaurants. At its southern end the street narrows into an alley on which the famous strip club Raymond Revuebar (once the comparatively respectable face of Soho sleaze) presented its "festival of erotica" from 1958 to 2004.

THE HEART OF SOHO

Beating a path through Soho is Old Compton Street, a busy thorough-fare of restaurants, bars, clubs and shops. Home for centuries to poets, writers and musicians, it's now an LGBT+ hub, the Admiral Duncan pub leading a pack of popular bars and clubs. Turn off on Frith Street to see iconic jazz club Ronnie Scott's and Bar Italia; above the latter, John Logie Baird first demonstrated TV in 1926.

11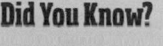

The Photographers' Gallery

Q1 **16-18 Ramillies St W1** **Oxford Circus** **10am-6pm Mon-Sat; 11am-6pm Sun** **thephoto graphersgallery.org.uk**

This fore-running gallery exhibits work from both new and well-known photographers, as well as staging regular talks, workshops (especially for young photographers) and film screenings. Entry is free before noon, and when exhibitions are staged, the gallery stays open late (until 8pm) on Thursdays. There's a bar-café, and the bookshop also sells cameras and prints.

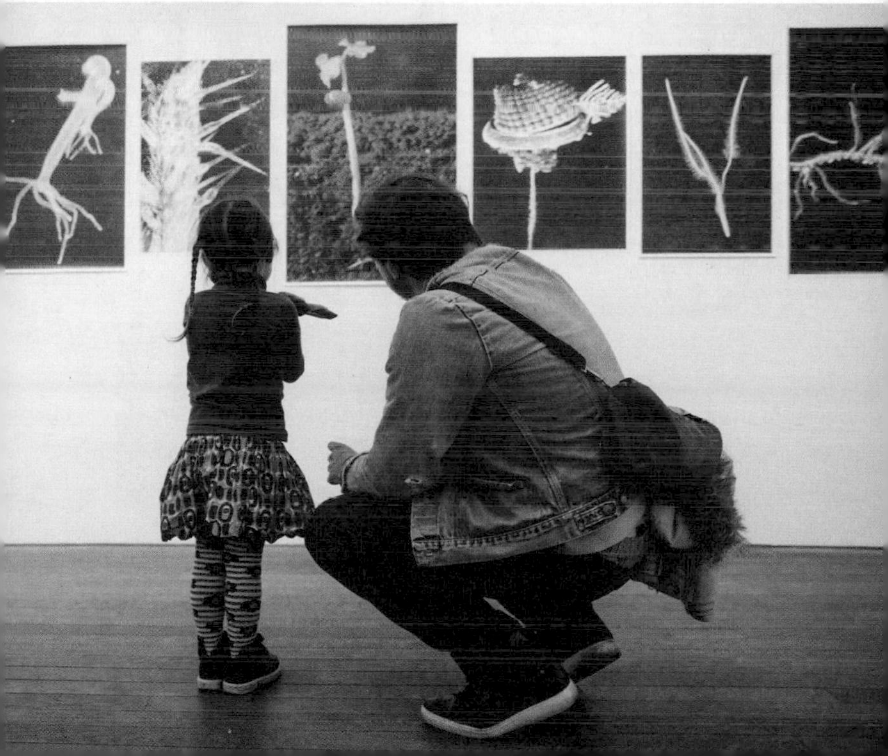

COVENT GARDEN AND THE STRAND

The site of a convent garden in medieval times, Covent Garden was laid out as an Italianate piazza in the 1630s by Inigo Jones, whose St Paul's Church still dominates the west side. Initially among the city's most fashionable addresses, coffee houses, then brothels and an increasing number of market stalls transformed the area's reputation and the wealthier residents trickled away. To accommodate the expansion of the market a permanent market building was commissioned and constructed in the 1830s, the elegant Neo-Classical structure dominating the centre of the piazza today. It housed a produce market until 1974 when the market moved to a larger site in Nine Elms, between Vauxhall and Battersea, better able to cope with its inflated size. Traders still occupy the building in Covent Garden but cater mostly to tourists now, operating from shops, craft stalls and restaurants.

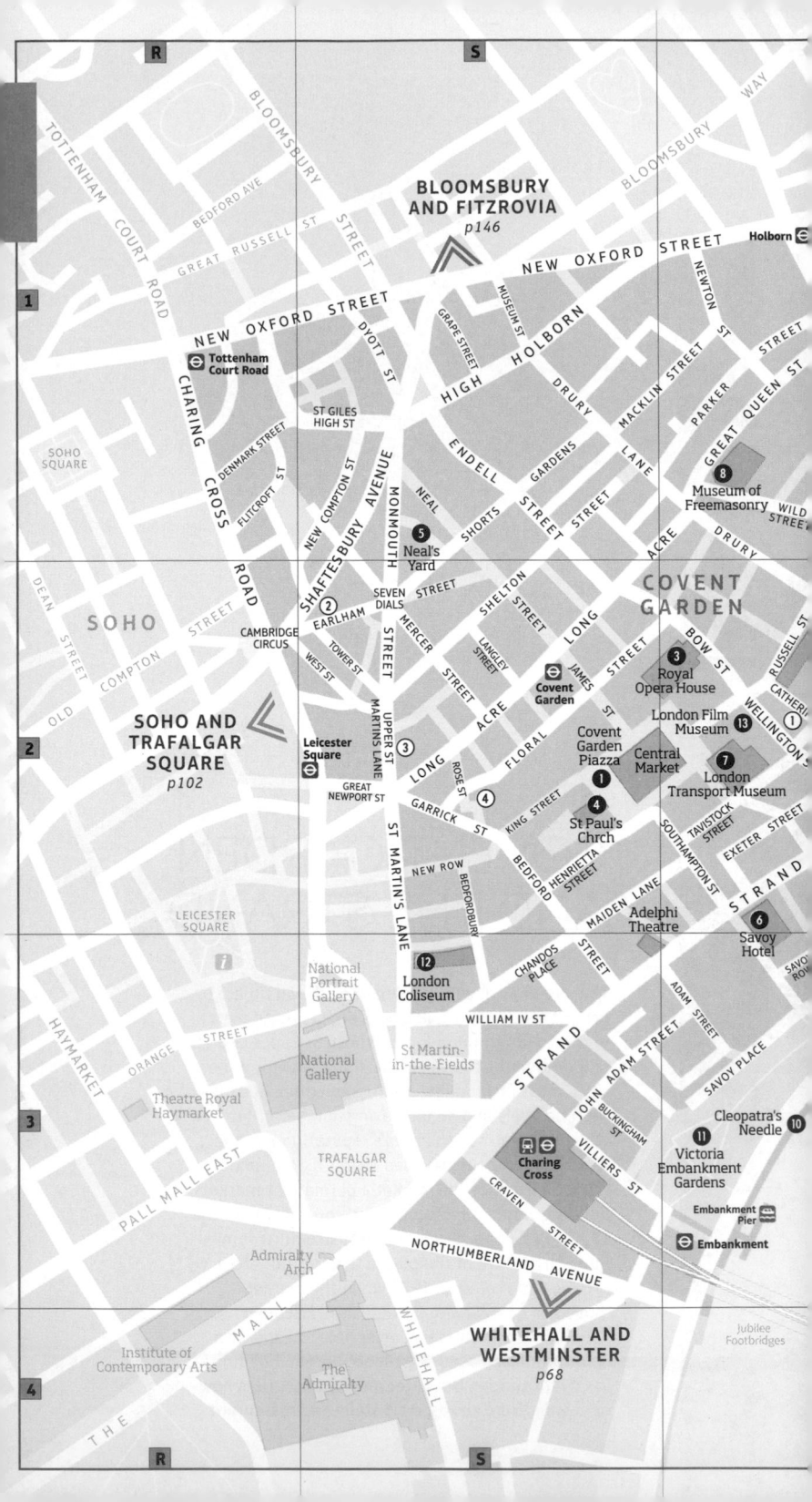

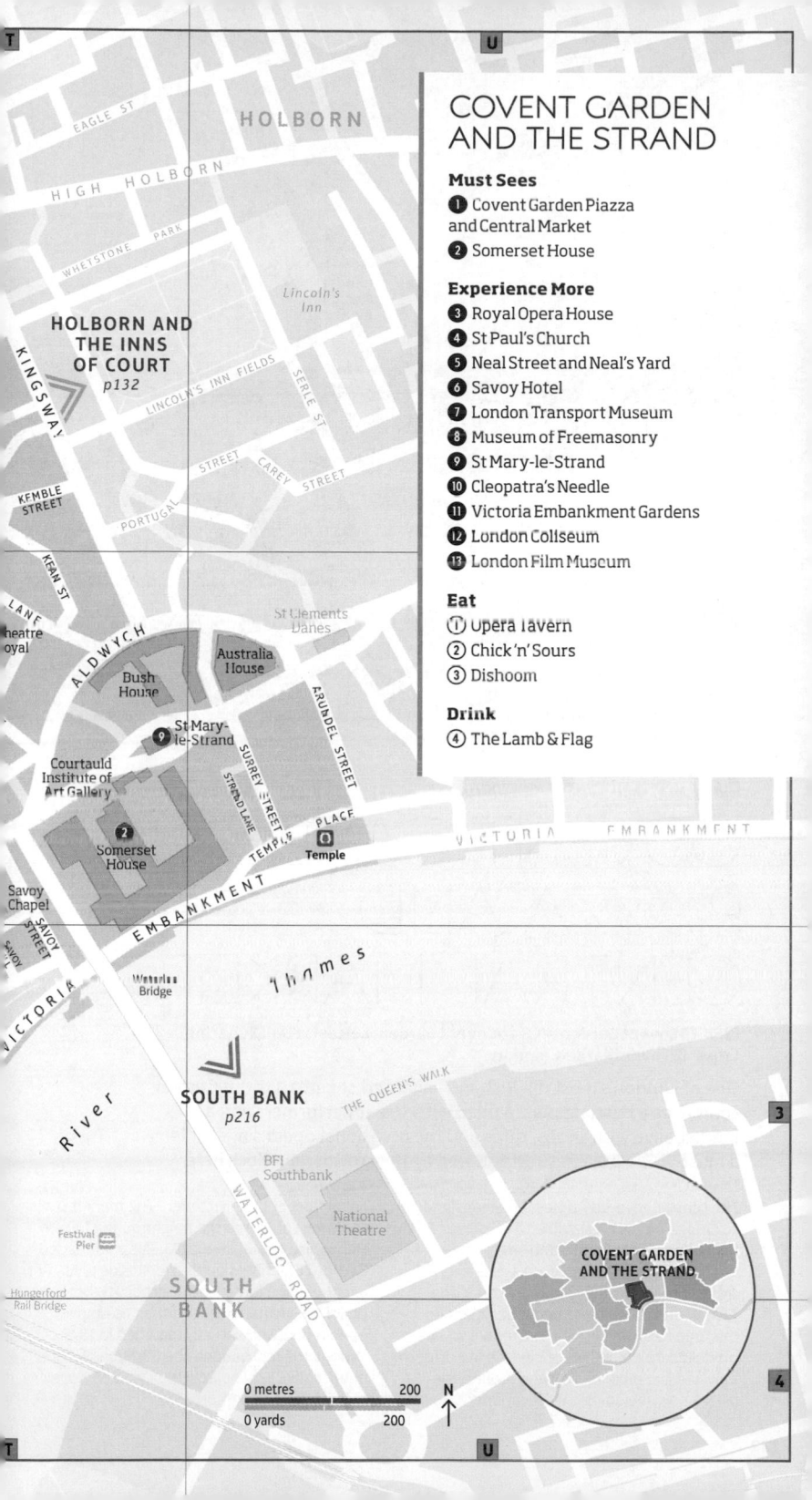

COVENT GARDEN AND THE STRAND

Must Sees
1 Covent Garden Piazza and Central Market
2 Somerset House

Experience More
3 Royal Opera House
4 St Paul's Church
5 Neal Street and Neal's Yard
6 Savoy Hotel
7 London Transport Museum
8 Museum of Freemasonry
9 St Mary-le-Strand
10 Cleopatra's Needle
11 Victoria Embankment Gardens
12 London Coliseum
13 London Film Museum

Eat
1 Opera Tavern
2 Chick 'n' Sours
3 Dishoom

Drink
4 The Lamb & Flag

Strolling and snacking under the iron and glass roof of the Apple Market ↑

COVENT GARDEN PIAZZA AND CENTRAL MARKET

📍 S2 🏠 Covent Garden WC2 🚇 Covent Garden, Leicester Sq 🚆 Charing Cross 🌐 coventgarden.london

One of London's most distinct and animated squares, Covent Garden comprises a bustling piazza filled with street performers and a market alive with shops, cafés and the occasional opera singer. It is a must-visit – a claim substantiated by the crowds who flock here.

The central, covered Apple Market, designed in 1833 for fruit and vegetable wholesalers, today houses an array of stalls and small shops selling designer clothes, books, arts and crafts, decorative items and antiques. The 17th-century architect Inigo Jones planned this area to be an elegant residential square, modelled on the piazza of Livorno in northern Italy, but the buildings on and around the piazza now, including the Royal Opera House,

are almost entirely Victorian. The market stalls continue south into the neighbouring Jubilee Hall, which was built in 1903. The colonnaded Bedford Chambers on the north side give a hint of Inigo Jones's plan, although these buildings are not original either, having been rebuilt and partially modified in 1879. Despite the renovations, the tradition of street entertainers in the piazza has endured since at least the 17th century.

EAT

The Ivy Market Grill

The first of the the once-exclusive Ivy restaurant's offshoots. Smart Art Deco interior and a menu heavy on seafood and steaks.

🏠 1a Henrietta St WC2
🌐 theivymarket
grill.com

ⓔⓔⓔ

Tuttons

Sit out on the piazza or in the refined dining area in this Covent Garden stalwart. Serves classic English food.

🏠 11/12 Russell St WC2
🌐 tuttons.com

ⓔⓔⓔ

1 The Punch & Judy is a popular market pub with tables inside the Apple Market and outside on the terrace overlooking the piazza.

2 Street entertainers are a much loved tradition in the piazza. These days musicians, circus performers and magicians must pass an audition in order to perform here.

3 Jubilee Market offers mainly souvenirs, jewellery and cheaper items, though on Mondays here and in the Apple Market antiques and vintage collectables are on sale.

Courtyard of Somerset House with fountains and café tables ↑

2 🎞️ 🍴 ☕ 🛍️

SOMERSET HOUSE

📍T2 🏛️Strand WC2 🚇Temple, Charing Cross
🚆Charing Cross ⛴️Embankment Pier 🕐8am–11pm daily
🌐Somerset House: somersethouse.org.uk; Courtauld Gallery: courtauld.ac.uk

This grand Georgian building, with four Neo-Classical wings around a huge stone courtyard, is an innovative arts and cultural centre offering a range of events and exhibitions in a marvellous riverside location.

Somerset House is best known as the home of the Courtauld Gallery, the city's premiere collection of Impressionist paintings. It is also a unique and popular venue for outdoor summer cinema and eclectic festivals, art fairs and installations.

Built in the 1770s, its first resident was the Royal Academy of Arts. Later tenants included the Navy Board at the end of the 1780s. The building retains some striking architectural features, including the classical grandeur of the Seamen's Waiting Hall and the spectacular five-storey rotunda staircase called Nelson's Stair, both in the South Wing. Strolling through the wing from the courtyard leads to a riverside terrace featuring an open-air summer café and a restaurant, perfect for a sundowner. Below are the modern Embankment Galleries with a range of contemporary arts exhibitions including photography, design and fashion.

EAT

Bryn Williams at Somerset House
Top-notch modern seasonal British cuisine with an emphasis on salads and grilled vegetables.

🏛️South Wing
🌐bryn-somerset house.co.uk

£££

Fernandez & Wells
This light-filled café, part of a respected London chain, serves quality breakfasts and light lunch dishes, plus cakes, tea and coffee.

🏛️East Wing
🌐fernandez andwells.com

£££

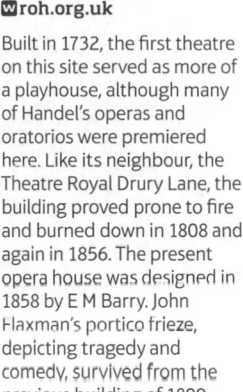

Did You Know?

The courtyard is turned over to a glittering tree and ice rink at Christmas time.

Courtauld Gallery

Most visitors to Somerset House are drawn here by the renown of the resident Courtauld Gallery, an exquisite collection of Impressionist and Post-Impressionist paintings but also of works by Botticelli, Bruegel, Bellini and Rubens. World-famous paintings by Monet, Gauguin, Pissarro, Renoir and Modigliani are here, as is Manet's *A Bar at the Folies-Bergères*, Van Gogh's *Self-Portrait with Bandaged Ear*, Cézanne's *The Card Players* and some evocative studies of dancers by Degas. The Courtauld Institute also hosts a series of temporary exhibitions through the year.

EXPERIENCE MORE

Royal Opera House

🅃2 🄰 Bow St WC2
🄴 Covent Garden
🅆 roh.org.uk

Built in 1732, the first theatre on this site served as more of a playhouse, although many of Handel's operas and oratorios were premiered here. Like its neighbour, the Theatre Royal Drury Lane, the building proved prone to fire and burned down in 1808 and again in 1856. The present opera house was designed in 1858 by E M Barry. John Flaxman's portico frieze, depicting tragedy and comedy, survived from the previous building of 1809.

The Opera House has had both high and low points during its history. In 1892, the first British performance of *Wagner's Ring* cycle was conducted here by Gustav Mahler. Later, during World War I, the building was used as a storehouse by the government. Today, it is home to the Royal Opera and Royal Ballet companies – the best tickets can cost over £100 (though restricted-view tickets up in the "slips" can be had for as little as £10). Backstage tours are available.

St Paul's Church

🅂2 🄰 Bedford St WC2
🄴 Covent Garden ⏰ 8:30am-5pm Mon-Fri, 9am-1pm Sun
🅆 actorschurch.org

St Paul's is the "Actors' Church" and plaques commemorate famed men and women of the theatre. Inigo Jones designed the altar at the west end to allow his grand portico to face east into Covent Garden Piazza. When clerics objected to this unorthodox placement, the altar was moved to its conventional position at the east end, but Jones went ahead with his original exterior design. Thus the church is entered from the west, and the east portico is a fake door.

The church grounds are a particularly pleasant place to pause – and surprisingly quiet in contrast to the hustle and bustle of neighbouring Covent Garden.

↑ The Floral Hall – now the Paul Hamlyn Hall – at the Royal Opera House

↑ The brightly painted former warehouses of Neal's Yard and the original branch of Neal's Yard Remedies

PICTURE PERFECT
Neal's Yard

A riot of rainbow-coloured walls, window frames and flower baskets, Neal's Yard – secreted in the triangle between Monmouth St, Neal St and Shorts Gardens – is the perfect subject to brighten any photo album.

5

Neal Street and Neal's Yard

S1 WC2 Covent Garden

In this attractive street, former warehouses dating from the 19th century can be identified by the hoisting mechanisms high on their exterior walls. Most buildings have been converted into shops and restaurants. Off Neal Street is Neal's Yard, a bright and cheerful courtyard of independent restaurants and shops, most displaying vividly painted façades. Seek out Homeslice for a 20" pizza or try veggie delights at Wild Food Café; either will set you up for an afternoon of shopping. Neal's Yard Remedies offers potions and lotions, while Neal's Yard Dairy is one of London's best cheese shops.

6

Savoy Hotel

T2 Strand WC2 Charing Cross, Embankment fairmont.com/savoy

Pioneer of en-suite bathrooms and electric lighting, the grand Savoy was built in 1889 on the site of the medieval Savoy Palace. A lavish £100 million refurbishment took place between 2008 and 2010, incorporating both the original Edwardian and the later Art Deco styles. The Gatsbyesque forecourt is the only street in Britain where traffic drives on the right.

Attached to the hotel are the Savoy Theatre, built for the D'Oyly Carte opera and famed for performing the operas of Gilbert and Sullivan, and the Simpson's in the Strand English restaurant, where traditional roasts are served ceremoniously from silver carving trolleys.

SEVEN DIALS

The pillar at this junction of seven streets features six sundials, the central spike forming the seventh. In the 19th century this was a slum area and a nexus for street thieves; with a choice of seven escape routes, pickpockets often evaded their pursuers. Today Seven Dials is a vibrant shopping and dining area that's perfect for strolling, its cobbled streets and charming hidden courtyards filled with one-off shops, boutiques, high-end cosmetics stores, bars and restaurants.

7 ⚡ Ⓜ 🖥 🏛

London Transport Museum

📍 T2 🏠 The Piazza WC2
🚇 Covent Garden 🕐 10am–
6pm daily (last adm: 5:15pm)
🌐 ltmuseum.co.uk

You don't have to be a train spotter to enjoy this museum. The intriguing collection is housed in the picturesque Victorian Flower Market and features public transport from the past and present. The history of London's transport is in essence a social history of the capital. Bus, tram and underground route patterns first reflected the city's growth and then promoted it; the northern and western suburbs began to develop only after their Tube connections were built.

The museum houses a fine collection of 20th-century commercial art. London's bus and train companies have long been prolific patrons of contemporary artists, and copies of some of the finest posters on display can be bought at the museum shop. They include the innovative Art Deco designs of E McKnight Kauffer, as well as work by renowned artists of the 1930s, such as Graham Sutherland and Paul Nash.

This museum is excellent for children (and they can enter free of charge). There are plenty of hands-on exhibits, including a London bus and an Underground train that children can climb aboard and pretend to drive.

---

8 Ⓜ 🏛

Museum of Freemasonry

📍 T1 🏠 Freemasons' Hall,
60 Great Queen St WC2
🚇 Covent Garden 🕐 10am–
5pm Mon-Sat 🌐 free
masonry.london.museum

Looming over a corner on Great Queen Street, the Art Deco Freemasons' Hall was built in 1933 as a memorial to some 3,000 freemasons who died in active service in World War I. The headquarters of English freemasonry, the cultish traditions of this secretive organization are in evidence in the building's museum. Ceremonial masks, pottery bearing masonic emblems and insignia, and ballot boxes used to vote new members in – or out– are among the exhibits. Peek into one of the lodge rooms where masons meet; redolent of a courtroom, it is hung with portraits of previous Grand Secretaries (leaders of this Masonic lodge).

EAT

Opera Tavern
Succulent braised pork cheeks are among the flavoursome tapas here.

📍 S2 🏠 23 Catherine St
WC2 🌐 saltyard
group.co.uk

£ £ £

Chick 'n' Sours
Deep-fried chicken, cocktails and a thumping soundtrack. This is fried chicken, but not as you know it.

📍 T2 🏠 1 Earlham St
WC2 🌐 chickn
sours.co.uk

£ £ £

Dishoom
Bombay brasserie serving Irani delights.

📍 T2 🏠 12 Upper St
Martin's Lane WC2
🌐 dishoom.com

£ £ £

←

Early motor buses on show in the London Transport Museum

9

St Mary-le-Strand

◻ T2 ◻ Strand WC2
◻ Temple ◻ 10am-4pm
Tue-Thu, 11am-4pm Sun
◻ stmarylestrand.org

Now beached on a road island at the east end of the Strand, this pleasing church was consecrated in 1724. It was the first public building by James Gibbs, who also designed the church of St Martin-in-the-Fields on Trafalgar Square (p114).

Gibbs was influenced by one of his early supporters, Sir Christopher Wren, but the exuberant external decorative detail here was inspired by the Baroque churches of Rome, where Gibbs studied. Its multi-arched tower is layered like a wedding cake, and culminates in a cupola and lantern. St Mary-le-Strand is now the official church of the Women's Royal Naval Service.

10

Cleopatra's Needle

◻ T3 ◻ Embankment WC2
◻ Embankment, Charing Cross

Erected in Heliopolis in about 1500 BC, this incongruous pink granite monument is much older than London itself. Its inscriptions celebrate the deeds of the pharaohs of ancient Egypt. It was presented to Britain by the then Viceroy of Egypt, Mohammed Ali, in 1819 and erected in 1878. It has a twin in New York's Central Park.

11

Victoria Embankment Gardens

◻ T3 ◻ WC2 ◻ Embankment, Charing Cross
◻ 7:30am-dusk Mon-Sat, 9am-dusk Sun & public hols

This narrow sliver of a public park, which was created when the Embankment was

DRINK

The Lamb & Flag
This popular pub sits in an alley linking Garrick and Floral Streets. Punters often spill out onto the street. It vies for the title of oldest pub in London - an inn has stood here since the 16th century.

◻ T2 ◻ 33 Rose St WC2
◻ lambandflag coventgarden.co.uk

built, boasts well-maintained flowerbeds, a clutch of statues of British worthies (including the Scottish poet Robert Burns) and, in summer, a season of concerts. Its main historical feature is the water gate at its northwest corner, which was built as a triumphal entry to the Thames for the Duke of Buckingham in 1626.

← Greenery by the Thames at Victoria Embankment Gardens

← Aston Martin V12
from *Die Another Day*,
London Film Museum

London Coliseum

**⬚ S3 🏠 St Martin's Lane
WC2 🚇 Leicester Sq, Charing
Cross 🕐 For performances
only 🌐 eno.org**

London's largest theatre and one of its most elaborate, this flamboyant building, topped with a large globe, was designed in 1904 by Frank Matcham and was equipped with London's first revolving stage. It was also the first theatre in Europe to have lifts. A former variety house, today it is the home of the English National Opera, and well worth visiting, if only for the Edwardian interior with its gilded cherubs and heavy purple curtains. In 2003, the original glass roof was restored, providing dramatic views over Trafalgar Square.

London Film Museum

**⬚ T2 🏠 45 Wellington St
WC2 🚇 Covent Garden
🕐 10am–6pm daily
(until 7pm Sat); last
entry 1 hr before closing
🌐 londonfilmmuseum.com**

Though previously an actual museum of film, this now misleadingly named place is really a James Bond museum,

the Bond in Motion exhibition having effectively become the permanent and only display. The Bond memorabilia on show includes outfits and posters but the exhibition revolves around an impressive collection of the original vehicles featured in the films. There are aircraft, boats, sleds and motorcycles but it's the

cars, many of them set against a moving backdrop from their respective movie, that usually attract the most excitement. Among the highlights are the instantly recognizable submersible white Lotus Esprit S1 from *The Spy Who Loved Me* and the quintessential Bond car, the Aston Martin DB5, first seen in 1964's *Goldfinger*.

THEATRELAND

So choc-a-bloc with theatres is the West End that it has earned the moniker Theatreland, which you will see written on street signs, particularly around Soho and Covent Garden. Theatre first took off in London in the late 16th century and in 1663 the West End had its first playhouse, the Theatre Royal, a previous incarnation of the theatre that stands on Drury Lane, Covent Garden, today. The present structure was completed in 1812, in a century when Theatreland really began to boom; the nearby Adelphi, on the Strand, had been built in 1806 and then, after the Theatres Act of 1843, dozens more followed to cater for the Victorian appetite for music hall. Today the West End has around 50 working theatres.

A SHORT WALK

COVENT GARDEN

Distance 1.5 km (1 mile) **Nearest Tube**
Leicester Square **Time** 15 minutes

Although no longer alive with the calls of fruit
and vegetable market traders going about their
business, visitors, residents and street entertainers
throng Covent Garden Piazza, much as they would
have done centuries ago. Pause to people
watch as you stroll through this buzzing
area, popping into vibrant boutiques
and historic pubs along the way.

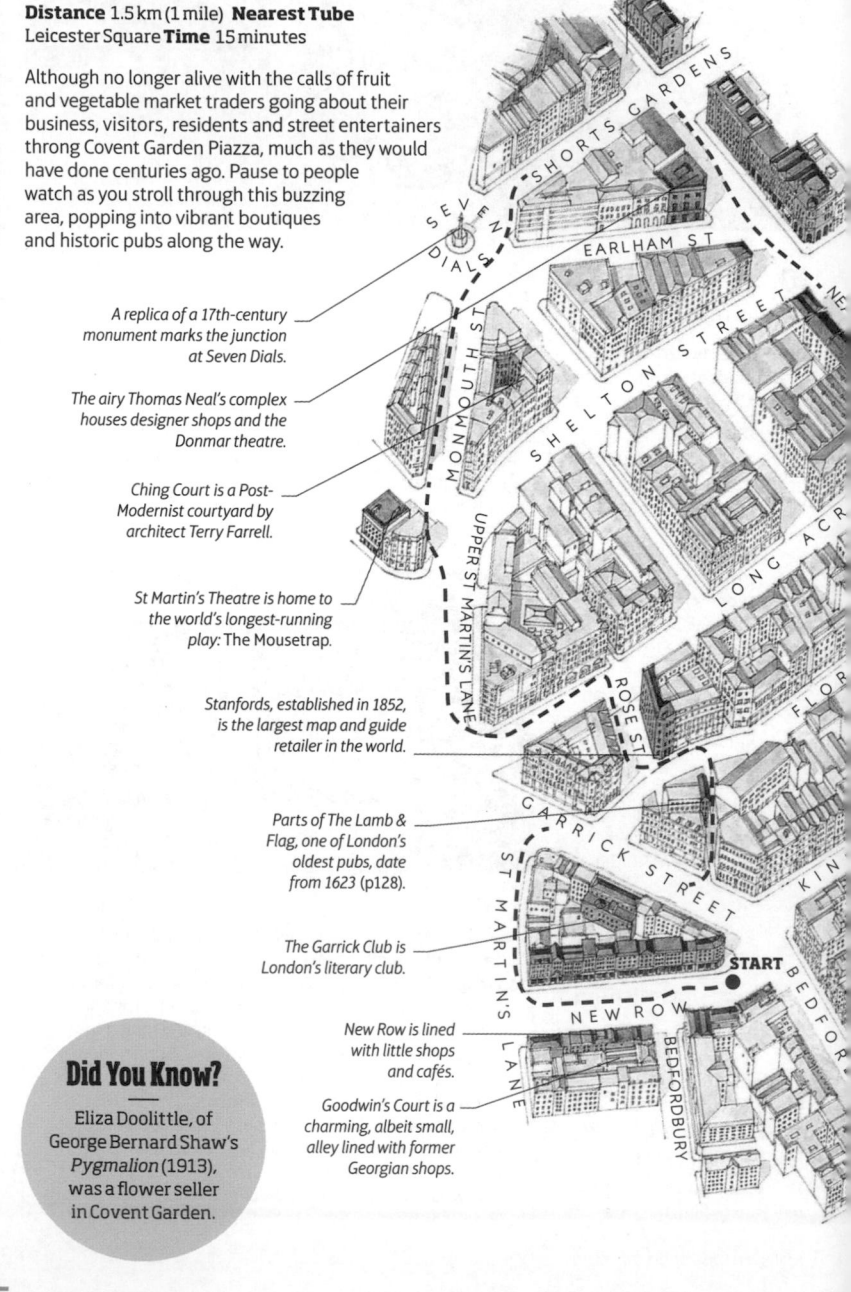

Bright and colourful
Neal Street and Neal's
Yard are home to lots of
charming shops and
cafés (p126).

A replica of a 17th-century
monument marks the junction
at Seven Dials.

The airy Thomas Neal's complex
houses designer shops and the
Donmar theatre.

Ching Court is a Post-
Modernist courtyard by
architect Terry Farrell.

St Martin's Theatre is home to
the world's longest-running
play: The Mousetrap.

Stanfords, established in 1852,
is the largest map and guide
retailer in the world.

Parts of The Lamb &
Flag, one of London's
oldest pubs, date
from 1623 (p128).

The Garrick Club is
London's literary club.

New Row is lined
with little shops
and cafés.

Goodwin's Court is a
charming, albeit small,
alley lined with former
Georgian shops.

START

Did You Know?

Eliza Doolittle, of
George Bernard Shaw's
Pygmalion (1913),
was a flower seller
in Covent Garden.

Locator Map
For more detail see p120

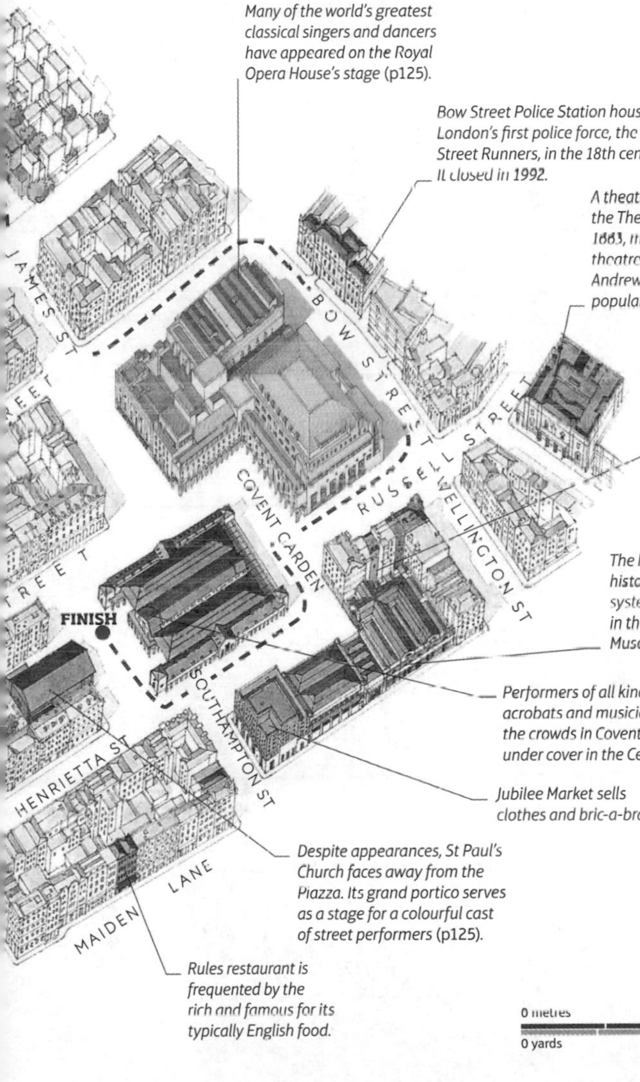

↑ Plants in a wooden market
barrow in Covent Garden

Many of the world's greatest
classical singers and dancers
have appeared on the Royal
Opera House's stage (p125).

Bow Street Police Station housed
London's first police force, the Bow
Street Runners, in the 18th century.
It closed in 1992.

A theatre has stood on the site of
the Theatre Royal Drury Lane since
1663, making it London's oldest
theatre. It is owned by composer
Andrew Lloyd Webber and stages
popular musicals.

Boswells, now a
coffee house, is where
Dr Johnson first met
his biographer,
James Boswell.

The history of the city's
historic public transport
system is brought to life
in the London Transport
Museum (p127).

Performers of all kinds – jugglers, clowns,
acrobats and musicians – entertain
the crowds in Covent Garden Piazza and
under cover in the Central Market (p122).

Jubilee Market sells
clothes and bric-a-brac.

Despite appearances, St Paul's
Church faces away from the
Piazza. Its grand portico serves
as a stage for a colourful cast
of street performers (p125).

Rules restaurant is
frequented by the
rich and famous for its
typically English food.

JAMES ST

BOW STREET

RUSSELL STREET

WELLINGTON ST

COVENT GARDEN

STREET

FINISH

SOUTHAMPTON ST

HENRIETTA ST

MAIDEN LANE

| 0 metres | | 100 | N |
| 0 yards | | 100 | ↑ |

HOLBORN AND THE INNS OF COURT

Holborn has been the home of the legal profession in London since the 13th century. The sprawling Royal Courts of Justice, the country's central civil courts, were built here, where The Strand meets Fleet Street, between 1873 and 1882. Much older are the Inns of Court, dating from the medieval period, which supply the courts here and elsewhere with their barristers and judges. Though the exact foundation dates for all four Inns of Court are uncertain, the reason for their location can be traced to a decree of Henry III, from 1234. It stated that no body providing legal education could be located in the City of London, forcing the legal profession to move just outside the boundary of the City to Holborn. Though student barristers can now study elsewhere, to graduate they must still belong to one of the Inns.

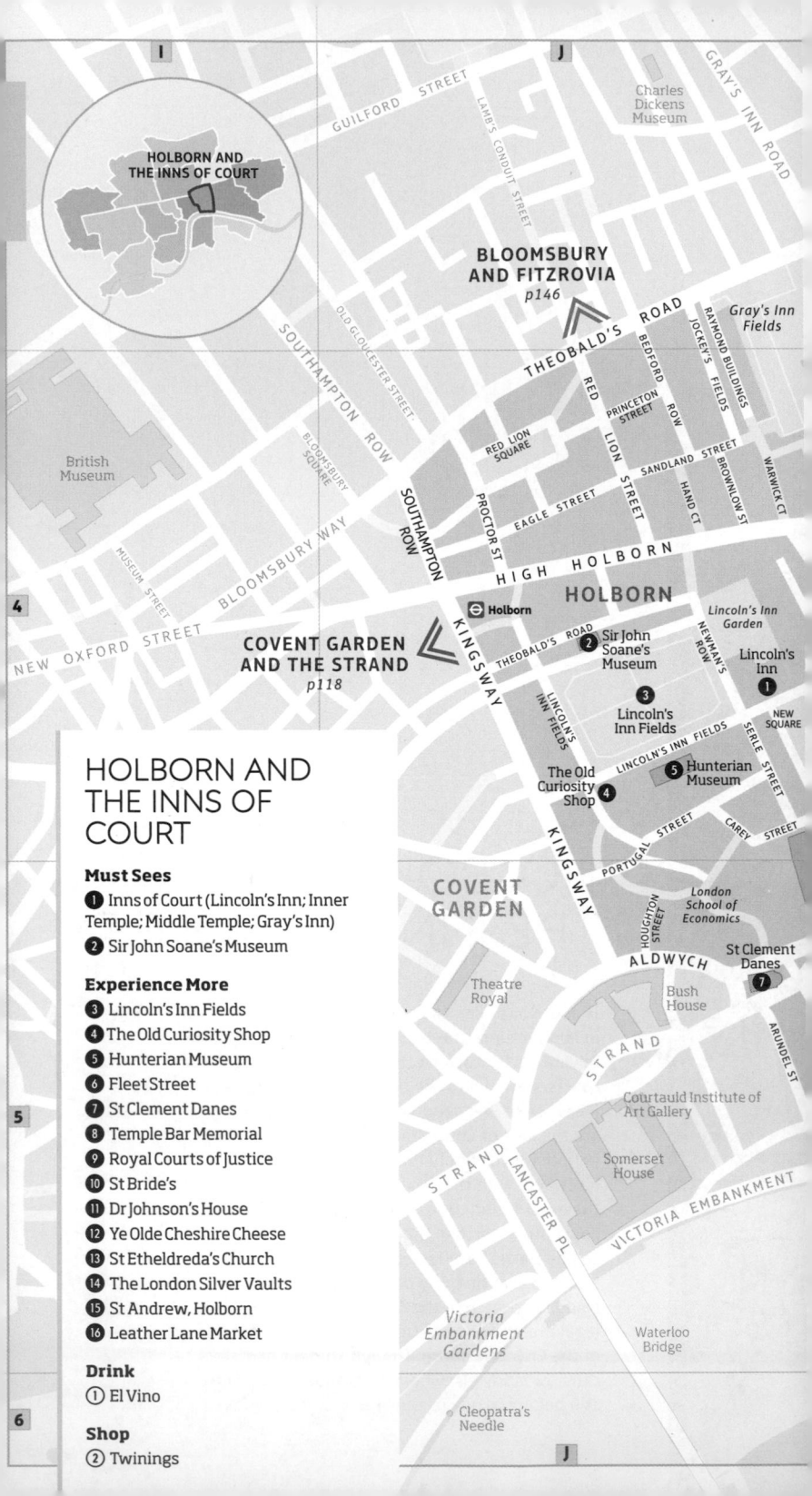

HOLBORN AND THE INNS OF COURT

Must Sees

1 Inns of Court (Lincoln's Inn; Inner Temple; Middle Temple; Gray's Inn)

2 Sir John Soane's Museum

Experience More

3 Lincoln's Inn Fields
4 The Old Curiosity Shop
5 Hunterian Museum
6 Fleet Street
7 St Clement Danes
8 Temple Bar Memorial
9 Royal Courts of Justice
10 St Bride's
11 Dr Johnson's House
12 Ye Olde Cheshire Cheese
13 St Etheldreda's Church
14 The London Silver Vaults
15 St Andrew, Holborn
16 Leather Lane Market

Drink

1 El Vino

Shop

2 Twinings

GRAY'S INN ROAD

GUILFORD STREET

LAMB'S CONDUIT STREET

Charles Dickens Museum

HOLBORN AND THE INNS OF COURT

BLOOMSBURY AND FITZROVIA p146

OLD GLOUCESTER STREET

THEOBALD'S ROAD

Gray's Inn Fields

JOCKEY'S FIELDS

RAYMOND BUILDINGS

BEDFORD ROW

PRINCETON STREET

RED LION STREET

SANDLAND STREET

BROWNLOW ST

WARWICK CT

SOUTHAMPTON ROW

BLOOMSBURY SQUARE

RED LION SQUARE

PROCTOR ST

EAGLE STREET

HAND CT

British Museum

BLOOMSBURY WAY

SOUTHAMPTON ROW

HIGH HOLBORN

HOLBORN

MUSEUM STREET

NEW OXFORD STREET

Holborn

COVENT GARDEN AND THE STRAND p118

KINGSWAY

THEOBALD'S ROAD

NEWMAN'S ROW

Lincoln's Inn Garden

2 Sir John Soane's Museum

Lincoln's Inn

1

NEW SQUARE

3 Lincoln's Inn Fields

LINCOLN'S INN FIELDS

SERLE STREET

The Old Curiosity Shop **4**

5 Hunterian Museum

CAREY STREET

PORTUGAL STREET

COVENT GARDEN

KINGSWAY

HOUGHTON STREET

London School of Economics

ALDWYCH

St Clement Danes **7**

Theatre Royal

Bush House

STRAND

ARUNDEL ST

Courtauld Institute of Art Gallery

STRAND

LANCASTER PL

Somerset House

VICTORIA EMBANKMENT

Victoria Embankment Gardens

Waterloo Bridge

Cleopatra's Needle

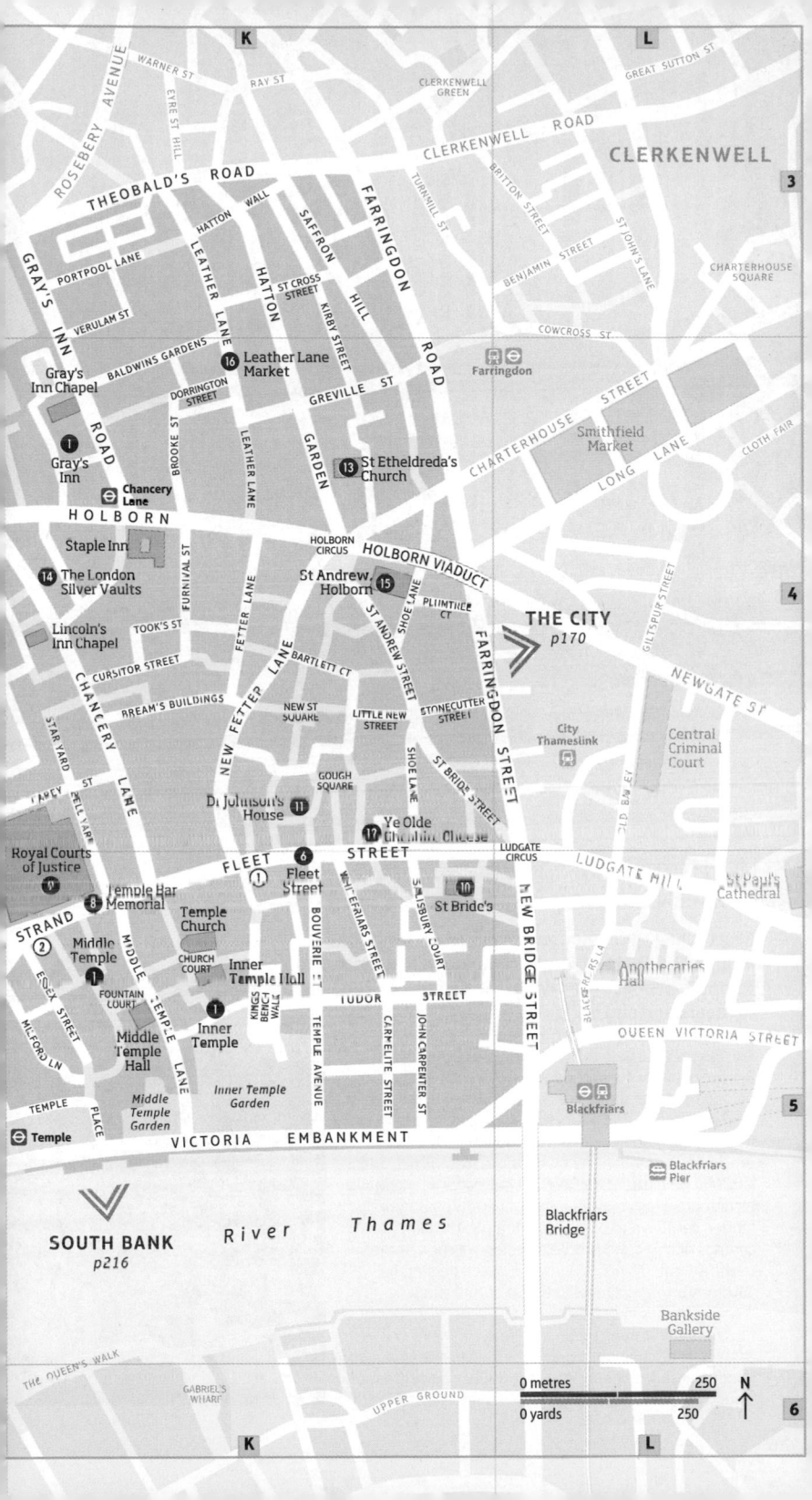

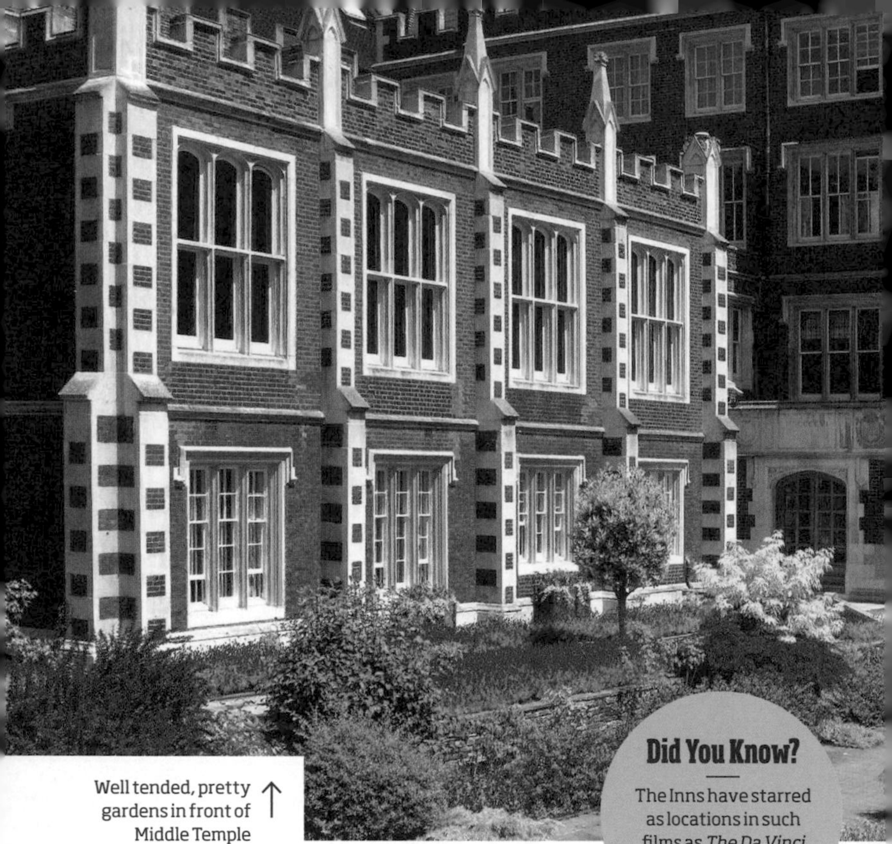

Well tended, pretty gardens in front of Middle Temple

Did You Know?

The Inns have starred as locations in such films as *The Da Vinci Code* and *Pirates of the Caribbean.*

1

INNS OF COURT

Resembling the campuses of Oxford or Cambridge University, the four Inns of Court – Lincoln's Inn, Gray's Inn, Inner Temple and Middle Temple – are oases of calm in the middle of London and perfect sites for a relaxing and intriguing wander through history.

The Inns of Court are the centuries-old homes of the Bar in England and Wales, and every barrister must belong to one of the four Inns. Established in the late medieval period, barristers have long used the Inns for training, study and as accommodation. The leafy precincts, each with their own chapel, historic hall and landscaped gardens, make great places for a lunchtime picnic or to explore their jumble of narrow passageways, hidden corners and courtyards. Temple, the joint campus of Inner and Middle Temples, was first home to the Knights Templar, who were based here in the 13th century, and a rebuilt version of their church is one of the highlights of all four Inns. It is among the most historic churches in London and one of only four "round churches" in the city.

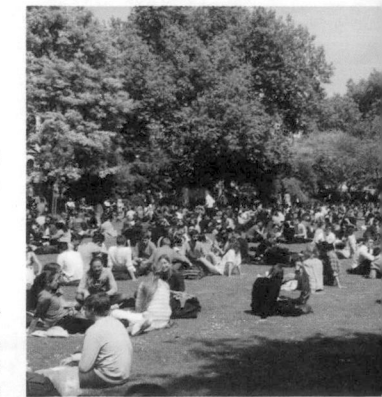

A perfect place to relax, on the grass of Lincoln's Inn Fields

Lincoln's Inn

📍 K7 🏛 Lincoln's Inn Fields WC2 🚇 Holborn, Chancery Lane 🕐 7am-7pm Mon-Fri 🌐 lincolnsinn.org.uk

Some of the buildings in Lincoln's Inn, the best-preserved of London's Inns of Court, date back to the late 15th century. The coat of arms above the arch of the Chancery Lane gatehouse is Henry VIII's, and the heavy oak door is from the same time. Shakespeare's contemporary, Ben Jonson, is believed to have laid some of the bricks of Lincoln's Inn during the reign of Elizabeth I. The chapel is early 17th-century Gothic. Lincoln's Inn has its share of famous alumni; Oliver Cromwell, John Donne, the 17th-century poet, and William Penn, founder of the US state of Pennsylvania were all students here.

Inner Temple and Middle Temple

📍 K5 🏛 Inner Temple: Kings Bench Walk EC4; Middle Temple: Temple Lane EC4 🚇 Temple 🕐 Inner Temple: 8am-7pm Mon-Fri 🌐 innertemple.org.uk; middletemple.org.uk

Temple's series of courtyards and buildings comprise two of the four Inns of Court: Middle Temple and Inner Temple. The name derives from the Knights Templar, a chivalrous order based here in medieval times, whose initiations probably took place in the crypt of Temple Church. Built in the 12th century, and maintained by the Inns since 1608, the circular Temple Church boasts an impressive Elizabethan organ and 13th-century effigies of the Knights Templar in its nave.

Among Temple's other ancient buildings is Middle Temple Hall. Completed in 1572, its fine Elizabethan interior survives. Behind Temple, peaceful lawns stretch lazily down towards the Embankment.

Gray's Inn

📍 K4 🏛 High Holborn WC1 🚇 Holborn, Chancery Lane 🕐 6am-8pm Mon-Fri, by prior arrangement 🌐 graysinn.org.uk

This ancient legal centre and law school dates to the 14th century though it was largely rebuilt after damage inflicted during World War II. At least one of Shakespeare's plays (*A Comedy of Errors*) was first performed in Gray's Inn hall in 1594. The hall's 16th-century interior screen still survives. The young Charles Dickens was employed as a clerk here between 1827 and 1828. The garden, known as "the Walks" and once a convenient site for staging duels, is open to lunchtime strollers for part of the year.

THE KNIGHTS TEMPLAR

The Knights Templar, who founded Temple and built Temple Church, was a religious order established to protect pilgrims on their way to and from Jerusalem in the 12th century. The Holy City had been seized in the late 11th century by Christian crusaders but pilgrimage routes were fraught with danger. The order was dissolved in 1312.

2

SIR JOHN SOANE'S MUSEUM

📍 J4 🏠 13 Lincoln's Inn Fields WC2 🚇 Holborn 🕐 10am–5pm Wed–Sun, 6–9pm first Tue of month 📅 24–26 Dec 🌐 soane.org

One of the most delightful and unusual museums in London, this extraordinary house, filled to bursting with an eclectic gathering of beautiful and peculiar objects, was left to the nation by the architect Sir John Soane in 1837.

Though laden with Classical statuary and other eye-catching and unusual artifacts, it is the interior design of the building itself that makes this place unlike any other museum. The house abounds with architectural surprises and illusions. Cunningly placed mirrors play tricks with light and space and in the centre of the basement an atrium stretches up to the roof, the glass dome of which illuminates the galleries on every floor. Up in the picture gallery on the first floor, walls turn out to be folding panels which open to reveal further paintings and, most unexpectedly, a floorless extension to the room itself, hung with yet more pictures.

↑ The museum, made up of three houses that Soane bought one by one

Rooms filled with an eclectic array of ancient statuary ↑

WHO WAS SIR JOHN SOANE?

Born in 1753, the son of a bricklayer, John Soane eventually became one of Britain's leading architects of the 19th century. Most of his buildings were Neo-Classical in style and he was responsible for designing Dulwich Picture Gallery *(p325)*, Pitzhanger Manor *(p330)* and the Bank of England *(p184)*.

EXPERIENCE MORE

③
Lincoln's Inn Fields

📍 J4 🏠 WC2 🚇 Holborn 🕐 Dawn-dusk daily

A former public execution site, many religious martyrs and those suspected of treachery to the Crown perished here under the Tudors and Stuarts. When the developer William Newton wanted to build on this site in the 1640s, students at Lincoln's Inn and other residents made him undertake that it would remain a public area forever. Thanks to this early protest, tennis is played on the public courts here in summer, while lawyers read their briefs in the fresh air.

④
The Old Curiosity Shop

📍 J4 🏠 13–14 Portsmouth St WC2 🚇 Holborn 🌐 the old-curiosity-shop.com

Whether it inspired Charles Dickens's 19th-century novel of the same name or not, the Old Curiosity Shop is a genuine 16th-century building. With its wooden beams and over-hanging first floor, it gives a rare impression of a London streetscape from before the Great Fire of 1666. The shop is still trading, currently as a handmade shoe shop.

⑤
Hunterian Museum

📍 J4 🏠 35–43 Lincoln's Inn Fields WC2 🚇 Holborn, Chancery Lane 🕐 For refurbishment until 2020 🌐 hunterianmuseum.org

Inside the Royal College of Surgeons, the Hunterian Museum started life as the personal collection of John Hunter (1728–93), one of the leading teachers of surgery in his day, who amassed a large collection of human and animal anatomical specimens to aid his teaching. Most famously the skeleton of Charles Byrne, the "Irish Giant" at 2.31 m (7 ft 7 in) tall, is here. It is not a museum for the squeamish, but the surgical instruments and interactive displays on modern surgery are fascinating for those with an interest in the subject.

↑ The Old Curiosity Shop provides a glimpse of London as it looked before 1666

↑ Fleet Street, one of the oldest streets in the City of London, which once rang with the sounds of printing presses

Fleet Street

📍K5 🏠EC4 🚇Temple, Blackfriars, St Paul's

England's first printing press was set up by William Caxton in the late 15th century. In around 1500, his assistant began his own business in Fleet Street, and the area became the centre of London's publishing industry. Playwrights Shakespeare and Ben Jonson were patrons of the old Mitre tavern, now No 37 Fleet Street. In 1702, England's first daily newspaper, *The Daily Courant*, was issued from Fleet Street – conveniently placed for the City and Westminster, which were the main sources of news. Later the street became synonymous with the Press. The grand Art Deco building with Egyptian-style detail at No 135 is the former headquarters of the *Daily Telegraph*.

Did You Know?

Sweeney Todd, the "Demon Barber of Fleet Street", is said to have had his parlour at No 152 Fleet St.

Next to the church of St-Dunstan-in-the-West (which largely dates from the 1830s) is a building adorned with the names of former newspapers.

The printing presses underneath the newspaper offices were abandoned in 1987, when new technology made it easy to produce papers away from the centre of town in areas such as Wapping and the Docklands. Today the newspaper offices have also left Fleet Street, even though some of the journalists' traditional watering holes remain, such as Ye Olde Cheshire Cheese public house *(p142)*, and the legendary El Vino wine bar, at the western end opposite Fetter Lane.

7
St Clement Danes

📍J5 🏠Strand WC2 📞020 7242 8282 🚇Temple
🕐9am–4pm Mon–Fri, 10am–3pm Sat, 9:30am–3pm Sun 🚫Noon 25–27 Dec, public hols

Sitting proudly isolated on a traffic island, this wonderful church was designed by Christopher Wren in 1680. Its name derives from an earlier church built here by the descendants of Danish invaders, whom Alfred the

Great had allowed to remain in London in the 9th century. From the 17th to the 19th centuries many people were buried here, and their memorial plaques are now in the crypt. The chain that hangs on the crypt wall was probably used to secure coffin lids against body snatchers, who stole fresh corpses and sold them to the teaching hospitals. Outside, to the east, is a statue (1910) of Dr Johnson *(p142)*, who often came to services here.

Nearly destroyed during World War II, the church was rebuilt and became the central church of the Royal Air Force (RAF). The interior is dominated by RAF symbols, memorials and monuments.

The church bells ring to various tunes, including that of the old nursery rhyme *Oranges and Lemons*, in whose lyrics the church features.

8
Temple Bar Memorial

📍K5 🏠Fleet St EC4
🚇Holborn, Temple, Chancery Lane

In the middle of Fleet Street stands a monument looking somewhat like a giant sentry box, with Queen Victoria and her son, the Prince of Wales,

DRINK

standing guard on either side. Dating from 1880, it marks the spot where Temple Bar, a magnificent gateway by Sir Christopher Wren, used to stand. This was the principal entrance to the City of London, where by tradition the monarch, when In State procession to the Tower of London or St Paul's Cathedral, had to pause and ask permission of the Lord Mayor to enter. The original gateway was dismantled when it began to cause traffic congestion, and spent over a century in the grounds of a country estate in Hertfordshire before being erected at the entrance of Paternoster Square near St Paul's (p174) in 2004.

---

9 Ⓜ 🖥

Royal Courts of Justice (the Law Courts)

📍 K5 🏠 Strand WC2
🚇 Holborn, Temple, Chancery Lane 🕐 9:30am-4:30pm Mon-Fri 🚫 Public hols 🌐 theroyalcourtsof justice.com

Knots of demonstrators and television cameras can often be seen outside this sprawling and fanciful Victorian Gothic building, waiting for the verdict of a contentious case. These are the nation's main civil courts, dealing with such matters as divorce, libel, civil liability and appeals. Cases involving criminal offences are dealt with at the Old Bailey (p187), ten minutes' walk to the east. The public are admitted to all the courtrooms and a list details which case is being heard in which one. The massive building was completed in 1882 and is said to contain 1,000 rooms and 5.6 km (3.5 miles) of corridors.

---

10 Ⓜ 🛍

St Bride's

📍 K5 🏠 Fleet St EC4
🚇 Blackfriars 🕐 8am-6pm Mon-Fri, 10am-3.30pm Sat, 10am-6.30pm Sun
🚫 Pub hols 🌐 stbrides.com

St Bride's is one of Wren's best-loved churches. Its position just off Fleet Street has made it the traditional venue for memorial services to departed journalists, and wall plaques commemorate notable pressmen and women and printers. The marvellous octagonal layered spire has been the model for tiered wedding cakes since shortly after it was added in 1703. The church was bombed during World War II, but its interior had been faithfully restored by 1957. The crypt contains remnants of earlier churches on the site, and a section of Roman pavement. Tours lasting 90 minutes are led at 2:15pm on Tuesdays.

↑ The Royal Courts of Justice, one of Britain's key courts of law

Ye Olde Cheshire Cheese, an icon of London's pub scene ↑

Dr Johnson's House

📍K4 📍17 Gough Sq EC4 🚇Blackfriars, Chancery Lane, Temple 🕐May-Sep: 11am-5:30pm Mon-Sat; Oct-Apr: 11am-5pm Mon-Sat 🚫Last two weeks Dec, public hols 🌐drjohnsonshouse.org

The oft-quoted Dr Samuel Johnson was an 18th-century scholar famous for the many witty (and often contentious) remarks that his biographer, James Boswell, recorded and published. Johnson lived at

↑ Hodge looking out from in front of Dr Johnson's House

17 Gough Square from 1748 to 1759. He compiled the first definitive English dictionary (published in 1755) in the attic, where six scribes and assistants stood all day at high desks.

The house, built before 1700, retains some period features and is furnished with 18th-century pieces. There is a small collection of exhibits relating to Johnson and the times in which he lived, including a tea set belonging to his friend Mrs Thrale and pictures of Johnson and his contemporaries. There are also replica Georgian costumes for children to try on. A statue of one of Johnson's favourite cats, Hodge, stands outside.

Ye Olde Cheshire Cheese

📍K4 📍145 Fleet St EC4 🚇Blackfriars 🕐11am-11pm Mon-Fri, noon-11pm Sat, noon-7pm Sun

There has been an inn here for centuries and parts of this building date back to 1667, when rebuilding took place

after the Great Fire of 1666. The diarist Samuel Pepys often drank here in the 17th century, but it was Dr Samuel Johnson's association with "the Cheese" that made it a place of pilgrimage for the 19th-century literati. Novelists Mark Twain and Charles Dickens were frequent visitors. In recent years it has been argued that there is no real evidence that Johnson actually drank here; nevertheless, this is a great old pub, one of few

SHOP

Twinings
The oldest tea shop in London. Learn about the history of Britain's favourite drink, and try (and buy) a variety of brews from the world-famous brand.

📍K5 📍216 Strand WC2 🌐twinings.co.uk

↑ The stained-glass west window of St Etheldreda's church

HATTON GARDEN

Named for Sir Christopher Hatton, Hatton Garden is the centre of London's diamond and jewellery district. Millions of pounds change hands daily in scores of small shops with sparkling window displays. In April 2015, an underground safe deposit facility was robbed of upwards of £25 million, in what has been described as the "largest burglary in English legal history".

to have kept the 18th-century arrangement of small rooms with fireplaces, tables and benches, rather than knocking through to make larger bars.

St Etheldreda's Church

K4 14 Ely Place Farringdon 8am-5pm Mon-Sat, 8am-12:30pm Sun stetheldreda.com

Built in 1290, this rare survivor is the oldest Catholic church in England. First the town chapel of the Bishops of Ely, it passed through various hands over the centuries, including those of Sir Christopher Hatton, an Elizabethan courtier, who built Hatton House in the grounds and used the church crypt as a tavern. Rebuilt and restored several times, the church has some stunning stained glass.

The London Silver Vaults

K4 53-64 Chancery Lane WC2 Chancery Lane, Holborn 9am-5:30pm Mon-Fri, 9am-1pm Sat silvervaultslondon.com

These silver vaults began life as the 19th-century Chancery Lane Safe Deposit Company.

Visitors are led down stairs, then through steel security doors to reach a nest of underground shops shining with antique and modern silverware. Prices range from modest to eye-watering.

St Andrew, Holborn

K4 5 St Andrew St EC4 Chancery Lane 9am-5pm Mon-Fri standrewholborn.org.uk

This has been a site of worship for over 1,000 years. The medieval church that stood here survived the Great Fire but in 1668, renowned architect Christopher Wren was asked to redesign it. The lower part of the tower is virtually all that remains of the earlier church. One of Wren's most spacious churches, it was gutted during World War II but faithfully restored as the church of the London trade guilds.

Benjamin Disraeli, the Jewish-born prime minister, was baptized here in 1817, at the age of 12. In the 19th century, a charity school was attached to the church.

Leather Lane Market

K4 Leather Lane Barbican, Chancery Lane 10am-2pm Mon-Fri

Running parallel to Hatton Garden is Leather Lane Market. A traditional London market, it sells a bit of everything, including some tasty street food, and is a perfect place to pick up a treat or two.

↑ The impressive silverware and antiques in the London silver vaults

A SHORT WALK
LINCOLN'S INN

Distance 2 km (1.25 miles) **Nearest Tube** Holborn **Time** 20 minutes

This is calm, dignified, legal London, packed with history and interest. Lincoln's Inn, adjoining one of the city's first residential squares, has buildings dating back to the late 15th century. Suited lawyers carry bundles of briefs between their offices here and the Neo-Gothic Law Courts. Nearby is Temple, another historic legal district, with a famous 13th-century round church.

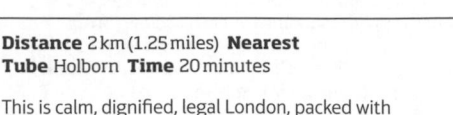

The Sir John Soane's Museum was the home of the Georgian architect. It was left, with his collection, to the nation (p38).

START

The mock-Tudor archway, leading to Lincoln's Inn and built in 1845, overlooks the Lincoln's Inn Fields (p139).

Lincoln's Inn (p137)

The Old Curiosity Shop is a rare 16th-century, pre-Great Fire building (p139).

The Hunterian Museum, part of the Royal College of Surgeons, was designed in 1836 by Sir Charles Barry (p139).

LINCOLN'S INN FIELDS

PORTSMOUTH ST

PORTUGAL STREET

CARE

↑ The peaceful green haven of the Lincoln's Inns Fields public square

| 0 metres | | 100 |
| 0 yards | | 100 |

N ↑

FINISH

The Gladstone Statue was erected in 1905 to commemorate William Gladstone, the Victorian statesman who served four terms as prime minister.

↑ The imposing façade of the Royal Courts of Justice, the nation's main civil courts

HOLBORN AND THE INNS OF COURT

Locator Map
For more detail see p134

Did You Know?

Lincoln's Inn Fields is the largest public square in London.

Look for the gold lions on the railings of the Law Society's headquarters.

For two centuries Fleet Street was the centre of the national press. The newspaper offices left in the 1980s (p140).

El Vino is a wine bar where Fleet Street's journalists once mingled with barristers (p141).

No 17 Fleet Street has a superb half-timbered façade (1610) that survived the Fire. James I's eldest son, Prince Henry, had a room on the first floor of this former tavern.

Temple was first home to the Knights Templar, who were based here in the 13th century.

A dragon marks where the City of London meets Westminster at the Temple Bar Memorial (p140).

Designed by Wren (1679), St Clement Danes is the Royal Air Force's church (p140).

The Royal Courts of Justice, the country's main court for civil cases and appeals, was built in 1882. It is made out of 35 million bricks faced with Portland stone (p141).

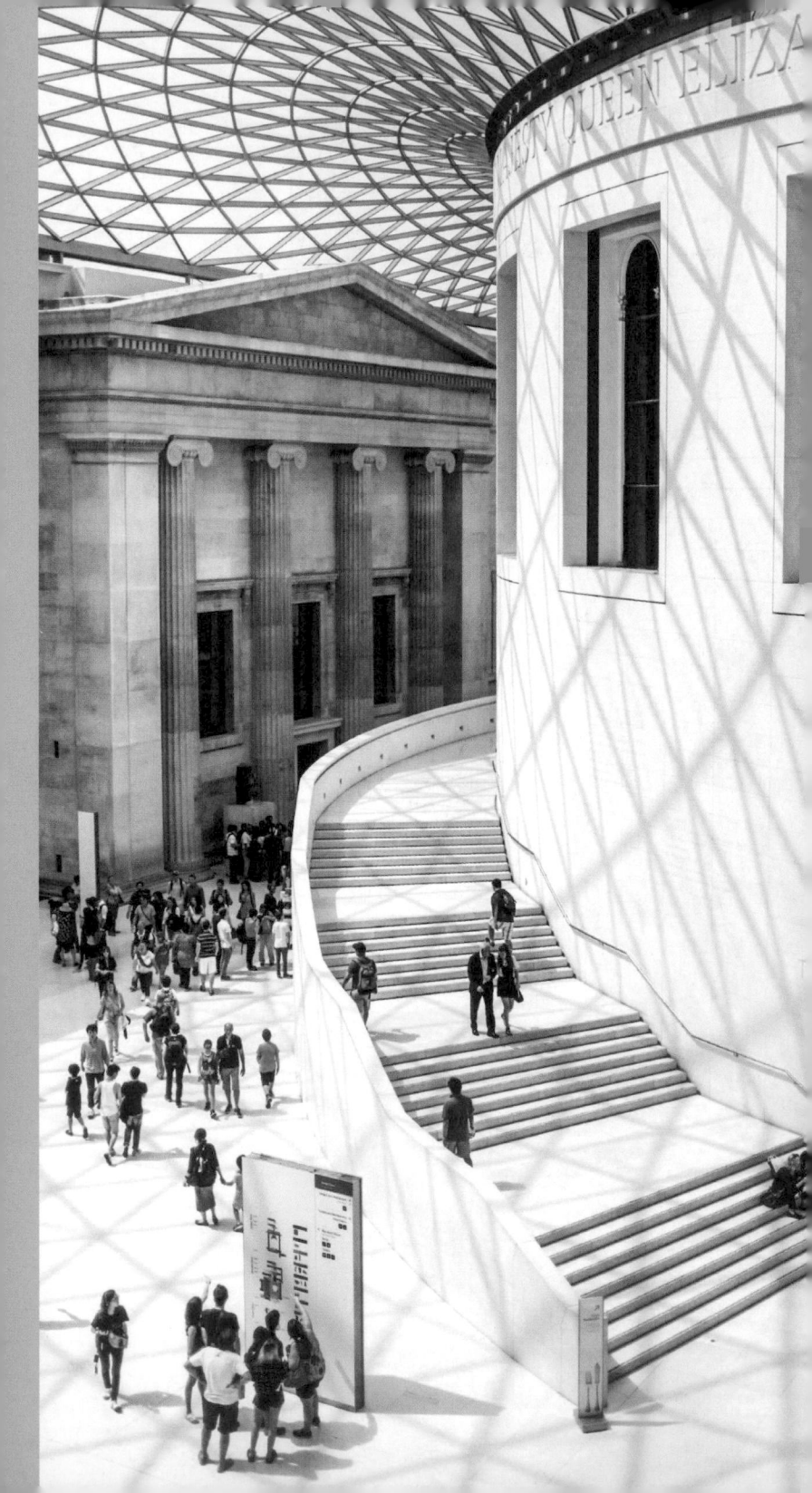

BLOOMSBURY AND FITZROVIA

The handsome garden squares of Fitzrovia and Bloomsbury date mainly from the late 18th and early 19th centuries but it wasn't until the early 20th century that the area became inseparably connected with the cultural and intellectual elite of London. By that time Bloomsbury was already established as a place of learning, home to the British Museum, founded in 1753, and the University of London, founded in 1826. Along with Fitzrovia it was an apt location, therefore, for the homes and haunts of the avant garde set known as the Bloomsbury Group, a network of mostly upper middle class, learned and artistic friends and associates. Since the Bloomsbury Group's heyday the university has expanded significantly, adding the School of Oriental and African Studies and the central library at monolithic Senate House to its collection of campuses, and cementing its place as the student capital of central London.

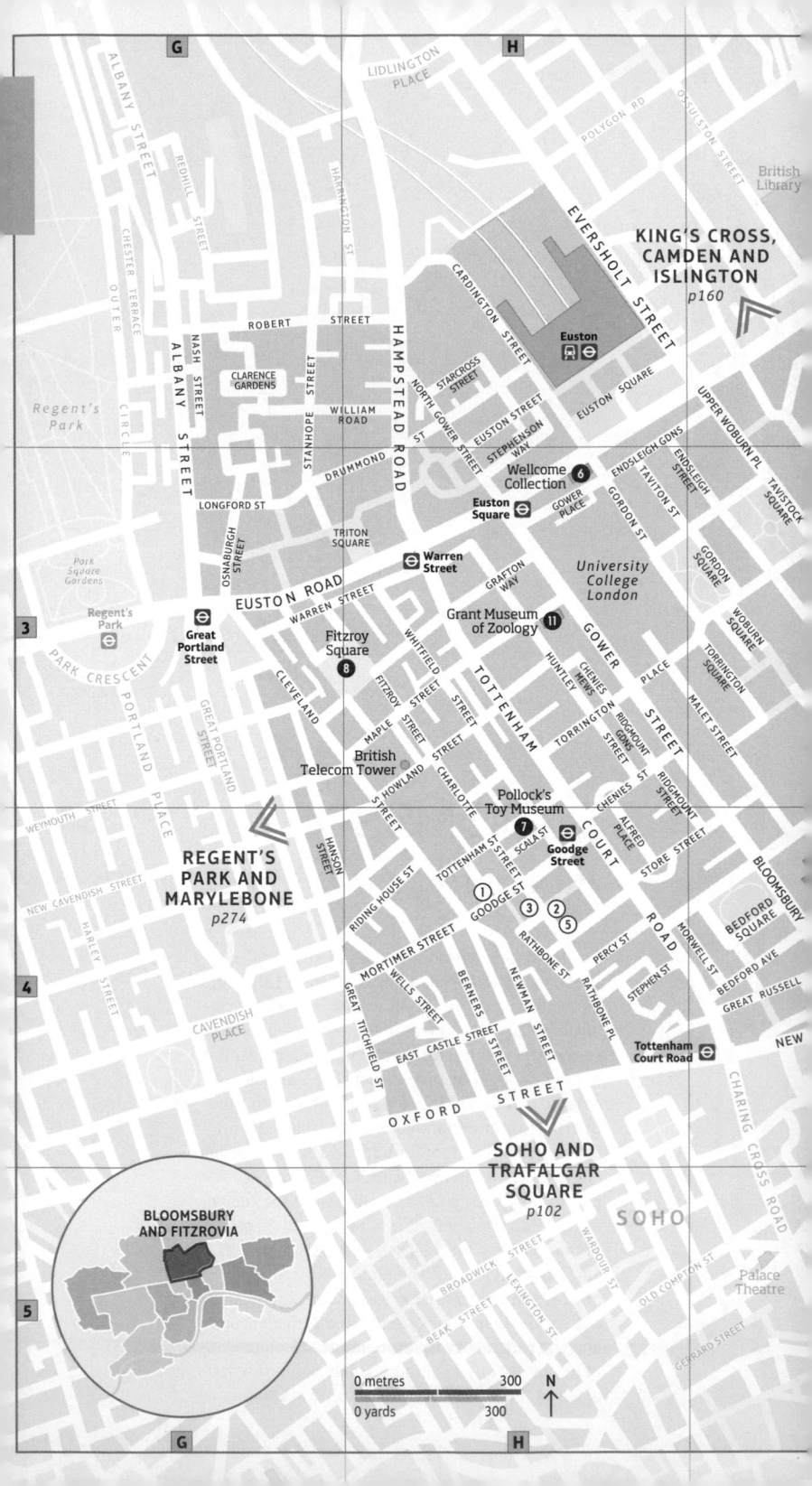

ALBANY STREET

REDHILL STREET

CHESTER TERRACE

OUTER CIRCLE

LIDLINGTON PLACE

POLYGON RD

OSULSTON STREET

British Library

KING'S CROSS, CAMDEN AND ISLINGTON
p160

Regent's Park

HARRINGTON STREET

EVERSHOLT STREET

CARDINGTON STREET

Euston

ROBERT   STREET

HAMPSTEAD ROAD

NORTH GOWER STREET

STARCROSS STREET

EUSTON STREET

STEPHENSON WAY

Euston Square

UPPER WOBURN PL

TAVISTOCK SQUARE

NASH STREET

ALBANY STREET

STANHOPE STREET

WILLIAM ROAD

DRUMMOND

CLARENCE GARDENS

LONGFORD ST

TRITON SQUARE

Wellcome Collection 6

GOWER PLACE

ENDSLEIGH GDNS

ENDSLEIGH STREET

TAVITON ST

GORDON ST

University College London

GORDON SQUARE

WOBURN SQUARE

TORRINGTON SQUARE

MALET STREET

Park Square Gardens

Regent's Park

OSNABURGH STREET

GREAT PORTLAND STREET

EUSTON ROAD

WARREN STREET

Warren Street

Grant Museum of Zoology 11

GRAFTON WAY

HUNTLEY

CHENIES MEWS

RIDGMOUNT STREET

GOWER STREET

PLACE

Great Portland Street

WARREN STREET

Fitzroy Square 8

CLEVELAND

WHITFIELD

FITZROY STREET

TOTTENHAM

TORRINGTON PLACE

RIDGMOUNT

CHENIES ST

ALFRED PLACE

STORE STREET

BLOOMSBURY

PARK CRESCENT

PORTLAND PLACE

MAPLE STREET

HOWLAND STREET

CHARLOTTE STREET

British Telecom Tower

Pollock's Toy Museum 7

SCALA ST

COURT

RIDGMOUNT STREET

BEDFORD SQUARE

WEYMOUTH STREET

NEW CAVENDISH STREET

HARLEY STREET

GREAT PORTLAND STREET

HANSON STREET

RIDING HOUSE ST

TOTTENHAM STREET

Goodge Street

ROAD

BEDFORD AVE

REGENT'S PARK AND MARYLEBONE
p274

GOODGE ST 1

RATHBONE ST

3 2 5

PERCY ST

STEPHEN ST

MORWELL ST

GREAT RUSSELL

CAVENDISH PLACE

MORTIMER STREET

WELLS STREET

BERNERS STREET

NEWMAN STREET

RATHBONE PL

Tottenham Court Road

NEW

EAST CASTLE STREET

GREAT TITCHFIELD ST

OXFORD   STREET

SOHO AND TRAFALGAR SQUARE
p102

SOHO

CHARING CROSS ROAD

Palace Theatre

BLOOMSBURY AND FITZROVIA

BROADWICK STREET

LEXINGTON STREET

WARDOUR ST

OLD COMPTON ST

BEAK STREET

GERRARD STREET

0 metres   300
0 yards   300

N

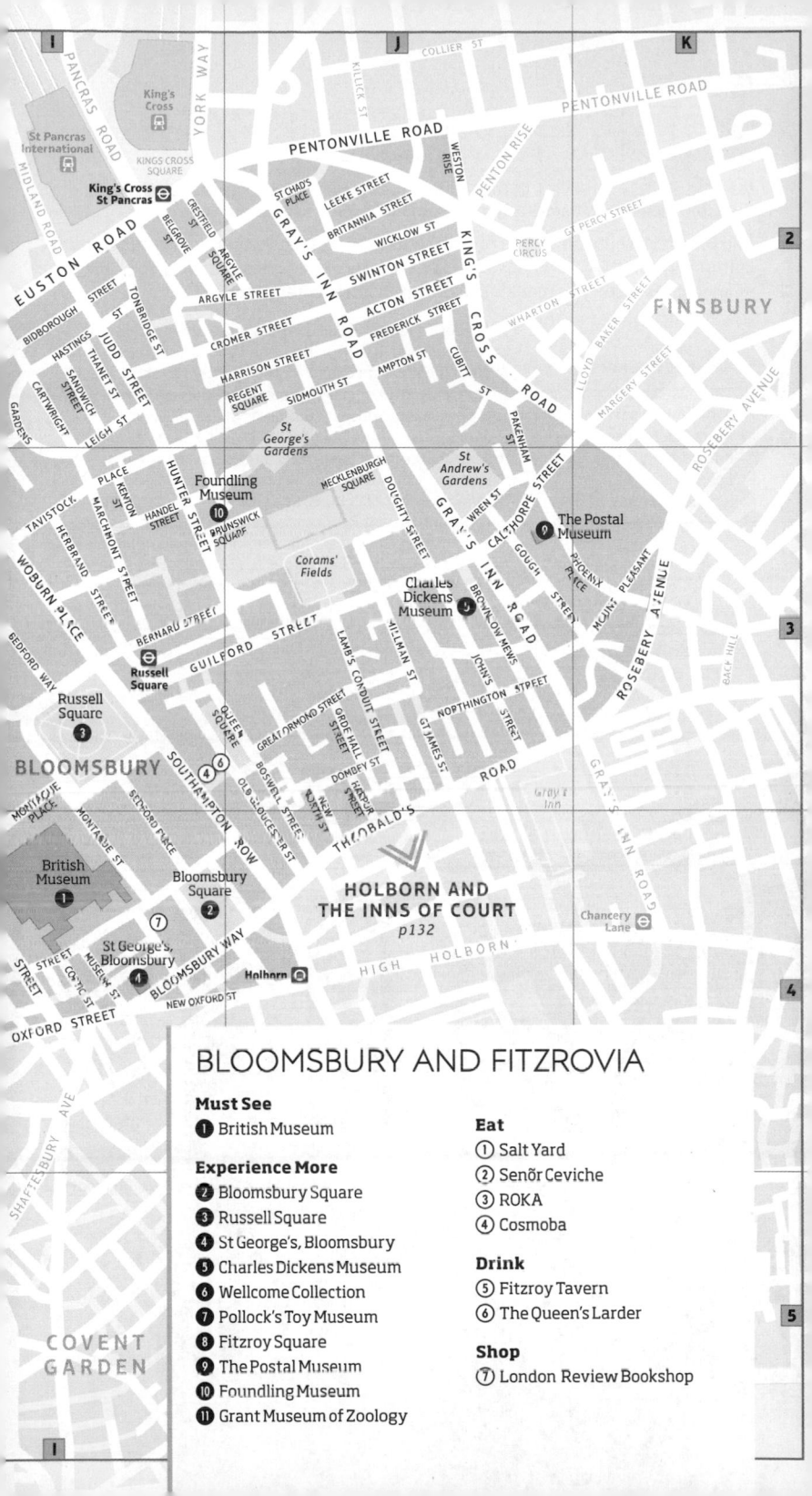

BLOOMSBURY AND FITZROVIA

Must See
① British Museum

Experience More
② Bloomsbury Square
③ Russell Square
④ St George's, Bloomsbury
⑤ Charles Dickens Museum
⑥ Wellcome Collection
⑦ Pollock's Toy Museum
⑧ Fitzroy Square
⑨ The Postal Museum
⑩ Foundling Museum
⑪ Grant Museum of Zoology

Eat
① Salt Yard
② Senõr Ceviche
③ ROKA
④ Cosmoba

Drink
⑤ Fitzroy Tavern
⑥ The Queen's Larder

Shop
⑦ London Review Bookshop

1

BRITISH MUSEUM

📍 I4 🏠 Great Russell St WC1 🚇 Tottenham Court Road, Holborn, Russell Square
🚉 Euston 🕐 Sat–Thu 10am–5.30pm, til 8.30pm Fri 🌐 britishmuseum.org

The British Museum holds one of the world's greatest collections of historical and cultural artifacts. This immense hoard of treasure comprises over 8 million objects spanning the history of mankind, from prehistoric times to today.

💬 INSIDER TIP
Eye Openers

The museum offers an excellent set of free tours. There are over a dozen daily "Eye-opener tours" of individual rooms; and on Friday evenings the "spotlight tours" focus on specific exhibits such as the Rosetta Stone. There's no need to book, simply check the website for where and when to meet.

The oldest public museum in the world, the British Museum was established in 1753 to house the books, antiquities, and plant and animal specimens of the physician Sir Hans Sloane (1660–1753). The collection expanded rapidly and during the 19th century the museum acquired a mass of Classical and Middle Eastern antiquities, some of which still make up the top attractions here, such as the Rosetta Stone and the Parthenon sculptures. You can now see items drawn from a dizzying number of cultures and civilizations, from Stone Age Europe and Ancient Egypt to modern Japan and contemporary North America. There are sculptures and statues, mummies and murals, coins and medals, ceramics, gold and silver, prints, drawings and innumerable other man-made objects from every corner of the globe and every period of history.

① The Rosetta Stone was the key to interpreting Egyptian hieroglyphs.

② The museum holds the largest collection of Egyptian mummies outside of Egypt.

③ Beautiful statues from the Parthenon in Ancient Greece

The Greek Revival-style main entrance to the British Museum on Great Russell Street ↓

A World of Treasures

There are 95 galleries covering 4 km (2.5 miles) over three floors and eight levels of the museum, though the majority of exhibits are on the ground and upper floors. Ancient Egyptian artifacts are on the upper floor in Rooms 61 to 66 and in Room 4, beside the Great Court. The Greece, Rome and Middle East collections are also spread across the two main floors, though major items such as the Parthenon sculptures are in the large rooms of the ground floor to the west of the Great Court. The Africa collection is on the lower floor, while Asia exhibits are found on ground and upper floors on the north side. The Americas collection is located in the north-east corner of the main floor. The Sainsbury Gallery hosts major temporary exhibitions.

← The world-famous Reading Room, designed by Sir Norman Foster, at the centre of the Great Court

Did You Know?

The Portland Vase, made before the birth of Christ, was reassembled after it was smashed by a visitor in 1845.

Inside the Enlightenment gallery, formerly the library of King George III ↑

GREAT COURT AND READING ROOM

The architectural highlight of the building is the Great Court, a breathtaking conversion of the original 19th-century inner courtyard. Opened in 2000, the court is now covered by a tessellated glass roof, creating Europe's largest indoor public square. At the centre of the Great Court is the glorious dome-roofed Reading Room of the former British Library where figures such as Mahatma Gandhi and Karl Marx studied.

Top Collections

Prehistoric and Roman Britain

▶ Relics of prehistoric Britain are on display in six galleries. The most impressive items include the gold "Mold Cape", a ceremonial Bronze Age cape found in Wales; an antlered headdress worn by hunter-gatherers 9,000 years ago; and "Lindow Man", a 1st-century AD victim of sacrifice preserved in a bog until 1984.

Europe

Sutton Hoo's treasure, the burial hoard of a 7th-century Anglo-Saxon king, is in Room 41. The artifacts include a helmet and shield, Celtic bowls, and gold and garnet jewellery. Exquisite timepieces include a 400-year-old clock from Prague, designed as a model galleon; in its day it pitched, played music and even fired a cannon. Nearby are the famous 12th-century Lewis chessmen. Baron Ferdinand Rothschild's (1839-98) Renaissance treasures are in Room 2a.

Middle East

Galleries devoted to the Middle East collections cover 7,000 years of history, with famous items such as 7th-century BC Assyrian reliefs from King Ashurbanpal's palace at Nineveh, two large human-headed bulls from 7th-century BC Khorsabad and the Black Obelisk of Shalmaneser III, an Assyrian king. The upper floors contain pieces from ancient Sumeria, part of the Oxus Treasure (which lay buried for over 2,000 years) and a collection of clay cuneiform tablets.

Egypt

Egyptian sculptures in Room 4 include a fine red granite head of a king, thought to be Amenophis III, and a huge statue of King Rameses II. Here too is the Rosetta Stone, used as a key for deciphering Egyptian hieroglyphs. An array of mummies, jewellery and Coptic art is upstairs. Room 61 houses paintings from the lost tomb-chapel of Nebamun.

Greece and Rome

◀ The Greek and Roman collections include the controversial Parthenon sculptures. These 5th-century BC reliefs decorated the temple to Athena on the Acropolis, Athens. Much of it was ruined, and what survived was removed by the British diplomat Lord Elgin. There is also the Nereid Monument and sculptures from the Mausoleum at Halicarnassus.

Asia

Fine porcelain, Shang bronzes (c 1500-1050 BC) and ceremonial bronze vessels are in the Chinese Collection. In the Sir Percival David gallery the Chinese ceramics date from the 10th to early 20th centuries. There is a fine collection of sculpture from the Indian subcontinent, including sculpted reliefs that once covered the walls of the Buddhist temple at Amaravati. A Korean section contains works of Buddhist art. Islamic art is in Room 34, and there is a traditional Japanese teahouse in Room 92.

Africa

African sculptures, textiles and graphic art are in Room 25. Famous bronzes from the Kingdom of Benin stand alongside modern African prints, paintings, drawings and colourful fabrics.

EXPERIENCE MORE

THE BLOOMSBURY GROUP

The Bloomsbury Group was an informal set of writers, artists and intellectuals who lived in and around Bloomsbury at the beginning of the 20th century. The group, with its passionate belief in the "aesthetic experience and the pursuit of knowledge", and modern attitudes towards feminism, sexuality and politics, first gathered at No 46 Gordon Square, home of the Stephen sisters, Virginia (later Woolf) and Vanessa (later Bell). Other key members included novelist E M Forster, economist John Maynard Keynes, the biographer Lytton Strachey and artists Duncan Grant and Dora Carrington.

② Bloomsbury Square

📍I4 🏠WC1 🚇Holborn

This is the oldest of the Bloomsbury squares. It was laid out in 1661 by the 4th Earl of Southampton, who owned the land. None of the original buildings survive and the square's shaded garden is encircled by a busy one-way traffic system. (There is a car park below the square that, unusually for central London, nearly always has a free space or two.)

From this square, the entire Bloomsbury area was gradually developed. Noted for the brilliance of many of its inhabitants, it gave its name most famously to the avant-garde Bloomsbury Group. Look out for their individual plaques throughout the area.

→

The austere, but bright interior of St George's, Bloomsbury

③ Russell Square

📍I3 🏠WC1 🚇Russell Sq

One of London's largest squares, Russell Square is a lively place, with a fountain, café and traffic roaring around its perimeter. The east side boasts perhaps the best of the Victorian grand hotels to survive in the capital. Designed by Charles Doll and opened in 1898, the former Russell Hotel – now the Principal London – remains a wondrous

of the **Museum of Comedy**, the first of its kind in the UK. Attached is a venue that hosts stand-up comedy performances in the evenings.

Museum of Comedy

🙂 ⏰ 1-6pm Mon-Fri; check website for performances 🌐 museumofcomedy.com

---

⑤ 🚳 Ⓜ 🖥 🍴

Charles Dickens Museum

📍 J3 🏠 48 Doughty St WC1 🚇 Chancery Lane, Russell Sq ⏰ 10am-5pm Tue-Sun (last adm: 4pm) 🚫 1 Jan, 25 & 26 Dec, and occasionally Sat for events 🌐 dickens museum.com

The novelist Charles Dickens lived in this early-19th-century terraced house for three of his most productive years (from 1837 to 1839). *Oliver Twist* and *Nicholas Nickleby* were entirely written here, and the *Pickwick Papers* was finished. Although Dickens had a number of London homes throughout his lifetime, this is the only one to have survived.

In 1923, it was acquired by the Dickens Fellowship and it is now a well-conceived museum with some of the principal rooms laid out exactly as they were in Dickens' time. Others have been adapted to display a varied collection of articles associated with him.

The museum houses over 100,000 exhibits, including manuscripts, paintings and personal items, papers and pieces of furniture from his other homes, and first editions of many of his best-known works.

The garden café (no entry fee required) provides respite from the city and a decent

→

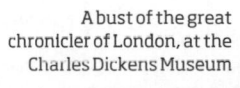

A bust of the great chronicler of London, at the Charles Dickens Museum

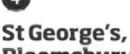

↑ Russell Square, an oasis in a whirl of busy traffic

confection of red terracotta, with colonnaded balconies and prancing cherubs beneath the main columns.

The poet T S Eliot worked at the west corner of the square from 1925 until 1965, in what were the offices of publisher Faber & Faber.

---

④

St George's, Bloomsbury

📍 I4 🏠 Bloomsbury Way WC1 🚇 Holborn, Tottenham Court Rd, Russell Sq ⏰ 1.30-3.30pm Wed & Fri, 1-3pm Thu 🌐 stgeorges bloomsbury.org.uk

St George's was designed by Nicholas Hawksmoor, a pupil of Christopher Wren, and completed in 1730. It was built as a place of worship for the residents of fashionable Bloomsbury. In 1913, the funeral of Emily Davison, the suffragette killed by King George V's racehorse at the Epsom Derby, was held here. The crypt is the unlikely home

London Review Bookshop

A bookshop for people who are serious about books. The carefully chosen stock is testament to the highly respected literary credentials of its owners, the *London Review of Books* journal. There are knowledgeable staff members to help and chat, and a great little coffee shop too.

📍 I4 🏠 14-16 Bury Pl WC1A 2JL 🌐 londonreview bookshop.co.uk

selection of drinks and treats. Note that as it is not possible to adapt this historic building, only the ground floor is wheelchair-accessible.

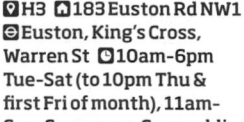

The cheerful home of Pollock's Toy Museum ↑

writers George Bernard Shaw and Virginia Woolf both lived at No 29 – although not at the same time. Shaw gave money to the artist Roger Fry to establish the Omega workshop at No 33 in 1913. Here young artists were paid a fixed wage to produce Post-Impressionist furniture, pottery, carpets and paintings for sale to the public.

9

The Postal Museum

Q J3 **🏛** 15-20 Phoenix Place WC1 **🚇** Farringdon **🕐** 10am-5pm daily **🌐** postalmuseum.org

Just over the road from the Mount Pleasant Royal Mail Sorting Office, once the largest sorting office in the world, the Postal Museum charts the 500 years of Britain's postal service in a series of engaging and interactive exhibits. The star attraction is Mail Rail, a 15-minute miniature train ride through tunnels that once formed part of the postal service's underground railway. The at times pitch-black, narrow, atmospheric tunnels feature audiovisual displays along the way and deposit you in the original engineering depot. The museum itself contains exhibits spanning the full life of the oldest postal service in the world.

6

Wellcome Collection

Q H3 **🏛** 183 Euston Rd NW1 **🚇** Euston, King's Cross, Warren St **🕐** 10am-6pm Tue-Sat (to 10pm Thu & first Fri of month), 11am-6pm Sun, noon-6pm public hols **🚫** 1 Jan, 24-26 Dec **🌐** wellcomecollection.org

Sir Henry Wellcome (1853–1936) was a pharmacist, entrepreneur and collector. His passionate interest in medicine and its history, as well as archaeology and ethnography, led him to gather more than one million objects from around the world, now housed in this building.

The museum's permanent exhibitions – Medicine Man and Medicine Now – include more than 900 objects, from Napoleon's toothbrush to Florence Nightingale's moccasins. Changing displays cover a range of engaging topics exploring medicine, art and the human condition. Visitors can also discover the reimagined Reading Room – a hybrid area bridging library, exhibition and event space – relax in the café or enjoy afternoon tea in the restaurant.

The Wellcome Library, which occupies the upper floors, is the world's largest collection of books devoted to the history of medicine.

7

Pollock's Toy Museum

Q H4 **🏛** 1 Scala St W1 (entrance on Whitfield St) **🚇** Goodge St, Warren St, Tottenham Court Rd **🕐** 10am-5pm Mon-Sat **🚫** Public hols **🌐** pollockstoys.com

Named for Benjamin Pollock, a renowned maker of toy theatres in the late 19th and early 20th centuries, this is a child-sized museum created in two 18th- and 19th-century houses. The small rooms have been filled with a fascinating assortment of historic toys from all over the world. There are dolls, puppets, trains, cars, construction sets, a fine rocking horse and a splendid collection of mainly Victorian doll's houses. Parents beware – the exit leads you through a toyshop.

8

Fitzroy Square

Q H3 **🏛** W1 **🚇** Warren St, Great Portland St

Designed by Robert Adam in 1794, the square's south and east sides survive in their original form, built in dignified Portland stone. Blue plaques record the homes of many artists, writers and statesmen:

10

Foundling Museum

Q I3 **🏛** 40 Brunswick Square WC1 **🚇** Russell Sq **🕐** 10am-5pm Tue-Sat, 11am-5pm Sun **🚫** 1 Jan, 24-26 & 31 Dec **🌐** foundling museum.org.uk

In 1722, Captain Thomas Coram, a retired sailor and shipbuilder recently returned from the Americas and horrified by the poverty on London's streets, vowed to set up a refuge for abandoned children. Assisted by two friends, the artist William Hogarth and the composer George Frideric Handel, Coram worked tirelessly to raise funds. Hogarth donated paintings to the hospital and other artists followed suit. The wealthy were encouraged to view the works of art and visit the children, in the hope that they would donate money to the cause.

On the ground floor, the story of the many children cared for here is told. The collection of 18th-century paintings, sculpture, furniture and interiors is displayed, with one room dedicated to Handel, on the upper floors.

Next to the museum, with its entrance on Guilford Street, is Coram's Fields, a unique park for children and youngsters under 16 (all adults must be accompanied by children). It includes a youth centre, a city farm and a café.

⓫
Grant Museum of Zoology

♥H3 **⌂**21 University St WC1 **Ⓢ**Warren St, Goodge St, Russell Square **Ⓞ**1–5pm Mon–Sat **W**ucl.ac.uk/ culture/grant-museum-zoology

The heart of Bloomsbury's university district is Gower Street: on one side is the Neo-Classical main building of University College London, designed by William Wilkins in 1826, and opposite is the original terracotta building of University College Hospital. UCL owns several museum collections, including the Grant Museum of Zoology, established in 1828. It houses around 68,000 specimens – animal skeletons, taxidermy, mounted insects and creatures preserved in jars (including one containing 18 preserved moles) – in crowded wooden cases, making it an atmospheric, occasionally gruesome, insight into the world of 19th-century science and collecting.

Unusual exhibits at the Grant Museum of Zoology (inset and below) ↓

A SHORT WALK
BLOOMSBURY

Distance 2 km (1.25 miles) **Nearest Tube**
Holborn **Time** 20 minutes

This so-called "brainy quarter" is dominated by the grand British Museum and, to its north, the main campus of University College London. A walk through the area will take you past Georgian buildings (formerly the homes of some of London's prolific writers and greatest minds) and pretty squares, as well as a good handful of bookshops to browse.

Senate House (1932), the administrative headquarters of the University of London, holds a priceless library.

↑ Bedford Square, one of London's best preserved Georgian squares

| 0 metres | 100 |
| 0 yards | 100 |

N ↑

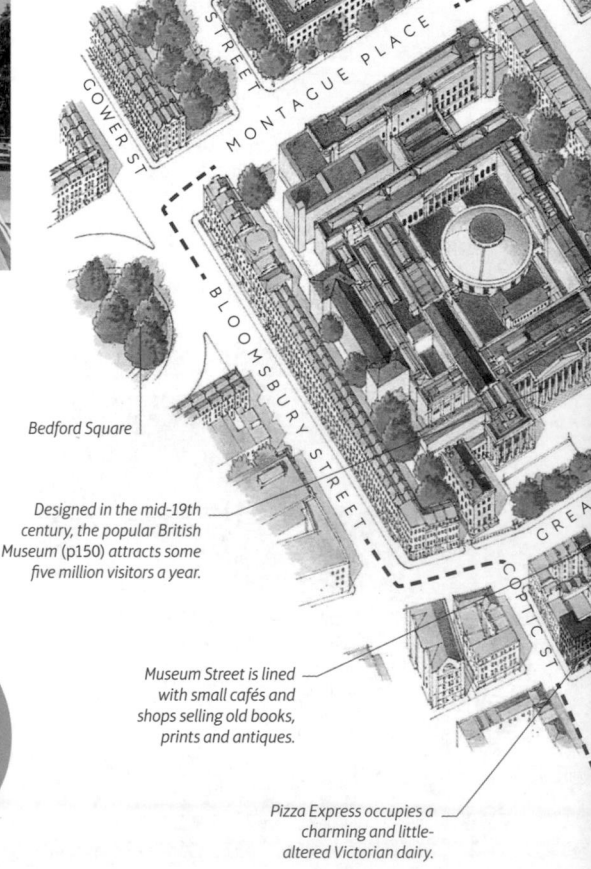

Bedford Square

Designed in the mid-19th century, the popular British Museum (p150) attracts some five million visitors a year.

Museum Street is lined with small cafés and shops selling old books, prints and antiques.

Pizza Express occupies a charming and little-altered Victorian dairy.

Did You Know?

Bloomsbury is older than you think – the area is mentioned in the 1086 Domesday Book as a "wood for 100 pigs".

Russell Square (p154), once part of the Duke of Bedford's estate, is now a shady retreat on a hot day.

The Duke of Bedford's statue commemorates the fifth duke, Francis Russell (1765–1805). An avid farmer, he is shown with sheep and a plough.

Locator Map
For more detail see p148

BLOOMSBURY AND FITZROVIA

SOUTHAMPTON ROW

BEDFORD PLACE

MONTAGUE ST

RUSSELL STREET

BURY PLACE

TLE RUSSELL STREET

BLOOMSBURY SQUARE

BLOOMSBURY WAY

↑ Bloomsbury Square, laid out in 1661

Bloomsbury Square

● FINISH

Sicilian Avenue is a small and unexpected pedestrian precinct dating from 1905, with colonnades that evoke Roman architecture.

● START

The tower on the typically flamboyant Hawksmoor church of St George's (p155) is modelled on the tomb of 4th-century Greek king Mausolus.

KING'S CROSS, CAMDEN AND ISLINGTON

King's Cross was predominantly rural until the late 18th century. Commonly referred to as Battle Bridge, after a mythical battle said to have taken place here between Boudicca and the Romans, the new name was adopted following the erection of a memorial to George IV in 1830 at the local crossroads. By this time King's Cross was becoming increasingly industrial, driven partly by the completion of the Regent's Canal in 1820, connecting it to the manufacturing cities of the north of England, and then by the construction of train depots, goods stations and passenger service termini. Decades of decline followed the Second World War but were reversed in the first years of this century when St Pancras Station became the terminus for international train routes to the rest of Europe, kick-starting a multi-billion-pound investment in the area. The urbanization of neighbouring Camden and Islington, connected to King's Cross by the canal, did not set in until the 19th century. Since then they have both undergone periods of boom and decline but, in keeping with King's Cross, are currently on an upward curve.

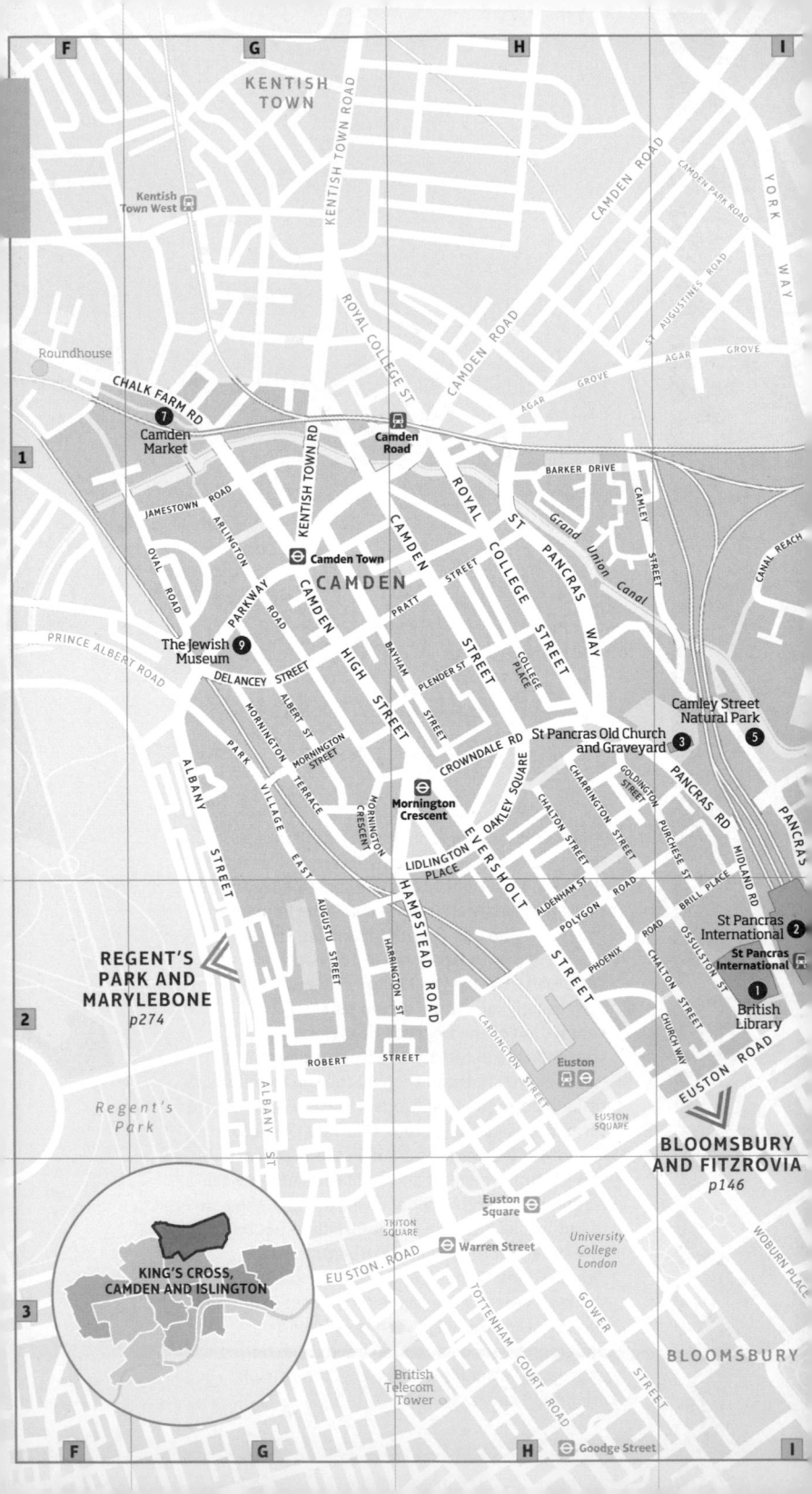

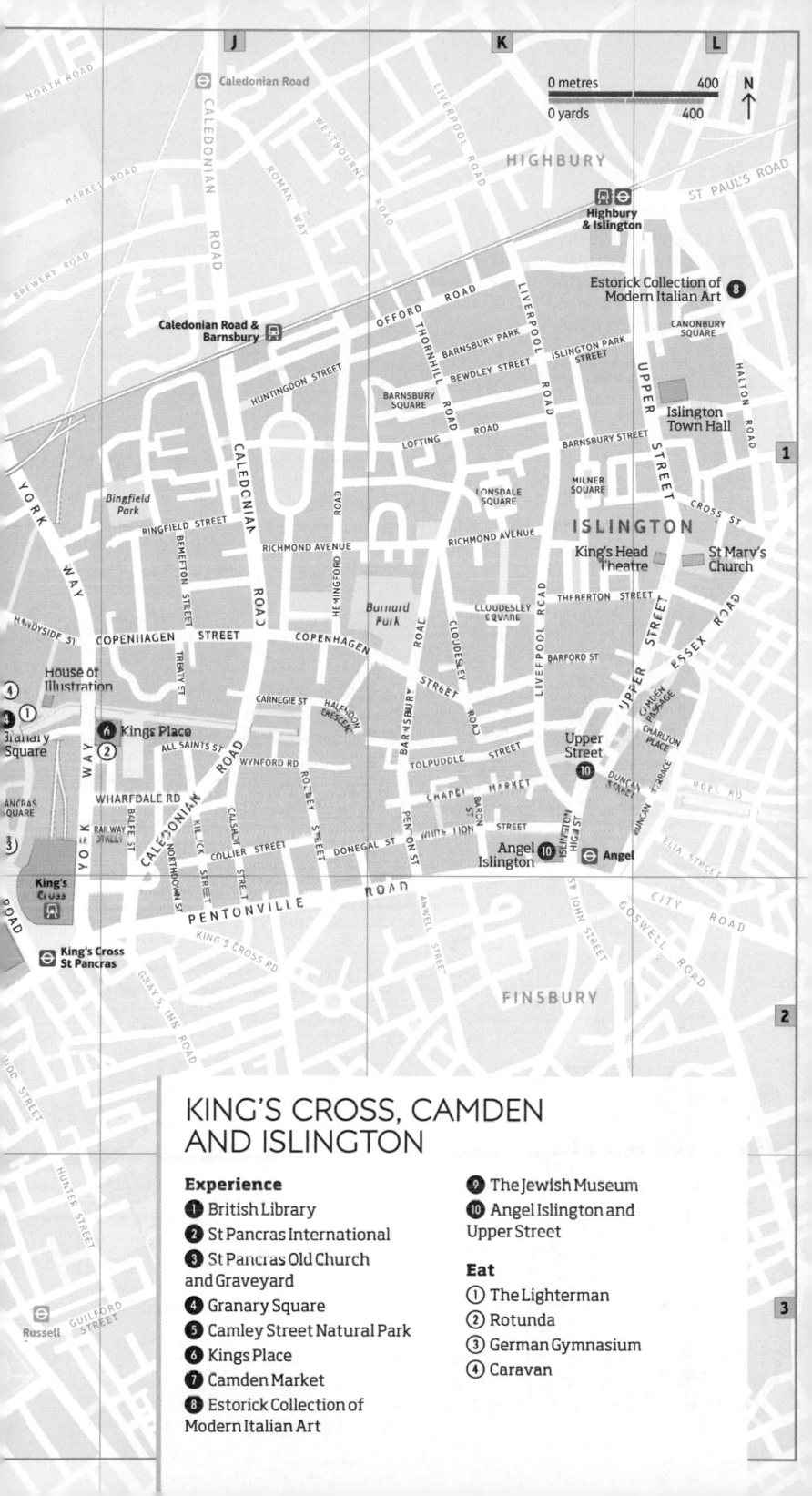

KING'S CROSS, CAMDEN AND ISLINGTON

Experience
1. British Library
2. St Pancras International
3. St Pancras Old Church and Graveyard
4. Granary Square
5. Camley Street Natural Park
6. Kings Place
7. Camden Market
8. Estorick Collection of Modern Italian Art
9. The Jewish Museum
10. Angel Islington and Upper Street

Eat
1. The Lighterman
2. Rotunda
3. German Gymnasium
4. Caravan

EXPERIENCE

① 🏛 🍴 📷 🛍
British Library

📍 I2 🏠 96 Euston Rd NW1
🚇 King's Cross St Pancras.
🕐 9:30am-8pm Mon-Thu,
9:30am-6pm Fri, 9:30am-
5pm Sat, 11am-5pm Sun
🌐 bl.uk

This modern building houses the national collection of books, manuscripts and maps, as well as the British Library Sound Archive. Designed in red brick by Sir Colin St John Wilson, it opened in 1997 after nearly 20 years of construction. A copy of nearly every printed book in the UK is held here – more than 14 million – and can be consulted by those with a Reader Pass (you can pre-register for one online). The real highlight, though, is the Treasures Gallery, which holds some extraordinary items, such as a Gutenberg Bible, Shakespeare's First Folio and lyrics by the Beatles. There are other free exhibitions, which change regularly (these often close earlier than the main building during the week), plus talks, discussions and workshops. Occasionally, a special exhibition has an entry charge. Tours are highly recommended; it's advisable to book at least two weeks in advance.

②
St Pancras International

📍 I2 🏠 Euston Rd NW1
🚇 King's Cross St Pancras
🌐 stpancras.com

St Pancras, London's terminus for Eurostar rail services to continental Europe, is hard to miss, thanks to the extravagant frontage, in red-brick gingerbread Gothic, of the former Midland Grand Hotel. Opened in 1874 it was one of the most sumptuous hotels of its time. Threatened with demolition in the 1960s, it was saved by a campaign led by the poet John Betjeman (there is a statue of him on the upper level of the station concourse). The hotel has since been magnificently restored and has a swish champagne bar.

③
St Pancras Old Church and Graveyard

📍 I1 🏠 Pancras Rd NW1
🚇 King's Cross St Pancras
🕐 9am-dusk daily (church usually closes around 3pm)
🌐 posp.co.uk

This site is thought to have been a place of Christian worship since the 4th century – there are fragments of Roman tiles embedded in one of the walls, and some Norman masonry – though much of the church building dates to 1847. There are lunchtime recitals here on Thursdays. The graveyard, now a green space with a few monuments dotted around, was until the 1850s one of the largest burial sites in London.

With the arrival of the railways, half the site was built over, and gravestones were moved – hence the remarkable sight of closely packed gravestones embedded into the base of a tree. This is the Hardy Tree, named after author Thomas Hardy, who worked as an

← Café tables set below towering shelves of books at the British Library

←

Relaxing on the steps
that lead from Granary
Square to the canal

graphic design, animation,
scientific drawings, picture
books and political cartoons.

House of Illustration

🎨 🏠 **☐** 2 Granary Sq N1
🚇 King's Cross St Pancras
🕐 10am–6pm Tue–Sun
🌐 houseofillustration.org.uk

architectural technician on the site. Sir John Soane *(p138)* designed his own family mausoleum, which is said to have inspired Sir Giles Gilbert Scott's design of London's famous red telephone box.

④ 🍴 💻 🏠 Granary Square

📍 I1 🚇 King's Cross St Pancras 🌐 kingscross.co.uk

Urban regeneration has transformed this area behind King's Cross station into a cultural and social hub, with major building projects still ongoing. The focus of the area is attractive Granary Square, which leads down to Regent's Canal. It is dominated by magnificent fountains that dance to an ever-changing pattern of lights, a magnet for small children on hot days. There are also a number of good restaurants and bars, and a popular food market.

Occupying the former King's Cross Goods Yards offices, built in 1850, is the **House of Illustration**. These three small rooms form the UK's only gallery dedicated to illustration. Founded by Sir Quentin Blake, best known for his illustrations of Roald Dahl's children's books, the gallery stages an eclectic programme of exhibitions, past examples featuring work from Soviet Russia, Japan, Thailand and North Korea. Displays cover a broad range of techniques and mediums, including

⑤ 💻 Camley Street Natural Park

📍 I1 🏠 12 Camley St N1 🚇 King's Cross St Pancras 🕐 10am–4pm daily (Apr–Sep to 5pm) 🌐 wildlondon.org.uk

Occupying land on the Regent's Canal once used as a coal drop for the nearby railways, this is a lovable little nature reserve run by the London Wildlife Trust. It packs in grassland, woodland and wetland habitats for birds, butterflies, bats and frogs in a small space. There is a visitor centre, paths around the reserve and some lovely places to sit and picnic.

PLATFORM 9¾

Wannabe witches and wizards flock to King's Cross station to find the elusive Platform 9¾, from where Harry Potter and his fellow students catch the Hogwarts Express. Though there's little to be found between platforms 9 and 10, a luggage trolley embedded into a concourse wall (conveniently, next to the Harry Potter Shop) provides a perfect photo op for those waiting for their owl from Hogwarts.

⑥ 💻 🍴 Kings Place

📍 J1 🏠 90 York Way N1 🚇 King's Cross St Pancras 🕐 Noon–8pm Mon–Sat 🌐 kingsplace.co.uk

This concert and arts venue is perched on the edge of the Regent's Canal and Battle-bridge Basin, a small wharf whose moorings are usually full of attractive narrowboats. Performances of classical, jazz, folk or world music are regularly staged, and there are two commercial art galleries. The open spaces are dotted with sculpture and art.

The bright lights of Granary Square, King's Cross

7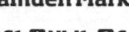

Camden Market

📍 G1 🏠 NW1 🚇 Camden Town, Chalk Farm 🕐 10am-6pm daily; some cafés and bars open later 🌐 camdenmarket.com

The huge Camden Market is really a series of interconnected markets running along Chalk Farm Road and Camden High Street. Packed at the weekends, most of the shops and some of the stalls are also open on weekdays.

The first market here was a small crafts market set up at Camden Lock in 1975, and today the lock, crossing the Regent's Canal, is the focus of this sprawling agglomeration.

Independent trading on an industrial scale, the warren of hundreds of stalls, units and shops occupy a network of restored and converted Victorian warehouses.

The market has been at the forefront of alternative fashion since the days of punk, and the current jumble of handmade and vintage clothes and jewellery, arts and crafts, records and music memorabilia, and all kinds of quirky one-offs maintain the market's place among the most original shopping destinations in the city. This is also street food heaven, with scores of stalls, cafés and likeably inelegant restaurants dishing out authentic nosh from all over the world.

Some of the more interesting stalls are in the Stables Market towards the Chalk Farm end, where there is also a statue of Camden habituée, the late singer Amy Winehouse.

8

Estorick Collection of Modern Italian Art

📍 L1 🏠 39a Canonbury Sq N1 🚇 Highbury & Islington 🕐 11am-6pm Wed-Sat, noon-5pm Sun 🌐 estorickcollection.com

Based on American and Anglo-German couple Eric and Salome Estorick's collection of modern Italian art, this is one of the more surprising of Islington's assets. It is housed in an unpretentious Georgian building with a delightful garden, partly occupied by an inviting café. At the core of the collection are important works of the Italian Futurism movement: paintings and drawings by the likes of Umberto Boccioni, Carlo Carrà, Luigi Russolo and Gino Severini. Spread over six galleries on three floors, there is plenty of striking modern Italian art of other genres, including sculpture.

←

Bronze statue of the late Amy Winehouse

←
Victorian industrial
heritage buildings
at Camden Lock

The Jewish Museum

⊠G1 🏠129-131 Albert
St NW1 🚇Camden Town
🕙10am-5pm Sat-Thu,
10am-2pm Fri 🚫Jewish
hols, 25 & 26 Dec, 1 Jan
🌐jewishmuseum.org.uk

London's Jewish Museum
was founded in 1932 in
Bloomsbury, and it has
occupied several locations –
at one point it was split
between two sites, in Finchley
and Camden. In 2007 the
museum celebrated its 75th
anniversary by starting work
to bring the two collections
together in a single building.
Reopened in 2010, the
museum today has large
galleries, education facilities
and displays for children.

Celebrating Jewish life in
Britain from the Middle Ages
onwards, the museum is
packed with memorabilia.

It has important collections of
Jewish ceremonial objects and
some illuminated marriage
contracts. The highlight is
a 17th- or 18th-century
Venetian synagogue ark.
There is also an exhibition
on the Holocaust.

Angel Islington and Upper Street

⊠K1 🏠Islington N1
🚇Angel, Highbury &
Islington

One of the destination high
streets in north London,
Upper Street runs for 1.5 km
(1 mile) between Angel and
Highbury & Islington tube
stations. Lively day and night,
the street is one long parade
of restaurants, cafés, pubs,
bars, fashion boutiques and
a contrasting mix of civic
buildings, churches, an
arthouse cinema and a live
music and clubbing venue.

Parallel to the main drag is
Camden Passage, an alleyway
even more densely packed
with shops, cafés and covered
markets. It's a popular place

⛰ GREAT VIEW
Primrose Hill

A 15-minute walk from
the Jewish Museum is
the delightful Primrose
Hill. A climb to the top of
this grassy promontory
provides spectacular
views of the city skyline
– look out for the
London Eye, the Shard
and St Paul's Cathedral.

for antiques hunters looking
for the latest bargain.

The area to the south
of the high street known as
Angel takes its name from
a 17th-century coaching inn
on the corner of Pentonville
Road, since replaced by the
current sand-coloured
structure, crowned with
an elegant domed cupola.
Built in 1903 as the Angel
Hotel it now houses a bank
and offices.

Cafés and restaurants
(inset and below) line
popular Upper Street ↓

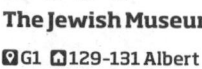
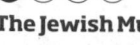

THE CITY

The capital's financial district, the City, built on the
site of the original Roman settlement, was, for
many centuries, London in its entirety – its full
name remains the "City of London". Royal government was moved from the City of London to the
City of Westminster by Edward the Confessor In
the 11th century but the area's importance as a
centre of trade remained, and indeed grew. In the
12th century, the City was granted autonomous
self-government, a privilege it has retained, and
dozens of tradesmen's guilds, known as livery
companies, were set up. Much of the early City,
including many of the grand halls of the liveries,
was obliterated by the Great Fire of 1666, but the
jumbled street plan, with names like Cheapside
and Poultry, stand as testament to the City's
medieval past. After the fire, Christopher Wren
rebuilt dozens of the city's churches, with his
magnificent dome for St Paul's Cathedral rising
above them all. Now the spires and financial institutions stand alongside dour postwar office blocks
and some extraordinary modern architecture, such
as the Lloyd's building and the Gherkin.

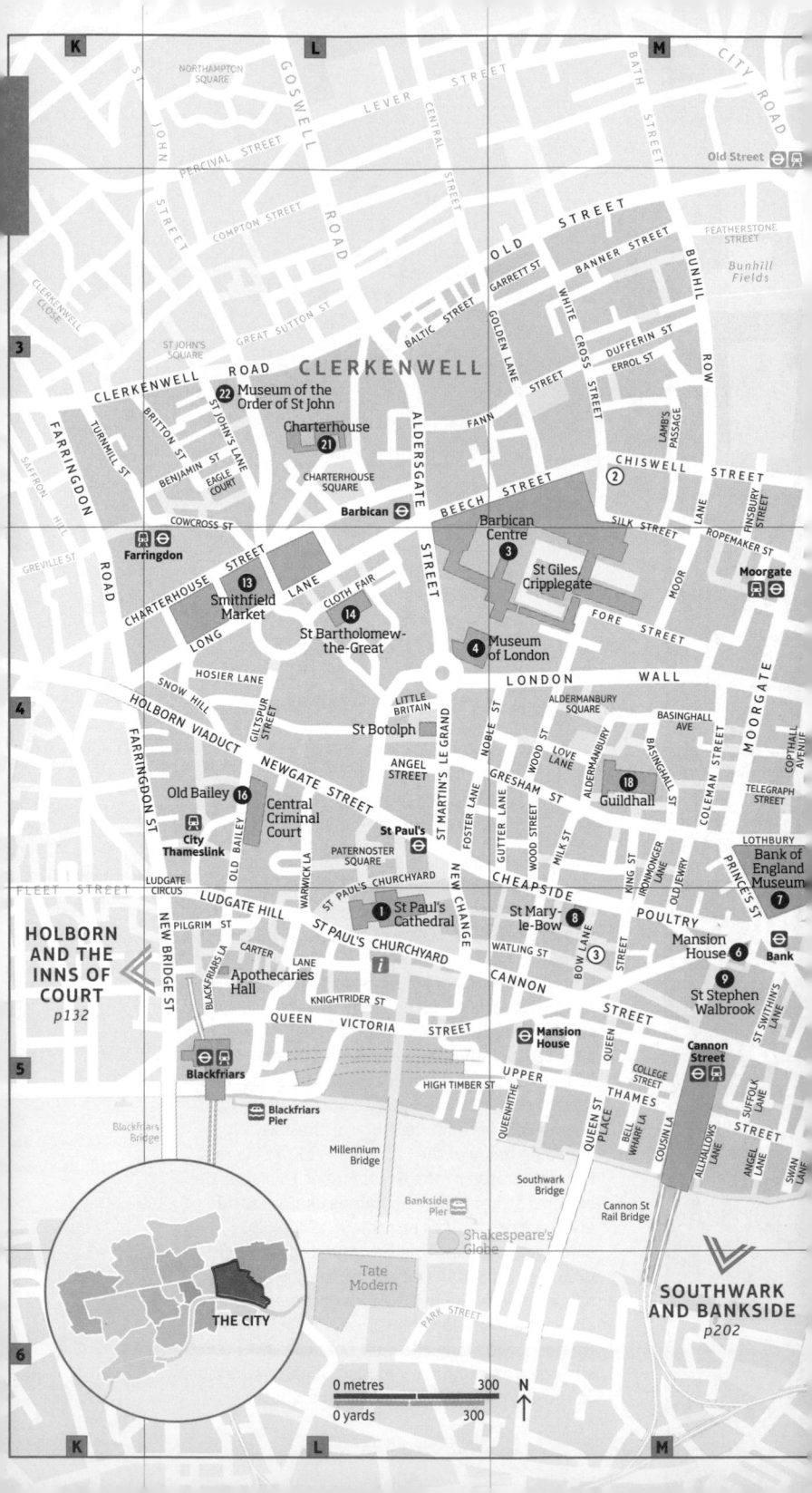

K · L · M

NORTHAMPTON SQUARE
GOSWELL ROAD
LEVER STREET
CENTRAL STREET
BATH STREET
CITY ROAD

Old Street ⊖≡

PERCIVAL STREET
COMPTON STREET
GREAT SUTTON STREET
OLD STREET
GARRETT ST
BANNER STREET
WHITE CROSS STREET
BUNHILL ROW
FEATHERSTONE STREET

Bunhill Fields

CLERKENWELL CLOSE
ST JOHN'S SQUARE

3

CLERKENWELL ROAD
CLERKENWELL
GOLDEN LANE
DUFFERIN ST
ERROL ST

FARRINGDON ROAD
TURNMILL ST
BRITTON ST
ST JOHN'S LANE
BENJAMIN ST
EAGLE COURT

22 Museum of the Order of St John
Charterhouse **21**

CHARTERHOUSE SQUARE

ALDERSGATE STREET
FANN STREET
BALTIC STREET

LAMB'S PASSAGE
CHISWELL STREET
2
FINSBURY STREET

Barbican ⊖

BEECH STREET
SILK STREET
ROPEMAKER ST
Moorgate ≡⊖

SAFFRON HILL
GREVILLE ST
FARRINGDON ROAD

Farringdon ≡⊖

COWCROSS ST
CHARTERHOUSE STREET

13 Smithfield Market

LONG LANE
CLOTH FAIR
14
St Bartholomew-the-Great

Barbican Centre
3 St Giles, Cripplegate

FORE STREET
MOOR LANE
MOORGATE
COPTHALL AVENUE

4

HOLBORN VIADUCT
SNOW HILL
HOSIER LANE
GILTSPUR STREET

NEWGATE STREET
LITTLE BRITAIN
St Botolph

4 Museum of London

LONDON WALL

ALDERMANBURY SQUARE
BASINGHALL AVE

ANGEL STREET
ST MARTIN'S LE GRAND
NOBLE ST
WOOD ST
LOVE LANE
ALDERMANBURY
BASINGHALL ST
COLEMAN STREET
TELEGRAPH STREET

Old Bailey **16**
Central Criminal Court

City Thameslink ≡

LUDGATE CIRCUS
FLEET STREET
LUDGATE HILL
PILGRIM ST
CARTER LANE

OLD BAILEY
WARWICK LA
PATERNOSTER SQUARE
St Paul's ⊖

ST PAUL'S CHURCHYARD

1 St Paul's Cathedral
ⓘ

FOSTER LANE
GUTTER LANE
WOOD STREET
MILK ST
GRESHAM ST
KING ST
IRONMONGER LANE
OLD JEWRY

18 Guildhall

LOTHBURY
Bank of England Museum **7**

CHEAPSIDE
St Mary-le-Bow **8**
3
POULTRY
Mansion House **6**
Bank ⊖

HOLBORN AND THE INNS OF COURT
p132

NEW BRIDGE ST
BLACKFRIARS LA
APOTHECARIES HALL

KNIGHTRIDER ST
QUEEN VICTORIA STREET

WATLING ST
BOW LANE
CANNON STREET

St Stephen Walbrook **9**
ST SWITHIN'S LANE

Mansion House ⊖

5

Blackfriars ⊖≡
Blackfriars Pier

UPPER THAMES STREET
HIGH TIMBER ST
QUEENHITHE
QUEEN STREET PLACE
COLLEGE STREET
BELL WHARF LA
COUSIN LANE
ALLHALLOWS LANE
SUFFOLK LANE

Cannon Street ⊖≡

ANGEL LANE
SWAN LANE

Blackfriars Bridge
Millennium Bridge
Bankside Pier ≡
Shakespeare's Globe

Southwark Bridge
Cannon St Rail Bridge

SOUTHWARK AND BANKSIDE
p202

THE CITY

Tate Modern

PARK STREET

6

| 0 metres | 300 |
| 0 yards | 300 |

N ↑

K · L · M

THE CITY

Must Sees
1 St Paul's Cathedral
2 Tower of London
3 Barbican Centre

Experience More
4 Museum of London
5 Royal Exchange
6 Mansion House
7 Bank of England Museum
8 St Mary-le-Bow
9 St Stephen Walbrook
10 Monument
11 All Hallows by the Tower
12 Tower Bridge
13 Smithfield Market
14 St Batholomew-the-Great
15 The Sky Garden
16 Old Bailey
17 Leadenhall Market
18 Guildhall
19 St Katharine Docks
20 St Katharine Cree
21 Charterhouse
22 Museum of the Order of St John

Eat
1 Jose Pizarro
2 The Jugged Hare

Drink
3 Merchant House

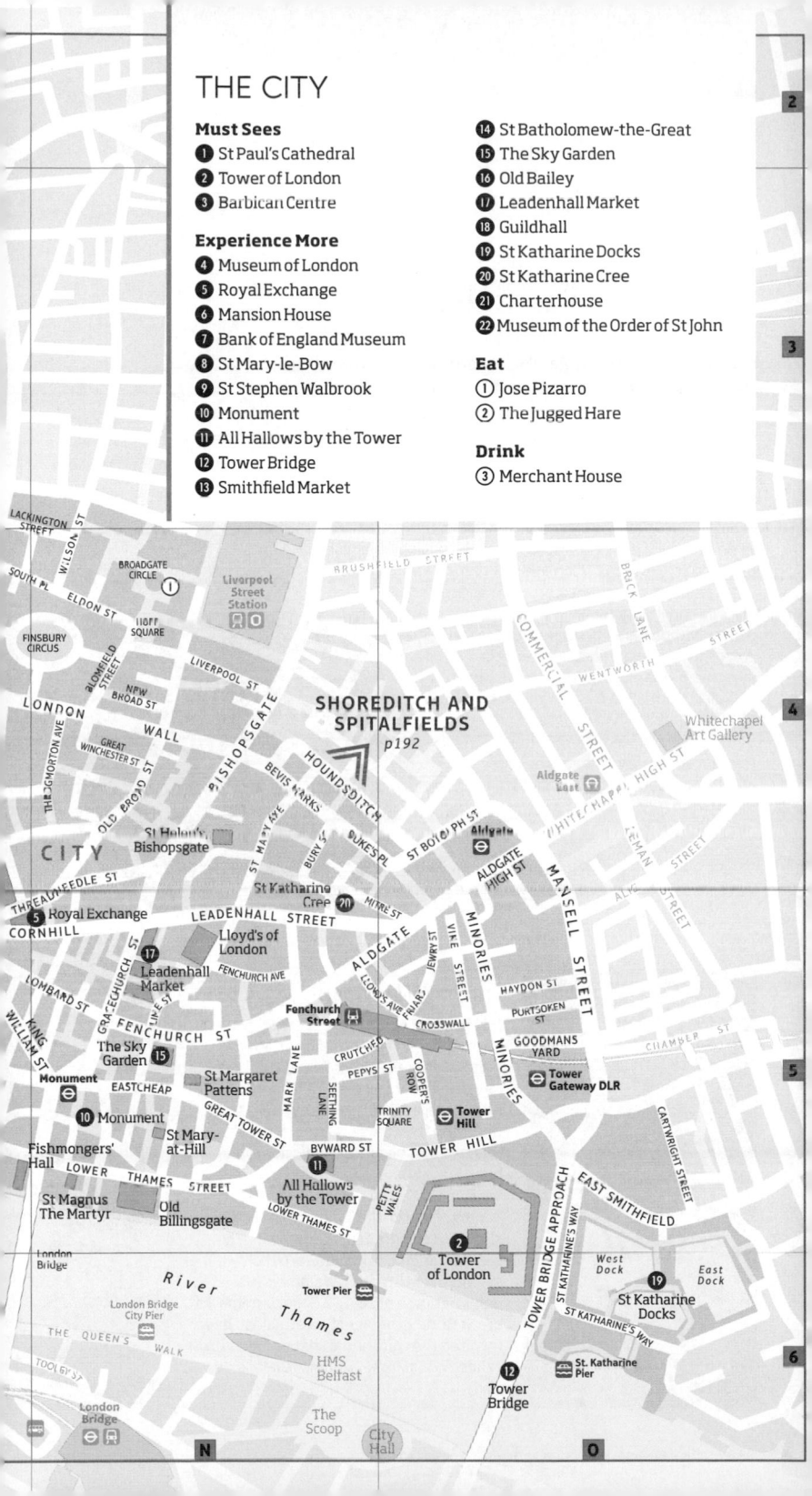

❶ ⬢ ⬢ ⬢ ⬢

ST PAUL'S
CATHEDRAL

📍 L5 🚇 Ludgate Hill EC4 🚇 St Paul's, Mansion House 🚉 City Thameslink, Blackfriars 🕐 Cathedral: 8:30am–4:30pm (last adm: 4pm) Mon–Sat; Galleries: 9:30am–4:15pm Mon–Sat 🌐 stpauls.co.uk

Holding its own against the towering skyscrapers of the City, the enormous dome of St Paul's Cathedral stands out as the star of the area's churches. Completed in 1711, Sir Christopher Wren's Baroque masterpiece was England's first purpose-built Protestant cathedral, and has many similarities with St Peter's in Rome, notably in its ornate dome.

Following the Great Fire of London in 1666, the medieval cathedral of St Paul's was left in ruins. The authorities turned to Christopher Wren to rebuild it, but his ideas met with considerable resistance from the conservative Dean and Chapter. Wren's 1672 Great Model plan was rejected and a watered-down plan was finally agreed in 1675. Wren's determination paid off, though: the cathedral is considered his greatest masterpiece. Its dome is one of the largest in the world, standing 111 m (365 ft) high and weighing 65,000 tonnes.

The cathedral has a strong choral tradition and is famed for its music, with regular concerts and organ recitals.

→

The cathedral's imposing West Front, dominated by two huge towers

CHRISTOPHER WREN

Sir Christopher Wren (1632–1723) played an integral part in the restoration of London after the Great Fire of 1666. He devised a new city plan, replacing the narrow streets with wide avenues radiating from piazzas. His plan was rejected, but he was commissioned to build 52 new churches; 31 have survived various threats of demolition and the bombs of World War II, although six are shells. Wren's great masterpiece is the massive St Paul's, while nearby as splendid is St Stephen Walbrook, his domed church of 1672–7. Other landmarks are St Bride's, off Fleet Street, said to have inspired the traditional shape of wedding cakes and St Mary-le-Bow in Cheapside.

GREAT VIEW
Vista of St Paul's

Cross the Millennium Bridge to the South Bank and look back to capture a great view of the cathedral.

↑ The elegant dome of St Paul's, viewed from the Millennium Bridge

Majestic Interior

Visitors to St Paul's will be immediately impressed by its cool, beautifully ordered and extremely spacious interior. The nave, transepts and choir are arranged in the shape of a cross, as in a medieval cathedral, but Wren's Classical vision shines through this conservative floorplan, which was forced on him by the cathedral authorities. Aided by some of the finest craftsmen of his day, he created an interior of grand majesty and Baroque splendour, a worthy setting for the many great ceremonial events that have taken place here. These include the funeral of Sir Winston Churchill in 1965 and the wedding of Prince Charles and Lady Diana Spencer in 1981.

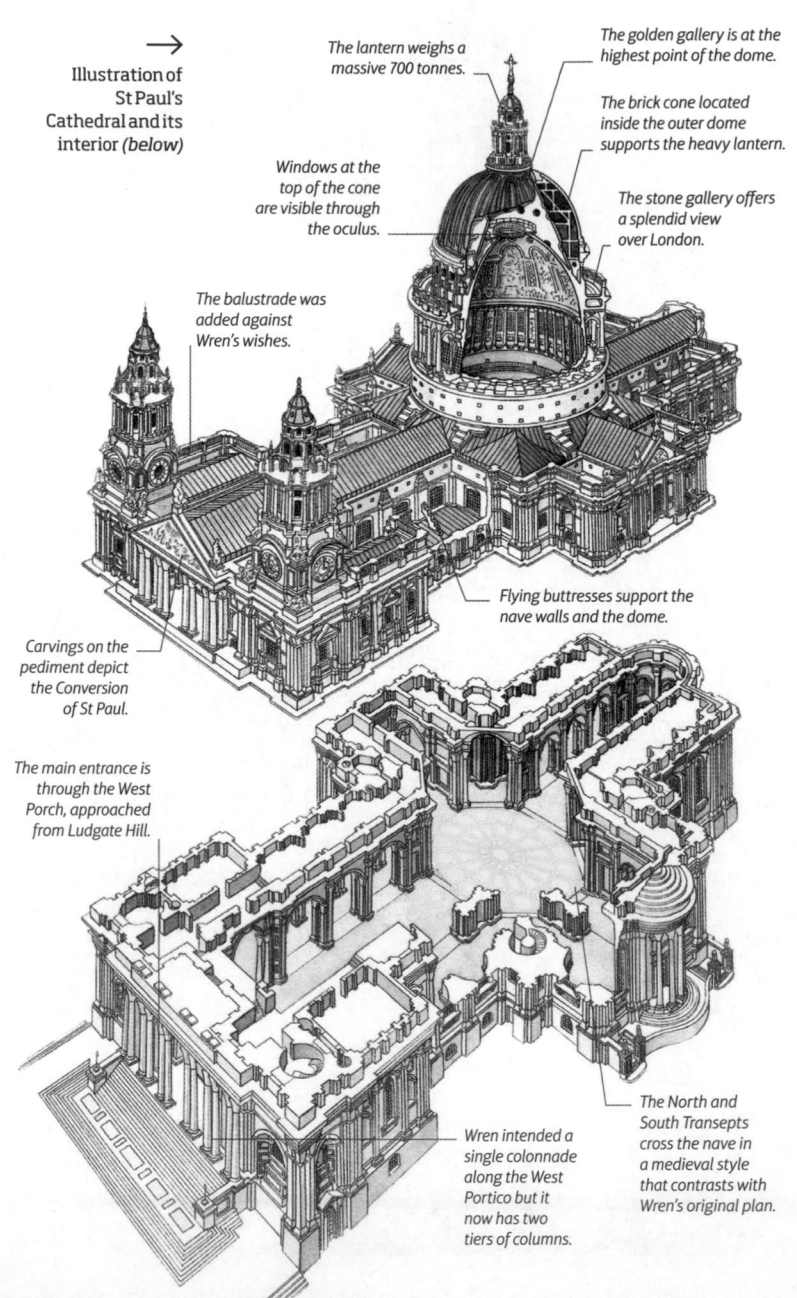

→

Illustration of St Paul's Cathedral and its interior *(below)*

The lantern weighs a massive 700 tonnes.

The golden gallery is at the highest point of the dome.

The brick cone located inside the outer dome supports the heavy lantern.

Windows at the top of the cone are visible through the oculus.

The stone gallery offers a splendid view over London.

The balustrade was added against Wren's wishes.

Flying buttresses support the nave walls and the dome.

Carvings on the pediment depict the Conversion of St Paul.

The main entrance is through the West Porch, approached from Ludgate Hill.

Wren intended a single colonnade along the West Portico but it now has two tiers of columns.

The North and South Transepts cross the nave in a medieval style that contrasts with Wren's original plan.

604
△ Bishop Mellitus builds the first St Paul's. It burned down in 1087

1087
△ Bishop Maurice begins Old St Paul's: a Norman cathedral built of stone

1708
△ Wren's son Christopher lays the last stone on the lantern

2011
△ Extensive restorations finished

1 The Whispering Gallery allows views down to the wide expanse of the crossing, the area under the dome.

2 Much of the fine wrought ironwork such as the screens, were made by Jean Tijou, a Hugenot refugee.

3 Intricate carvings of cherubs, fruit and garlands adorn the cathedral.

4 In the crypt are the tombs of famous figures and popular heroes, such as Lord Nelson.

The imposing walls of the historic Tower of London. ↑

2 🗡️ 🎨 🍴 🖥️ 🛍️

TOWER OF LONDON

📍 O5 🏰 Tower Hill EC3 🚇 Tower Hill, DLR Tower Gateway 🚆 Fenchurch Street ⏰ Check website for tours and opening hours 🌐 hrp.org.uk

A former fortress, palace and prison, the Tower of London attracts over three million visitors a year, who come to see the Crown Jewels and to hear tales of its dark and intriguing history.

For much of its 900-year history, the Tower was somewhere to be feared. Those who had committed treason or threatened the throne were held within its dank walls – many did not get out alive, and some were tortured before meeting violent deaths on nearby Tower Hill.

The Tower has been a tourist attraction since the reign of Charles II (1660–85), when both the Crown Jewels and the collection of armour were first shown to the public, and it remains popular today. Come to discover the brutality of royal regimes, the curious menagerie that once called the Tower home and the regalia of Britain's kings and queens.

💬 INSIDER TIP
Tour with a Beefeater

Join a Yeoman Warder, or Beefeater, on a tour of the Tower. A lively retelling of tales of executions, plots and prisoners, it's an entertaining way to explore the Tower's history. Tours are included in the entry fee and set off every 30 minutes from near the main entrance, lasting for an hour.

Timeline

1066
△ William I erects a temporary castle

1534–35
△ Thomas More imprisoned and executed

Did You Know?
—
The Tower has a colony of ravens. Legend has it that if they leave the Tower, the kingdom will fall.

↑ Yeoman Warders guarding the Tower

↑ King Edward I's bedchamber inside St Thomas's Tower

1553
△ Lady Jane Grey held and executed

1603–16
△ Walter Raleigh imprisoned in Tower

1671
△ "Colonel Blood" tries to steal Crown Jewels

1941
△ Prominent Nazi Rudolf Hess held in Queen's House

Life Within the Tower

The area within the mighty walls houses the remaining parts of the Medieval Palace built by Henry III, as well as several towers that held prisoners, including Anne Boleyn, Thomas Cromwell and Catherine Howard. High-ranking prisoners could live in some comfort with their own servants but the rest suffered hardship, torture and, ultimately, death.

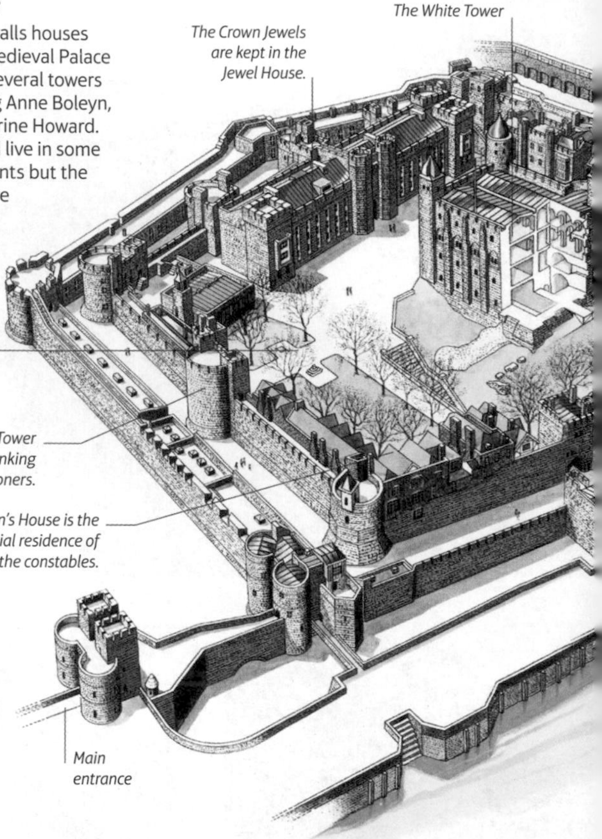

The White Tower

The Crown Jewels are kept in the Jewel House.

The aristocratic prisoners were executed on Tower Green.

Beauchamp Tower held high-ranking prisoners.

Queen's House is the official residence of the constables.

Did You Know?

In 1952, London gangsters the Kray twins were among the last to be held at the Tower.

Main entrance

1 A sentry from the Tower Guard stands on duty outside the Jewel House.

2 Many were imprisoned in the Tower, some tortured or held in solitary confinement.

3 The Tower of London enclosure is in the centre of the city, beside the Thames. There are several towers, a palace, residences, a chapel and open areas within the walls.

The beautiful Romanesque Chapel of St John made of stone from France.

Wakefield Tower was part of the Medieval Palace.

Prisoners entered the tower by boat through Traitors' Gate.

Henry III created the Medieval Palace in 1220. His son Edward I enlarged it.

Gallery Rooms

The Crown Jewels

Comprising crowns, sceptres and orbs used at coronations and other state occasions, the priceless Crown Jewels *(below)* have enormous historical significance. They mostly date from 1661 when a new set was created for the coronation of Charles II.

Coronation Regalia

Apart from the crowns, other items that are used during coronation ceremonies *(left)* include the Orb, the jewelled State Sword and the Sceptre with the Cross containing the biggest cut diamond in the world.

Royal Castle and Armour Gallery

In these adjoining chambers, discover the history of the White Tower and admire suits of armour from Tudor and Stuart times *(right)*, including three made for Henry VIII and one for his horse.

THE PRINCES IN THE TOWER

One of the Tower's darkest mysteries concerns two boy princes, sons and heirs of Edward IV. They were put into the Tower by their uncle, Richard of Gloucester, when their father died in 1483. Neither was seen again and Richard was crowned later that year. In 1674, the skeletons of two children were found nearby.

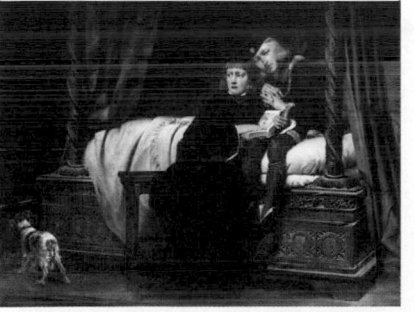

The Ordnance Gallery

Created when the roof of the White Tower was raised in 1490, this room *(below)* was used mainly for storage. In 1603 a new floor was added as a place to keep gunpowder. There were 10,000 barrels of it in the Tower by 1667. Gilt panels and ornaments from the barge of the Master of the Ordnance are also on display here.

The Barbican's concrete Brutalist architecture with lake and fountains ↑

③ 🐎 🍴 🖥 🛍

BARBICAN CENTRE

📍 M3 🏠 Barbican Estate EC2 🚇 Barbican, Moorgate 🚉 Moorgate, Liverpool Street 🕐 9am-11pm Mon-Sat, from 11am Sun, from noon public hols; Art gallery: 10am-6pm daily (to 9pm Thu & Fri); Conservatory: 11am-5pm Sun (but check website for days) 🌐 barbican.org.uk

A Brutalist masterpiece, this residential, commercial and cultural complex is a formidable, fabulous anomaly in the City: an oasis of culture and community in London's largest financial district. Look out for world-class theatrical performances and concerts here.

The soul at the concrete heart of the Barbican Estate, the Barbican Centre is one of London's largest and most complete arts institutions, with two cinemas, a concert hall, two theatres and gallery spaces all celebrating the arts. The centre is also home to a public library, three restaurants, three cafés, four bars and a tropical conservatory. A dynamic programme of events typically includes seasons of plays by the Royal Shakespeare Company, concerts by the resident London Symphony Orchestra, and plenty of independent cinema. The centre has always made room for experimental, genre-defying performers and artists, so expect anything from multimedia art exhibitions to street dance operas. Jazz and world music also feature frequently, with musicians and singers from Latin American and Africa often on the bill, but at any time you will find a broad range of one-off shows and events.

↑ The Barbican Hall, well known for its world music performances

EXPERIENCE MORE

④ 🍴 🍽 🛍

Museum of London

📍L4 🏛150 London Wall EC2 🚇Barbican, St Paul's, Moorgate ⏰10am–6pm daily 🌐museumoflondon.org.uk

Opened in 1976 on the edge of the Barbican Estate, this museum provides a lively account of London life from prehistoric times to the present day. The eclectic set of displays, which are laid out chronologically, range from detailed models and life-sized sets to items recovered from archaeological digs, photographs and recordings of Londoners talking about their lives.

Prehistory exhibits, such as flint hand axes found in the gravels under the modern city, begin on the entrance level and visitors can walk through Roman and medieval London galleries to the War, Plague and Fire exhibit, which includes a display on the Great Fire of 1666.

On the lowest level, the history of London after the disastrous fire up to the present day is explored. The Lord Mayor of London's spectacular State Coach is on show here. Finely carved and painted, this gilded coach from c 1757 is paraded once a year during the Lord Mayor's Show. The Victorian Walk uses several original shopfronts to re-create the atmosphere of late-19th-century London. There are also the bronze and cast iron Brandt Edgar lifts from Selfridges department store on Oxford Street and unusual items such as a 1964 Beatles dress printed with the faces of the fab four.

One of the newest permanent galleries is the London 2012 Cauldron, the centrepiece of the opening and closing ceremonies at the London Olympics. Photographs, videos, diagrams and the copper petal elements which rose together to form the Olympic Flame combine to describe the spectacle and the ingenuity of the design.

THE BARBICAN ESTATE

Housing over 4,000 residents in its Brutalist tower and terrace blocks, this ambitious piece of post-war city planning was designed by Chamberlin, Powell & Bon and built on a site devastated by World War II bombs. It is a maze of concrete pavements, overhead walkways, stone staircases and Soviet-style buildings but it is softened considerably by islands of green – small gardens dotted around the estate – and by an ornamental lake and fountains.

↑ Visitors examining exhibits at the fascinating Museum of London

⑤

Royal Exchange

**⑨ N5 ⌂ EC3 ⊜ Bank
ⓦ theroyalexchange.co.uk**

Sir Thomas Gresham, an Elizabethan merchant and courtier, founded the Royal Exchange in 1565 as a centre for commerce of all kinds. The original building was centred on a vast courtyard where merchants and tradesmen did business. Queen Elizabeth I gave it its royal title and it is still one of the sites from which a new monarch is announced. Dating from 1844, this is the third splendid building on the site since Gresham's.

The building now contains a luxurious shopping centre with designer stores such as Hermès and Paul Smith, and an elegant central bar and café.

⑥

Mansion House

**⑨ M5 ⌂ Walbrook EC4
⊜ Bank, Mansion House
🕐 To group tours by appt
only ⓦ cityoflondon.gov.uk**

The official residence of the Lord Mayor was designed by George Dance the Elder and completed in 1758. The Palladian front with its six Corinthian columns is one of the most familiar City land-

marks. The state rooms have a dignity appropriate to the office of mayor, one of the most spectacular being the 27-m (90-ft) Egyptian Hall. An impressive collection of 17th-century Dutch art includes works by Frans Hals.

The cellars once housed 11 holding cells, a reminder of the building's other function as a magistrate's court; the mayor is chief magistrate of the City during his year of office. Emmeline Pankhurst, who campaigned for women's suffrage in the early 20th century, was once held here.

---

⑦

Bank of England Museum

**⑨ M4 ⌂ Bartholomew Lane
EC2 ⊜ Bank 🕐 10am–5pm
Mon–Fri 🕐 Public hols
ⓦ bankofengland.co.uk**

The Bank of England was set up in 1694 to raise money for foreign wars. It grew to become Britain's central bank, and also issues currency notes. Sir John Soane (*p138*) was the architect of the 1788 bank building on this site, but only the exterior wall of his design has survived. The rest was destroyed in the 1920s and

↑ Gold bar that visitors can try to lift in the Bank of England Museum

30s when the building was enlarged by Sir Herbert Baker. The only part of Soane's design left today is the curtain wall around the outside of the building. There is now a reconstruction of Soane's stock office of 1793 in the museum. As well as images illustrating the architectural history of the building, there is also an interactive exhibit where visitors can set monetary policy.

Glittering gold bars (which you can touch), silver-plated decoration and a Roman mosaic floor, which was discovered during the rebuilding, are among the items on display, along with a unique collection of bank-notes. The museum illustrates the work of the Bank and the financial system.

↓ The Neo-Classical façade of the Royal Exchange

↑ St Mary-le-Bow's steeple, housing Bow bells

9
St Stephen Walbrook

📍 M5 🏠 39 Walbrook EC4
🚇 Bank, Cannon St
🕐 10am–4pm Mon, Tue &
Thu, 11am–3pm Wed,
10am–3:30pm Fri
🌐 ststephenwalbrook.net

The Lord Mayor's parish church was built by architect Christopher Wren in 1672–9 and it is considered the finest of his City churches. The deep, coffered dome, with its ornate plasterwork, was a forerunner of St Paul's Cathedral.

St Stephen's airy columned interior comes as a surprise after its plain exterior. The font cover and pulpit canopy are decorated with exquisite carved figures that contrast strongly with the stark simplicity of Henry Moore's massive white stone altar (1972), installed in 1987.

However, perhaps the most moving monument of all is a telephone in a glass box. This is a tribute to Rector Chad Varah who, in 1953, founded the Samaritans, a volunteer-staffed telephone helpline for people in emotional need.

The church is also the home of the London Internet Church, which brings together people from all over the world to worship and discuss Christianity. There is a sung Mass on Thursdays at 12:45pm, and a free organ recital at lunchtime on Friday (1pm), to which you are welcome to bring and eat a packed lunch.

> Bow bells have significance for Londoners: traditionally only those born within their sound can claim to be true Cockneys.

8

St Mary-le-Bow

📍 M5 🏠 Cheapside EC2
🚇 St Paul's, Mansion House
🕐 7:30am–6pm Mon–Wed, 7:30am–6:30pm Thu, 7:30am–4pm Fri
🌐 stmarylebow.co.uk

The church takes its name from the bow arches in the Norman crypt. When Wren rebuilt the church (in 1670–80) after the Great Fire, he continued this pattern through the arches on the steeple. The weathervane is an enormous dragon.

The church was bombed in 1941, leaving only the steeple and two walls standing. It was restored in 1956–62, when the bells were recast and rehung. Bow bells have significance for Londoners: traditionally only those born within their sound can claim to be true Cockneys. Tours of the church are offered by arrangement.

THE CITY'S LIVERY HALLS

There are around 110 livery companies in London, each traditionally representing a specific profession or trade. They were first created by groups of medieval tradesmen who formed associations, or guilds, to protect, promote and regulate their trades, setting up headquarters in large houses or halls around the City. Though many did not survive the Great Fire, several dozen companies maintain their own hall to this day, while blue plaques mark former halls. Some have grand, ornate interiors worthy of a palace but they are difficult places to visit – a few allow group tours, others are not publicly accessible.

10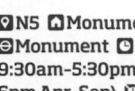

Monument

📍 N5 🏠 Monument St EC3
🚇 Monument ⏰ Platform:
9:30am–5:30pm daily (to
6pm Apr–Sep) 🚫 24–26 Dec
🌐 themonument.info

The column designed by Wren
to commemorate the Great
Fire of London of 1666 is the
tallest isolated stone column
in the world. It is 61.5 m (202 ft)
high and is said to be 61.5 m
west of where the fire started,
in Pudding Lane. Reliefs around
the column's base show Charles
II restoring the city. It's a tough
climb up 311 steps to the top
of the column, but the views
from the viewing platform
are spectacular.

11

All Hallows by
the Tower

📍 N5 🏠 Byward St EC3
🚇 Tower Hill ⏰ 8am–6pm
Mon–Fri, 10am–5pm Sat &
Sun 🚫 26 Dec–2 Jan 🌐 all
hallowsbythetower.org.uk

The oldest church in the city
retains some original Saxon
features and a Roman pavement, discovered in the

crypt in 1926. There is a
small charge to enter the
undercroft. The church carried
out the temporary burials of
those executed on nearby
Tower Hill, including Thomas
More, and it was from the
church tower that Samuel
Pepys watched the Great Fire
consume London in 1666.

12

Tower Bridge

📍 O6 🏠 SE1 🚇 Tower Hill
⏰ Exhibition: Apr–Sep:
10am–5:30pm daily; Oct–
Mar: 9:30am–5pm daily
(from 10am 1 Jan) 🚫 24–26
Dec 🌐 towerbridge.org.uk

Completed in 1894, this
flamboyant piece of Victorian
engineering is a symbol of
London. Its pinnacled towers
and linking catwalk support
the mechanism for raising
the roadway when big ships
have to pass through, or for
special occasions. When
raised, the bridge is 40 m
(135 ft) high and 60 m (200 ft)
wide. In its heyday it was
opened five times a day.

The Tower Bridge Exhibition
features interactive displays
on the bridge's history, views
from the glass-floored

catwalk and a close-up look
at the steam engine that
powered the lifting machinery
until 1976, when the system
was electrified.

13

Smithfield Market

📍 L4 🏠 Charterhouse
St EC1 🚇 Farringdon,
Barbican ⏰ 2–9am
Mon–Fri 🚫 Public hols
🌐 smithfieldmarket.com

Animals have been traded
here since the 12th century,
but the site was granted its
first official charter in 1400.

In 1648, Smithfield was
officially established as a
cattle market and live cattle
continued to be sold here
until the mid-19th century.
It now confines itself to
wholesale trading in meat
and poultry. It was originally
sited in Smithfield, outside
the City walls and, although
moved to its present location
in Charterhouse Street in the
1850s and called the London
Central Meat Market, the
original name stuck. The
old buildings are by Victorian
architect Horace
Jones, but
there

are 20th-century additions. Some pubs in the area keep market hours, serving hearty breakfasts from dawn. Modernized, the market is now one of the best-equipped meat markets in the world. Visitors should aim to arrive by 7am.

⑭ 🖼 🎭 🖥 🏛
St Bartholomew-the-Great

📍 L4 🏠 West Smithfield EC1 🚇 Barbican 🕐 8:30am-5pm Mon-Fri (to 4pm mid-Nov-mid-Feb), 10:30am-4pm Sat, 8:30am-8pm Sun 🔒 Christmas week 🌐 greatstbarts.com

One of London's oldest churches, St Bart's was founded in 1123 by the monk Rahere, whose tomb is inside. A courtier of Henry I, he dreamed that the saint saved him from a winged monster.

The 13th-century arch used to be the door; the gatehouse above it is from a later period. The crossing and chancel are original, with fine Norman detailing. There are also some Tudor monuments. In the south transept is a gilded statue of St Bartholomew by

↑ The Sky Garden, top deck of the "Walkie-Talkie" building

Damien Hirst. In 1725, US statesman Benjamin Franklin worked for a printer in the Lady Chapel. The church also featured in the films *Four Weddings and a Funeral*, *Shakespeare in Love* and *The Other Boleyn Girl*. The cloister café is a peaceful spot.

⑮ 🍴
The Sky Garden

📍 N5 🏠 20 Fenchurch St EC3 🚇 Bank, Monument 🕐 10am-6pm Mon-Fri (last adm: 5pm), 11am-9pm Sat & Sun (last adm. 8pm) 🌐 skygarden.london

The Rafael Viñoly-designed 20 Fenchurch Street is commonly known as the "Walkie-Talkie", thanks to its unusual shape. Not without controversy (its shape and position make it particularly obtrusive on the city skyline), it is one of few skyscrapers with free public access, provided that you book ahead for the Sky Garden, a three-level viewing deck. Tickets are released three weeks ahead, and go quickly for popular times. There is also a bar and restaurants.

This is a perfect place from which to view London's other mega-structures. To the south is the Shard *(p212)*; north are Tower 42, the "Gherkin" and the Leadenhall Building aka the "Cheesegrater".

⑯
Old Bailey

📍 L4 🏠 EC4 🚇 St Paul's 🕐 9:55am-12:40pm & 1:55-3:40pm Mon-Fri (reduced times Aug; hours vary from court to court) 🔒 Public hols 🌐 cityoflondon.gov.uk

The new Central Criminal Courts opened here in 1907 on the site of the infamous and malodorous Newgate prison. Across the road, the Magpie and Stump pub served "execution breakfasts" until 1868, when mass public hangings outside the gates were stopped. Today, the courts are open to the public when in session.

←
Tower Bridge, an enduring symbol of London, at sunset

→ Elegant wrought-iron
and glass vaulting at
Leadenhall Market

17

Leadenhall Market

📍N5 🚇Whittington Ave
EC3 🚇Bank, Monument
🕐10am-6pm Mon-Fri
🌐leadenhallmarket.co.uk

There has been a food market
here, on the site of a Roman
forum, since the Middle Ages.
Today's ornate Victorian
covered shopping arcade was
designed in 1881 by Sir Horace
Jones. Leadenhall is now home
to boutique wine shops,
cheesemongers, florists and
fine food shops, along with
several traditional pubs and
wine bars. At Christmas the
decorated stores are an
attractive sight.

18

Guildhall

📍M4 🚇Guildhall Yard EC2
🚇St Paul's 🕐Great Hall:
10am-4.30pm Mon-Sat,
(daily May-Sep) 🚫1 Jan,
25 & 26 Dec, occasionally
for events 🌐guildhall.
cityoflondon.gov.uk

Guildhall has been the
administrative centre of the

City for at least 800 years. For
centuries its Great Hall was
used for trials and many
people were condemned to
death here, including Henry
Garnet, one of the Gunpowder
Plot conspirators.

Overlooking the Great Hall
at one end are the figures of
legendary giants Gog and
Magog, the guardians of the
City, while statues of notable
figures such as Churchill and
Nelson line its 46-m- (150-ft-)
long sides. Each year, a few
days after the Lord Mayor's
parade, the prime minister
addresses a banquet here.

On the south side of
Guildhall Yard is a Wren-
designed church, St Lawrence
Jewry, while on the east side
is the **Guildhall Art Gallery**.
It houses the studio collection
of 20th-century artist Sir
Matthew Smith, portraits from
the 16th century to the present
day, 18th-century works
including John Singleton
Copley's *Defeat of the Floating
Batteries at Gibraltar*, and
numerous Victorian works.

In 1988, the foundations
of a Roman amphitheatre
were discovered beneath the
gallery. Built in AD 70 and with
a capacity of about 6,000

spectators, the arena would
have hosted animal hunts,
executions and gladiatorial
combat. Access to the
atmospheric ruins is through
the art gallery.

**Guildhall Art Gallery and
Roman Amphitheatre**
🕐10am-5pm Mon-Fri, noon-
4pm Sun 🚫1 Jan, 24-26 Dec
🌐cityoflondon.gov.uk

19 🍴 🛍 🏛

St Katharine Docks

📍O6 🚇E1 🚇Tower Hill
🌐skdocks.co.uk

This most central of all
London's docks was designed
by Thomas Telford and
opened in 1828 on the site
of St Katharine's Hospital.
Commodities as diverse as
tea, marble and live turtles
(turtle soup was a Victorian
delicacy) were unloaded here.

During the 19th and early
20th centuries, the docks
flourished, but by the mid-
20th century, cargo ships
were delivering their wares
in massive containers. The old
docks became too small and
closed in 1968.

The redevelopment of St Katharine's has been one of the City's most successful – the old warehouse buildings have shops and restaurants on their ground floors and offices above. In front is a marina, and there are other entertainment facilities.

The dock is well worth wandering through after visiting the Tower (p178) or Tower Bridge (p186). A weekly street food market is held here on Fridays from 11am to 3pm.

---

⑳ St Katharine Cree

🚇 N5 🏠 86 Leadenhall St EC3 🚇 Aldgate, Tower Hill 🕐 9:30am-4pm Mon-Fri 🗓 Aug 🌐 sanctuaryinthecity.net

A rare pre-Wren 17th-century church with a medieval tower, this was one of only eight churches in the City to survive the fire of 1666. Some of the elaborate plasterwork on and beneath the high ceiling of the nave portrays the coats of arms of the guilds, with which the church has special links. The 17th-century organ, supported by magnificent carved wooden columns, has in the past been played by both Purcell and Handel.

㉑ Charterhouse

🚇 L3 🏠 Charterhouse Sq EC1 🚇 Barbican 🏛 Museum: 11am-4:45pm Tue-Sun 🗓 1 Jan, 24-26 Dec 🌐 thecharterhouse.org

The Tudor gateway on the north side of Charterhouse square leads to the site of a former Carthusian monastery, which was dissolved under Henry VIII. In 1611, the buildings were converted into a hospital for poor pensioners, and a charity school – called Charterhouse – whose pupils included Methodism founder John Wesley, writer William Thackeray and Robert Baden-Powell, founder of the Boy Scouts.

In 1872, the school relocated to Godalming in Surrey. Part of the original site was subsequently taken over by St Bartholomew's Hospital medical school. Some of the old buildings remain, including the chapel and part of the cloisters. Today Charterhouse is still home to more than 40 pensioners supported by the charitable foundation. There is a small museum open to all, but access to the rest of the site is by guided tour only, conducted every day except Monday; book online.

EAT

Jose Pizarro
Classic Spanish tapas and inventive dishes.

🚇 N4 🏠 36 Broadgate Circle EC2 🌐 jose pizarro.com

£££

The Jugged Hare
Gastropub serving excellent game dishes.

🚇 M3 🏠 49 Chiswell St EC1 🌐 thejuggedhare.com

£££

㉒ Museum of the Order of St John

🚇 L3 🏠 St John's Lane EC1 🚇 Farringdon 🕐 10am-5pm Mon-Sat (daily Jul-Sep) 🗓 Christmas week, bank holiday weekends 🌐 museumstjohn.org.uk

The Tudor gatehouse and parts of the 12th-century church are all that remain of the priory of the Knights of St John, which flourished here for 400 years and was the precursor of the St John Ambulance. Over the years, the priory buildings have had many uses, such as offices for Elizabeth I's Master of the Revels and a coffee shop run by the artist William Hogarth's father.

In 2009–10, the museum was renovated to create gallery spaces and a learning space in the priory church, and to reveal even more of the Tudor architecture. The rest of the building can be seen on guided tours, at 11:30am and 2:30pm on Tuesdays, Fridays and Saturdays. Tours are free, but a donation is appreciated.

St Katharine Docks, a working quay turned marina

A SHORT WALK
THE CITY

Distance 1.5 km (1 mile) **Nearest Tube**
St Paul's **Time** 15 minutes

This route through the business centre of London
unsurprisingly takes in vast financial institutions,
such as the Stock Exchange and the Bank of England.
Alongside these 19th- and 20th-century buildings
stand the majestic architectural visions of
Christopher Wren, England's most sublime and
probably most prolific architect (p174). Marvel
at his genius as you pass some of his churches.

Did You Know?

Bread Street was
named for the bread
market located here in
medieval times.

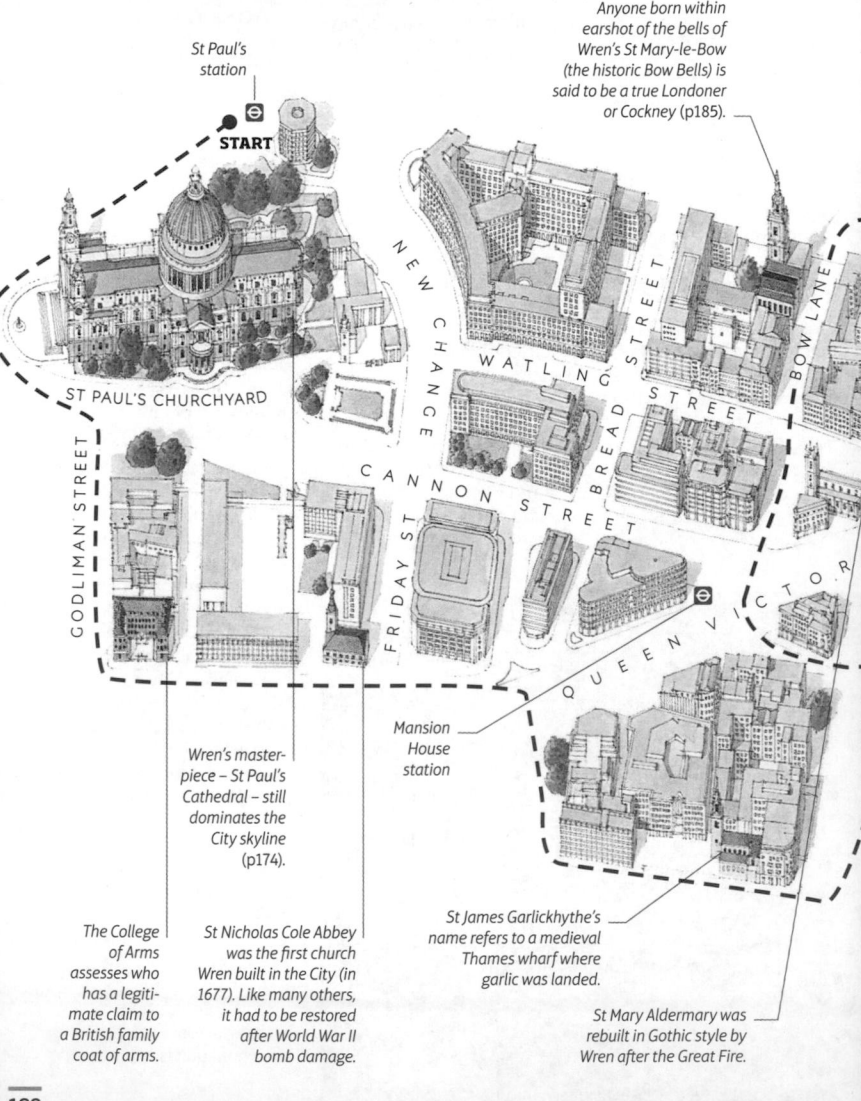

St Paul's
station

START

Anyone born within
earshot of the bells of
Wren's St Mary-le-Bow
(the historic Bow Bells) is
said to be a true Londoner
or Cockney (p185).

NEW CHANGE

WATLING STREET

BREAD STREET

BOW LANE

ST PAUL'S CHURCHYARD

CANNON STREET

GODLIMAN STREET

FRIDAY ST

QUEEN VICTOR

Mansion
House
station

Wren's master-
piece – St Paul's
Cathedral – still
dominates the
City skyline
(p174).

The College
of Arms
assesses who
has a legiti-
mate claim to
a British family
coat of arms.

St Nicholas Cole Abbey
was the first church
Wren built in the City (in
1677). Like many others,
it had to be restored
after World War II
bomb damage.

St James Garlickhythe's
name refers to a medieval
Thames wharf where
garlic was landed.

St Mary Aldermary was
rebuilt in Gothic style by
Wren after the Great Fire.

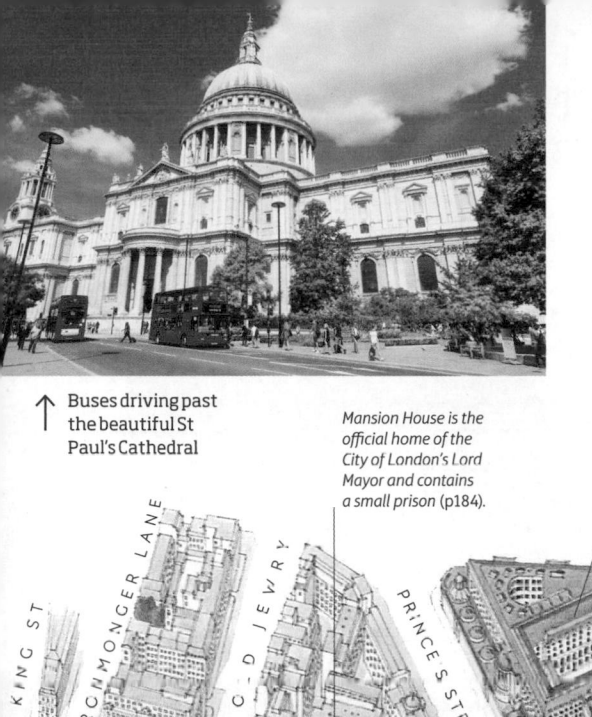

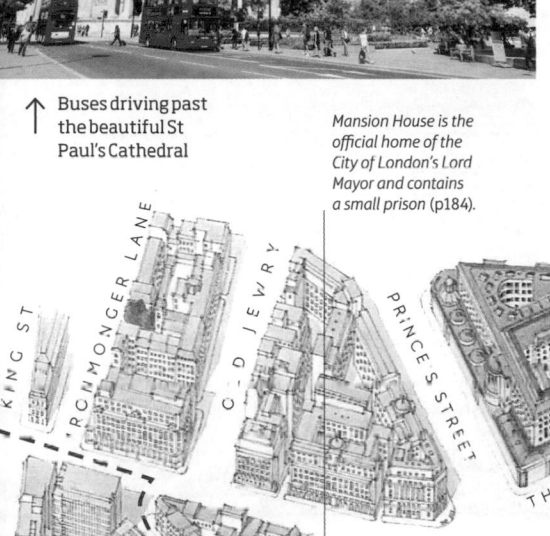

Locator Map
For more detail see p172

Buses driving past the beautiful St Paul's Cathedral

Mansion House is the official home of the City of London's Lord Mayor and contains a small prison (p184).

The intriguing story of England's financial system is explored at the Bank of England Museum (p184).

Bank station

Since its foundation in Tudor times, the Royal Exchange has been at the heart of London's commerce (p184).

Lombard Street is named after Italian bankers who settled here from Lombardy in the 13th century. It is still a banking centre.

St Mary Woolnoth is a characteristically powerful work by Wren's pupil, Nicholas Hawksmoor.

St Mary Abchurch owes its unusually spacious feel to the large dome designed by Wren. Admire the altar carving by Grinling Gibbons.

The dome of St Stephen Walbrook (p185) is a forerunner to that atop St Paul's.

FINISH

0 metres 100
0 yards 100
N

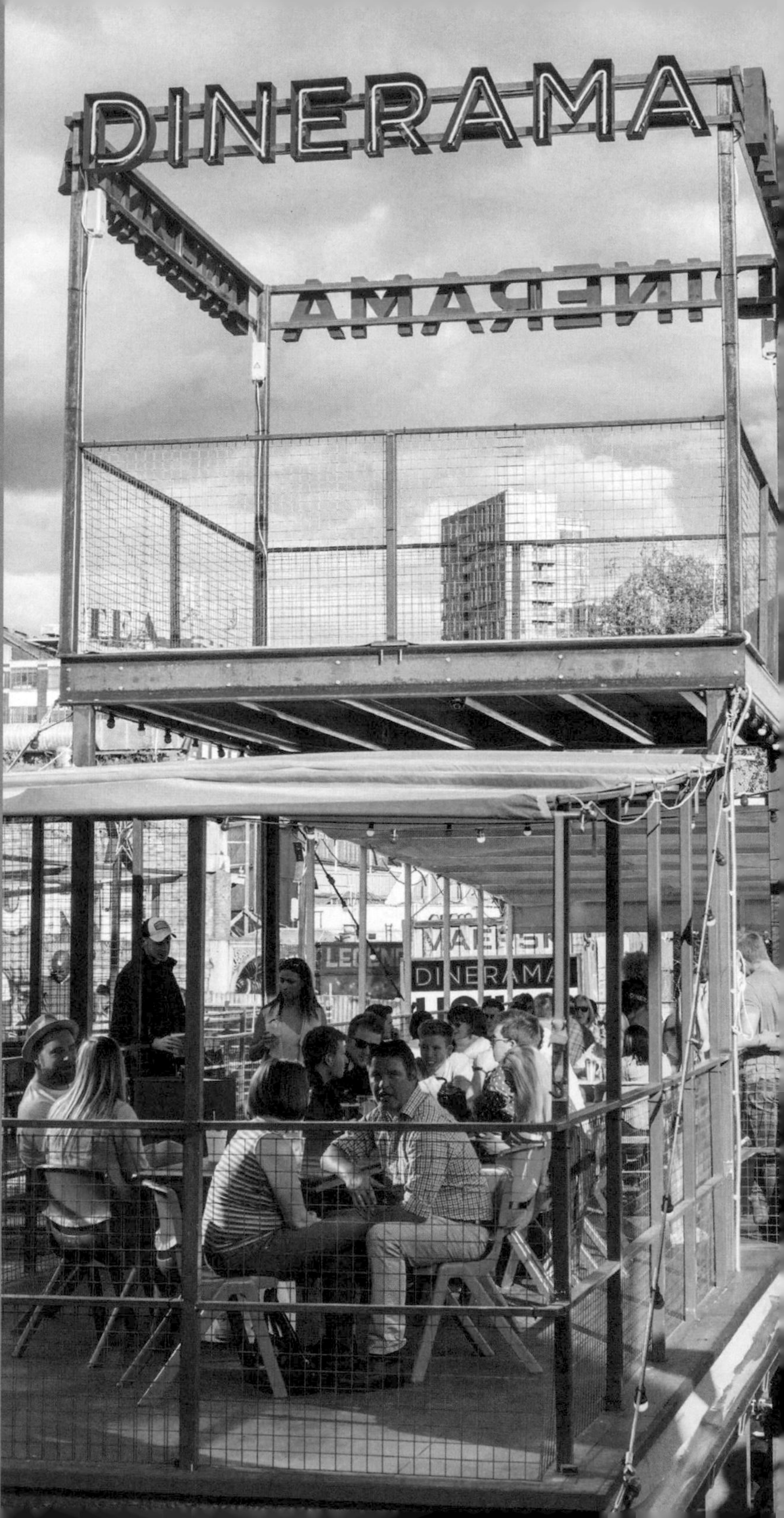
DINERAMA
DINERAMA

SHOREDITCH AND SPITALFIELDS

Just outside the boundaries of the City, Spitalfields has long rotated around its market, which first emerged in the late 17th century after traders had begun operating outside the city gates. As the market expanded people began to settle in its vicinity, notably Huguenots fleeing religious persecution in France. The Huguenots also moved to nearby Shoreditch and their skilled weavers soon dominated the textile industry in the area. Waves of Irish, then Jewish and most recently Bangladeshi immigrants followed. The market survived, was given its own building in the late 19th century and flourished for decades as a wholesale market. It was saved from destruction in the early years of this century and reborn as a market for vintage clothing, antiques, arts and crafts, in keeping with the recent gentrification of the area, extending across Shoreditch and beyond.

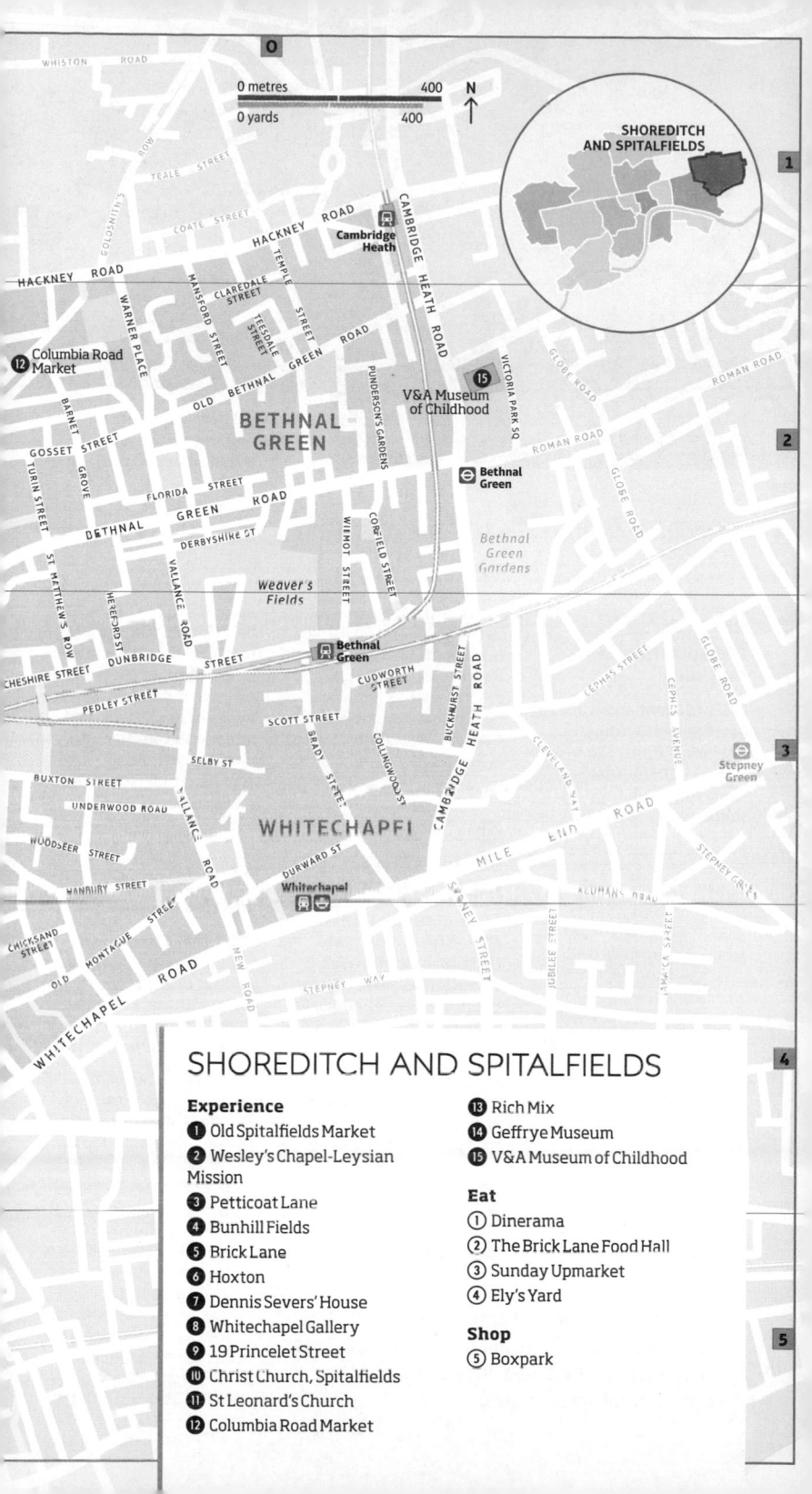

0 metres 400
0 yards 400

N ↑

SHOREDITCH
AND SPITALFIELDS

WHISTON ROAD
TEALE STREET
ROW
GOLDSMITH'S
COATE STREET
HACKNEY ROAD
Cambridge
Heath
CAMBRIDGE HEATH ROAD
HACKNEY ROAD
WARNER PLACE
MANSFORD STREET
TEMPLE STREET
CLAREDALE STREET
TEESDALE STREET
OLD BETHNAL GREEN ROAD
PUNDERSON'S GARDENS
VICTORIA PARK SQ.
GLOBE ROAD
ROMAN ROAD
12 Columbia Road Market
BETHNAL GREEN
15 V&A Museum of Childhood
ROMAN ROAD
BARNET GROVE
GOSSET STREET
TURIN STREET
FLORIDA STREET
DETHNAL GREEN ROAD
DERBYSHIRE ST
Bethnal Green
GLOBE ROAD
ST MATTHEWS ROW
VALLANCE ROAD
HEREFORD ST
WILMOT STREET
CORFIELD STREET
Bethnal Green Gardens
DUNBRIDGE STREET
Weaver's Fields
Bethnal Green
CUDWORTH STREET
BUCKHURST STREET
LEOPAS STREET
CEPHAS AVENUE
GLOBE ROAD
CHESHIRE STREET
PEDLEY STREET
SCOTT STREET
BRADY STREET
COLLINGWOOD ST
CAMBRIDGE HEATH ROAD
CLEVELAND WAY
ROAD
Stepney Green
BUXTON STREET
SELBY ST
UNDERWOOD ROAD
WOODSEER STREET
VALLANCE ROAD
WANBURY STREET
WHITECHAPEL
DURWARD ST
MILE END ROAD
ALDHAMS ROAD
STEPNEY CRES
CHICKSAND STREET
OLD MONTAGUE STREET
Whitechapel
NEW ROAD
STEPNEY WAY
STEPNEY STREET
JUBILEE STREET
JAMAICA STREET
WHITECHAPEL ROAD

SHOREDITCH AND SPITALFIELDS

Experience

1 Old Spitalfields Market
2 Wesley's Chapel-Leysian Mission
3 Petticoat Lane
4 Bunhill Fields
5 Brick Lane
6 Hoxton
7 Dennis Severs' House
8 Whitechapel Gallery
9 19 Princelet Street
10 Christ Church, Spitalfields
11 St Leonard's Church
12 Columbia Road Market

13 Rich Mix
14 Geffrye Museum
15 V&A Museum of Childhood

Eat

1 Dinerama
2 The Brick Lane Food Hall
3 Sunday Upmarket
4 Ely's Yard

Shop

5 Boxpark

↑ Independent traders with their wares on display at Old Spitalfields Market

EXPERIENCE

① 🍴 💻 🛍
Old Spitalfields Market

📍 O3 🏠 Commercial St E1
🚇 Liverpool St, Aldgate
🕐 Market stalls: 10am–5pm Sun–Fri, 10am–6pm Sat
🌐 oldspitalfields market.com

Produce has been traded at Spitalfields market since 1682, though the original covered market buildings date to 1887. The vegetable market finally moved out in 1991, after which today's version of the market – known for antiques, fashion, bric-a-brac and crafts stalls – started to take shape. Today the market space is a mix of restaurants, shops and traditional market stalls. It is open every day; Thursdays are good for antiques and collectibles, and Fridays for fashion, but it is on Sundays that the crowds really arrive, in search of vintage clothing and unique items. This is also a major foodie destination, with superb street food from top names, both global and local – from Pacific pokè and Burmese tea leaf salad to East Anglian oysters and the unrivalled Reuben sandwich from iconic Monty's Deli.

----

②
Wesley's Chapel-Leysian Mission

📍 M3 🏠 49 City Rd EC1
🚇 Old Street, Moorgate
🕐 10am–4pm Mon–Sat
🔒 Christmas to New Year, public hols except Good Fri
🌐 wesleyschapel.org.uk

John Wesley, the founder of the Methodist Church, laid this chapel's foundation stone in 1777. He preached here until his death in 1791, and is buried behind the chapel. Next door is the house where he lived, in which some of his furniture, books and other possessions can be seen. The chapel, in accordance with Wesley's austere religious principles, has columns made from ships' masts. Baroness Thatcher, Britain's first female prime minister, was married here. Beneath the chapel is a small museum devoted to the history of Methodism. There are free lunchtime recitals on Tuesdays.

----

③
Petticoat Lane

📍 O4 🏠 Middlesex St E1
🚇 Aldgate East, Aldgate, Liverpool St 🕐 9am–2pm Sun (main market); 8am–4pm Mon–Fri (smaller market on Wentworth St)

During Queen Victoria's prudish reign, the name of this street, long famous for its market, was changed to the respectable but colourless Middlesex Street. That is still its official designation, but the old name, derived from the petticoats and lace sold here by the Huguenots who came from France, has stuck, and is now applied to the market held every Sunday morning in this and the surrounding streets. Though the street is not particularly attractive, the

> Thursdays are good for antiques and collectibles, and Friday for fashion, but it is on Sundays that the crowds really arrive, in search of vintage clothing and unique items.

lively market creates plenty of atmosphere. A great variety of goods are sold but there is still a bias towards clothing, especially leather coats. It's a noisy and cheerful scene, with Cockney stallholders making use of their wit to attract custom. There are scores of snack bars for pitstops.

④

Bunhill Fields

🗺 M3 📍 City Rd EC1
🚇 Old Street ⏰ Apr-Sep: 8am-dusk Mon-Fri, 9:30am-dusk Sat, Sun & public hols; Oct-Mar: 8am-4pm Mon-Fri; 9:30am-4pm Sat, Sun & public hols 🚫 1 Jan, 25 & 26 Dec 🌐 cityoflondon.gov.uk

This burial ground was first designated a cemetery after the Great Plague of 1665, when it was enclosed by a brick wall and gates. Twenty years later it was allocated to Nonconformists, who were banned from being buried in churchyards because of their refusal to use the Church of England prayer book.

The cemetery is situated on the edge of the City, and shaded by large plane trees. There are monuments to the well-known writers Daniel Defoe, John Bunyan and William Blake, as well as to members of the Cromwell family. John Milton wrote his epic poem *Paradise Lost* while he lived in Bunhill Row, located on the west side of the cemetery.

↑ Taking a selfie in front of street art by Alexis Diaz and Elian

⑤ 🍴 🥤 🛍
Brick Lane

🗺 O4 📍 E1 🚇 Liverpool St, Aldgate East, Shoreditch ⏰ Market. 10am-5pm Sun 🌐 visitbricklane.org

Once a lane running through brickfields, Brick Lane has long been synonymous with the area's British-Bangladeshi community. Now their curry houses sit next to hip galleries and quirky boutiques. Shops and houses, some dating from the 18th century, have seen immigrants of many nationalities, and ethnic foods, spices, silks and saris are all on sale here. In the 19th century this was a predominantly Jewish quarter, and some Jewish shops remain, including a 24-hour bagel shop at No 159.

On Sundays, a large market is held here and in the surrounding streets. At the northern end of Brick Lane is the Old Truman Brewery, home to a mix of bars, shops and stalls: five separate markets at weekends sell food, vintage clothes and new fashion.

←

A monument to William Blake and his wife in Bunhill Fields

NEAR BY LIE THE REMAINS OF
THE POET-PAINTER
WILLIAM BLAKE
1757 — 1827
AND OF HIS WIFE
CATHERINE SOPHIA
1762 — 1831

EAT

Dinerama
Best spot for street food after dark, this old truck depot offers craft beer and cocktails

🗺 N3 📍 19 Great Eastern St EC2 ⏰ Sun-Tue

£ £ £

The Brick Lane Food Hall
Treats from Poland, Jamaica, Japan, Korea and more inside a red-brick warehouse.

🗺 O3 📍 Old Truman Brewery, Brick Lane E1 ⏰ Mon-Fri

£ £ £

Sunday Upmarket
International street food is found among artsy stalls.

🗺 O3 📍 Old Truman Brewery, Brick Lane E1 ⏰ Mon-Sat

£ £ £

Ely's Yard
The food trucks and stalls are here all week.

🗺 O3 📍 Old Truman Brewery, Dray Walk, E1

£ £ £

Hoxton

📍 N2 📍 N1, E2
🚇 Old St

Hoxton, at the heart of hipster London, is a loosely defined district that revolves around its two main streets: Old Street and Kingsland Road. This once-gritty landscape of Victorian warehouses is now home to trendy places to eat, increasingly pricey clothes stores and a significant percentage of the city's newer street art. The converted warehouses house some of the city's most rambunctious nightlife, with clubs and bars radiating out from the Shoreditch High Street and Old Street junction, some of them on neatly proportioned Hoxton Square, just behind Old Street.

Dennis Severs' House

📍 O3 📍 18 Folgate St E1
🚇 Liverpool St ⏰ Noon-2pm & 5-9pm Mon, 5-9pm Wed & Fri, noon-4pm Sun
🌐 dennissevershouse.co.uk

At No 18 Folgate Street, built in 1724, the late designer and performer Dennis Severs re-created a historical interior that takes you on a journey from the 17th to the 19th centuries. It offers what he called "an adventure of the imagination… a visit to a time-mode rather than… merely a look at a house".

The rooms are like a series of *tableaux vivants*, as if the occupants had simply left for a moment. There is bread on the plates, wine in the glasses, fruit in the bowl; the candles flicker and horses' hooves are heard clattering on the cobbles outside.

This highly theatrical experience is far removed from the usual museum re-creations and is not suitable for the under-12s. Praised by many, including artist David Hockney, it is truly unique. The house's motto is "you either see it or you don't".

↑ The immaculately re-created interior of Dennis Severs' House

For an even more intimate experience, private tours can be arranged.

Around the corner on Elder Street are two of London's earliest surviving terraces, where many of the Georgian red-brick houses have been carefully restored.

Whitechapel Gallery

📍 O4 📍 77-82 Whitechapel High St E1 🚇 Aldgate East, Aldgate ⏰ 11am-6pm Tue-Sun (to 9pm Thu) 🚫 1 Jan, 24-26 Dec
🌐 whitechapelgallery.org

A striking Art Nouveau façade by C Harrison Townsend

→ Industrial chic in the gentrified Hoxton district

fronts this light, airy gallery, founded in 1901 and expanded in the 1980s and again in 2007–9. Situated close to Brick Lane and the area's burgeoning art scene, this independent gallery was founded with the aim of bringing great art to the people of East London. Today it enjoys an international reputation for high-quality shows of major contemporary artists and for events, talks, live performances, films and art-themed evenings (especially on the first Thursday of each month, when many galleries in the area open late).

In the 1950s and 60s, the likes of Jackson Pollock, Anthony Caro, Mark Rothko, Robert Rauschenberg and John Hoyland all displayed their work in the gallery. In 1970 David Hockney's first exhibition was held here.

The gallery has a well-stocked arts bookshop and a relaxed café which on Thursday evenings becomes a popular wine bar. There is an entry charge occasionally for some special exhibitions.

→
Contemporary photography at the Whitechapel Gallery

9
19 Princelet Street

📍03 🏠19 Princelet St E1 ⊜Liverpool St ⏰ Check website for dates 🌐19princeletstreet.org.uk

This 1719 Huguenot silk merchant's house, with a Victorian synagogue hidden within, epitomizes the area's multicultural history as a refuge for the dispossessed. Now it exists as a museum of immigration, with exhibitions celebrating the people who have arrived and settled in London's East End. It is hoped that, with funding, this historic gem can be further developed into a permanent centre. For now, one-off group visits can be booked in advance via the website (booking at least four weeks ahead is advisable).

🔟 Ⓜ
Christ Church, Spitalfields

📍04 🏠Commercial St E1 ⊜Liverpool St ⏰10am-4pm Mon-Fri (unless in use as venue), 1-4pm Sun 🌐ccspits.org

Christopher Wren's pupil Nicholas Hawksmoor built six London churches, and this is his finest. It was commissioned by parliament in the Fifty New Churches Act of 1711, aimed at combating the threat of Nonconformism. It was intended to make a powerful statement in an area fast becoming a Huguenot stronghold. (The Protestant Huguenots had fled here from religious persecution in Catholic France, see below.)

Completed in 1729, the building was mauled by alterations in the 1850s. By 1960 it had become derelict, narrowly escaping demolition. In 1976 the Friends of Christ Church Spitalfields was formed to restore the building to its former glory – a goal achieved in 2004. The impression of size and strength created by its portico and spire is continued inside by such features as the high ceiling and the gallery. Now used for musical events, it is one of the main venues for the Spitalfields music festivals in June and December.

HUGUENOTS IN LONDON

Among the first really significant waves of immigration into east London was the influx of tens of thousands of Huguenots from France in the late 17th century. These were Protestant refugees, fleeing persecution in their home country, and their numbers were highest in Spitalfields. Many were weavers by trade and they came to dominate the silk and textile industry that already existed in this part of the city. Spitalfields became known as "Weaver Town".

Beautiful blooms at the Columbia Road flower market ↑

11

St Leonard's Church

📍 O2 🏠 Shoreditch High St E1 🚇 Old St, Liverpool St 🕐 Mar–Oct: noon–2pm Mon–Fri 🌐 shoreditch church.org.uk

Standing as it does on the spot where several major Roman roads converged, this has been a site of worship for millennia. The Norman-era St Leonard's was the original "Actors' Church" *(p125)* and many famous names of Tudor theatre are buried in the crypt, including Richard Burbage, who played the first Hamlet, Macbeth and Romeo, and his brother Cuthbert, founder of the Globe Theatre.

Erected in 1736–40, the current Palladian-style church is the oldest building in Shoreditch. Its fine acoustics make it still popular today as a performance space for actors and musicians. Sunday service is at 10:30am; see the website for details of musical events.

12

Columbia Road Market

📍 O2 🏠 Columbia Rd E2 🚇 Liverpool St, Old St, Bethnal Green 🕐 8am–3pm Sun 🌐 columbiaroad.info

A visit to this flower and plant market is one of the most delightful things to do on a Sunday morning in London, whether you want to take advantage of the exotic species on offer or not – though it's hard to resist, as prices are competitive and the range impressive. Set in a well-preserved street of small Victorian shops, it is a lively, sweet-smelling and colourful affair. Apart from the stalls, there are several shops selling, among other things, home-made bread and farmhouse cheeses, antiques and interesting objects, many flower-related. There are also cafés, a tapas bar and pubs to refuel at along the street.

13

Rich Mix

📍 O3 🏠 35–47 Bethnal Green Rd E1 🚇 Shoreditch High St 🕐 10am–late 🌐 richmix.org.uk

This hip independent cultural centre spread over five floors offers a diverse programme of live music, theatre, dance, spoken word, comedy and

SHOP

Boxpark

Independent clothing brands, accessories, cosmetics, homewares and kooky gifts are traded from repurposed shipping containers in this fun, popup-style retail park.

📍 O3 🏠 Bethnal Green Rd E1

film. There's an emphasis on both multiculturalism and local talent, with a marked international outlook reflected in the African, Latin American, Ukrainian and other film festivals for which its three-screen cinema has become a major venue. The building is a converted leather factory with an unusual mishmash of performance and exhibition spaces giving off an industrial chic vibe. There are three bars buried within its straight-edged interior, but the Indian street food café facing the street is much easier to find.

14

Geffrye Museum

📍 01 🏠 136 Kingsland Rd
🚇 Hoxton ⏰ Museum and gardens closed until 2020; restored almshouse open for tours (see website)
🌐 geffrye-museum.org.uk

This delightful museum is housed in a set of restored almshouses that were built in 1715 on land bequeathed by Sir Robert Geffrye, a 17th-century Lord Mayor of London. Inside, you take a trip through historical room settings, each providing an insight into the domestic interiors of the urban middle classes from 1600 to the present day, reflecting changes in society, behaviour, style and taste. Each room contains superb examples of British furniture of the period. Outside, a series of period garden "rooms" show designs and planting schemes popular in urban gardens between the 16th and 20th centuries.

The museum is currently closed until 2020 for a £15m redevelopment, which will bring to life more of the almshouse buildings and more than double the exhibition space. One of the almshouses remains open for tours, and there are events in the green space in front of the buildings: check the website for details.

---

15 🖥 🎭

V&A Museum of Childhood

📍 02 🏠 Cambridge Heath Rd E2 🚇 Bethnal Green
⏰ 10am–5:45pm daily (to 9pm first Thu of month)
🌐 vam.ac.uk/moc

With an amazing array of toys, games, lavish dolls' houses, model trains and costumes, dating from the 16th century to the present day, this museum has the largest collection of childhood-related objects in the UK.

There are plenty of activities to keep children amused, including story-telling, arts and crafts workshops, and fun trails.

↑ Four centuries of fun and games *(inset)* at the V&A Museum of Childhood

SOUTHWARK AND BANKSIDE

Southwark and its stretch of riverbank, known as Bankside, once offered an escape from the City, a place to indulge in the many forms of entertainment that were banned across the river. Among the illicit pleasures that thrived here from the late 16th century were brothels, theatres, and bear and cock pits. Borough High Street was lined with taverns – the medieval courtyards that run off it mark where they stood, and The George survives as the only galleried inn in London. Shakespeare's company was famously based at the Globe Theatre, which has been rebuilt close to its original site. Docks, wharves and warehouses were built along Bankside in the 18th and 19th centuries as the area industrialized, but a century later, bomb damage during World War II, and the decline in river trade that followed, ushered in a period of decline. Southwark's riverside renaissance as one of the capital's top visitor destinations began in the 1990s and since the turn of the millennium Tate Modern, the Millennium Bridge and The Shard, have all opened, accompanied by a sweeping regeneration of the whole area.

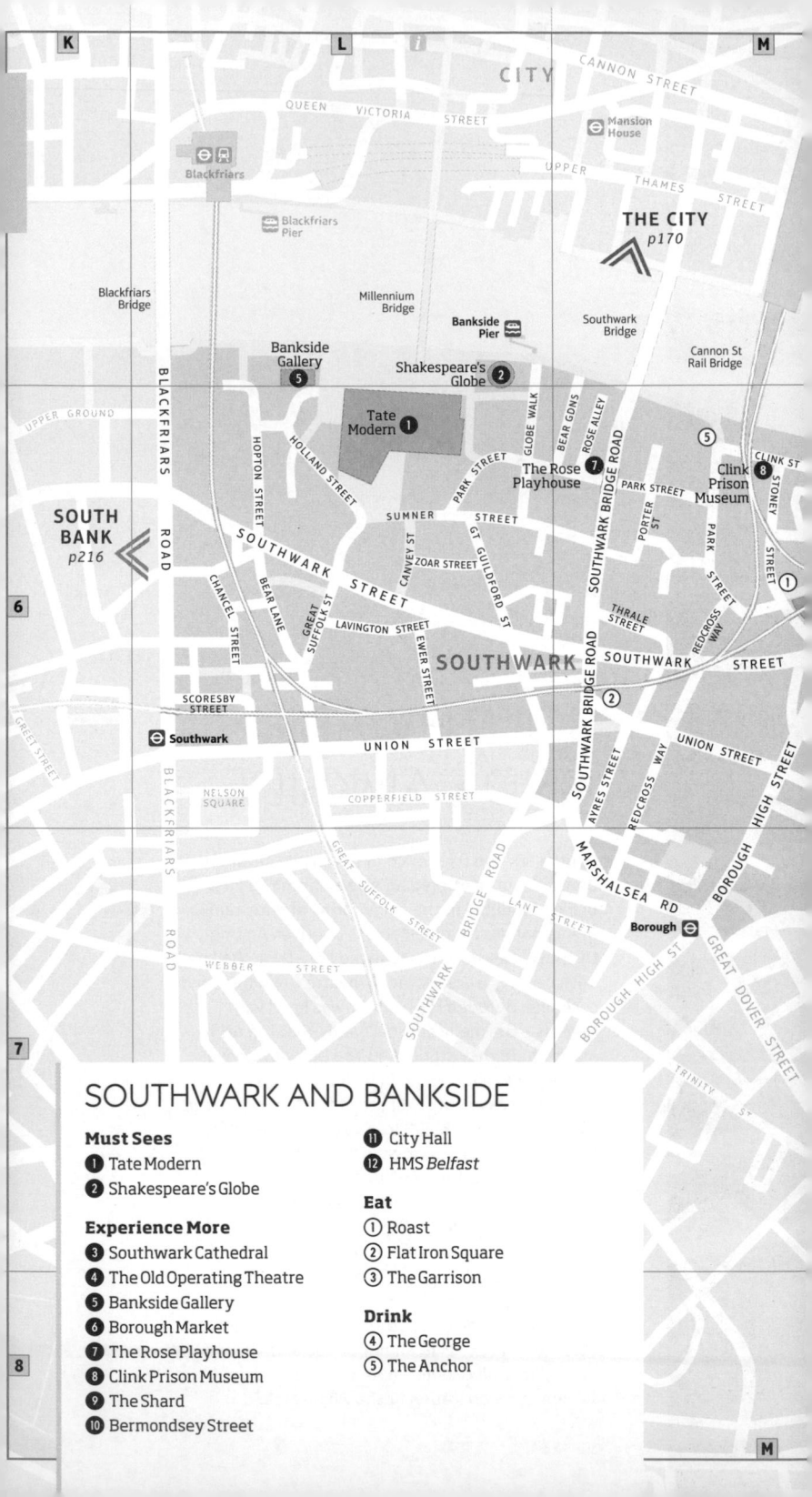

SOUTHWARK AND BANKSIDE

Must Sees
1. Tate Modern
2. Shakespeare's Globe

Experience More
3. Southwark Cathedral
4. The Old Operating Theatre
5. Bankside Gallery
6. Borough Market
7. The Rose Playhouse
8. Clink Prison Museum
9. The Shard
10. Bermondsey Street

11. City Hall
12. HMS *Belfast*

Eat
1. Roast
2. Flat Iron Square
3. The Garrison

Drink
4. The George
5. The Anchor

THE CITY
p170

SOUTH BANK
p216

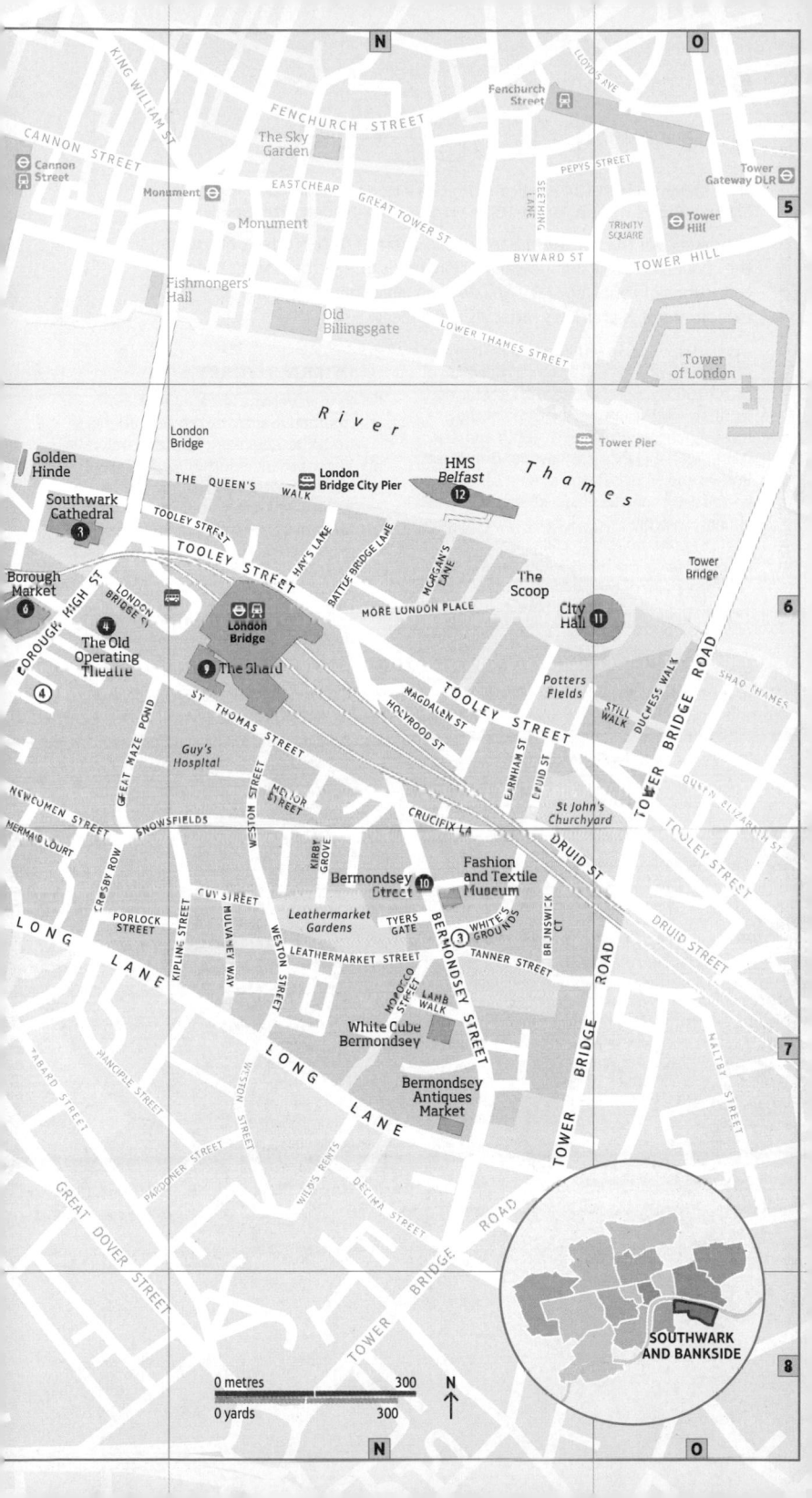

TATE MODERN

📍L6 🏠Bankside SE1 🚇Pimlico 🚉Blackfriars, Southwark 🚆Blackfriars
🕐10am–6pm Sun–Thu, 10am–10pm Fri–Sat 🗓24–26 Dec 🌐tate.org.uk

Looming over the southern bank of the Thames, Tate Modern, housed in the converted Bankside power station, holds one of the world's premier collections of contemporary art. With an ever-changing roster of exhibitions, it is London's most visited gallery.

Opened to coincide with the new millennium, this Goliath of a gallery boasts a collection of over 70,000 works of modern art, featuring paintings and sculptures by some of the most significant artists of the 20th and 21st centuries, Pablo Picasso, Salvador Dalí, Mark Rothko and Francis Bacon among them. Lesser known artists and less mainstream media also abound, with pieces composed of bottle tops or, most famously, a porcelain urinal, in the guise of Marcel Duchamp's notorious *Fountain*. The focal point of the building is the awesome Turbine Hall, which is often filled by a specially commissioned work. Other exhibition spaces, including the galleries of the towering Blavatnik Building, feature collections on a single theme or hugely popular temporary shows.

INTERACTIVE ART

Tate Modern has created a series of interactive activities and experiences under its Bloomberg Connects umbrella. These products, including the Tate app, the digital Drawing Bar and the digital gallery, in which you can immerse yourself in the studios and cities of artists, enable members of the public to actively connect with art, artists and other visitors. The award-winning handheld multimedia guides present audio commentary alongside images, film clips and games.

One Two Three Swing!
by SUPERFLEX, an
installation in the Turbine Hall ↓

4.2 million

The number of bricks
used to build the
original Bankside
power station.

① The striking 99-m- (325-ft-) high chimney of Tate Modern reveals the building's former role as a power station.

② Sculptures by French artist Louise Bourgeois (1911–2010), featuring body parts, cages and giant spiders, are in the Tate's permanent collection.

③ The cool interior of the Blavatnik Building extension, which has added a large number of galleries and performance spaces to the Tate.

GREAT VIEW
Top of the Tower

On Level 10, the top floor of the new extension, the Blavatnik Building, the 360-degree viewing terrace gives spectacular views of London. You can enjoy more or less the same views, taking in St Paul's Cathedral, the rest of the City and beyond, from the restaurant on Level 9.

2 🏛 🎭 🍴 🏪 🛍

SHAKESPEARE'S GLOBE

📍L5 🏠New Globe Walk SE1 🚇Southwark, London Bridge 🕐9am–5pm
📅24 & 25 Dec 🌐shakespearesglobe.com

To see a Shakespeare play at the reconstructed Globe is a magical experience. Time-travel to the 1600s and watch Romeo woo Juliet, Beatrice and Benedick squabble, and Hamlet seek revenge.

Built along the south bank of the Thames, Shakespeare's Globe is a fine reconstruction of the Elizabethan theatre where many of the famous playwright's works were first performed. The circular wooden structure is open in the middle, leaving some of the audience exposed to the elements. Those holding seat tickets enjoy a roof over their heads. Performances (staged from late April until mid-October) are thrilling, with first-rate acting. A second theatre, the Sam Wanamaker Playhouse, is a splendidly atmospheric reproduction of a Jacobean indoor candlelit theatre, with performances year-round. The Globe also houses an exhibition telling the history of Elizabethan theatre in Southwark, the process of building the Globe and the exquisite costumes made for shows there. You can also listen to classic performances of speeches from Shakespeare's works.

↑ The theatre, built with green oak beams and lime plaster to replicate the 1599 original

💬 INSIDER TIP
Wrap Up

Got tickets? Dress warmly: plays tend to run for several hours and even during the summer months London evenings can be very cool.

Must See

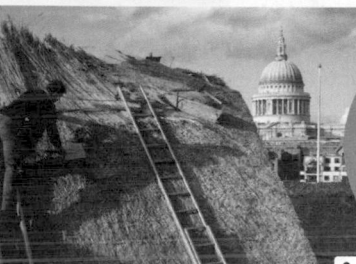

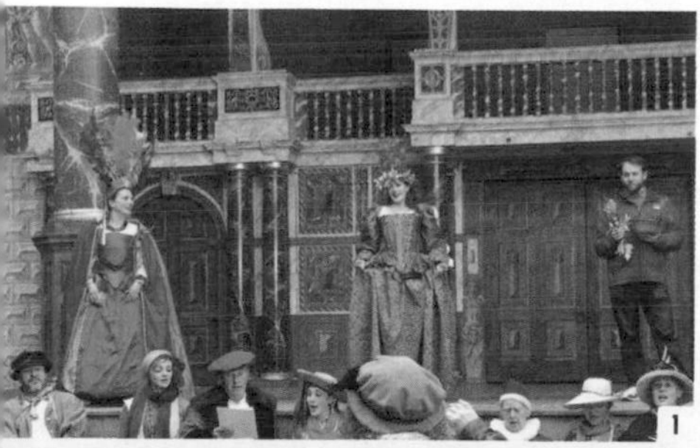
1

2

3

1 A performance at the Globe is always a lively experience.

2 The ornate and intimate Sam Wanamaker playhouse is indoors.

3 The roof of the Globe is made of water reed thatch. There has been a law banning the use of thatch in the city since the Great Fire of London in 1666, so the theatre had to have special permission to use it and had to line the roof with fire-retardant material.

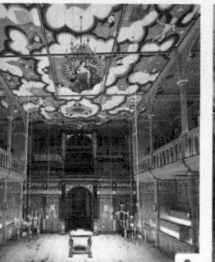

Did You Know?

The Taming of the Shrew is considered Shakespeare's first play, written before 1592.

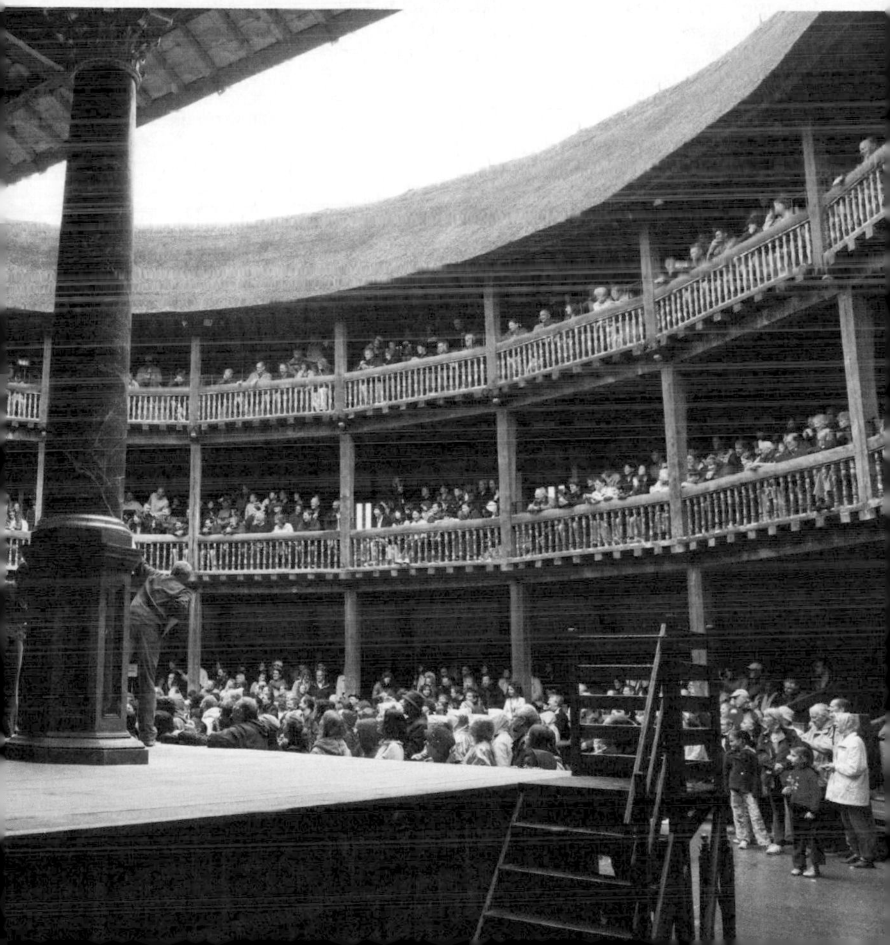

EXPERIENCE MORE

3

Southwark Cathedral

📍 M6 🏛 Montague Close SE1 🚇 London Bridge ⏰ 7:30am–6pm Mon–Fri, 8:30am–6pm Sat & Sun 🌐 cathedral.southwark.anglican.org

This church did not become a cathedral until 1905 – yet some parts of it date back to the 12th century, when the building was attached to a priory, and many of its medieval features remain. The memorials are quite fascinating and include a late-13th-century wooden effigy of a knight. John Harvard, the first benefactor of Harvard University, was baptized here in 1607 and there is a chapel named after him.

In 2000, the cathedral was restored in a multi-million-pound programme, which included the addition of new buildings housing a shop and a refectory. The exterior has been landscaped to create a herb garden and an attractive Millennium Courtyard that leads to the riverside.

4 🎭 Ⓜ 🏛

The Old Operating Theatre

📍 M6 🏛 9a St Thomas St SE1 🚇 London Bridge ⏰ 10:30am–5pm daily 🚫 15 Dec–5 Jan 🌐 oldoperatingtheatre.com

St Thomas' Hospital, one of the oldest in Britain, stood here from its foundation in the 12th century until it was moved west in 1862. At this time, nearly all of its buildings were demolished in order to make way for the railways. The women's operating theatre survived only because it had been constructed in a garret

↑ Surgical items forming a *memento mori* at The Old Operating Theatre

over the hospital church. The UK's oldest operating theatre, dating from 1822, it remained bricked up and forgotten until the 1950s. It has now been fitted out just as it would have been in the early 19th century, before the discovery of either anaesthetics or antiseptics. Another section of the garret, which was once used by the hospital apothecary to store herbs, houses a collection of traditional herbs and remedies, plus displays of antiquated medicines.

As the museum is upstairs in a historic building, wheelchair access is problematic.

5 🏛

Bankside Gallery

📍 L5 🏛 48 Hopton St SE1 🚇 Blackfriars, Southwark ⏰ 11am–6pm daily during exhibitions 🚫 1 Jan, 24–26 Dec 🌐 banksidegallery.com

This modern riverside gallery is the headquarters of two historic British societies: the

←

The tower and east end of Southwark Cathedral, built in golden sandstone and flint

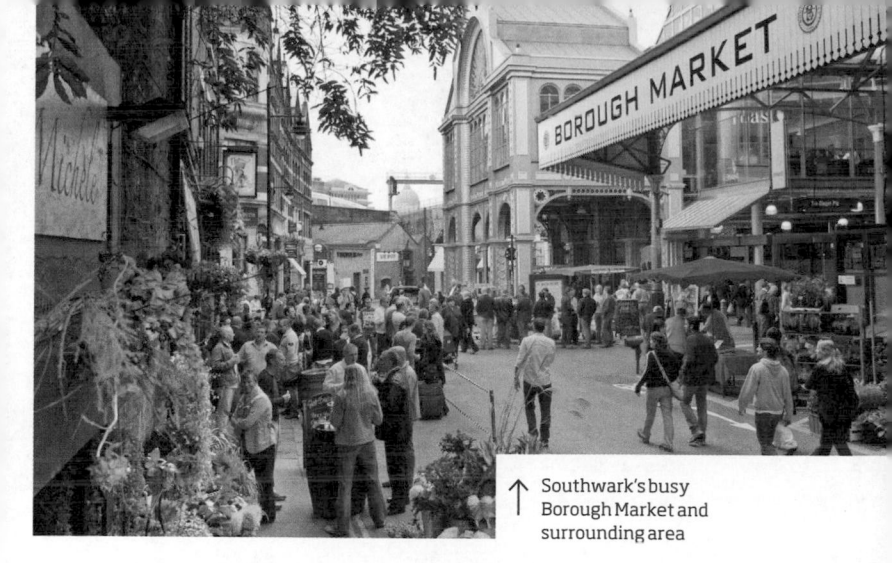

↑ Southwark's busy Borough Market and surrounding area

Royal Watercolour Society and the Royal Society of Painter-Printmakers. The members of these societies are elected by their peers in a tradition that dates back over 200 years. The exhibitions held here feature the work of both societies and many of the pieces on display are for sale. There is also a superb specialist art shop that sells both books and materials.

There is an unparalleled view of St Paul's Cathedral from the nearby pub, the Founders' Arms – built on the site of the foundry where the cathedral's bells were cast.

crowds can be huge, especially on Fridays and Saturdays), it is known for gourmet goods from Britain and Europe, as well as quality fruit and vegetables, and organic meat, fish and dairy produce. A growing number of hot food stalls, selling a tempting array of dishes from around the world, share the space with produce stalls. Food demonstrations take place in the glass atrium on Borough High Street on Thursdays and Fridays. The specialist food shops and pubs on the streets around the market are also well worth checking out.

⑥ Borough Market

📍 M6 🏠 8 Southwark St SE1 🚇 London Bridge 🕐 10am-5pm Wed-Thu, 10am-6pm Fri, 8am-5pm Sat (some stalls also 10am-5pm Mon & Tue) 🌐 boroughmarket.org.uk

Borough Market was once an exclusively wholesale fruit and vegetable market, which had its origins in medieval times. It moved to its current atmospheric position beneath the railway tracks in 1756. Today an extremely popular fine food market (beware: the

⑦ The Rose Playhouse

📍 M6 🏠 56 Park St SE1 🚇 London Bridge 🕐 10am-5pm Sat, plus performances 🌐 rosetheatre.org.uk

In 1989 the remains of the Rose theatre, dating from Elizabethan times, were discovered during excavations ahead of building work for a new office block. The Rose, built in 1587, was the first of the Bankside theatres, and it staged plays by Shakespeare and Christopher Marlowe. The site of the original Globe theatre was just over the road

on Park Street (a plaque marks the spot). Preserved in a specially designed space, with a modern building overhead, the archaeological remains are submerged in water, with lights indicating the shape of the theatre. A small volunteer-run exhibition tells the story of the excavation. The atmospheric space is also sometimes used as a small theatre – check the website for details.

Scary skeletons spook
visitors at the Clink
Prison Museum ↑

EAT

Roast

Traditional British food
at its best in a smart
dining room overlooking
Borough Market.

M6 **The Floral Hall,
Stoney St SE1** **roast-
restaurant.com**

£££

Flat Iron Square

A sociable hub for street
food and quality
independent fast food
restaurants in the
railway arches near
Borough Market.

M6 **68 Union St SE1**
flatironsquare.co.uk

£££

The Garrison

The British seasonal
menu served here is
a mixture of the
creatively modern and
the satisfyingly
traditional.

N7 **99-101
Bermondsey St SE1**
thegarrison.co.uk

£££

8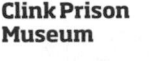

Clink Prison Museum

M6 **1 Clink St
SE1** **London Bridge**
**Jul-Sep: 10am-9pm daily;
Oct-Jun: 10am-6pm Mon-
Fri, 10am-7:30pm Sat & Sun**
clink.co.uk

The prison that was once
located here was founded
in the 12th century. It was
owned by successive Bishops
of Winchester, who lived in
the adjoining palace, of which
all that now remains is a lovely
rose window on Clink Street.
During the 15th century, the
prison became known as the
"Clink", and this has become
a British slang term for any
prison or jail cell. It closed
down in 1780.

The museum alongside
the remains of the palace
illustrates the history of the
prison. Tales are told of the
inmates incarcerated here,
including prostitutes, debtors,
and priests imprisoned by the
bishopric as heretics. Visitors
can handle instruments of
torture that leave little to the
imagination – a trip here is
not for the faint-hearted.

9

The Shard

N6 **London Bridge St
London Bridge **The
View from the Shard: Apr-
Oct: 10am-10pm daily;
Nov-Mar: 10am-10pm Thu-
Sat, 10am-7pm Sun-Wed;
last adm 1 hour before
closing** **theviewfrom
theshard.com**

Designed by Renzo Piano, the
Shard is the tallest building in
western Europe. At 310 m
(1,016 ft) high with a crystalline
façade, the 95-storey tower
houses offices, restaurants,
a five-star hotel, exclusive
apartments and the country's
highest observation gallery,
the View from the Shard.

→

The Shard, rising up
behind the visor-
shaped City Hall

Take a high-speed lift from the entrance on Joiner St to the top of the building for spectacular, unobstructed views of the capital. There are two viewing floors, the higher of which is right among the "shards" with the breeze blowing overhead.

Bermondsey Street

◎ N7 ◉ SE1 ◉ London Bridge, Borough

Bermondsey's winding streets still hold traces of its past in the form of medieval, 18th-century and Victorian buildings. Today, Bermondsey Street is home to galleries, coffee shops and a few great restaurants. The area is also famous for its antiques market, held in Bermondsey Square at the bottom end of the street. Each Friday morning from 6am, seriously committed antiques dealers trade their latest acquisitions, and the best bargains tend to go before most people are even awake.

The **Fashion and Textile Museum** at No 83 puts on a programme of exhibitions covering all aspects of fashion design, and also runs an education programme. Further along the street, White Cube Bermondsey is a major

space for international contemporary art.

Fashion and Textile Museum

◎ 11am–6pm Tue–Sat (to 8pm Thu), 11am–5pm Sun ◉ ftmlondon.org

---

City Hall

◎ O6 ◉ The Queen's Walk SE1 ◉ London Bridge ◎ 8:30am–6pm Mon–Thu, 8:30am–5:30pm Fri ◉ london.gov.uk/city-hall

The Norman Foster-designed domed glass building just by Tower Bridge is the headquarters for London's mayor and the Greater London Authority. Anyone can visit the building and head up the walkway to the second floor to look in on the assembly chamber, or sit in on Mayor's Question Time, when assembly members interrogate the mayor on London issues; this takes place ten times a year on Wednesday mornings (check website for dates). On the lower ground floor are temporary exhibitions and a café. Outside, the stone amphitheatre known as

the Scoop hosts free events in summer, including plays, music and screenings.

---

⑫ 〰 🚫 🍴 💻 🛍

HMS Belfast

◎ N6 ◉ The Queen's Walk SE1 ◉ London Bridge, Tower Hill ◎ Mar–Oct: 10am–6pm daily (last adm: 5pm); Nov–Feb: 10am–5pm (last adm: 4pm) ◎ 24–26 Dec ◉ iwm.org.uk/visits/hms-belfast

Launched in 1938 to serve in World War II, HMS *Belfast* was instrumental in the destruction of the German battle cruiser *Scharnhorst* in the battle of North Cape, and also played a role in the Normandy Landings. After the war, the battle cruiser was sent to work for the United Nations in Korea, and remained in service with the Royal Navy until 1965. The only surviving World War II cruiser, it has been used as a floating naval museum since 1971. Ideal for inquisitive children and adults alike, visitors can climb down narrow ladders to the engine room 4.5 m (15 ft) below sea level, and experience what it was like in the gun turrets during a battle. Exhibits also explore the ship's history post-World War II, including during the Cold War.

A SHORT WALK AROUND SOUTHWARK

Distance 2 km (1.25 miles) **Nearest Tube** Southwark
Time 20 minutes

Out of the jurisdiction of the City authorities, Southwark was the place for illicit pleasures from medieval times until the 18th century. The 18th and 19th centuries brought new business, and docks, warehouses and factories were built to meet the demand. Today, a riverside walk here provides spectacular views of St Paul's and takes in Tate Modern, a regenerated Borough Market, the recreation of Shakespeare's Globe Theatre and the Shard.

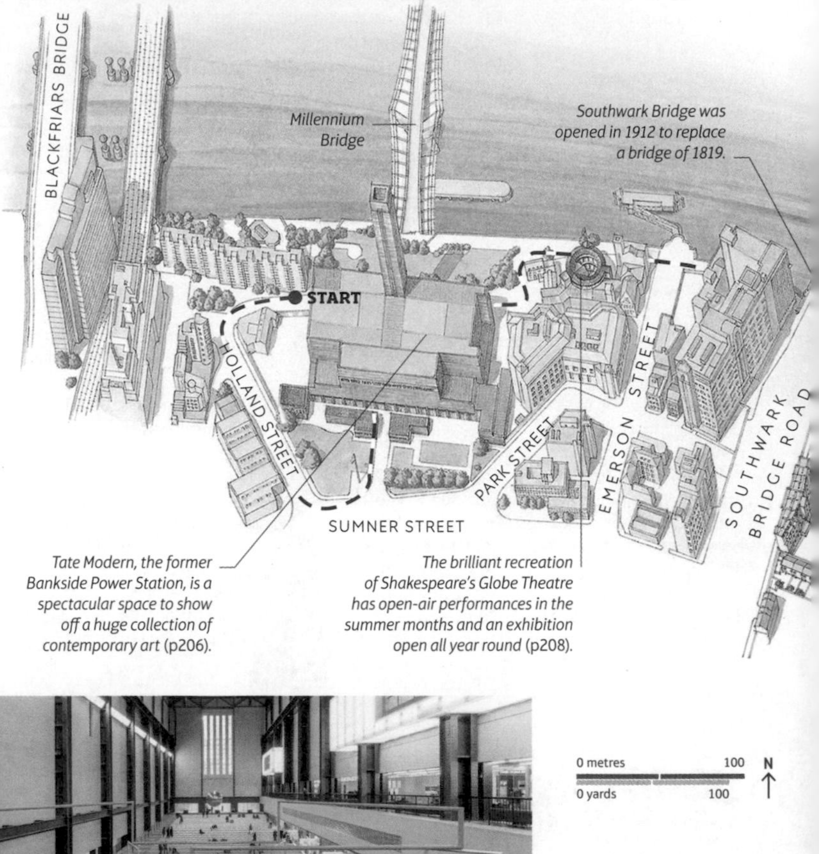

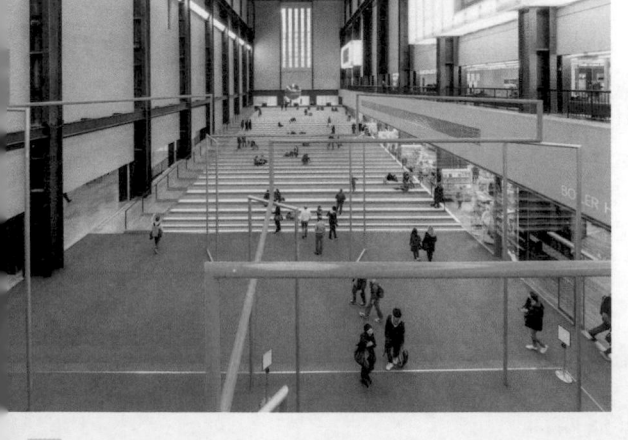

BLACKFRIARS BRIDGE
Millennium Bridge
Southwark Bridge was opened in 1912 to replace a bridge of 1819.
START
HOLLAND STREET
SUMNER STREET
PARK STREET
EMERSON STREET
SOUTHWARK BRIDGE ROAD
Tate Modern, the former Bankside Power Station, is a spectacular space to show off a huge collection of contemporary art (p206).
The brilliant recreation of Shakespeare's Globe Theatre has open-air performances in the summer months and an exhibition open all year round (p208).
0 metres 100
0 yards 100
N

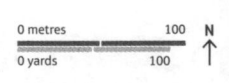

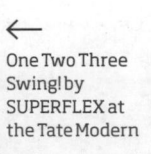

← One Two Three Swing! by SUPERFLEX at the Tate Modern

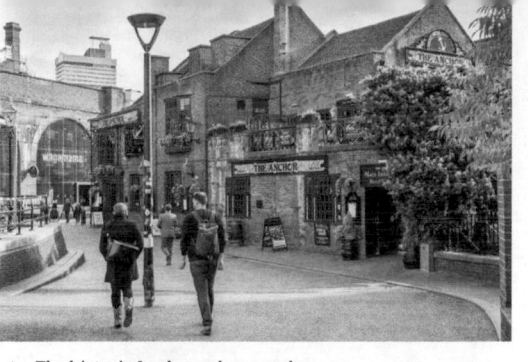

↑ The historic Anchor pub, a popular drinking establishment since the time of Shakespeare

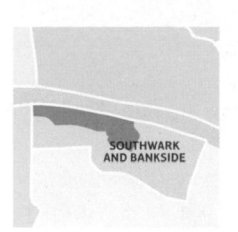

Locator Map
For more detail see p204

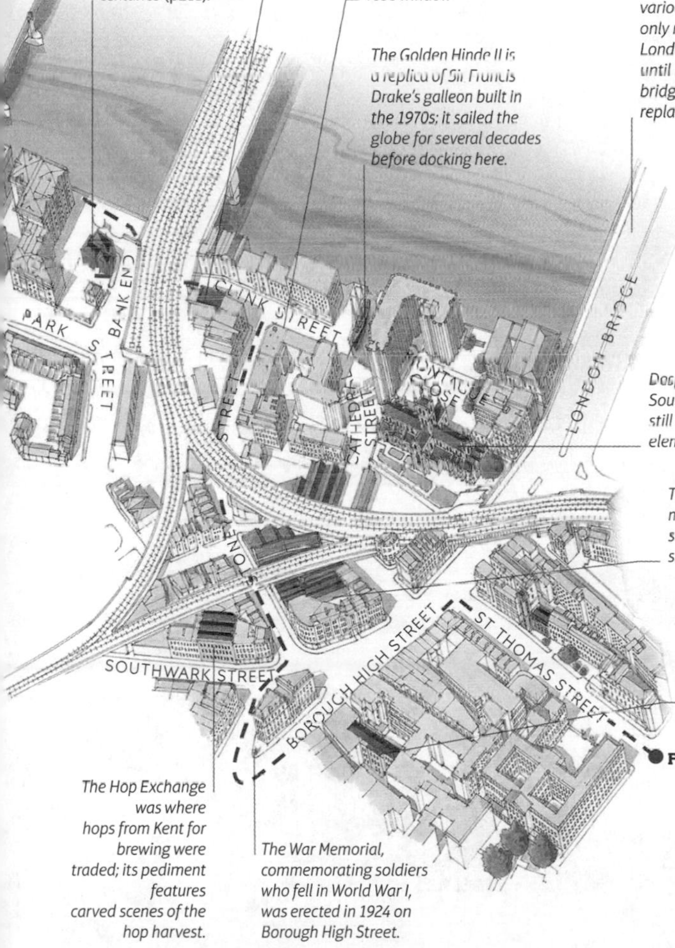

Clink Prison Museum, on the site of the notorious old prison, looks back at Southwark's colourful past (p212).

The riverside pub The Anchor has been a firm favourite for centuries (p211).

14th-century rose window

The Golden Hinde II is a replica of Sir Francis Drake's galleon built in the 1970s; it sailed the globe for several decades before docking here.

London Bridge, in its various forms, was the only river crossing in London from Roman times until 1750. The present bridge, completed in 1972, replaced the one of 1831.

Despite major alterations, Southwark Cathedral still contains medieval elements (p210).

There has been a market on or near the site of Borough Market since 1276 (p211).

The George is London's only surviving traditional galleried inn (p211).

● **FINISH**

The Hop Exchange was where hops from Kent for brewing were traded; its pediment features carved scenes of the hop harvest.

The War Memorial, commemorating soldiers who fell in World War I, was erected in 1924 on Borough High Street.

PARK STREET

BANK END

CLINK STREET

CATHEDRAL STREET

MONTAGUE CLOSE

LONDON BRIDGE

SOUTHWARK STREET

BOROUGH HIGH STREET

ST THOMAS STREET

SOUTH BANK

It was not until the 18th century that the stretch of marshy land over the river from Westminster, opposite what would later become the Victoria Embankment, was drained and developed, and referred to as the South Bank. Pleasure gardens gave way to industrialization and by the late 1830s the riverfront was dominated by the Lion Brewery, which stood here until it was demolished in 1949, by which time it had already been abandoned. After World War II the land lay bomb-damaged and derelict until London County Council decided to develop it for the 1951 Festival of Britain. Conceived as a much-needed tonic for a war-worn population, a large exhibition site full of cultural and leisure venues and installations was created for the festival. The only permanent construction was the Royal Festival Hall, and the Southbank Centre, which now dominates the site, grew up around that building. It was in the spirit of the Festival of Britain that the new millennium was marked on the South Bank with the raising of the London Eye, a gigantic ferris wheel.

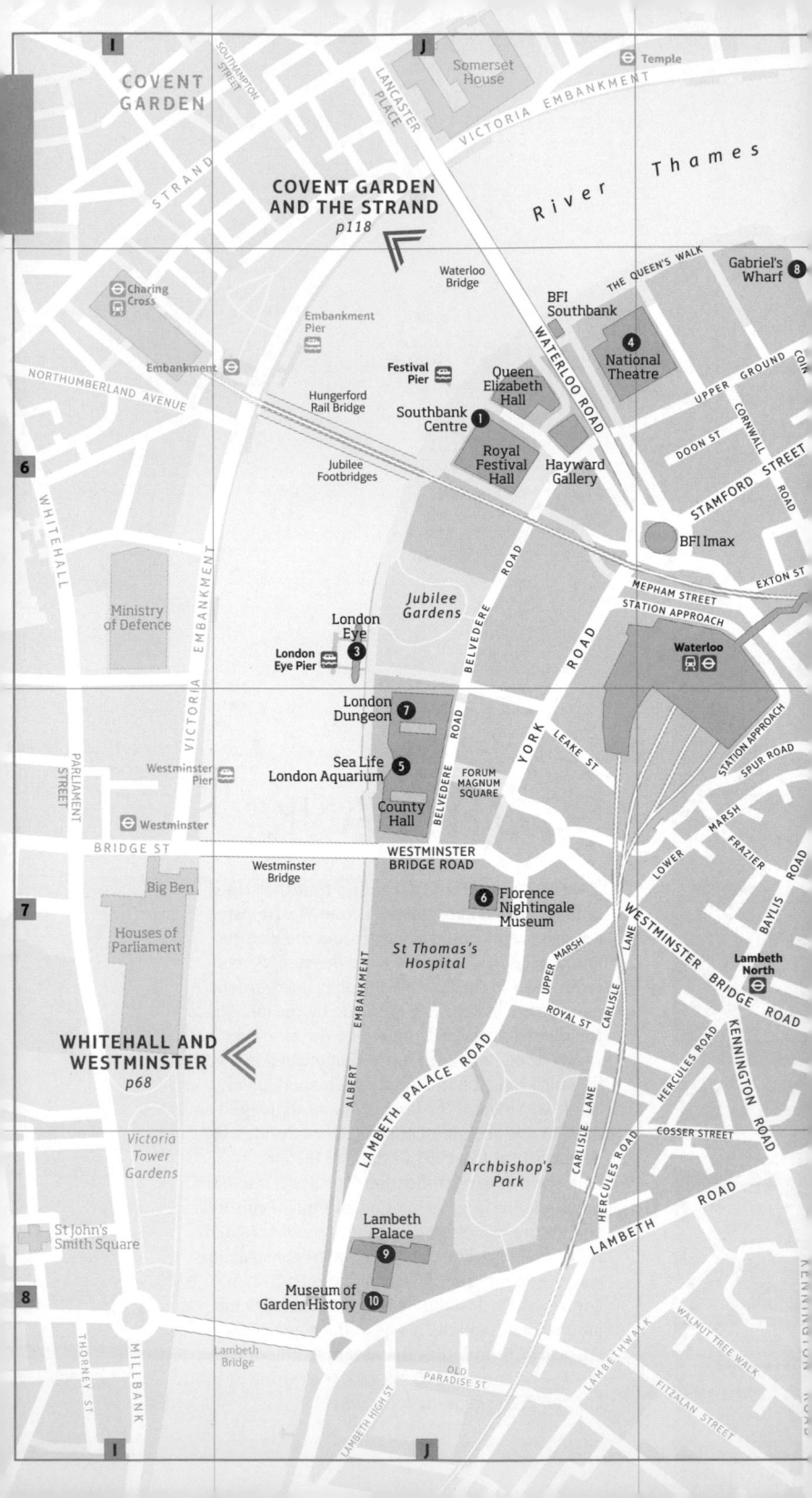

COVENT GARDEN
AND THE STRAND
p118

WHITEHALL AND
WESTMINSTER
p68

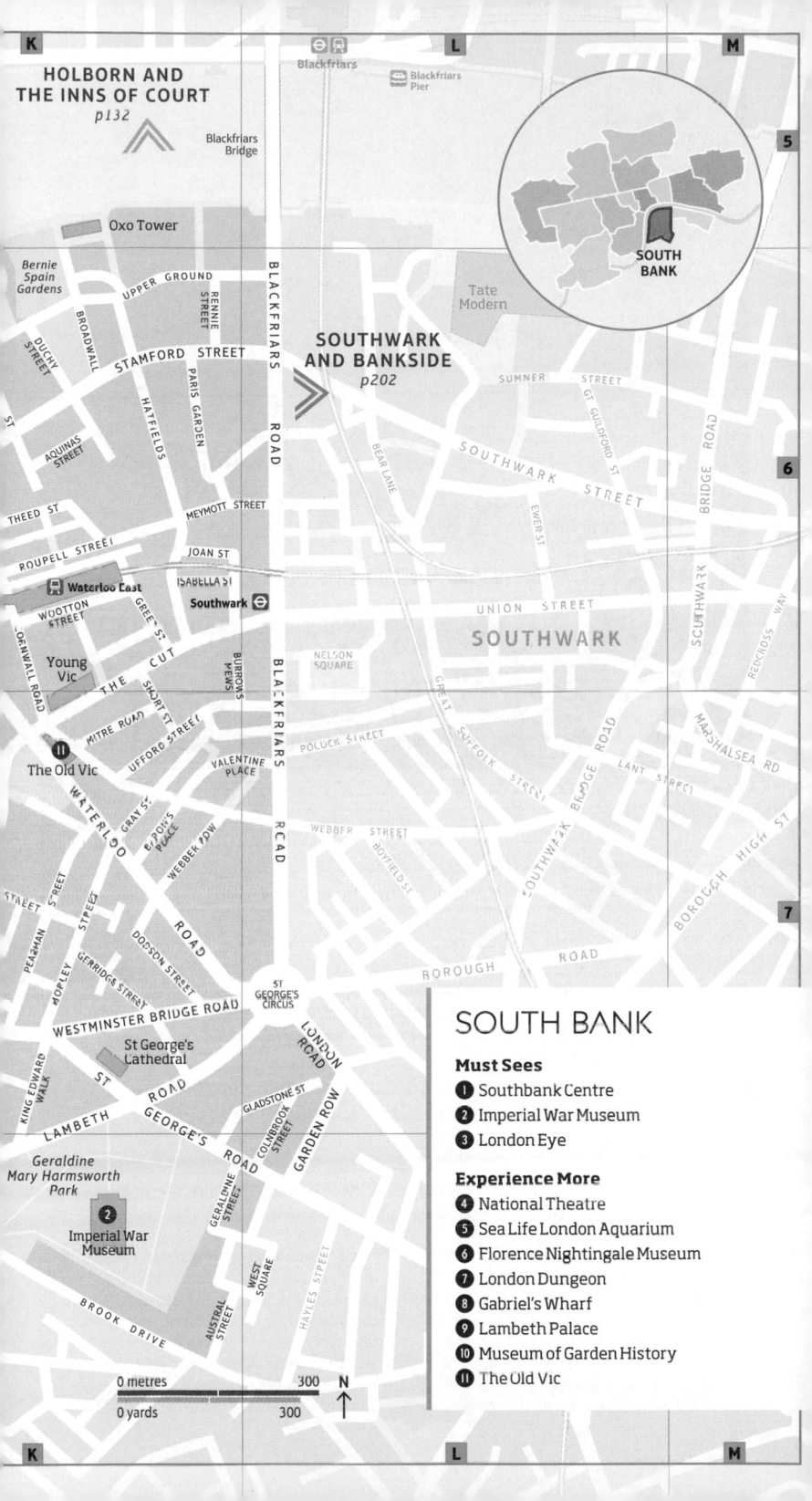

Blackfriars

Blackfriars Pier

L

M

5

HOLBORN AND THE INNS OF COURT
p132

Blackfriars Bridge

Oxo Tower

Tate Modern

SOUTH BANK

SOUTHWARK AND BANKSIDE
p202

Bernie Spain Gardens

UPPER GROUND

BLACKFRIARS ROAD

RENNIE STREET

STAMFORD STREET

DUCHY STREET

BROADWALL

ST

PARIS GARDEN

HATFIELDS

SUMNER STREET

GT GUILDFORD ST

SOUTHWARK STREET

BRIDGE ROAD

6

AQUINAS STREET

BEAR LANE

EWER ST

THEED ST

MEYMOTT STREET

POUPELL STREET

JOAN ST

Waterloo East

ISABELLA ST

Southwark

SOUTHWARK

SCROSS WAY

UNION STREET

SOUTHWARK

WOOTTON STREET

CORNWALL ROAD

THE CUT

GREET ST

SHORT ST STREET

BURROWS MEWS

BLACKFRIARS ROAD

NELSON SQUARE

Young Vic

MITRE ROAD

UFFORD STREET

VALENTINE PLACE

POLLOCK STREET

GREAT SUFFOLK STREET

SOUTHWARK BRIDGE ROAD

LANT STREET

MARSHALSEA RD

The Old Vic

WATERLOO

GRAY ST

ST PHILIP'S PLACE

WEBBER ROW

WEBBER STREET

BOLFIELD ST

BOROUGH HIGH ST

7

STREET

STREET

PEARMAN ST

MORLEY ST

GERRIDGE STREET

DODSON STREET

WESTMINSTER BRIDGE ROAD

ST GEORGE'S CIRCUS

LONDON ROAD

BOROUGH ROAD

St George's Cathedral

KING EDWARD WALK

ST GEORGE'S ROAD

GLADSTONE ST

COLNBROOK STREET

GARDEN ROW

LAMBETH ROAD

GERALDINE STREET

Geraldine Mary Harmsworth Park

Imperial War Museum

BROOK DRIVE

AUSTRAL STREET

WEST SQUARE

HAYLES STREET

0 metres 300
0 yards 300
N

SOUTH BANK

Must Sees

1 Southbank Centre
2 Imperial War Museum
3 London Eye

Experience More

4 National Theatre
5 Sea Life London Aquarium
6 Florence Nightingale Museum
7 London Dungeon
8 Gabriel's Wharf
9 Lambeth Palace
10 Museum of Garden History
11 The Old Vic

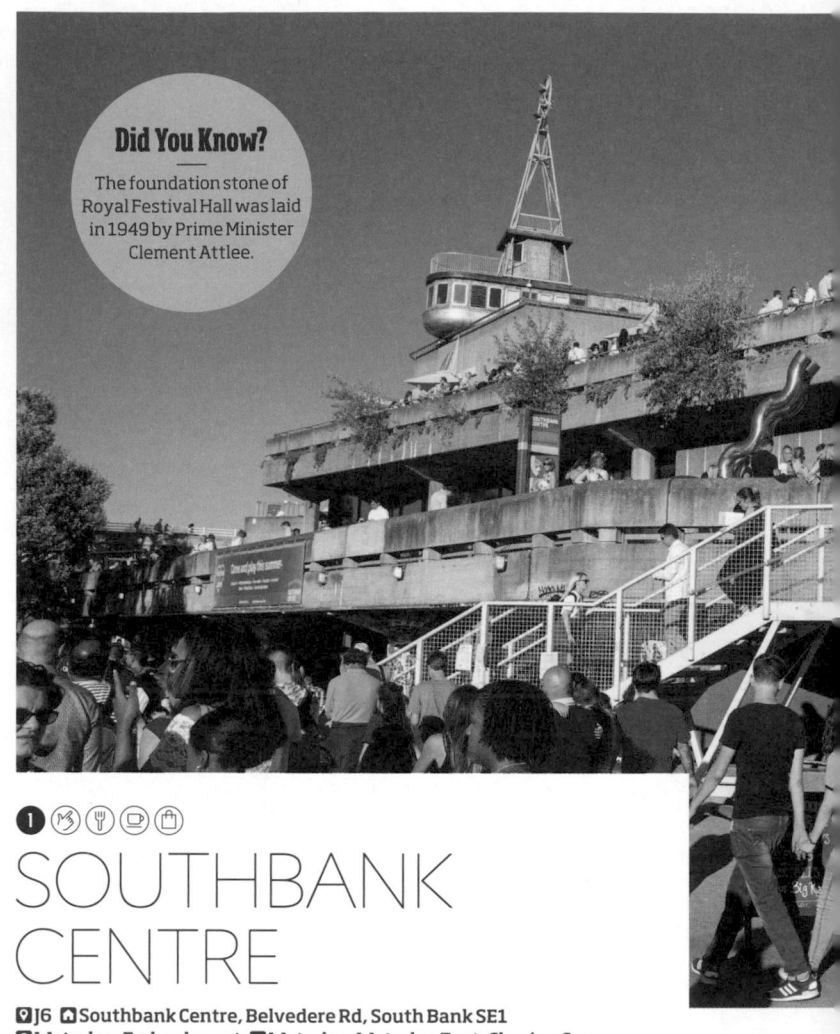

❶ 🛼 🍴 🖥 🏠

SOUTHBANK CENTRE

📍 J6 🏠 Southbank Centre, Belvedere Rd, South Bank SE1
🚇 Waterloo, Embankment 🚆 Waterloo, Waterloo East, Charing Cross
⛴ Festival Pier, every 40 min and London Eye Pier, every 20 min Mon-Fri 🌐 southbankcentre.co.uk

With a major art gallery and three world-class auditoriums for music and dance lined up along the river, the Southbank Centre is one of London's pre-eminent cultural and performance venues.

London's high-profile, much-respected and visited multi-dimensional arts centre takes centre stage among the other great arts institutions on the South Bank: the National Theatre and the British Film Institute. The Southbank Centre itself comprises four main venues: the Royal Festival Hall, the Hayward Gallery, the Queen Elizabeth Hall and the Purcell Room. The centre's always buzzing, with bustling bars and restaurants slotted into and between the terraces, platforms, walkways and rooftops of this concrete complex. There are always innumerable visitors making their way to performances, primarily of classical music but also of opera, folk, world music and all kinds of contemporary leftfield genres. Comedy, talks and dance all feature too, while there is a multitude of regular festivals, seasons and weekends staged here, including the London Jazz Festival, Women of the World (WOW) Festival, the London Literature Festival and the New Music Biennial.

↑ Crowds enjoying the sun outside the Royal Festival Hall

↑ Strolling along the riverfront past the Southbank Centre, towards the London Eye

1951 FESTIVAL OF BRITAIN

The 1951 Festival of Britain was timed to mark the centenary of the Great Exhibition but also to provide some optimism and cultural celebration in the aftermath of war. The wharves and factories that once stood on this site suffered considerable bomb damage during World War II, so the area was cleared for the event and a set of weird and wonderful temporary structures were erected in their place, forming a kind of cultural theme park. The one permanent structure was the Royal Festival Hall.

The South Bank

Hugging the curve of the River Thames, the Southbank Centre is a sprawling complex, with the Royal Festival Hall at its heart. Just a little further along the bank is the enormous London Eye and County Hall, home to other top attractions the London Dungeon and the London Aquarium. There is plenty to entertain here, making it perfect for a gentle afternoon.

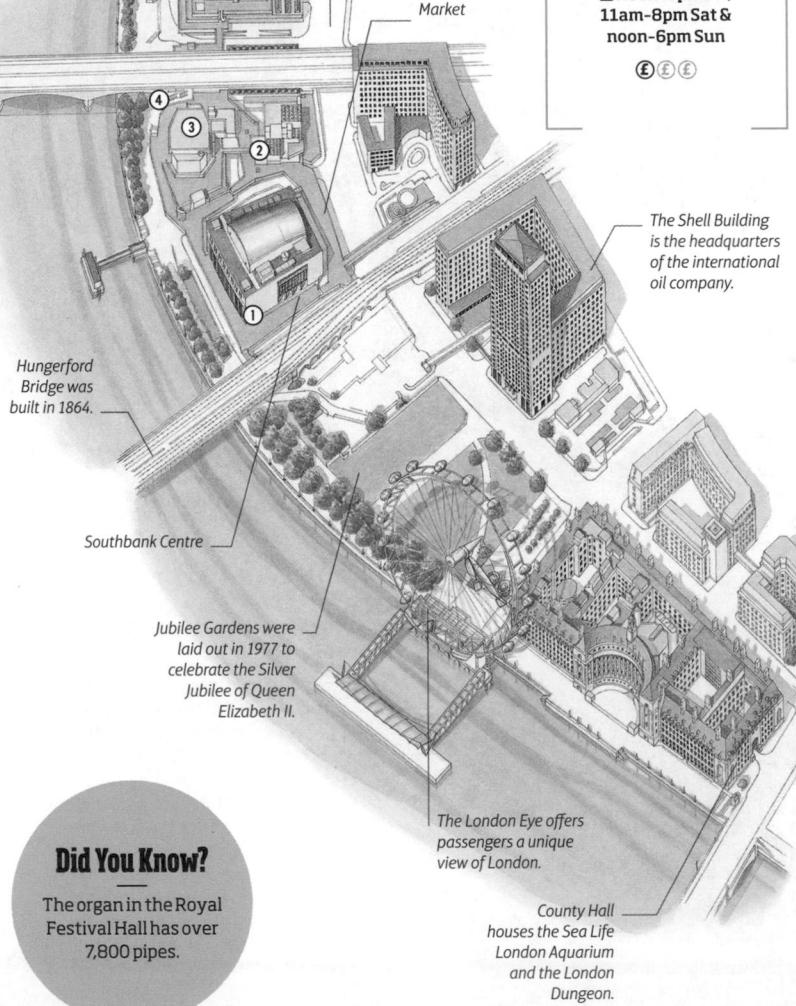

Plays at the National Theatre range from classics to modern works.

Waterloo Bridge was designed by Sir Giles Gilbert Scott.

Southbank Centre Food Market

The Shell Building is the headquarters of the international oil company.

Hungerford Bridge was built in 1864.

Southbank Centre

Jubilee Gardens were laid out in 1977 to celebrate the Silver Jubilee of Queen Elizabeth II.

The London Eye offers passengers a unique view of London.

County Hall houses the Sea Life London Aquarium and the London Dungeon.

Did You Know?

The organ in the Royal Festival Hall has over 7,800 pipes.

[1] The Southbank Centre Food Market takes place on Fridays, Saturdays and Sundays, in the square behind the Royal Festival Hall.

[2] The concrete exterior of the Hayward Gallery is well suited to the modern works that it displays within. The building's stark design is a landmark of Brutalist architecture.

[3] BFI Southbank, previously the National Film Theatre, was originally established to show historic films; today it offers an eclectic programme of films from around the world.

① 🍽 🖥 🏠
Royal Festival Hall

📍 J6

With its 2,500-seat auditorium, this modernist building is the Southbank Centre's largest concert hall and the city's principal classical music venue. The airy halls outside the auditorium house the open-sided Clore Ballroom, where free concerts are frequently staged in sight of the casual bar. The foyer is also used for exhibitions and contains a café whilst above is the Skylon restaurant. In summer, temporary venues and bars are installed and DJ-led parties take place on the riverside terrace.

② 🎨 🖥 🏠
Hayward Gallery

📍 J6

Reopened in 2018 after a lengthy refurbishment, the Hayward Gallery, an icon of 1960s Brutalist architecture with its slabby grey concrete exterior and its distinctive and pyramidal glass roof panels, is one of London's foremost venues for large contemporary art exhibitions. The gallery exhibits paintings, drawings, photography, sculpture, installation art and more, by interesting, innovative and internationally renowned artists from around the world. Paul Klee, Andreas Gursky, Bridget Riley and Anthony Caro are among the artists who have had exhibitions here.

③
Queen Elizabeth Hall and Purcell Room

📍 J6

After three years of renovations, the Queen Elizabeth Hall reopened in 2018. Smaller orchestral performances, genre-bending music and dance, stand-up comedy, spoken word poetry and literary events are all staged in this relatively intimate, comfortable concert venue. The Purcell Room, in the same building, is smaller still and also hosts readings, while its music events tend to be small ensembles, piano recitals, chamber music and the like. The foyer is also regularly used as a performance venue, hosting free events day and night plus a club night on Fridays.

④ 🍽 🍷 🏠
BFI Southbank

📍 J6 🌐 bfi.org.uk

BFI Southbank, previously the National Film Theatre, was established in 1953 and though adjacent to the Southbank Centre it's not actually part of it. It has four cinema screens and offers a huge and diverse selection of films, both British and international. It also holds regular screenings of rare and restored films and television programmes and has a free Mediatheque where the BFI's archives can be browsed.

↑ Military aircraft on display in the main atrium at the Imperial War Museum

② 🏍 🍴 🖥 🎒

IMPERIAL WAR MUSEUM

📍K8 🏠Lambeth Rd SE1 🚇Waterloo, Lambeth North, Elephant & Castle
🚆Waterloo, Elephant & Castle 🕐10am–6pm daily 🚫24–26 Dec
🌐iwm.org.uk

With great creativity and sensitivity, the immersive exhibitions at the terrific Imperial War Museum provide a fascinating insight into the history of war and themes of conflict.

Inevitably the two World Wars feature heavily at the Imperial War Museum but they are covered in innovative ways. In the First World War galleries, there are original exhibits such as a recreated trench, while some of the most fascinating Second World War exhibits relate more to the impact on the lives of people at home, than to the business of fighting. One display focuses on the experiences of a London family, including the effects of food rationing and regular air raids. The Holocaust Exhibition is a particularly poignant experience while other highly original permanent displays include Curiosities of War, full of unexpected items such as a wooden training horse from the First World War. More conventionally, there are tanks, artillery and aircraft, including a Mark 1 Spitfire and a Harrier jet, on show in the main atrium.

> 💬 **INSIDER TIP**
> **Get a Guide**
>
> There is a guide book to the museum aimed specifically at children aged 7 and above. There are also daily 40-minute tours (£10, children £5) at noon and 3pm that introduce the museum's collections. Tickets must be bought in person.

① The museum is housed in what used to be the Bethlehem Royal Hospital for the Insane (commonly known as "Bedlem"), built in 1811.

② Military hardware on display includes a T-34 World-War-II-era Russian tank captured in 1973 by Israeli forces.

③ Hanging in the atrium is the famous Battle of Britain fighter plane, the Spitfire, from 1940.

80 spokes made from 6 km (3.7 miles) of tensioned cable support the wheel.

The wheel rim was floated down the Thames in sections.

The glass capsules are mounted on the outside of the rim.

The Eye turns slowly enough that the capsules are boarded while they are moving.

↑ Illustration of the London Eye, on the South Bank

THE LONDON EYE

📍J6 🏛 Jubilee Gardens SE1 🚇 Waterloo, Westminster 🕐 Apr–Jun: 10am–9pm; Jul–Aug: 10am–9:30pm; Sep–Mar: 10am–8:30pm (times can vary, check website) 🗓 25 Dec and mid-Jan for maintenance 🌐 londoneye.com

Stunning views of London's historic skyline can be had from the glass capsules of the London Eye. Situated right beside the River Thames, visitors enjoy a 360-degree view of the city.

The London Eye is a 135-m- (443-ft-) high observation wheel. Opened in 2000 as part of London's millennium celebrations, it immediately became one of the city's most recognizable landmarks, notable not only for its size, but for its circularity amid the block-shaped buildings flanking it. Thirty-two capsules, each holding up to 25 people, take a gentle 30-minute round trip. On a clear day, the Eye affords a 40-km (25-mile) view, which sweeps over the capital in all directions and on to the countryside beyond.

BOOKING TICKETS

Queues for the London Eye can be long so pre-book your tickets online to secure a timed slot and to make the most of online offers. The Merlin's Magical London Pass combines a trip on the London Eye with another top London attraction such as the London Dungeon. Print your tickets at home to save time.

↑ A capsule mid-tour with unimpeded views of the city

↑ Taking a selfie against the London skyline

↑ The London Eye peering over the Thames

EXPERIENCE MORE

4

National Theatre

📍J6 🚇 South Bank SE1 🚆 Waterloo 🕐 9:30am-11pm Mon-Sat (Sherling Walkway closes 7:30pm), noon-6pm Sun 🚫 Good Fri, 24 & 25 Dec
🌐 nationaltheatre.org.uk

Even if you don't want to see a play, this complex is worth a visit, especially for a backstage tour. These are offered Monday to Saturday, and it is advisable to book in advance. You can also get a glimpse of the backstage area from the Sherling High-Level Walkway (entrance near the Dorfman theatre), which runs above the prop-building areas.

Sir Denys Lasdun's building opened in 1976 after 200 years of debate: should there be a national theatre and, if so, where? The theatre company was formed in 1963, under Laurence (later Lord) Olivier. The largest of the three theatres is named after him; the others are the Dorfman and the Lyttleton. Prestigious productions are streamed live to theatres and cinemas all over the UK via the National Theatre Live initiative.

5

Sea Life London Aquarium

📍J7 🏛 County Hall, Westminster Bridge Rd SE1 🚆 Waterloo 🕐 10am-6pm Mon-Fri, 9:30am-7pm Sat & Sun (last adm: 6pm) 🌐 visit sealife.com/london

Once the home of London's elected government, County Hall now houses the Sea Life London Aquarium and London Dungeon (*p228*), alongside a hotel, restaurants and other themed attractions.

The aquarium is home to myriad aquatic species from all over the world, including stingrays, turtles, jellyfish, starfish (which you can stroke) and penguins. There's a 25-m (82-ft) glass tunnel walkway through a tropical ocean environment, and a large tank housing numerous shark species, which you can view from several levels. Book ahead to guarantee entry and skip large queues.

↑ The controversial Brutalist architecture of the National Theatre

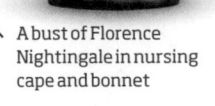

↑ A bust of Florence Nightingale in nursing cape and bonnet

6

Florence Nightingale Museum

◉ J7 **⌂** 2 Lambeth Palace Rd SE1 **⊖** Waterloo, Westminster **◷** 10am–5pm daily **⌚** 1 Jan, 23–26 Dec **w** florence-nightingale. co.uk

This determined woman captured the nation's imagination as the "Lady of the Lamp" who nursed the wounded soldiers of the Crimean War (1853–6). She founded the country's first school of nursing at old St Thomas' Hospital in 1860, and revolutionized modern nursing. She was also an advocate for women in the workplace.

Sited near the entrance to St Thomas' Hospital, this museum gives an account of Nightingale's career through displays of original documents and personal memorabilia. They illustrate her life and the developments she pioneered in health care, until her death in 1910 at the age of 90. Tours are led on Tuesdays at 3:30pm.

→

Riverside shopping and refreshment at Gabriel's Wharf

7

London Dungeon

◉ J7 **⌂** County Hall, Westminster Bridge Rd SE1 **⊖** Waterloo **◷** 10am–5pm Mon–Fri & Sun (from 11am Thu), 10am–6pm Sat; extended hours in school holidays **w** thedungeons.com

This scary attraction is a great hit with older children. Illustrating the most bloodthirsty events in British history with live actors and special effects, the dungeon plays strictly for terror, and screams abound during the 90-minute tour. Gory scenes recount tales of such characters as Guy Fawkes and Jack the Ripper. Don't miss the Tyrant Boat Ride along a black River Thames to find out what happened to Tudor Queen Anne Boleyn and her co-conspirators.

8

Gabriel's Wharf

◉ K6 **⌂** 56 Upper Ground SE1 **⊖** Waterloo

This pleasant enclave of boutiques, craft shops and cafés was the product of a long and stormy debate over the future of what was once an industrial riverside area. Residents of Waterloo strongly opposed various schemes for office developments before a community association was able to acquire the site in 1984 and build cooperative housing.

Adjoining the market area is a small public garden with grass to sit on and a riverside walkway with fine views of the City. The Oxo Tower to the east was adapted from an older power station in 1928 to surreptitiously advertise a well-known meat extract by means of its window shapes. It now houses galleries and design shops on the lower floors and a restaurant and bar on the top floor.

GREAT VIEW
Waterloo Bridge

Making any Londoner's list of favourite views is this one from a busy bridge spanning the Thames. Whether you look up or down river, the scene in front of you is a reminder of the beauty of Britain's capital city.

↑ The centuries-old Lambeth Palace and its grounds

Lambeth Palace

Q J8 **A** SE1 **E** Lambeth North, Westminster, Waterloo, Vauxhall **C** For tours only **W** archbishopof canterbury.org

This Grade-I listed palace has housed Archbishops of Canterbury since the 13th century and today remains the archbishop's official London residence. The chapel and its undercroft contain elements from the 13th century, but a large part of the rest of the building is far more recent. It has been frequently restored, most recently by Edward Blore in 1828. The Tudor gatehouse, however, dates from 1485 and is one of London's most familiar riverside landmarks.

The garden, planted with many mature trees, is open in summer occasionally, while you can visit the palace year-round by pre-booking a place on a guided tour (the website has dates and times).

Until the first Westminster Bridge was built, the horse ferry that operated between here and Millbank was a principal river crossing. The revenues from it went to the archbishop, who received compensation when the bridge opened in 1750.

Museum of Garden History

Q J8 **A** Lambeth Palace Rd SE1 **E** Waterloo, Lambeth North, Westminster **C** 10:30am–5pm Sun–Fri, 10:30–4pm Sat **W** garden museum.org.uk

The world's first museum of garden history is housed in the restored church of St Mary of Lambeth Palace, where it is set around a central knot garden. In the grounds are the tombs of John Tradescant, father and son, who, as well as being gardeners to Charles I and Charles II, were adventurous plant hunters and collectors of curiosities. The tomb of William Bligh of *The Bounty*, the ship set adrift in the Pacific Ocean after the fateful mutiny, can also be seen here. Coincidentally, his vessel had been on a plant-collecting voyage.

The museum presents a history of gardening in Britain, including objects collected by the Tradescants, and an archive of garden design. It also runs a programme of exhibitions, events and lectures, and has an excellent shop and café.

The Old Vic

Q K7 **A** Waterloo Rd SE1 **E** Waterloo **C** For performances and tours **W** oldvictheatre.com

This splendid building dates back to 1818, changing its name to the Royal Victoria in 1833 in honour of the future queen. The theatre became a centre for music hall, the immensely popular Victorian entertainment. In 1912, Lillian Baylis became manager and from 1914 to 1923 staged all of Shakespeare's plays here.

The National Theatre (*p227*), founded in the 1960s, was formerly based at this site. In 2003 the Old Vic Theatre Company was set up as the resident company. There are cheap seats for younger people and pantomimes at Christmas. Theatre tours (which can be booked online) are fascinating, full of backstage snippets and anecdotes.

Did You Know?

Despite the fact that it was named in her honour, Queen Victoria only visited the Old Vic once, aged 14.

CHELSEA AND BATTERSEA

Chelsea was last in vogue in the 1960s when showy young shoppers, including the Rolling Stones, paraded along the King's Road. Formerly a riverside village, it first became fashionable in Tudor times with Henry VIII liking it so much that he had a small palace (long vanished) built here. In the 18th century it featured renowned riverside pleasure gardens, painted by Canaletto. Later artists, including Turner, Whistler and Rossetti, were attracted by the river views from Cheyne Walk over to Battersea. From the mid-19th century those views featured picturesque Battersea Park, whose landscaping was enhanced in 1951 when it too was laid out as pleasure gardens for the Festival of Britain. In graceless but impressive contrast, just east of Chelsea Bridge, the colossal chimneys of Battersea Power Station clouded the skies with smoke between its opening in 1933 and its decommissioning in 1983. Decades of failed bids to make use of the vast site – including turning it into a theme park and football stadium – ensued until a Malaysian consortium bought it for £400 million in 2012. It is now part of London's largest area of urban regeneration, stretching down to Vauxhall, featuring apartment blocks, shops and restaurants.

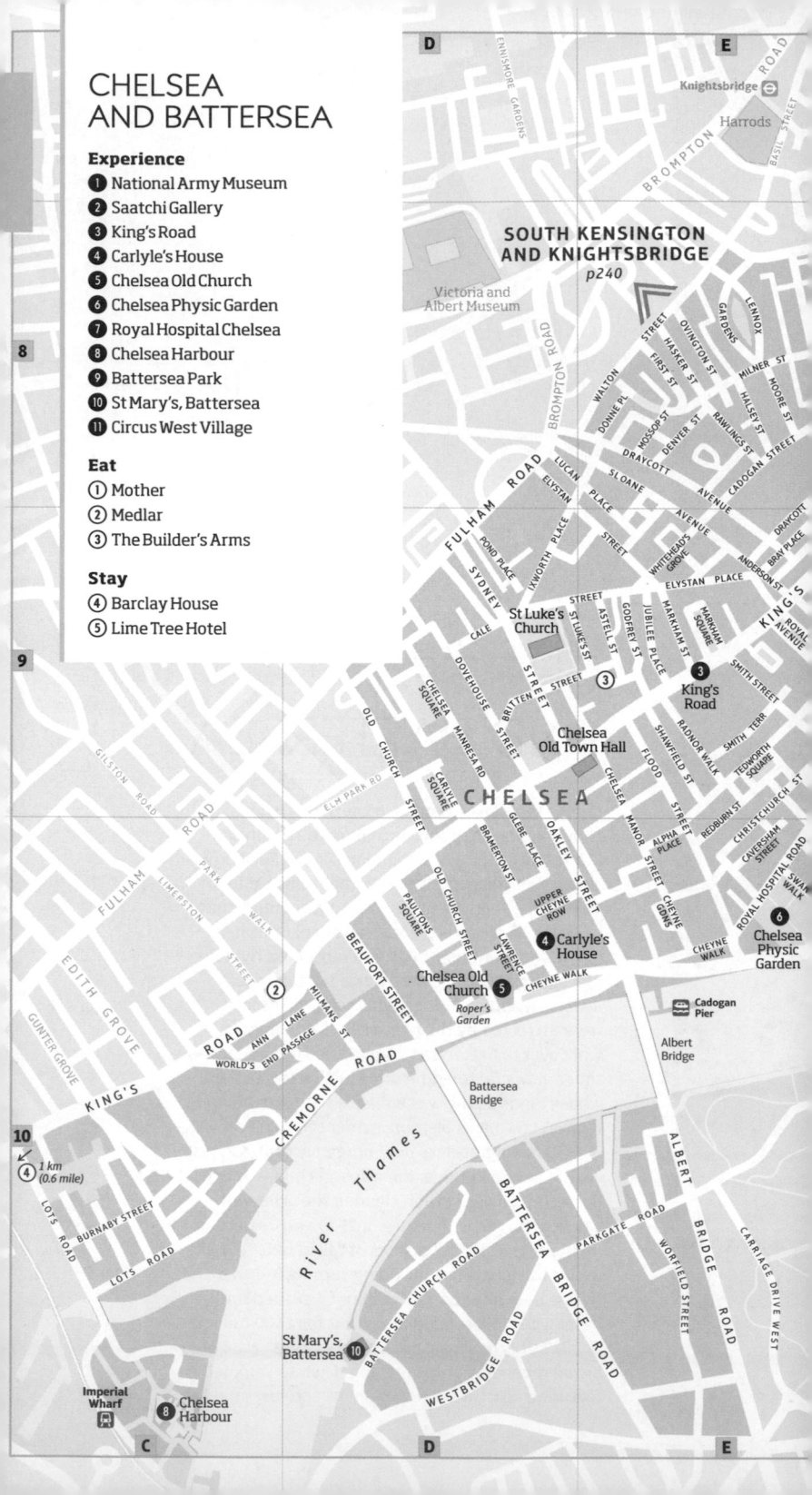

CHELSEA AND BATTERSEA

Experience

1. National Army Museum
2. Saatchi Gallery
3. King's Road
4. Carlyle's House
5. Chelsea Old Church
6. Chelsea Physic Garden
7. Royal Hospital Chelsea
8. Chelsea Harbour
9. Battersea Park
10. St Mary's, Battersea
11. Circus West Village

Eat

1. Mother
2. Medlar
3. The Builder's Arms

Stay

4. Barclay House
5. Lime Tree Hotel

Knightsbridge

Harrods

SOUTH KENSINGTON AND KNIGHTSBRIDGE
p240

Victoria and Albert Museum

St Luke's Church

③

King's Road 3

Chelsea Old Town Hall

CHELSEA

④ Carlyle's House

Chelsea Old Church 5

②

Roper's Garden

Chelsea Physic Garden 6

Cadogan Pier

Albert Bridge

Battersea Bridge

River Thames

Imperial Wharf

Chelsea Harbour 8

St Mary's, Battersea 10

1 km (0.6 mile)

④

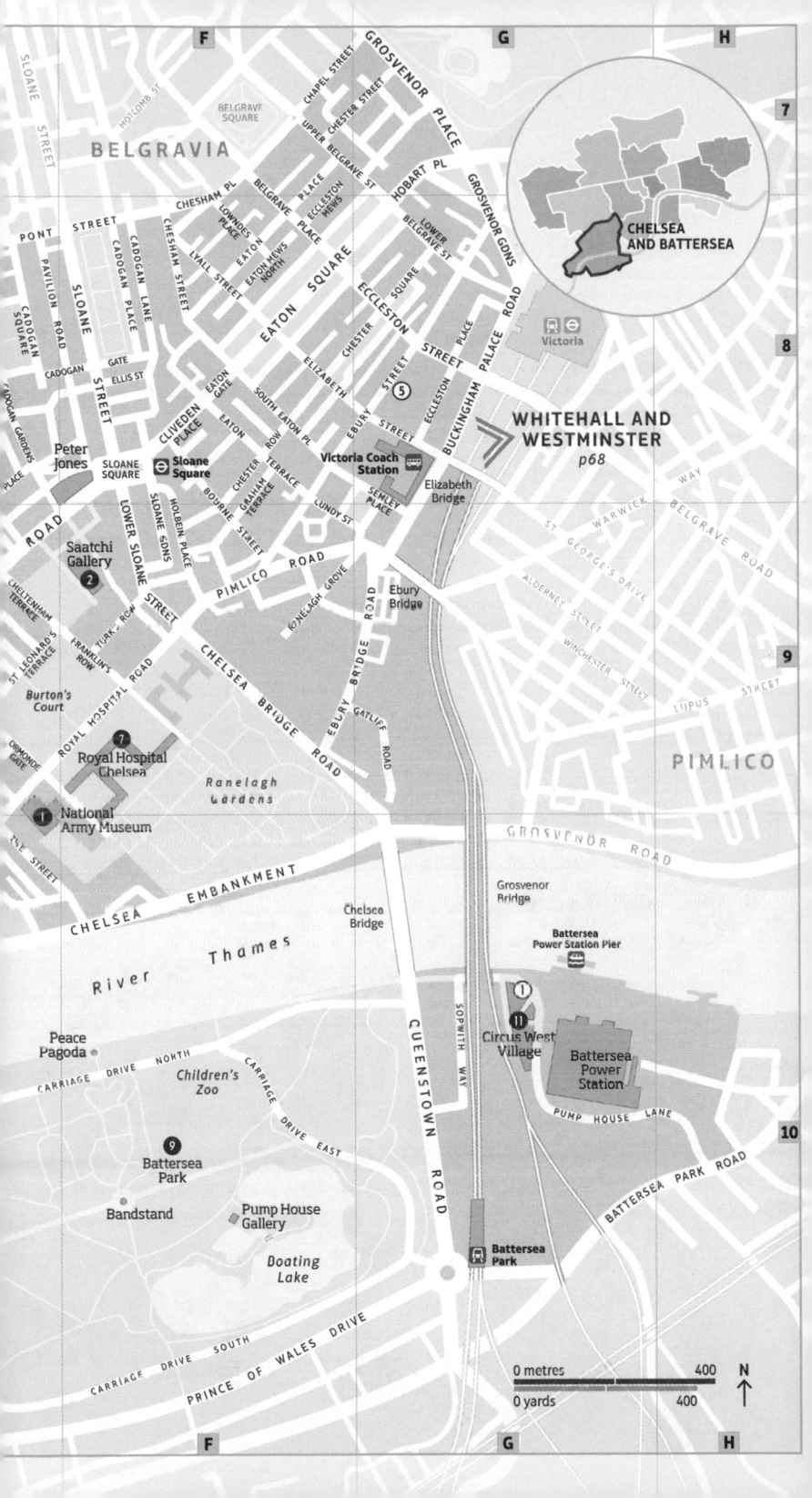

F **G** **H**

7

SLOANE STREET

HOLBEIN ST

BELGRAVE SQUARE

CHAPEL STREET

GROSVENOR PLACE

CHELSEA
AND BATTERSEA

BELGRAVIA

UPPER CHESTER ST

CHESHAM PL

BELGRAVE PLACE

HOBART PL

GROSVENOR PLACE

PONT STREET

CADOGAN PLACE

CHESHAM STREET

ECCLESTON MEWS

LOWER BELGRAVE ST

LOWNDES PLACE

PLACE

LYALL STREET

EATON MEWS NORTH

LOWER BELGRAVE ST

GROSVENOR GDNS

8

Victoria

CADOGAN LANE

CADOGAN SQUARE

PAVILION ROAD

SLOANE STREET

CADOGAN GATE

ELLIS ST

EATON GATE

EATON SQUARE

ELIZABETH STREET

CHESTER STREET

ECCLESTON STREET

SQUARE

CHESTER SQUARE

ECCLESTON PLACE

BUCKINGHAM PALACE ROAD

**WHITEHALL AND
WESTMINSTER**
p68

WAY

CADOGAN GARDENS

Peter
Jones

SLOANE
SQUARE

**Sloane
Square**

SOUTH EATON PL

EATON ROW

CHESTER TERRACE

GRAHAM TERRACE

CUNDY ST

SEMLEY PLACE

EBURY STREET

ECCLESTON STREET

PLACE

**Victoria Coach
Station**

Elizabeth
Bridge

ST GEORGES DRIVE

WARWICK WAY

BELGRAVE ROAD

9

ROAD

LOWER SLOANE STREET

Saatchi
Gallery
2

HOLBEIN PLACE

BOURNE STREET

PIMLICO ROAD

CHELSEA BRIDGE ROAD

RANELAGH GROVE

EBURY BRIDGE ROAD

Ebury
Bridge

GATLIFF ROAD

ALDERNEY STREET

WINCHESTER STREET

LUPUS STREET

ST

CHELTENHAM TERRACE

YORK RD ROW

FRANKLIN'S ROW

ST LEONARD'S TERRACE

*Burton's
Court*

ROYAL HOSPITAL ROAD

7
Royal Hospital
Chelsea

*Ranelagh
Gardens*

EBURY BRIDGE

PIMLICO

ORMONDE GATE

1 National
Army Museum

TITE STREET

CHELSEA EMBANKMENT

River Thames

Chelsea
Bridge

Chelsea
Bridge

QUEENSTOWN ROAD

SOPWITH WAY

GROSVENOR ROAD

Grosvenor
Bridge

**Battersea
Power Station Pier**

1

11
Circus West
Village

Battersea
Power
Station

Peace
Pagoda

CARRIAGE DRIVE NORTH

*Children's
Zoo*

CARRIAGE DRIVE EAST

PUMP HOUSE LANE

BATTERSEA PARK ROAD

9
Battersea
Park

Bandstand

Pump House
Gallery

*Boating
Lake*

**Battersea
Park**

10

CARRIAGE DRIVE SOUTH

PRINCE OF WALES DRIVE

| 0 metres | 400 |
| 0 yards | 400 |

N

F **G** **H**

EXPERIENCE

❶ 💻 🛍
National Army Museum

📍 E9 🏛 Royal Hospital Rd SW3 Ⓔ Sloane Square
🕐 10am–5.30pm daily
🌐 nam.ac.uk

Adjoining the Royal Hospital Chelsea is the official museum of the British Army, with a collection that spans its 600-year history, including many uniforms, paintings and portraits. Recently refurbished, its five galleries explore the role of the armed forces in society, and in addition to displays of militaria there are some thought-provoking audiovisual presentations and loads of great interactive stuff for kids.

❷ 💻 🛍
Saatchi Gallery

📍 F9 🏛 Duke of York's HQ, King's Rd SW3 Ⓔ Sloane Square 🕐 10am–6pm daily during exhibitions (last adm: 5pm) 🗓 For private events
🌐 saatchigallery.com

Set up by advertising mogul Charles Saatchi in order to showcase his impressive contemporary art acquisitions, the Saatchi Gallery has moved location several times in London. Now, however, it is firmly established in Chelsea at the Duke of York's Headquarters building, which dates from 1801. Saatchi is perhaps best known for his espousal, in the 1980s and 90s, of the Young British Artists movement led by Damien Hirst. Today, the exhibitions of contemporary art staged here are wide-ranging and international in scope, covering everything from new Chinese artists to fashion illustration and Pop Art.

❸ 🍴 💻 🛍
King's Road

📍 E9 🏛 SW3 and SW10 Ⓔ Sloane Square

This is Chelsea's central artery, with a wealth of upmarket high-street shops and smaller boutiques. The miniskirt revolution of the 1960s – the birth of so-called "Swinging London" – began here, with Mary Quant's first shop, Bazaar, and so have many subsequent style trends, perhaps the most famous of them being punk.

Look out for the Pheasantry at No 152, with its columns and statuary. Built in 1881 as the shopfront of a furniture-maker's premises, it now conceals a modern restaurant.

At the top of King's Road is attractive 18th-century Sloane Square, named after Sir Hans Sloane, the wealthy physician and collector who bought the manor of Chelsea in 1712. On the west side is the Royal Court Theatre, which for over a century has fostered new drama.

STAY

Barclay House
A classy B&B in an exquisite Victorian property, with an impressive attention to detail in the three luxurious guest rooms, from the underfloor heating to the rainforest showers.

📍C10 🏠21 Barclay Rd SW6 🌐barclayhouse london.com

💷💷💷

Lime Tree Hotel
Very comfy, spotlessly maintained rooms, each individually decorated and homely enough to make this large boutique hotel a cut above the rest.

📍G8 🏠135 Ebury St SW1 🌐limetreehotel.co.uk

💷💷💷

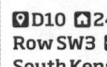

↑ Statue of Thomas More located outside Chelsea Old Church

4
Carlyle's House

📍D10 🏠24 Cheyne Row SW3 🚇Sloane Square, South Kensington 🕐Mar-Oct: 11am-5pm Wed-Sun 🌐nationaltrust.org.uk

The historian Thomas Carlyle moved into this modest 18th century house in 1834, and wrote many of his best-known books here, notably *The French Revolution*. His presence at this address made Chelsea more fashionable and the house became a mecca for literary figures, including novelists Charles Dickens and William Thackeray, poet Alfred Lord Tennyson and naturalist Charles Darwin. The house has been restored and looks as it would have done during Carlyle's lifetime.

5
Chelsea Old Church

📍D10 🏠64 Cheyne Walk SW3 🚇Sloane Square, South Kensington 🕐2-4pm Tue-Thu 🌐chelseaoldchurch.org.uk

Rebuilt after World War II, this square-towered building is a careful replica of the medieval church here that was largely

← "Untitled" by Maha Mullah in the Champagne Life exhibition at the Saatchi Gallery *(inset)*

destroyed in World War II. The glory of this church is its Tudor monuments. One to Sir Thomas More, who built a chapel here in 1528, contains an inscription he wrote (in Latin) asking to be buried next to his wife. Among other monuments is a 17th-century memorial to Lady Jane Cheyne, after whose husband Cheyne Walk was named. Outside the church is a statue in memory of More, "statesman, scholar, saint", gazing piously across the river.

6
Chelsea Physic Garden

📍E10 🏠66 Royal Hospital Rd SW3 🚇Sloane Square 🕐Apr-Oct: 11am-6pm Mon-Fri & Sun; Nov-Mar: 11am-4pm Mon-Fri 🌐chelsea physicgarden.co.uk

Established by the Society of Apothecaries in 1673 to study plants for medicinal use, this garden was saved from closure in 1722 by a gift from Sir Hans Sloane, whose statue adorns it. New varieties nurtured in its glasshouses have included cotton sent to the plantations of the southern United States. Visitors to London's oldest botanic garden can see ancient trees and one of Britain's first rock gardens, installed in 1772.

The fine Georgian architecture of Chelsea

 **7**

Royal Hospital Chelsea

📍F9 🏠Royal Hospital Rd SW3 🚇Sloane Square 🕐Museum, chapel and Great Hall: 10am–4pm Mon–Fri (no access to Hall noon–2pm) 🚫23 Dec–6 Jan, public hols, for functions 🌐chelsea-pensioners.co.uk

This graceful complex was commissioned by Charles II from Christopher Wren in 1682 as a retirement home for old or wounded soldiers, who have been known as Chelsea Pensioners ever since. The hospital opened ten years later and is still home to about 300 retired soldiers, whose distinctive uniform of scarlet coat and tricorn hat dates from the 17th century. The Pensioners lead guided tours of the hospital, but only for prebooked groups.

Flanking the northern entrance are Wren's two main public rooms: the chapel, notable for its wonderful simplicity, and the panelled Great Hall, still used as the dining room. A small museum covers the history of the Chelsea Pensioners.

A statue of Charles II by Grinling Gibbons is to be found on the terrace outside, from where there is a fine view of Battersea Power Station across the river.

8

Chelsea Harbour

📍C10 🏠SW10 🚇Fulham Broadway

This is an impressive development of modern apartments, shops, offices, restaurants, a hotel and a marina. It is near the site of Cremorne Pleasure Gardens, which closed in 1877 after more than 40 years as a venue for dances and circuses. The centrepiece of the harbour is the Belvedere, a 20-storey apartment tower with an external glass lift and a pyramid roof, topped with a golden ball on a rod that rises and falls with the tide.

---

9 💻

Battersea Park

📍F10 🏠Albert Bridge Rd SW11 🚇Sloane Square then bus 137 🚆Battersea Park 🕐6:30am–10:30pm daily 🌐wandsworth.gov. uk/batterseapark

This was the second public park created to relieve the growing urban stresses of

---

EAT

Mother
The hip Copenhagen pizza joint has opened under the hangar-like railway arch in Circus West Village.

📍G10 🏠Circus West Village SW11 🌐mother restaurant.co.uk

£££

Medlar
Refined French cuisine in a romantic, low-key environment. Good fixed-price menus.

📍C10 🏠438 King's Rd SW10 🌐medlar restaurant.co.uk

£££

The Builder's Arms
Smart neighbourhood pub serving traditional British food. It's a congenial place to drink, too.

📍E9 🏠13 Britten St SW3 🌐thebuildersarms chelsea.co.uk

£££

The Great Hall at the Royal Hospital Chelsea, laid out for the Pensioners' lunch

Victorian Londoners – the first was Victoria Park *(p322)* in the East End. It opened in 1858 on the former Battersea Fields, a swampy area notorious for vice centred on the Old Red House, a disreputable pub.

The new park was immediately popular, especially for its man-made boating lake, with its romantic rocks, gardens and waterfalls. In 1985, the Peace Pagoda was unveiled, a 35-m- (100-ft-) high monument built by Japanese Buddhist nuns and monks and presented to the park as a gift. There is also an excellent children's zoo (entry fee), a playground, sports activities and an art gallery, the Pumphouse.

🔟
St Mary's, Battersea

🔵 D10 🏛 Battersea Church Rd SW11 🚇 Sloane Sq then bus 19 or 219 🕐 By arrangement 🌐 stmarys battersea.org.uk

There has been a church here since at least the 10th century. The present brick building dates from 1775, but the

17th-century stained glass, commemorating Tudor monarchs, comes from the former church. In 1782, the poet and artist William Blake was married in the church. Later, J M W Turner painted views of the Thames from the church tower. Benedict Arnold, who served George Washington in the American War of Independence but defected to the British side, is buried here in the crypt.

BATTERSEA POWER STATION

This is one of the London landmarks least known to visitors but best known to locals - and, of course, to Pink Floyd fans: the monstrous industrial building with its four towering smoke stacks graces the cover of their album *Animals*. Since it was decommissioned in 1983, numerous proposals for its redevelopment have come and gone. Now, finally, the colossal Grade II-listed structure is coming back into use. A new riverside park, an extension to the Thames Path, a new Tube station and a myriad restaurants, shops and pricey housing all form part of the new district already visibly emerging.

1️⃣1️⃣ 🚇 🍴 🛍
Circus West Village

🔵 G10 🏛 Battersea Power Station 🚇 Sloane Sq then bus 452 or 137; Victoria then bus 44 🌐 batterseapower station.co.uk

Circus West is the first stage of the gargantuan redevelopment of Battersea Power Station, part of the regeneration of riverside land stretching between Battersea Park and Vauxhall. Squeezed into what still feels like a secret passage between the towering power station and the train lines heading into Victoria Station, its development, though certainly commercially driven, just about bridges the gap between the independent and corporate business worlds.

An interesting mix of restaurants, bars and shops have been installed inside the railway arches and by the new-builds gathering around the site, including a gin specialist, a cocktail bar and a cave-like pizzeria.

← Battersea Park's Peace Pagoda, which looks out over the river

SOUTH KENSINGTON AND KNIGHTSBRIDGE

The tone was set for Kensington from the late 17th century when William III and Mary II bought Kensington Palace. With the arrival of the royal court it soon became a highly desirable residential area, as it still is today, attracting the wealthy as well as those who sought to sell them goods. It remained largely rural until the late 18th century when a period of urban expansion slowly began, with Knightsbridge among the first spots to be developed. It was in the 1850s that the pace of transformation really exploded, the fuse lit by the Great Exhibition of 1851. Held in Hyde Park, the exhibition was the brainchild of Queen Victoria's husband, Prince Albert, who sought to demonstrate and promote British industry and invention. It was a huge success and the profits were ploughed into the creation of a permanent showcase for the arts and sciences in South Kensington. The great museums, the Royal Albert Hall and the Royal Colleges of Art and Music are all part of that legacy.

Map Grid Labels

| A | B | C |

WESTBOURNE GROVE

BAYSWATER

PORCHESTER GARDENS

🚇 Bayswater

KENSINGTON, HOLLAND PARK AND NOTTING HILL
p260

🚇 Notting Hill Gate

🚇 Queensway

BAYSWATER ROAD

🚇 Lancaster Gate

The Fountains

CRAVEN ROAD

LEINSTER GARDENS

GLOUCESTER TERRACE

WESTBOURNE TERRACE

SUSSEX GARDENS

LANCASTER WALK

⑫ The Diana, Princess of Wales Memorial Playground

Peter Pan Statue

The Long Water

⑪ Kensington Gardens

THE BROAD WALK

Round Pond

⑩ Kensington Palace

KENSINGTON PALACE GARDENS

KENSINGTON CHURCH ST

HOLLAND ST

PALACE GREEN

PALACE AVENUE

LANCASTER WALK

Serpentine Gallery ⑨

THE RING

FLOWER WALK

⑧ Albert Memorial

KENSINGTON ROAD

Royal College of Art ⑥

⑦ Royal Albert Hall

KENSINGTON

PALACE GATE

KENSINGTON GATE

HYDE PARK GATE

QUEEN'S GATE MEWS

QUEEN'S GATE

JAY MEWS

PRINCE CONSORT ROAD

Museum of Instruments

⑤ Royal College of Music

Science ③ Museum

EXHIBITION ROAD

PRINCE

IMPERIAL COLLEGE ROAD

QUEEN'S GATE TERRACE

ELVASTON PLACE

GLOUCESTER

QUEEN'S GATE GARDENS

Natural ② History Museum

CROMWELL

GARDENS

CROMWELL PLACE

🚇 Gloucester Road

STANHOPE GARDENS

STANHOPE MEWS EAST

QUEEN'S GATE GARDENS

QUEEN'S GATE

SOUTH KENSINGTON

ROAD

GLOUCESTER

STANHOPE GARDENS

CLAREVILLE STREET

OLD BROMPTON ROAD

ROLAND GARDENS

CRANLEY GARDENS

ONSLOW GARDENS

FOULIS TERRACE

SUMNER PLACE

FULHAM ROAD

SOUTH KENSINGTON AND KNIGHTSBRIDGE

Must Sees
1. Victoria and Albert Museum
2. Natural History Museum
3. Science Museum

Experience More
4. Brompton Oratory
5. Royal College of Music
6. Royal College of Art
7. Royal Albert Hall
8. Albert Memorial
9. Serpentine Gallery
10. Kensington Palace
11. Kensington Gardens
12. The Diana, Princess of Wales Memorial Playground
13. Marble Arch
14. Hyde Park
15. Speakers' Corner

Shop
① Harrods

D | E | F

Bond Street 🚇

CONNAUGHT STREET
EDGWARE RD
SEYMOUR STREET

🚇 Marble Arch

HYDE PARK STREET

BAYSWATER ROAD

Marble Arch **13**

CUMBERLAND GATE

NORTH AUDLEY ST

DUKE STREET

5

THE RING

Speakers' Corner **15**

BROOK GATE

PARK STREET

MAYFAIR AND ST JAMES'S *p86*

SOUTH AUDLEY STREET

MAYFAIR

HILL WALK

THE RING

Hyde Park **14**

GROSVENOR GATE

PARK LANE

6

SERPENTINE ROAD

The Serpentine

SERPENTINE ROAD

Diana, Princess of Wales Memorial Fountain

Apsley House

HAMILTON PL

ROTTEN ROW

ROTTEN ROW

Hyde Park Corner 🚇

Wellington Arch

SOUTH CARRIAGE DRIVE

KNIGHTSBRIDGE

GROSVENOR PLACE

ROAD

KNIGHTSBRIDGE

Knightsbridge 🚇

KINNERTON ST

WILTON PLACE

WILTON ROW

WILTON CRESCENT

GROSVENOR CRESCENT

HALKIN STREET

GROSVENOR PL

CHAPEL STREET

7

Ennismore Gardens

ENNISMORE GARDENS

RUTLAND GATE

KNIGHTSBRIDGE

RAPHAEL ST

TREVOR PL

TREVOR SQUARE

LANCELOT PL

BROMPTON ROAD

LOWNDES SQUARE

WILLIAM STREET

WILLIAM MEWS

MOTCOMB ST

BELGRAVE SQUARE

BELGRAVE MEWS

UPPER BELGRAVE ST

BELGRAVIA

GARDENS

ENNISMORE GDNS MEWS

MONTPELIER PLACE

MONTPELIER WALK

MONTPELIER SQUARE

CHEVAL PLACE

Harrods **ℹ**

HANS ROAD

HANS CRESCENT

HANS STREET

SLOANE STREET

HANS PLACE

CADOGAN PLACE

LOWNDES ST

CHESHAM PL

CHESHAM STREET

BELGRAVE PLACE

EATON PLACE

EATON

8

PRINCE'S GATE MEWS

Brompton Oratory **4**

BROMPTON SQUARE

BROMPTON ROAD

BEAUCHAMP PL

YEOMAN'S ROW

WALTON STREET

PAVILION ROAD

PONT STREET

CADOGAN PLACE

CADOGAN GARDENS

EATON SQUARE

ELIZABETH STREET

Victoria and Albert Museum **1**

THURLOE PLACE

THURLOE SQUARE

ALEXANDER PLACE

EGERTON PLACE

EGERTON GDNS

EGERTON TERR

SLOANE STREET

CHELSEA AND BATTERSEA *p230*

South Kensington 🚇

PELHAM STREET

SOUTH TERRACE

PELHAM CRES

DRAYCOTT AVENUE

CADOGAN STREET

SLOANE AVENUE

AVENUE

FULHAM ROAD

ELYSTAN PLACE

ELYSTAN STREET

WALTON PLACE

SLOANE AVENUE

SOUTH KENSINGTON AND KNIGHTSBRIDGE

SYDNEY STREET

0 metres 400

0 yards 400

N ↑

9

D | E | F

1 🖾 🍴 🖵 🛍

VICTORIA AND
ALBERT MUSEUM

📍D8 🏠Cromwell Road SW7 🚇South Kensington 🕐10am–5:45pm
daily (til 10pm Fri) 🚫24–26 Dec 🌐vam.ac.uk

Housed in Victorian splendour, as well as modern state-of-the-art
galleries, the V&A is the world's leading museum of art and design,
with its collection spanning 5,000 years of furniture, glass, textiles,
fashion, ceramics and jewellery.

The Victoria and Albert Museum (the V&A)
contains one of the world's broadest
collections of art and design, with exhibits
ranging from early Christian devotional
objects to cutting-edge furniture. Originally
founded in 1852 to inspire design students as
the Museum of Manufactures, it was renamed
by Queen Victoria in 1899 in memory of Prince
Albert. The museum underwent an extensive
renovation in the early 2000s, including a new
opening on Exhibition Road leading into a
large courtyard with a café. Inside, a dramatic
staircase leads down to a vast new gallery
beneath the courtyard.

↑ The grand Cromwell Road
entrance to the museum

←
Dale Chihuly's
chandelier over the
information desk

GALLERY GUIDE

The V&A has six levels. Level 1
houses the China, Japan and
South Asia Galleries, the Fashion
Gallery and Cast Courts. The
British Galleries are on levels
2 and 4. Level 3 contains the
20th Century Galleries and
silver, ironwork, paintings,
photography and design works.
The glass display is on level 4.
The Ceramics Galleries and
Furniture are on level 6.
European galleries from
300 to 1800 are on Level 0.

↑ The reading room of
the National Art Library
in the V&A

Did You Know?

The V&A was the first museum to have its own restaurant. The original refreshment rooms are still in use today.

↑ Large-scale works that were once part of buildings in the Renaissance City gallery

British Galleries

A sequence of grand rooms starting on level 2 and continuing on level 4 are devoted to British design and decorative arts from 1500 to 1900. The luxurious galleries chart Britain's rise from obscure island to "workshop of the world".

The galleries present the evolution of British design and the numerous influences, whether technological or aesthetic, it has absorbed from all over the world. Beautiful textiles, furniture, costumes and household objects illustrate the tastes and lifestyles of the country's ruling classes. Among the highlights are the wedding suit of James II, the opulent State Bed from Melville House, and a number of carefully preserved period rooms, including the stunning Rococo Norfolk House Music Room. Discovery Areas give visitors a chance to delve even deeper into the past by trying out a Tudor ruff or viewing 3D images through a Victorian stereoscope.

Asia: China, Japan, Middle East and South Asia

The Jameel Gallery of Islamic Art was opened in July 2006 and houses a significant collection of more than 400 objects, including ceramics,

Vibrant examples of stained glass in the Sacred Silver and Stained Glass galleries ↑

textiles, carpets, metalwork, glass and woodwork. The exhibits date from the great days of the Islamic caliphate of the 8th and 9th centuries through to the years preceding World War I. Middle Eastern art from Syria, Iraq, Iran and Egypt, and art from Turkey, is found in room 42. Beautifully crafted textiles and ceramics illustrate the Islamic influence on fine and decorative arts. A dramatic arc of burnished steel fins, representing the spine of a Chinese dragon, spans the China gallery (room 44). Covering the several millennia from 3000 BC to the present, the impressive collection includes a giant Buddha's head from 700–900 AD, a huge yet elegant Ming canopied bed, and rare jade and ceramics. Japanese art is

concentrated in the gallery in room 45, and is particularly notable for lacquer, Samurai armour and woodblock prints.

Architecture Gallery

The Architecture Gallery features drawings, models, photographs and architectural fragments from the V&A and the Royal Institute of British Architects (RIBA) in both permanent displays and temporary exhibitions.

A superb collection of artifacts and illustrations from around the world explores key themes, such as construction techniques and the role of public buildings. Don't miss the exquisitely detailed architectural scale models, including a traditional Japanese house, Modernist constructions from Ernö Goldfinger and others, and British designs such as Charles Barry's Gothic plans for the Palace of Westminster.

Europe

Ten galleries, occupying an entire wing of the museum, house some of the world's greatest treasures of medieval and Renaissance Europe. Among the many remarkable exhibits are the notebooks of Leonardo da Vinci; sculptures by Italian masters such as Donatello and Giambologna, some set in a Renaissance courtyard garden setting; the fine enamel Becket Casket (c 1180);

Ancient kimonos on display in the Toshiba Gallery of Japanese Art ↑

and the reconstructed Santa Chiara Chapel, the only one of its kind outside Italy.

The Europe collection continues in the level 0 galleries of the opposite wing, which cover the period 1600 to 1800, and include several recreated period rooms. Room 48a on the ground floor is dedicated to the famous Raphael cartoons – huge designs for tapestries planned for the Sistine Chapel, dating from 1515.

Another of the most famous sights at the V&A are the extraordinary cast courts, which have been part of the museum since its founding. They house large plaster casts of major European sculptures, such as Rome's Trajan's Column (in two pieces) and a 5 m (16 ft) tall reproduction of Michaelangelo's David, created so that visitors to the museum could see these works without travelling.

Textiles and fashion

The popular Fashion Gallery displays items from the largest and most compre-hensive collection of dress in the world. Around 100 exhibits, including men's and women's wear, footwear and accessories, spanning five centuries, are arranged chronologically. They feature a magnificent mantua from the 1760s; an 1850s wedding dress with veil and shoes; a

→
Enamelled casket depicting the murder of Thomas Becket

Schiaparelli evening coat embroidered with a design by Jean Cocteau; a punk outfit designed by Vivienne Westwood; and stunning dresses from Alexander McQueen. Textiles are also found throughout the museum's collections; the Japanese galleries in particular have some exquisite kimonos and other traditional textiles.

Metalwork

This group of galleries is located on level 3. In the Silver Galleries, 3,500 pieces from 1400 to the present day are displayed in the beautifully refurbished Victorian rooms 65 to 69. Arms and armour, European metalwork from the 1500s to the present, and Islamic brass and bronze can be found in rooms 81, 82 and 87 to 89.

The Sacred Silver and Stained Glass galleries situated in rooms 83 and 84 display devotional treasures. The highlight of the Ironwork galleries, which are located in rooms 113 to 114e, is the dazzling Hereford Screen, which was designed by Sir George Gilbert Scott in 1862. The screen became

the V&A's largest-ever conservation project.

The Gilbert Collection of gold, silver, micromosaics and gold boxes, formerly housed at Somerset House, was relocated here in 2009.

Glass and Ceramics

The museum has the most comprehensive collection of glass and ceramics in the world. Examples of glass covering 2,000 years are largely housed in room 131, which has a stunning glass balustrade on the staircase and mezzanine by artist Danny Lane. Displays of international contemporary glass are on display in this room and in room 129.

The ceramics collection has an introductory gallery presenting the history and development of ceramics across the world. All of the major British pottery factories are represented.

Alexander McQueen's animal print dress Plato's Atlantis, from 2010 ↑

🔍 HIDDEN GEM
Relax and Refresh

Be sure to visit the museum's original refreshment rooms off room 16a (one of which was designed by William Morris), which are now being used again as a café. If the weather is good, don't miss a wander in the John Madejski Garden, with a coffee in hand.

② Ⓜ 🍴 🖥 🏛

NATURAL HISTORY MUSEUM

📍 D8 🏠 Cromwell Rd SW7 🚇 South Kensington 🕐 10am-5:50pm daily (til 10pm last Fri of month), last admission 5:30pm 🚫 24-26 Dec 🌐 nhm.ac.uk

A paradise for budding botanists, explorers and geologists, the superlative Natural History Museum, with its specimens, skeletons and simulators, is quite simply a national treasure and an absolute must for any visitor to the capital.

Using interactive techniques and traditional displays, life on earth and the earth itself are vividly explained at this awe-inspiring museum. And the building that houses the vast collection is a masterpiece in itself. Founded as just one of the Victorian temples to learning, it opened in 1881 and was designed by Alfred Waterhouse using revolutionary building techniques. It is built on an iron and steel framework concealed behind arches and columns, richly decorated with sculptures of plants and animals.

The museum is divided into four zones, plus the Hintze Hall, the grand centrepiece of the building dominated by a huge skeleton of a blue whale. In the Blue Zone discover Human Biology, Mammals, Dinosaurs and Images of Nature. The Green Zone has Creepy Crawlies, Fossils and The Vault. The giant escalator in the Earth Hall leads through a stunning globe to Red Zone highlights Restless Surface and Earth's Treasury. The Orange Zone includes the Darwin Centre's Cocoon and, outside, the Wildlife Garden.

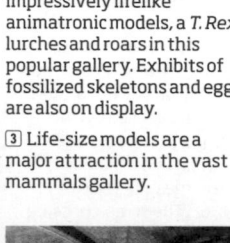

① The elegant museum is set in grounds that include a peaceful wildlife garden.

② One of the museum's impressively lifelike animatronic models, a *T. Rex* lurches and roars in this popular gallery. Exhibits of fossilized skeletons and eggs are also on display.

③ Life-size models are a major attraction in the vast mammals gallery.

TOP 5 UNMISSIBLE EXHIBITS

Triceratops Skull
The gigantic skull of a plant-eating *Triceratops* dinosaur.

Latrobe Gold Nugget
A rare crystalized gold nugget from Australia weighing 717 g (25 oz).

Butterflies
A tropical butterfly house filled with these beautiful flying insects.

Archaeopteryx
This valuable fossil of a feathered dinosaur provided the link between birds and dinosaurs.

Earthquake Simulator
Experience the effects of an earthquake in this simulation.

Did You Know?

Kids can spend a night at the museum at Dino Snores, a monthly event for those aged 7–11

↑ The 25.5-m- (84-ft-) long skeleton of "Hope", the blue whale hanging over Hintze Hall

③ Ⓜ️ 🖥️ 🏛️

SCIENCE MUSEUM

⚲ D8 ⌂ Exhibition Rd SW7 🚇 South Kensington 🕐 10am–6pm daily (last entry 5:15pm) 🚫 24–26 Dec 🌐 sciencemuseum.org.uk

Centuries of continuing scientific and technological innovation lie at the heart of the Science Museum's huge collection. Discover the science fact behind science fiction and explore humanity's achievements so far – and where we might be heading next.

From steam engines to aeroengines, space-craft to the first computers, this museum has a vast range of scientific objects. Equally important is the social context of science – what discoveries and inventions mean for day-to-day life – and the process of discovery itself. The high-tech Wellcome Wing has hands-on displays, an IMAX cinema, a 3D theatre and galleries devoted to scientific advancements.

The Science Museum is spread over seven floors, balconies and mezzanine levels. The Wellcome Wing, with four floors of interactive technology, is at the west end of the museum, accessible from the ground floor and third floor of the main building. The museum is undergoing renovations, so some galleries may be closed and others may have temporary exhibitions; check the website for up-to-date information before you visit.

↑ The unassuming exterior of the fascinating Science Museum

💬 INSIDER TIP
Get Some Air

Though there are several places to eat in the museum, pack a picnic and walk five minutes to Hyde Park – a perfect place for kids to let off some steam.

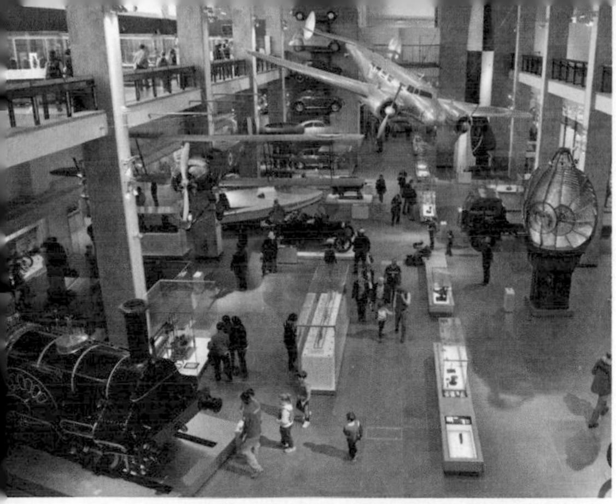

↑ Early flying machines and fighter planes suspended over the Flight and Fly Zone galleries on the third floor

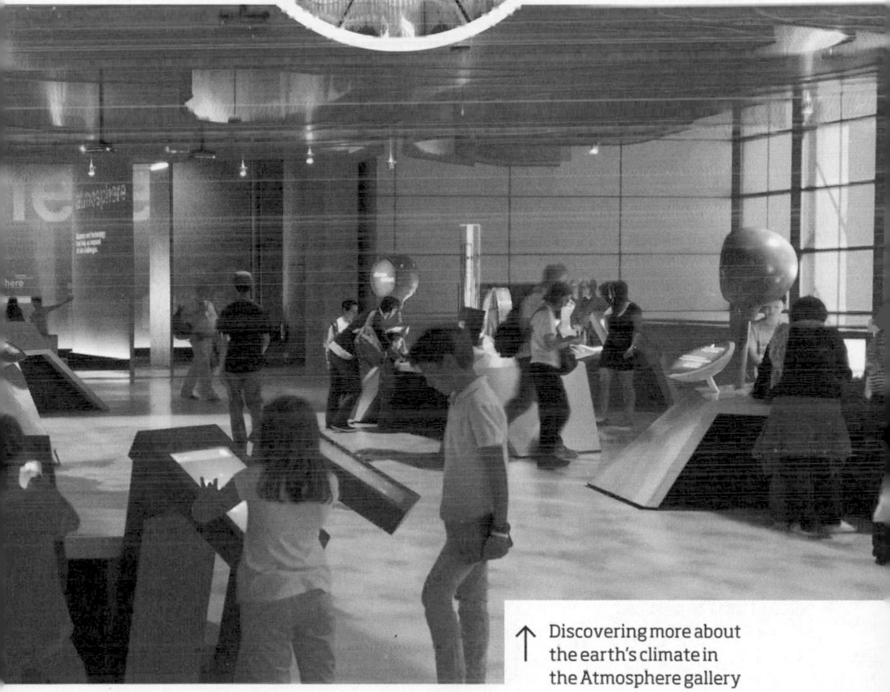

→ A child enjoying the hands-on exhibits in the immersive and imaginative Wonderlab, which has over 50 mind-boggling exhibits, shows and demonstrations

TOP 5 UNMISSABLE EXHIBITS

Apollo 10
US astronauts orbited the moon in May 1969 in the Apollo 10 capsule.

Who Am I?
Explore how your genetics and your upbringing make you who you are.

Flight Simulator
An adrenaline ride with high-definition 3D and motion effects.

Space Descent VR
A virtual reality 400-km (250-mile) journey from space back to earth.

The Garden
Hands-on galleries for younger children.

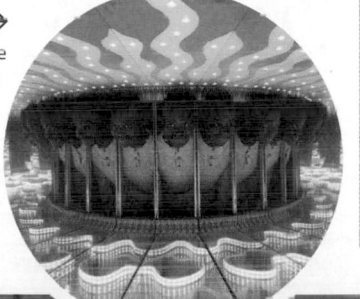

↑ Discovering more about the earth's climate in the Atmosphere gallery

← The soaring interior of the Brompton Oratory, rich in Italianate decoration

EXPERIENCE MORE

4

Brompton Oratory

📍D8 🏛Brompton Rd SW7
🚇South Kensington
🕐6:30am–8pm daily
🌐bromptonoratory.co.uk

Famous for its splendid musical tradition, the Italianate Oratory is a rich (some think a little too rich) monument to the English Catholic revival of the late 19th century. It was established by John Henry Newman (later Cardinal Newman).

The church was opened in 1884; its façade and dome were added in the 1890s, and the interior has been progressively enriched ever since. Inside, all the most eye-catching treasures predate the church – many of them were brought here from Italian churches. Giuseppe Mazzuoli carved the huge marble figures of the 12 apostles for Siena Cathedral in the late 17th century. The beautiful Lady Altar was originally created in 1693 for the Dominican church in Brescia, and the 18th-century altar in St Wilfrid's Chapel came from a church in Rochefort, Belgium.

5

Royal College of Music

📍C7 🏛Prince Consort Rd SW7 🚇Knightsbridge, South Kensington
🌐rcm.ac.uk

Sir Arthur Blomfield designed the turreted Gothic palace, with Bavarian overtones, that has housed this distinguished institution since 1894. Pupils have included the composers Benjamin Britten and Ralph Vaughan Williams. The Museum of Music (currently closed for redevelopment) contains instruments from many parts of the world, together with portraits of great musicians and composers. Check the website for details of concerts and masterclasses hosted by the college.

6

Royal College of Art

📍C7 🏛Kensington Gore SW7 🚇High St Kensington, South Kensington 🕐For exhibitions, lectures, film screenings 🌐rca.ac.uk

Sir Hugh Casson's mainly glass-fronted building (1962) is in stark contrast to the Victoriana around it. The college was founded in 1837 to teach design and practical art for the manufacturing industries. It became noted for modern art in the 1950s and 60s, when David Hockney, Peter Blake and Eduardo Paolozzi attended.

7

Royal Albert Hall

📍C7 🏛Kensington Gore SW7 🚇High St Kensington, South Kensington 🕐For tours & performances daily 🌐royalalberthall.com

Designed by an engineer, Francis Fowke, and completed

in 1871, this huge concert hall was modelled on Roman amphitheatres. On the red-brick exterior the only ostentation is a frieze symbolizing the triumph of arts and science. The building was planned as the Hall of Arts and Science but Queen Victoria renamed it the Royal Albert Hall, in memory of her husband, when she laid the foundation stone in 1868.

The hall is often used for classical concerts, most famously the "Proms", but it also hosts other large gatherings, such as tennis matches, comedy shows, rock concerts and circus shows.

8

Albert Memorial

📍C7 🚇South Carriage Drive, Kensington Gdns SW7 🚉High St Kensington, South Kensington 🌐royalparks.org.uk

This grand memorial to Prince Albert, Queen Victoria's beloved consort,

was completed in 1872, 11 years after his death. Fittingly, it is near the site of the 1851 Exhibition, which Albert co-organized. The statue, by John Foley, shows him with an exhibition catalogue on his knee.

The Queen chose Sir George Gilbert Scott to design the monument, which stands 55 m (175 ft) high. It is loosely based on a medieval market cross – although considerably more elaborate, with a black and gilded spire, multi-coloured marble canopy, stones, mosaics, enamels, wrought iron and nearly 200 sculpted figures. In October 1998, the re-gilded statue was unveiled by Elizabeth II; it had

Did You Know?

There are 169 carvings of notable figures from the arts in the frieze around the Albert Memorial.

been painted black in 1915 to prevent it attracting attention during World War I.

9

Serpentine Gallery

📍D6 🚇Kensington Gdns W2 🚉Lancaster Gate, South Kensington 🕙10am-6pm Tue-Sun 🚫1 Jan, 24-26, 31 Dec & between exhibitions 🌐serpentinegalleries.org

The Serpentine Gallery houses temporary exhibitions of major and rising contemporary artists' and architects' work, excitingly transforming its space to suit the exhibits. Every summer, a temporary pavilion is commissioned from a major architect. A second building, the Serpentine Sackler Gallery, in a former gunpowder store a 5-minute walk away, displays similarly ambitious exhibits. An extension, designed by the late Zaha Hadid, houses the Magazine restaurant, and there is also an art bookshop

The Royal Albert Hall, home to musical events across a wide variety of genres ↑

The magnificent Royal Albert Hall in South Kensington

⑩ 🛝 🍴 🛍

Kensington Palace

📍 B6 🏠 Kensington Palace Gdns W8 🚇 High St Kensington, Queensway, Notting Hill Gate 🕐 Mar-Oct: 10am-6pm daily; Nov-Feb: 10am-4pm daily (last adm: 1 hr before closing) 🌐 hrp.org.uk

Half of this spacious palace is used as royal apartments; the other half, which includes the 18th-century state rooms, is open to the public. When William of Orange and his wife Mary came to the throne in 1689, they bought a mansion, dating from 1605, and commissioned Christopher Wren to convert it into a royal palace.

The palace has seen some important royal events. In 1714, Queen Anne died here from apoplexy brought on by over-eating and, on 20 June 1837, Princess Victoria of Kent was woken at 5am to be told that her uncle William IV had died and she was now queen – the start of her 64-year reign. After the death in 1997 of Diana, Princess of Wales, the gold gates to the south were deluged with bouquets in their thousands.

Visitors can explore inside the King's and Queen's state apartments, the latter little changed since it was designed for Mary in the 17th century. The palace also often displays clothes worn by many of the royals, including the Queen and Princess Diana.

---

⑪ 🚻

Kensington Gardens

📍 C6 🏠 W8 🚇 Bayswater, High St Kensington, Queensway, Lancaster Gate 🕐 6am-dusk daily 🌐 royalparks.org.uk

The former grounds of Kensington Palace became a public park in 1841. The gardens are full of charm, starting with Sir George Frampton's statue (1912) of J M Barrie's fictional Peter Pan, playing his pipes for the bronze fairies and animals that cling to the column below. Just north of here, in Hyde Park, are ornamental fountains and statues, including Jacob Epstein's *Rima* and George Frederick Watts' muscular horse and rider, *Physical Energy*. Close by is a summer house designed by William Kent in 1735. The Round Pond, built in 1728, is often packed with model boats navigated by enthusiasts young and old.

In the north, near Lancaster Gate, is a dogs' cemetery, created in 1880 by the Duke of Cambridge.

→

Passing the time aboard a rowing boat on Hyde Park's Serpentine

⑫ 🚻

The Diana, Princess of Wales Memorial Playground

📍 B6 🏠 Kensington Gardens 🚇 Bayswater, Queensway 🕐 Daily, from 10am; closing times vary, from 4:45pm in midwinter to 7:45pm in midsummer 🌐 royalparks.org.uk

The newest of Kensington Gardens' three playgrounds, on the site of an earlier playground funded by J M Barrie, takes the boy who didn't want to grow up as its theme and includes a beach cove with a 15-m (50-ft) pirates' galleon, a tree house and a mermaid's fountain with a slumbering crocodile. Though all children under 13 must be accompanied by an adult, staff are on hand too. Many features of the playground are accessible to children with specific needs.

←

The sunken garden with reflecting pool adjoining Kensington Palace

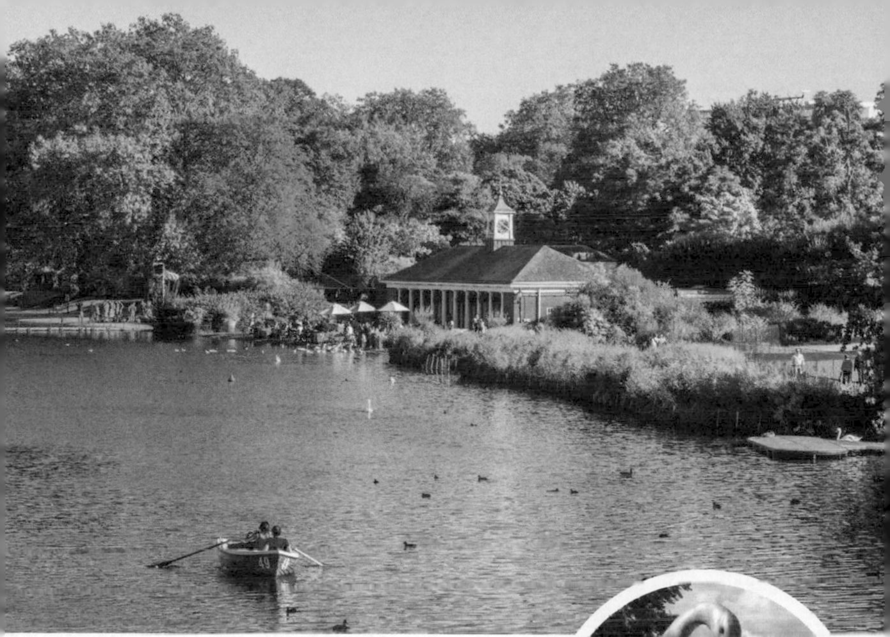

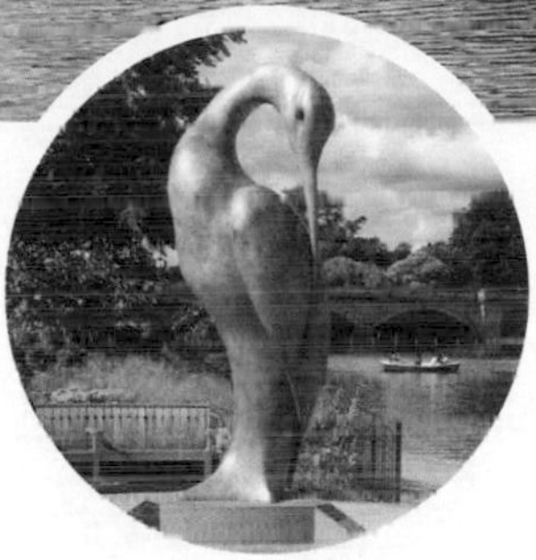

↑ The Isis statue, one of the most recent additions to Hyde Park's statuary and buildings

INSIDER TIP
On the Water

Rent a pedalo or rowing boat from the Boathouse (late Mar–end Oct) and enjoy a tranquil tour of Hyde Park's Serpentine lake. The brave can dive in for a swim at the lido during the summer months (Jun–Aug).

13

Marble Arch

E5 Park Lane W1 Marble Arch

John Nash designed the arch in 1827 as the main entrance to Buckingham Palace. It was, however, too narrow for the grandest coaches and in 1851 it was moved here. Historically, only senior members of the royal family and one of the royal artillery regiments are allowed to pass under it.

The arch stands near the site of the old Tyburn gallows, where until 1783 the city's most notorious criminals were hanged in front of crowds of bloodthirsty spectators.

14

Hyde Park

E6 W2 Hyde Park Corner, Knightsbridge, Lancaster Gate, Marble Arch 5am-midnight daily royalparks.org.uk

The ancient manor of Hyde was part of the lands of Westminster Abbey seized by Henry VIII on the Dissolution of the Monasteries in 1536. It has remained a royal park ever since. Henry used it for hunting but James I opened it to the public in the early 17th century. The Serpentine, an artificial lake used for boating and bathing, was created when Caroline, George II's queen, dammed the flow of the Westbourne River in 1730. There is a Princess Diana Memorial fountain to the south of the Serpentine.

In its time, the park has been a venue for duelling, horse racing, demonstrations and musical performances. The 1851 Great Exhibition was held here in a vast glass palace. Come Christmas time, the festive Winter Wonderland takes over, with markets, an ice rink funfair.

15

Speakers' Corner

E5 Hyde Park W2 Marble Arch

An 1872 law made it legal for anyone to assemble an audience and address them on whatever topic they chose. Since then, this corner of Hyde Park has become the established venue for budding public orators and a fair number of eccentrics. On Sundays, speakers from fringe groups and one-member political parties reveal their plans for the betterment of humanity (or otherwise) while assembled onlookers heckle them without mercy.

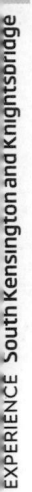

A SHORT WALK
SOUTH KENSINGTON

Distance 1.5 km (1 mile) **Nearest Tube**
South Kensington **Time** 15 minutes

This area is characterized by its world-renowned museums, which are housed in grandiose buildings celebrating Victorian self-confidence. Take a stroll from the Albert Memorial in Hyde Park, past the Royal Albert Hall, to the Victoria and Albert Museum and admire the monuments to the royal couple that made London a world capital of industry and knowledge.

Did You Know?

The Royal Albert Hall was partly funded by selling seats on a 999-year lease.

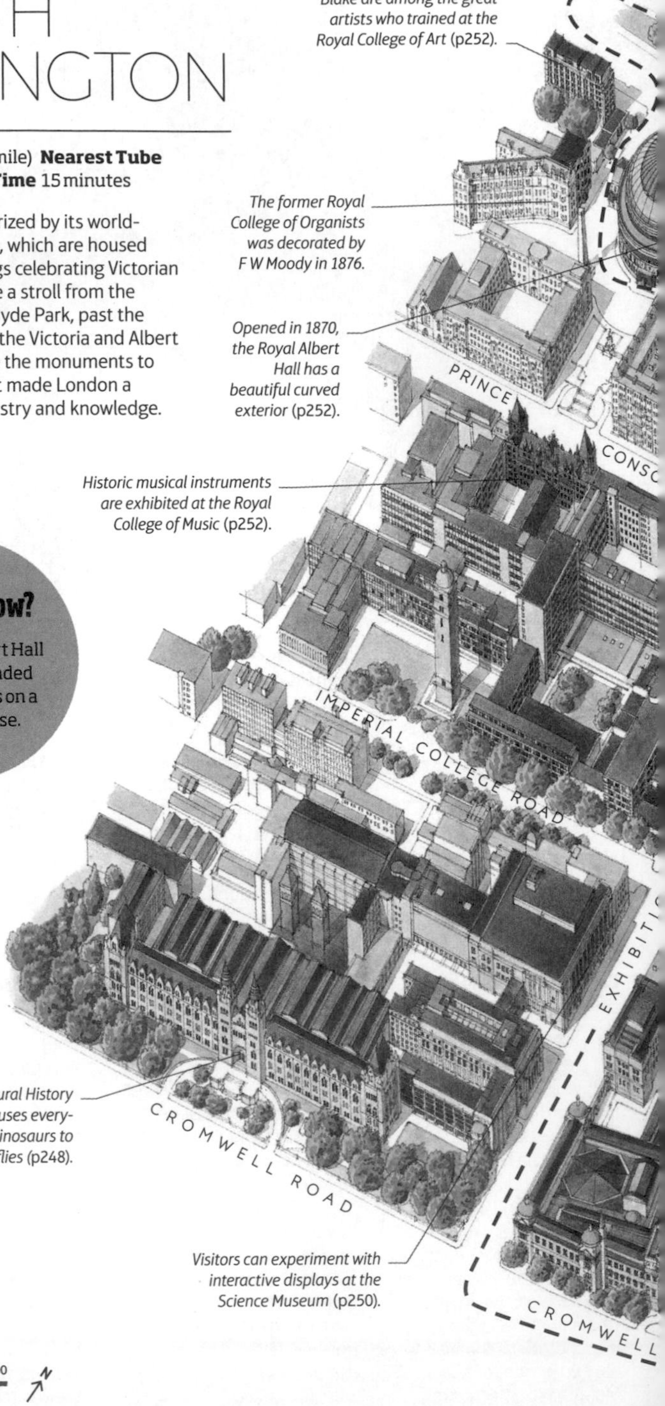

David Hockney and Peter Blake are among the great artists who trained at the Royal College of Art (p252).

The former Royal College of Organists was decorated by F W Moody in 1876.

Opened in 1870, the Royal Albert Hall has a beautiful curved exterior (p252).

Historic musical instruments are exhibited at the Royal College of Music (p252).

The Natural History Museum houses everything from dinosaurs to butterflies (p248).

Visitors can experiment with interactive displays at the Science Museum (p250).

PRINCE
CONS
IMPERIAL COLLEGE ROAD
EXHIBITI
CROMWELL ROAD
CROMWELL

0 metres 100
0 yards 100

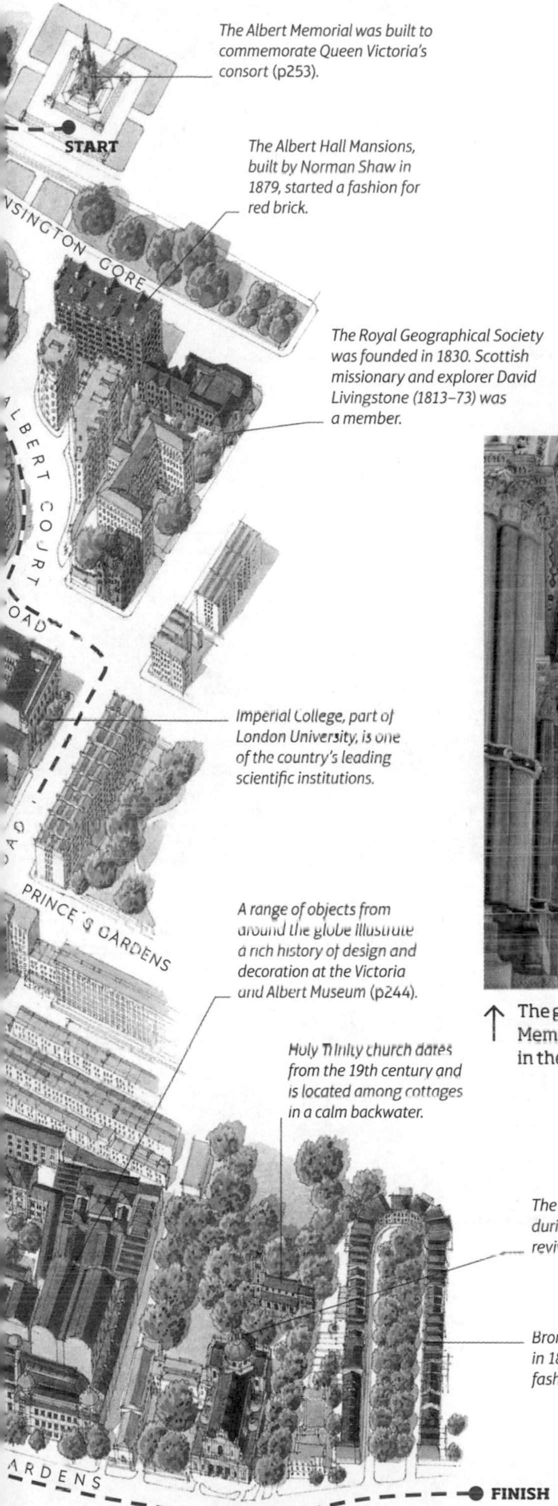

The Albert Memorial was built to commemorate Queen Victoria's consort (p253).
START
The Albert Hall Mansions, built by Norman Shaw in 1879, started a fashion for red brick.
The Royal Geographical Society was founded in 1830. Scottish missionary and explorer David Livingstone (1813–73) was a member.
ALBERT COURT
Imperial College, part of London University, is one of the country's leading scientific institutions.
PRINCE'S GARDENS
A range of objects from around the globe illustrate a rich history of design and decoration at the Victoria and Albert Museum (p244).
Holy Trinity church dates from the 19th century and is located among cottages in a calm backwater.
The Brompton Oratory was built during the 19th-century Catholic revival (p252).
Brompton Square, begun in 1821, established this as a fashionable residential area.
FINISH

SOUTH KENSINGTON AND KNIGHTSBRIDGE

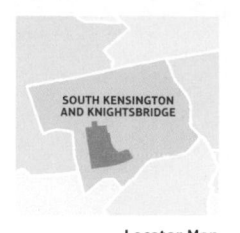

Locator Map

For more detail see p242

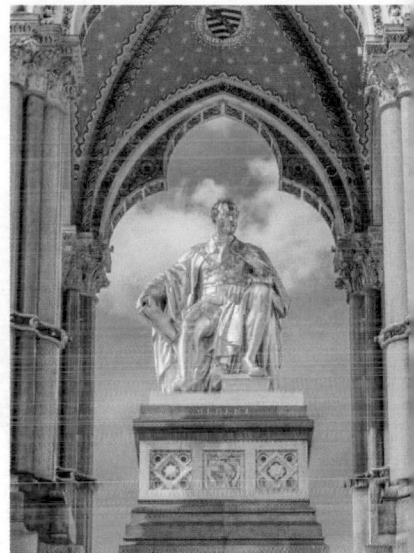

↑ The gilded Albert Memorial gleams in the sunshine

KENSINGTON, HOLLAND PARK AND NOTTING HILL

Kensington remained a country village of market gardens and mansions until the 1830s. Outstanding among these mansions was Holland House, part of whose grounds are now Holland Park. The area grew up rapidly in the mid-19th century and most of its buildings date from then – mainly expensive apartments, mansion flats and fashionable shops. It was during that century that a slew of famous artists and writers settled in the area, notable among them Henry James, William Thackeray, Edward Linley Sambourne and Lord Leighton, the striking homes of the latter two, 18 Stafford Terrace and Leighton House, now open to the public. It was also during the 19th century that Notting Hill emerged as a suburb, initially attracting well-to-do residents in much the same vein as elsewhere in Kensington. By the end of World War II, however, many of the stuccoed terraced houses had been converted to multiple-occupancy tenements. They became homes, during the 1950s, to West Indian immigrant families who began arriving in the area in large numbers – their presence spawned the first Notting Hill Carnival, in 1965.

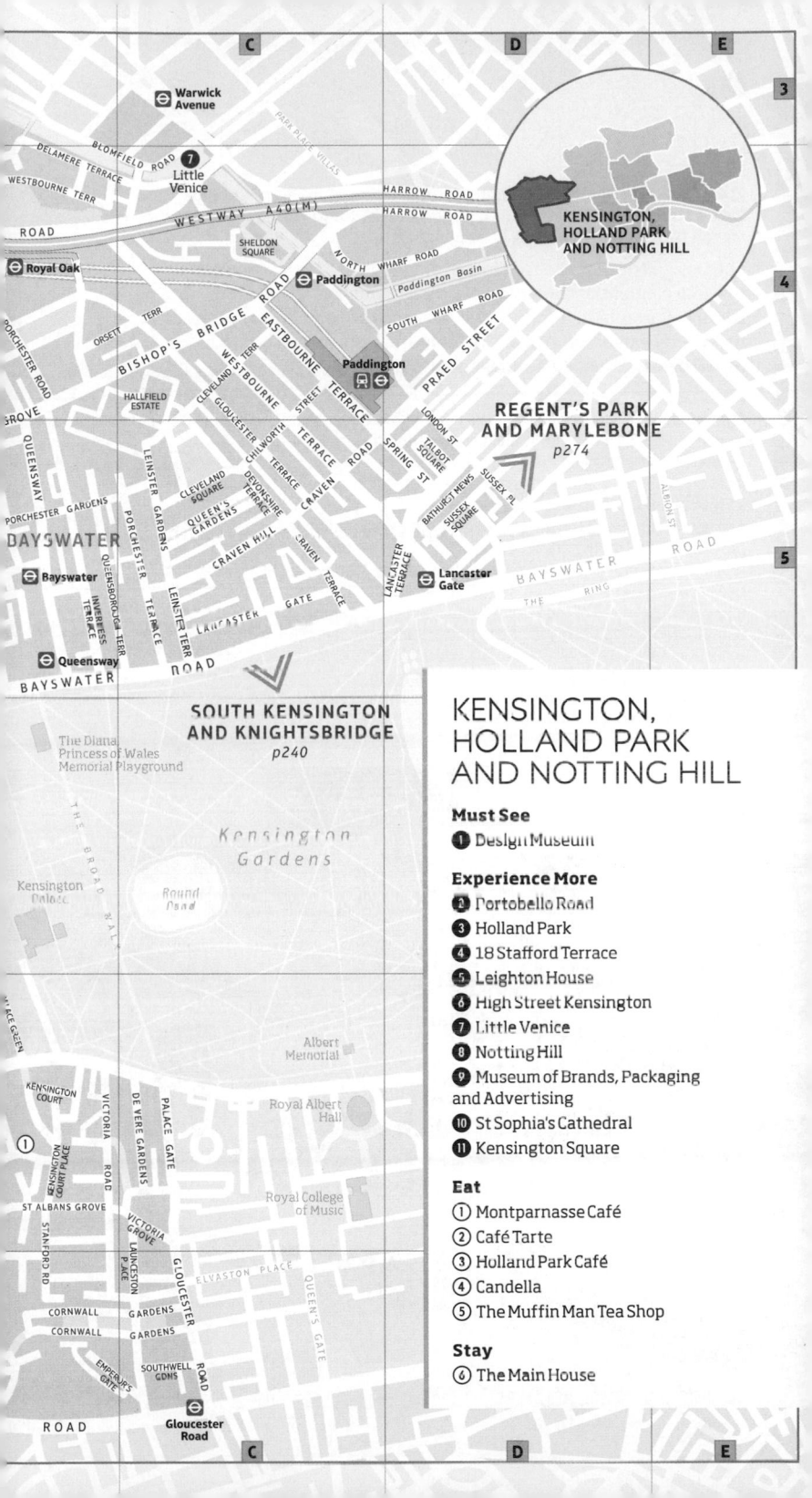

Warwick
Avenue

BLOMFIELD ROAD

DELAMERE TERRACE

7 Little
Venice

WESTBOURNE TERR

PARK PLACE VILLAS

HARROW   ROAD

WESTWAY   A40(M)

HARROW   ROAD

ROAD

SHELDON
SQUARE

NORTH   WHARF   ROAD

KENSINGTON,
HOLLAND PARK
AND NOTTING HILL

Royal Oak

Paddington

Paddington Basin

BISHOP'S

PORCHESTER ROAD

ORSETT   TERR

BRIDGE   ROAD

EASTBOURNE

SOUTH   WHARF   ROAD

PRAED   STREET

Paddington

WESTBOURNE

CLEVELAND   TERRACE

GLOUCESTER   TERRACE

HALLFIELD
ESTATE

TERRACE

STREET

LONDON ST

TALBOT
SQUARE

SPRING ST

REGENT'S PARK
AND MARYLEBONE
p274

GROVE

QUEENSWAY

PORCHESTER GARDENS

BAYSWATER

Bayswater

PORCHESTER

LEINSTER   GARDENS

CLEVELAND
SQUARE

QUEEN'S
GARDENS

CHILWORTH   TERRACE

DEVONSHIRE
TERRACE

CRAVEN   ROAD

CRAVEN   HILL

CRAVEN   TERRACE

LANCASTER   TERRACE

BATHURST MEWS   SUSSEX PL

SUSSEX
SQUARE

ALBION   ST

BAYSWATER

THE   RING

ROAD

PORCHESTER   TERRACE

QUEENSBOROUGH   TERR

Queensway

INVERNESS
TERRACE

LEINSTER   TERR

LANCASTER   GATE

Lancaster
Gate

BAYSWATER   ROAD

SOUTH KENSINGTON
AND KNIGHTSBRIDGE
p240

The Diana
Princess of Wales
Memorial Playground

THE   BROAD   WALK

Kensington
Gardens

Kensington
Palace

Round
Pond

PALACE   GREEN

KENSINGTON
COURT

KENSINGTON COURT PLACE

VICTORIA   ROAD

DE VERE GARDENS

PALACE   GATE

Albert
Memorial

Royal Albert
Hall

ST ALBANS GROVE

STANFORD RD

VICTORIA
GROVE

LAUNCESTON
PLACE

ELVASTON   PLACE

QUEEN'S   GATE

Royal College
of Music

CORNWALL   GARDENS

CORNWALL   GARDENS

GLOUCESTER   ROAD

SOUTHWELL
GDNS

EMPEROR'S
GATE

ROAD

Gloucester
Road

KENSINGTON, HOLLAND PARK AND NOTTING HILL

Must See

① Design Museum

Experience More

② Portobello Road
③ Holland Park
④ 18 Stafford Terrace
⑤ Leighton House
⑥ High Street Kensington
⑦ Little Venice
⑧ Notting Hill
⑨ Museum of Brands, Packaging and Advertising
⑩ St Sophia's Cathedral
⑪ Kensington Square

Eat

① Montparnasse Café
② Café Tarte
③ Holland Park Café
④ Candella
⑤ The Muffin Man Tea Shop

Stay

⑥ The Main House

DESIGN MUSEUM

📍 A7 🏠 234-238 Kensington High St W8 🚇 Kensington High St, Holland Park 🕐 10am-6pm daily (last entry 5pm) and till 8pm on first Fri of every month 🌐 designmuseum.org

The Design Museum, housed in a truly unique building, is dedicated to every element of contemporary design, ranging architecture, transport, graphics, furniture and fashion. Its imaginatively curated temporary exhibitions usually outshine its rather small but nevertheless engaging permanent display.

Appropriately housed in what was the Commonwealth Institute, an inventively designed 1960s building, the Design Museum reopened in 2016, having moved from its previous riverside location near Tower Bridge. The redeveloped building is itself a joy to behold, with its arresting interior of sweeping spaces and geometric lines all crowned by a dramatically cascading roof. Famed for this hyperbolic paraboloid copper-plated roof, the exterior has been kept intact, but the interior has been completely re-fashioned. There is room enough for four galleries – three of them for the superlative programme of temporary exhibitions and one to house the permanent collection, called Designer Maker User, which is free to explore. The building also houses a lecture theatre, café and two appealing shops. The beautiful green woodland of Holland Park is right next door.

SHOP

Designer Shopping

The Design Museum shop is one of the best museum shops in London for the originality and diversity of its carefully selected stock. Items include clothing, stylish stationery, models and miniatures, prints, kitchenware and more.

Exhibits displayed beneath the museum's remarkable roof ↓

GALLERY GUIDE

The permanent exhibition, called
Designer Maker User, examines some
of the most iconic product designs of
the modern world. It also shows a cross-
section of recent innovations from
the three perspectives of its title.

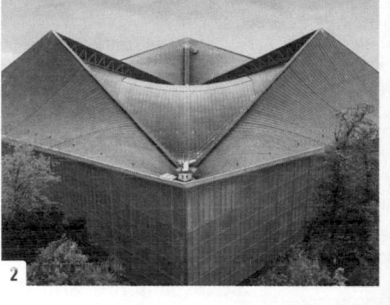

1 Attractive displays of innovative design
feature in the permanent collection.

2 The Grade II-listed building has an
unusual sweeping roof design.

3 The Design Museum's new home is the
former Commonwealth Institute building,
which was originally opened in 1962.

EXPERIENCE MORE

2

Portobello Road

 A5 W11 Notting Hill Gate, Ladbroke Grove
Main market: 9am-7pm Fri & Sat; general market, bric-a-brac: 9am-6pm Mon-Wed & 9am-1pm Thu
w portobelloroad.co.uk

There has been a market here since 1837. Today the southern end of the road consists mostly of stalls that sell antiques, jewellery, souvenirs and other collectables. The market is extremely popular with tourists and tends to be very crowded, but it is well worth visiting, if only to experience its bustling, cheerful atmosphere. The busiest day is Saturday, when the antiques arcades are open. If you are looking for bargains, be warned – the stallholders have a sound idea of the value of what they are selling. Other markets run along the rest of the street on different days, with vintage and new clothes featured around Portobello Green, under Westway near Ladbroke Grove Tube.

3

Holland Park

 A7 Ilchester Place, W8 Holland Park, High Street Kensington, Notting Hill Gate 7:30am-dusk daily (hours vary with season)
w rbkc.gov.uk

This small but delightful park, more wooded and intimate than the large royal parks to its east, Hyde Park (*p257*) and Kensington Gardens (*p256*), was opened in 1952 on what remained of the grounds of the Jacobean Holland House – the rest had been sold off in the late 19th century for the construction of new, large houses. During its heyday in

the 19th century, the mansion was a noted centre of social and political intrigue. Statesmen such as Lord Palmerston and Benjamin Disraeli mixed here with the likes of the poet Lord Byron.

The house suffered heavy bomb damage during World War II, but surviving parts and outbuildings have been put to various uses: exhibitions are held in the orangery and the ice house, and the old Garden Ballroom is now a restaurant. The former front terrace of the house is often used as a backdrop for summer musical events and open-air film screenings, and theatre, opera and dance performances.

The park still contains some of the formal gardens laid out in the early 19th century. Surprisingly, there is also a Japanese garden, created for the 1991 London Festival of Japan. Look out for koi carp in the pond beneath the waterfall. The park is full of wildlife, including peacocks, and there is a well-equipped playground perfect for kids to while away an afternoon in.

Did You Know?

Lord Leighton held Britain's shortest peerage: made a baron on 24 January 1896 he died the next day.

4

18 Stafford Terrace

 A7 W8 High St Kensington Wed, Sat & Sun; tours am, free access pm **w** rbkc.gov.uk/subsites/museums.aspx

The former home of Linley Sambourne, built in about 1870, remains much as Sambourne furnished it – in the Victorian manner, with Oriental ornaments and heavy velvet curtains. Some rooms have William Morris wallpaper. Sambourne was a cartoonist for the satirical magazine *Punch*; drawings cram the walls of the house. It's advisable to book tours ahead.

↑ Exquisite tilework in Eastern style in Leighton House's Arab Hall

5 (⌀)(Ⓜ)(⌂)

Leighton House

📍 A7 🏠 12 Holland Park Rd W14 🚇 High St Kensington 🕐 10am-5:30pm Wed-Mon, occasional late openings 🌐 rbkc.gov.uk/subsites/museums.aspx

Lord Leighton was one of the most respected Victorian painters. His work *Flaming June* is regarded by many as the apotheosis of the Pre-Raphaelite movement. His house, built in 1864–79, has been preserved with its opulent decoration as an extraordinary monument to the Victorian aesthetics Leighton embodied. The highlight is the Arab Hall, added in 1879 to house Leighton's collection of Islamic tiles, some inscribed with text from the Koran. There are paintings and drawings displayed, including some by Edward Burne-Jones, John Millais, G F Watts and many works by Leighton himself. There are free guided tours at 3pm on Wednesday and Sunday. "Leighton Lates" once a month (usually a Friday) give you the chance to enjoy the house until 9pm, with complimentary live music and a glass of wine.

STAY

The Main House
A chic guest house with suites combining modern luxuries with antique furniture.

📍 A5 🏠 6 Colville Road W11 🌐 themain house.co.uk

6 (🍴)(🖥)(⌂)

High Street Kensington

📍 B7 🏠 W8 🚇 High St Kensington

This is one of the main shopping streets in west London, and it reflects the tastes of this affluent neighbourhood, with lots of rather conservative clothing stores and a spread of British and international high-street names. There is a good number of cafés and some decent restaurants. Holland Park and Kensington Gardens bookend the main shopping drag with green space away from the bustle.

←

Stylized Japanese elegance in the Kyoto Garden, Holland Park

Colourful houses at Portobello Road, one of the city's most popular street markets

7

Little Venice

📍 C4 🚇 W2 🚉 Warwick Avenue, Edgware Road

This is a charming corner of London where the western end of the Regent's Canal, the eastern end of the Grand Union Canal and the short waterway to the Paddington Basin converge. Three bridges frame a small triangle of water populated with floating cafés and even a puppet theatre – there are plenty of delightful pubs and restaurants in the nearby terraced streets, too. Towpath walks will take you for miles in either direction along the canals, and narrowboats sail up to Camden Lock (*p168*).

8 🍴 💻 🛍️

Notting Hill

📍 A6 🚇 W11 🚉 Notting Hill Gate

Now the home of Europe's biggest street carnival, most of this area was farmland until the 19th century. In the 1950s and 60s, it became a centre for the Caribbean community, many of whom lived here when they first arrived in Britain. The carnival started in 1966 and takes over the area every August over the bank holiday weekend, when costumed parades meander through the streets.

9

Museum of Brands, Packaging and Advertising

📍 A5 🏠 111–117 Lancaster Rd W11 🚉 Ladbroke Grove 🕐 10am–6pm Tue–Sat, 11am–5pm Sun 🌐 museum ofbrands.com

This out-of-the-ordinary museum is at once a perm-anent exhibition for the history of product packaging in the UK, a study of the changing tastes and fashions since the Victorian period and a gleeful trip down memory lane. The sheer volume of items on display is dizzying: tins, bottles, boxes, magazines, toys, games, household appliances and much more besides. In the main exhibition space, the twisty Time Tunnel, familiar products appear multiple times, their packaging updated as the years pass. Other displays reflect past trends, like the Egyptomania of the 1920s and the militar-ization of marketing during the two World Wars. There's a section for every decade of the 20th century and some substantial and intriguing 19th-century displays, such as the teapots, gift sets and guides from the Great Exhibition of 1851.

NOTTING HILL CARNIVAL

The centrepiece in Europe's largest street carnival is a procession of flamboyant floats accompanied by steel bands, costumed dancers and mobile sound systems, transforming the area around Notting Hill, Ladbroke Grove and Westbourne Park into a celebration of Caribbean culture. Along the parade route are static sound systems, stages and food stalls. Born out of the black and West Indian experience in London, the carnival has expanded exponentially, and today over two million people attend.

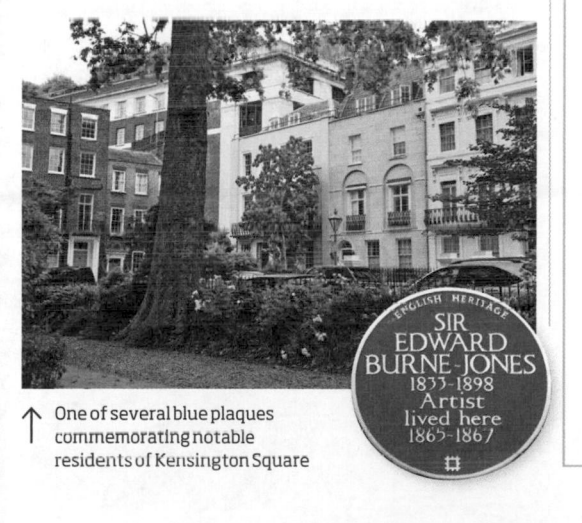

↑ Houseboats packed along the moorings at Little Venice

⑩ St Sophia's Cathedral

📍B5 🏛Moscow Rd W2
🚇Queensway 🕐2-4pm
Mon, 10am-noon Wed
🌐stsophia.org.uk

The richly decorated interior of this Greek Orthodox cathedral is a riot of coloured marble and gilded mosaics. On the second Sunday of each month it's possible to visit the treasury down in the crypt. The services feature a superb polyphonic choir.

⑪ Kensington Square

📍B7 🏛W8 🚇High St Kensington

This is one of London's oldest squares. It was laid out in the 1680s, and a few early 18th-century houses still remain (Nos 11 and 12 are the oldest). The renowned philosopher John Stuart Mill lived at No 18, and the Pre-Raphaelite painter and illustrator Edward Burne-Jones at No 41.

↑ One of several blue plaques commemorating notable residents of Kensington Square

ENGLISH HERITAGE
SIR
EDWARD
BURNE-JONES
1833-1898
Artist
lived here
1865-1867

EAT

Montparnasse Café
Homely French café and pâtisserie offering simple breakfasts, lunches and pastries.

📍B7 🏛22 Thackeray St W8

£££

Café Tarte
Nicely prepared light lunches at this friendly café - the irresistible cakes steal the show.

📍A7 🏛270 Kensington High St W8 🌐cafetarte.co.uk

£££

Holland Park Café
Great location, on the edge of the picturesque park. Enjoy soups, sandwiches and cakes.

📍A7 🏛Holland Park, W8 🌐cooksandpartners.co.uk

£££

Candella
Teas on vintage china, dainty sandwiches and light meals.

📍B7 🏛34 Kensington Church St W8 🌐candellatearoom.com

£££

The Muffin Man Tea Shop
Archetypally quaint, traditional tea shop with a hint of English village about it.

📍B7 🏛12 Wrights Lane W8 🌐themuffinmanteashop.co.uk.

£££

A SHORT WALK
KENSINGTON
AND HOLLAND PARK

Distance 3 km (2 miles) **Nearest Tube** High
Street Kensington **Time** 40 minutes

Although now part of central London, as recently as
the 1830s this was a country village of market gardens
and mansions. Outstanding among these was Holland
House; part of its grounds are now Holland Park. A walk
through the area takes you past many of its attractive
mid-19th century buildings, including expensive
apartments, mansion flats and fashionable shops.

Did You Know?

Holland Park was once
notorious as a location
for highway robbers.

Parts of the old formal
gardens of Holland House
feature in the delightful
Holland Park (p266).

Holland House, a
rambling Jacobean
mansion started in 1605,
was largely demolished
in the 1950s.

The Orangery, now a
restaurant, has parts
that date from the
1630s, when it was
within the grounds of
Holland House.

Melbury Road is lined with
large Victorian houses. Many
were built for fashionable
artists of the time.

The Design Museum is an
international showcase for the
many design skills at which
Britain excels (p264).

START

Leighton House is preserved
as it was when the Victorian
painter Lord Leighton lived
here (p267).

The Victorian letter box on
the High Street is one of the
oldest in London.

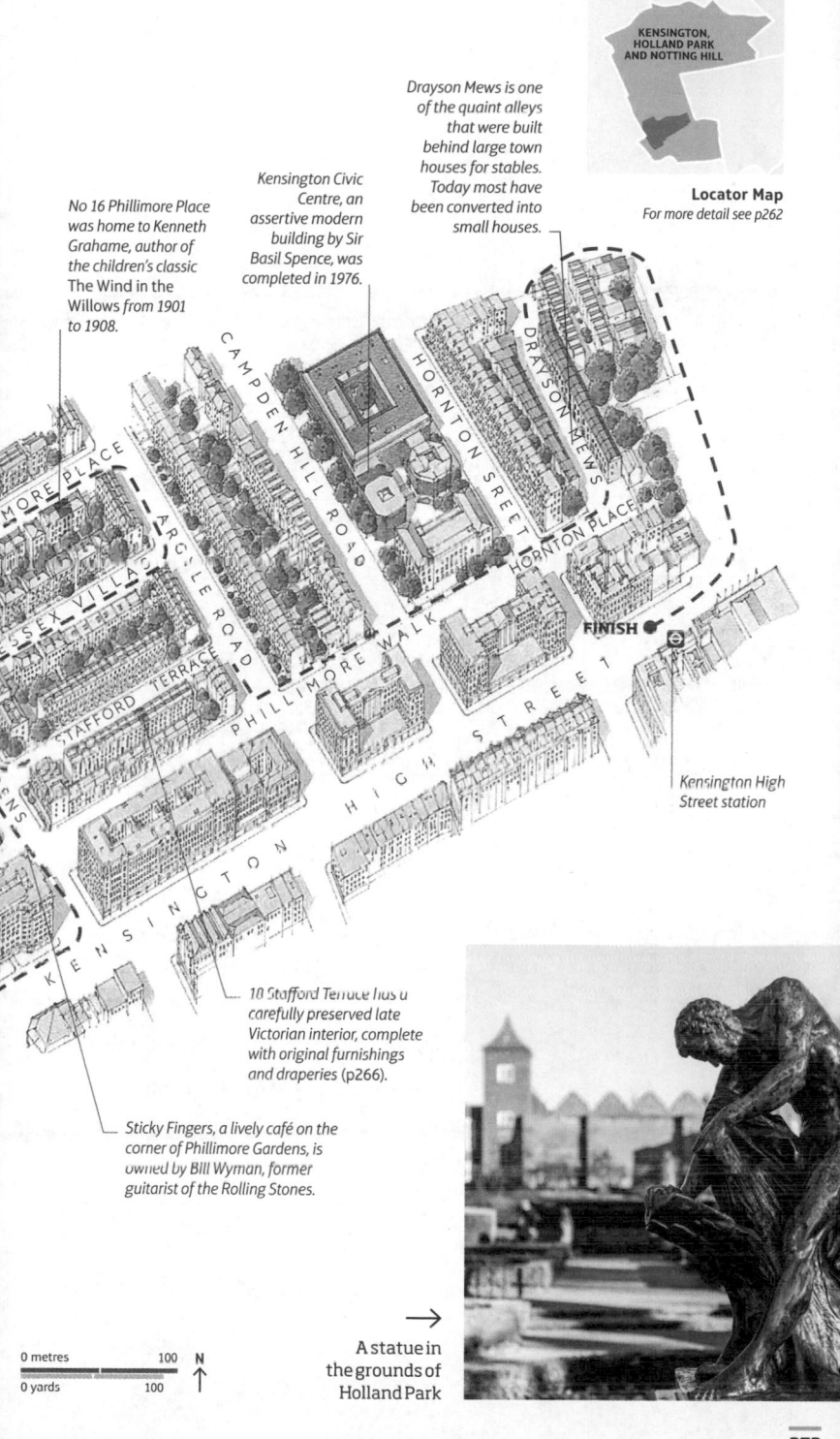

No 16 Phillimore Place was home to Kenneth Grahame, author of the children's classic The Wind in the Willows from 1901 to 1908.

Kensington Civic Centre, an assertive modern building by Sir Basil Spence, was completed in 1976.

Drayson Mews is one of the quaint alleys that were built behind large town houses for stables. Today most have been converted into small houses.

Locator Map
For more detail see p262

KENSINGTON, HOLLAND PARK AND NOTTING HILL

CAMPDEN HILL ROAD

ARGYLE ROAD

HORNTON STREET

DRAYSON MEWS

HORNTON PLACE

PHILLIMORE PLACE

ESSEX VILLAS

STAFFORD TERRACE

PHILLIMORE WALK

KENSINGTON HIGH STREET

GARDENS

KENSINGTON

FINISH

Kensington High Street station

18 Stafford Terrace has a carefully preserved late Victorian interior, complete with original furnishings and draperies (p266).

Sticky Fingers, a lively café on the corner of Phillimore Gardens, is owned by Bill Wyman, former guitarist of the Rolling Stones.

0 metres 100
0 yards 100

N ↑

→
A statue in the grounds of Holland Park

273

REGENT'S PARK AND MARYLEBONE

The name Marylebone is a derivation of "St Mary by the Bourne", the church that once stood next to the River Tyburn (also called Tybourne), long since buried underground. Many of the street names around Marylebone, including Wigmore Street and Portland Place, are taken from ancestral connections to the Howard de Walden family whose estate still occupies more or less the entire district. The estate dates from the early 18th century but before this time the land had been in royal hands. Henry VIII established hunting grounds to the north of Marylebone, some of which became Regent's Park when it was formally laid out from 1812 by John Nash, the architect responsible for the design of much of Regency London. Along the northern perimeter of the park runs the Regent's Canal, also laid out by Nash in the early 19th century. Not long after its completion, the recently founded Zoological Society of London opened their Zoological Gardens in five acres of the park – the beginnings of London Zoo.

REGENT'S PARK
AND MARYLEBONE

0 metres 400
0 yards 400

N

Primrose Hill

ST EDMUND'S TERRACE

PRINCE ALBERT ROAD

Grand Union Canal (Regent's Canal)

OUTER

St John's
Wood

ALLITSEN ROAD

ST JOHN'S WOOD TERRACE

ACACIA ROAD

CIRCLE

ROAD

WELLINGTON ROAD

COCHRANE STREET

ST JOHN'S WOOD HIGH STREET

NEWCOURT ST

MACKENNAL ST

PRINCE ALBERT ROAD

ST JOHN'S
WOOD

ABERCORN PLACE

GROVE END ROAD

ST JOHN'S WOOD ROAD

Lord's Cricket
Ground
9

LODGE ROAD

HALL ROAD

MAIDA VALE

Winfield
House

London
Central
Mosque **12**

HANOVER
GATE

OUTER

CIRCLE

*Boating
Lake*

PARK

PAVLEY STREET

LISSON

GROVE

LILESTONE ST

ROSSMORE ROAD

ROAD

SUSSEX PLACE

ROAD

CORNWALL TERR

LINHOPE STREET

BALCOMBE STREET

GLENTWORTH STREET

Sherlock
Holmes
Museum **11**

**Baker
Street** ⊖

CLIFTON GARDENS

BLOMFIELD ROAD

MAIDA AVENUE

FRAMPTON ST

CAPLAND ST

ASHBRIDGE

CHURCH STREET

PENFOLD STREET

BROADLEY ST

BROADLEY TERR

HAREWOOD AVENUE

LISSON GROVE

BOSTON PLACE

Marylebone 🚆⊖

ROAD

MARYLEBONE

EDGWARE ROAD

BELL STREET

**Edgware
Road** ⊖

PADDINGTON
GREEN

WESTWAY A40(M)

HARROW ROAD

ROAD

CHAPEL STREET

OLD MARYLEBONE RD

MARYLEBONE

ENCORD ST

KNOX ST

UPPER MONTAGU ST

YORK ST

YORK ST

Paddington

Paddington

Paddington Basin

SOUTH WHARF ROAD

PRAED STREET

SALE PLACE

ST MICHAELS ST

STAR STREET

NORFOLK

SUSSEX GARDENS

CAMBRIDGE SQUARE

NORFOLK CRESCENT

SHOULDHAM ST

YORK

CRAWFORD

BRYANSTON PLACE

SEYMOUR

HARROWBY ST

FORSET ST

EDGWARE

ROAD

MONTAGU PLACE

MONTAGU SQUARE

BRYANSTON SQUARE

GEORGE STREET

MONTAGU STREET

GLOUCESTER PLACE

DORSET ST

UPPER BERKELEY ST

PADDINGTON

NORFOLK SQUARE

LONDON ST

GLOUCESTER SQUARE

SUSSEX PL

HYDE PARK CRES

OXFORD SQUARE

HYDE PARK SQUARE

CONNAUGHT ST

ALBION ST

CONNAUGHT SQUARE

SEYMOUR STREET

BRYANSTON STREET

STREET

STREE

Marble Arch ⊖

*Marble
Arch*

**KENSINGTON,
HOLLAND PARK AND
NOTTING HILL**
p260

GARDEN MEWS

HYDE PARK GARDENS

BAYSWATER ROAD

**SOUTH KENSINGTON
AND KNIGHTSBRIDGE**
p240

CRAVEN HILL

Lancaster
Gate ⊖

REGENT'S PARK AND MARYLEBONE

Must See

1 London Zoo

Experience More

2 Regent's Park
3 Wallace Collection
4 Madame Tussauds
5 St Marylebone Parish Church
6 Broadcasting House
7 All Souls, Langham Place
8 Royal Academy of Music Museum
9 Lord's Cricket Ground
10 Oxford Street
11 Sherlock Holmes Museum
12 London Central Mosque
13 Wigmore Hall
14 Cumberland Terrace
15 Marylebone High Street

Stay

① The Langham

Shop

② Daunt Books

❶

LONDON ZOO

Q F1 🅰 Regent's Park NW1 ⓔ Camden Town, Regent's Park ⓞ Apr-Aug: 10am-6pm; Sep-Oct & Mar: 10am-5:30pm; Nov-Feb: 10am-4pm (last adm 1 hr before closing) 🆆 zsl.org

By international standards, London Zoo is relatively small but it packs a lot in, including Sumatran tigers, Western lowland gorillas, spider monkeys, giraffes, iguanas, pythons and bird-eating tarantulas.

Despite its dense population, many of the larger animals here enjoy relatively spacious and interesting enclosures, especially since the zoo embarked on an extensive series of imaginative redevelopments in the early 2000s. Since then they have opened Penguin Beach, Gorilla Kingdom, the Meet the Monkeys and In With The Lemurs walk-through exhibits, as well as a humid rainforest enclosure with sloths and anteaters. The largest and most captivating enclosure is the Land of the Lions, where Asiatic lions prowl around the zoo's rendering of the Gir Forest in western India. Visitors look on from overhead walkways and a reconstruction of a Gujarat village, complete with train station, high street and temple ruins.

← Entrance to the ever popular London Zoo

STAY

Gir Lion Lodge
Wake up to the roaring of lions after spending the night at the zoo's Gir Lion Lodge, a set of comfortable, charming cabins inside the zoo. Tours of the zoo at sunset, after dark and in the morning are included, as well as a two-course dinner.

🆆 zsl.org/gir-lion-lodge

£££

Children get close to a giant moth at Butterfly Paradise ↑

EXPERIENCE MORE

Regent's Park

F2 **NW1** **Regent's Park, Baker St, Great Portland St** **5am–dusk daily** **royalparks.org.uk**

This area of land became enclosed as a park in 1812. John Nash designed the scheme and originally envisaged a kind of garden suburb, dotted with 56 villas in a variety of Classical styles, and a pleasure palace for the Prince Regent. In the event only eight villas – but no palace – were built inside the park (three survive round the edge of the Inner Circle).

The boating lake, which is home to many varieties of water birds, is marvellously romantic, especially when music drifts across from the bandstand. Queen Mary's Gardens are a mass of wonderful sights and smells in summer, when visitors can also enjoy a full programme of outdoor theatre, including Shakespeare, musicals and children's plays, at the Open Air Theatre nearby. The park is also renowned for its excellent sports facilities.

Nash's master plan for the park continues just beyond its northeastern edge in Park Village East and West. These elegant stucco buildings date from 1828, the same year in which London Zoo, which ranged across the north of the park, first opened.

↑ Eighteenth-century European art in the Wallace Collection

Wallace Collection

F4 **Hertford House, Manchester Sq W1** **Bond St, Baker St** **10am–5pm daily** **wallacecollection.org**

This is one of the world's finest private collections of art. It has remained intact since it was bequeathed to the government in 1897 with the stipulation that it should go on permanent public display with nothing added or removed. The product of passionate collecting for four generations of the Hertford family, it is a must for anyone with even a passing interest in the progress of European art up to the late 19th century. The house itself is magnificent, with dozens of rooms, including the superb great gallery, rich with period detail.

Among the 70 masterworks are Frans Hals's *The Laughing Cavalier*, Titian's *Perseus and Andromeda* and Rembrandt's *Titus*. There are superb portraits by Reynolds, Gainsborough and Romney. Other highlights include Sèvres porcelain and sculpture by Houdon and Roubiliac. The fine European and Oriental armour collection is the second largest in the UK.

There are tours and talks daily; details are on the website, along with some excellent podcasts.

↑ Enjoying the underwater view of penguins swimming at Penguin Beach

4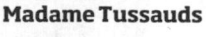

Madame Tussauds

⊕F3 ⊕Marylebone Rd NW1 ⊜Baker St ⊙9:30am-5:30pm Mon-Fri, 9am-6pm Sat & Sun ⊞madame tussauds.com

Madame Tussaud began her wax-modelling career rather morbidly, making death masks of well-known victims of the French Revolution. In 1835 she set up an exhibition of her work in Baker Street, not far from the present site.

Traditional wax-modelling techniques are still used to recreate politicians, royals, actors, rock stars and sporting heroes, the displays changing fairly regularly to keep up with who's in and who's out.

The exhibition features "A-List Party", where visitors can "attend" a celebrity bash; "Film", devoted to Hollywood's finest, such as Marilyn Monroe and ET; and "World Leaders", including Donald Trump, Boris Johnson and Nelson Mandela. "Culture" has the likes of Shakespeare and Picasso, and the "Music Zone" includes Madonna, Rihanna and Lady Gaga. There are also sections dedicated to franchises such as Marvel and Star Wars, with detailed walk-in sets and a 4D Marvel film experience. The Chamber of Horrors features gruesome episodes in the grim catalogue of crime and punishment, and in "Spirit of London" visitors travel in stylized London taxi-cabs through momentous events in the city's history, from the Great Fire of 1666 to 1960s Swinging London.

Ticket prices are fairly steep, but cheaper if you buy online in advance. Opting for timed tickets can help reduce queuing times.

5

St Marylebone Parish Church

⊕F3 ⊕Marylebone Rd NW1 ⊜Regent's Park ⊙9am-5pm daily ⊞stmarylebone.org

This is where the poets Robert Browning and Elizabeth Barrett were married in 1846 after eloping from her strict family home on nearby Wimpole Street. The large, stately church by Thomas Hardwick was built in 1817 after the former church, where Admiral Lord Nelson worshipped and where Lord Byron was christened in 1778, had become too small. Hardwick was determined that the same should not happen to his new church – so everything is on a grand scale.

→

Eric Gill's *Prospero and Ariel*, at the BBC's Broadcasting House

↑ The spacious interior of St Marylebone Parish Church

6

Broadcasting House

⊕G4 ⊕Portland Place W1 ⊜Oxford Circus ⊞bbc.co.uk

Broadcasting House was built in 1931 as a suitably modern Art Deco setting for the new medium of broadcasting. Its front, curving with the street, is dominated by Eric Gill's stylized relief *Prospero and Ariel*, inspired by characters in Shakespeare's play *The Tempest*. As the invisible spirit of the air, Ariel was considered

an appropriate personification of broadcasting. The character appears in two other sculptures on the western frontage, and again over the eastern entrance in the frieze *Ariel Piping to Children*.

Broadcasting House is the London headquarters of BBC news, radio, television and online departments. The only way to get a look inside is to book yourself a place, via the website, on one of the BBC's television or radio shows as a studio audience member.

A new wing added in 2005 was named after the disc jockey John Peel. Further refurbishment in 2011 created a public piazza, a BBC shop and a café that overlooks the central newsroom.

 7

All Souls, Langham Place

📍 G4 🏛 Langham Place W1 🚇 Oxford Circus 🕐 9:30am-5:30pm Mon-Fri, 9am-3pm & 5:30-8:30pm Sun 🌐 allsouls.org

John Nash designed this church in 1824. Its quirky round frontage is best seen from Regent Street. When it was first built, the spire was ridiculed as it appeared too slender and flimsy, and the church itself was described as "one of the most miserable structures in the metropolis".

The only Nash church in London, it had close links with the BBC, based across the street at Broadcasting House; the daily service, a stalwart of the radio schedule, was broadcast from here for many years. It maintains this broadcasting tradition with a "sermon streaming" resource on its website.

 **8** 🍴 🛍

Royal Academy of Music Museum

📍 F3 🏛 Marylebone Rd NW1 🚇 Baker Street, Regent's Park 🕐 11:30am-5:30pm Mon-Fri, noon-4pm Sat 🌐 ram.ac.uk

This simple museum in one of the country's finest music schools showcases the Royal Academy's collection of historical instruments. The three small rooms, staffed by volunteer students, are dispersed across three floors. On the ground floor you can find out about the history of the institution; in the Strings Gallery and the Piano Gallery upstairs are a prized Stradivari violin and viola and a 17th-century harpsichord. There's a restaurant and free lunchtime and evening concerts given elsewhere in the buildings.

 9 🚲 🏛 🛍

Lord's Cricket Ground

📍 D2 🏛 NW8 🚇 St John's Wood 🕐 For guided tours: Jan-Feb 11am-2pm; Apr-Oct 10am-3pm; Mar, Nov & Dec 10am-2pm 🕐 Last week of Dec 🌐 lords.org

Set up in 1814 by professional cricketer Thomas Lord, the ground can be visited on guided tours that take in the honour boards, dressing rooms

and the MCC (Marylebone Cricket Club) Museum. This is full of memorabilia from cricketing history, including a stuffed sparrow killed by a cricket ball and the Ashes. This tiny urn contains, supposedly, the burned remains of a cricket bail signifying "the death of English cricket" after a notable defeat by Australia. It is still the object of ferocious competition between the two national teams. The museum explains the history of the game, and mementos of notable cricketers make it a place of pilgrimage for devotees of the sport. Tours are hourly and it is essential to book ahead; there are no tours on major match days, but ticket holders do get free access to the museum.

→ The late Victorian pavilion at Lord's Cricket Ground

Another case for the great detective unfolding in the Sherlock Holmes Museum

and is furnished exactly as described in the books. Visitors are greeted by Holmes's "housekeeper" and shown to his recreated rooms on the first floor. The shop sells souvenirs including short stories and deerstalker hats.

Nike, UNIQLO and Gap plus British favourites like Marks & Spencer and Topshop.

Did You Know?

There have been more films starring Sherlock Holmes than any other (human) character.

10

Oxford Street

9 F5 **🏠** W1 **🚇** Marble Arch, Bond St, Oxford Circus, Tottenham Court Rd

This is London's biggest, brashest and busiest shopping street, running from Marble Arch at the western end right along Marylebone's southern border and then beyond, dividing Soho and Fitzrovia and ending at the Centre Point tower block. The western half is home to several department stores, most notably Selfridges, the largest and most famous (don't miss its magnificent Food Hall), although John Lewis, opened in 1864, predates it by half a century. Along the street's length and its shopper-clogged pavements are the UK flagship stores of international brands such as

→

Immaculate Cumberland Terrace, among London's most desirable addresses

11

Sherlock Holmes Museum

9 E3 **🏠** 221b Baker St NW1 **🚇** Baker St **🕐** 9:30am–6pm daily **🌐** sherlock-holmes.co.uk

Sir Arthur Conan Doyle's fictional detective lived at 221b Baker Street, an address that did not exist at the time, because Baker Street was then much shorter. This building, dating from 1815, is on what Conan Doyle would have known as Upper Baker Street, above Marylebone Road. It has been converted to resemble Holmes's flat,

12

London Central Mosque

9 E2 **🏠** 146 Park Rd NW8 **🚇** Marylebone, St John's Wood, Baker St **🕐** Dawn–dusk daily **🌐** iccuk.org

Surrounded by trees on the edge of Regent's Park, this large, golden-domed mosque was designed by Sir Frederick Gibberd and completed in 1978. Built to cater for the increasing number of Muslim residents in and visitors to London, the mosque is capable of holding 1,800 worshippers. The main hall of worship is a plain square chamber with a domed roof and a magnificent carpet. Visitors must remove their shoes before entering the mosque, and women should remember to cover their head.

Welcoming pubs and bars offering refreshment on Marylebone High Street ↑

13 🍽️

Wigmore Hall

📍 G4 🏠 36 Wigmore St W1
🚇 Bond St, Oxford Circus
🌐 wigmore-hall.org.uk

This appealing little concert hall for chamber music was designed by T E Collcutt, architect of the Savoy hotel, in 1900. At first it was called Bechstein Hall because it was attached to the Bechstein piano showroom; the area used to be the heart of London's piano trade. Opposite is the Art Nouveau emporium built in 1907 as Debenham and Freebody's department store – now Debenham's on Oxford Street.

14

Cumberland Terrace

📍 G2 🏠 NW1 🚇 Great Portland St, Regent's Park, Camden Town

Architect James Thomson is credited with the detailed design of this, the longest and most elaborate of the Neo-Classical terraces created by John Nash that border Regent's Park. Completed in 1828, it was designed to be visible from a palace Nash planned for the Prince Regent (later George IV). The palace was never built because the prince was too busy with his plans for Buckingham Palace (p90).

15

Marylebone High Street

📍 F4 🏠 NW1 🚇 Baker St, Regent's Park, Bond St

This boutique-heavy high street, the most villagey part of central London, is often overlooked by many visitors. Inside smart Victorian and Edwardian red-and-yellow brick townhouses are organic food shops, independent fashion stores and refined restaurants, all frequented by a well-dressed set of local shoppers. Must-sees are iconic design depot the Conran Shop and the incomparable Daunt Books. A few paces away, Cramer Street hosts the Marylebone Farmers' Market every Sunday (10am-2pm), one of the largest and most upmarket in London.

SHOP

Daunt Books
The most wonderful feature of this original Edwardian bookshop is its long oak galleries. Shelves carry travel guides and literature on each country.

📍 F4 🏠 83 Marylebone High St W1
🌐 dauntbooks.co.uk

A SHORT WALK
MARYLEBONE

Distance 2.5 km (1.5 miles) **Nearest Tube** Regent's Park
Time 30 minutes

Just south of Regent's Park lies the medieval village of
Marylebone (originally Maryburne, the stream by St Mary's
church). Until the 18th century it was surrounded by fields,
but these were built over as fashionable London drifted
west. The area has maintained its elegance, and your walk
will take you past the spacious houses that professionals,
especially doctors, used in the mid-19th century to receive
wealthy clients. The route also takes in Marylebone High
Street, full of interesting, high-quality food and clothes
shops, bookshops and cafés.

↑ The splendid Edwardian
interior of Daunt Books,
built in 1910

John Nash laid out Regent's
Park (p279), one of the city's
royal parks, in 1812 as a setting for classically designed
villas and terraces.

FINISH

The Royal Academy of Music
(p281), England's first music
academy, was founded in 1774.
The present brick building, with
its own concert hall, is from 1911.

Poets Robert Browning
and Elizabeth Barrett
were married in 1846 in
St Marylebone Parish
Church (p280).

The Madame Tussauds
waxworks museum
(p280) has been
in business since
1835 and remains one
of London's most
popular attractions.

Baker Street
station

Marylebone High Street (p283) is lined with attractive
shops. At No 83 is Daunt Books with its galleried interior. On the corner of Marylebone Lane, V V Rouleaux
is a gloriously colourful haberdashery shop.

Park Crescent's breathtaking façades by Nash
have been preserved, although the interiors
were rebuilt as offices in the 1960s. The
crescent seals the north end of Nash's
ceremonial route from St James's to Regent's
Park via Regent Street and Portland Place.

Regent's Park
station

START

0 metres   100
0 yards   100

N

Consulting rooms of
eminent medical
specialists have been
located at Harley Street
for more than a century.

In the centre of broad
Portland Place is a
statue of Field Marshal
Sir George Stuart
White, who won the
Victoria Cross for
gallantry in the
Afghan War of 1879.

PARK SQUARE WEST

PARK CRESCENT

PORTLAND PLACE

HARLEY   STREET

DEVONSHIRE   STREET

UPPER WIMPOLE ST

BEAUMONT STREET

The Royal Institute of
British Architects is
housed in a striking
Art Deco building
designed by Grey
Wornum in 1934.

→
Enjoying café life
along the pleasant
Marylebone High Street

HAMPSTEAD AND HIGHGATE

These rather exclusive north London neighbourhoods, perched on either side of the vast,
bucolic Hampstead Heath, were distinct villages
centuries before they were swallowed up by the
metropolis, an apartness still tangible to this day.
There has been a settlement in Highgate since at
least the Middle Ages, when an important staging
post on the Great North Road from London was
established, with a gate to control access.
Hampstead is known to have existed as far back
as the 10th century. From around the 17th century
both became fashionable retreats from the capital,
an allure only partially dampened in the 19th
century by their own urban expansion, the arrival
of the railway and the encroachment of the city.
They also share illustrious literary and artistic
connections, though Hampstead's arguably have
the edge, with the likes of John Keats having set
up home there. Though they may have lived in
Hampstead, many of the city's intellectuals are
buried in Highgate's cemetery – among them
political theorist Karl Marx.

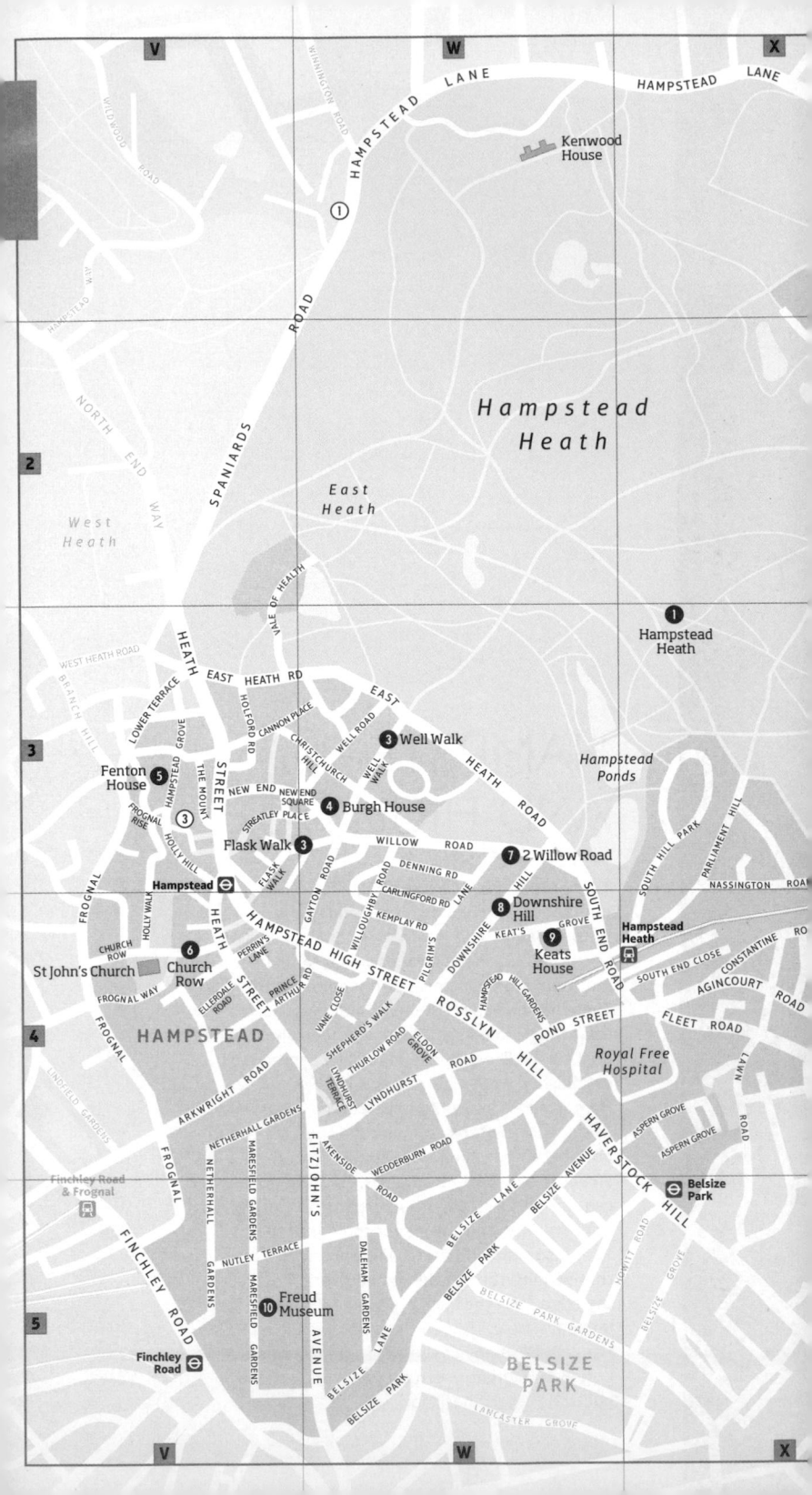

V **W** **X**

HAMPSTEAD LANE

HAMPSTEAD LANE

WINNINGTON ROAD

Kenwood House

①

SPANIARDS ROAD

WILD WOOD ROAD

NORTH END WAY

2

West Heath

Hampstead Heath

East Heath

WEST HEATH ROAD

BRANCH HILL

VALE OF HEALTH

❶
Hampstead Heath

Hampstead Ponds

3

HEATH STREET

EAST HEATH RD

LOWER TERRACE

HAMPSTEAD GROVE

THE MOUNT

HOLFORD RD

CANNON PLACE

CHRISTCHURCH HILL

WELL ROAD

WELL WALK

❸ Well Walk

EAST HEATH ROAD

Fenton House ❺

FROGNAL RISE

③

NEW END

NEW END SQUARE

STREATLEY PLACE

❹ Burgh House

Flask Walk ❸

FLASK WALK

WILLOW ROAD

WILLOUGHBY ROAD

GAYTON ROAD

DENNING RD

CARLINGFORD RD

❼ 2 Willow Road

DOWNSHIRE HILL

SOUTH HILL PARK

PARLIAMENT HILL

NASSINGTON ROAD

Hampstead ⊖

HOLLY HILL

HOLLY WALK

FROGNAL

CHURCH ROW

KEMPLAY RD

PILGRIM'S LANE

❽ Downshire Hill

KEAT'S GROVE

❾ Keats House

HAMPSTEAD HILL GARDENS

Hampstead Heath ⊖

SOUTH END CLOSE

CONSTANTINE RD

AGINCOURT ROAD

St John's Church

❻ Church Row

FROGNAL WAY

HEATH STREET

HAMPSTEAD HIGH STREET

PERRIN'S LANE

ELLERDALE ROAD

PRINCE ARTHUR RD

VANE CLOSE

SHEPHERD'S WALK

ELDON GROVE

ROSSLYN HILL

POND STREET

Royal Free Hospital

FLEET ROAD

LAWN ROAD

4

HAMPSTEAD

FROGNAL

ARKWRIGHT ROAD

THURLOW ROAD

LYNDHURST TERRACE

LYNDHURST ROAD

HAVERSTOCK HILL

ASPERN GROVE

ASPERN GROVE

LINDFIELD GARDENS

NETHERHALL GARDENS

MARESFIELD GARDENS

FITZJOHN'S AVENUE

AKENSIDE ROAD

WEDDERBURN ROAD

Finchley Road & Frognal ⊕

NETHERHALL GARDENS

NUTLEY TERRACE

MARESFIELD GARDENS

DALEHAM GARDENS

BELSIZE LANE

BELSIZE AVENUE

Belsize Park ⊖

NORWICH ROAD

FINCHLEY ROAD

BELSIZE PARK

BELSIZE PARK

BELSIZE PARK GARDENS

BELSIZE GROVE

5

Finchley Road ⊖

❿ Freud Museum

BELSIZE LANE

BELSIZE PARK

LANCASTER GROVE

V **W** **X**

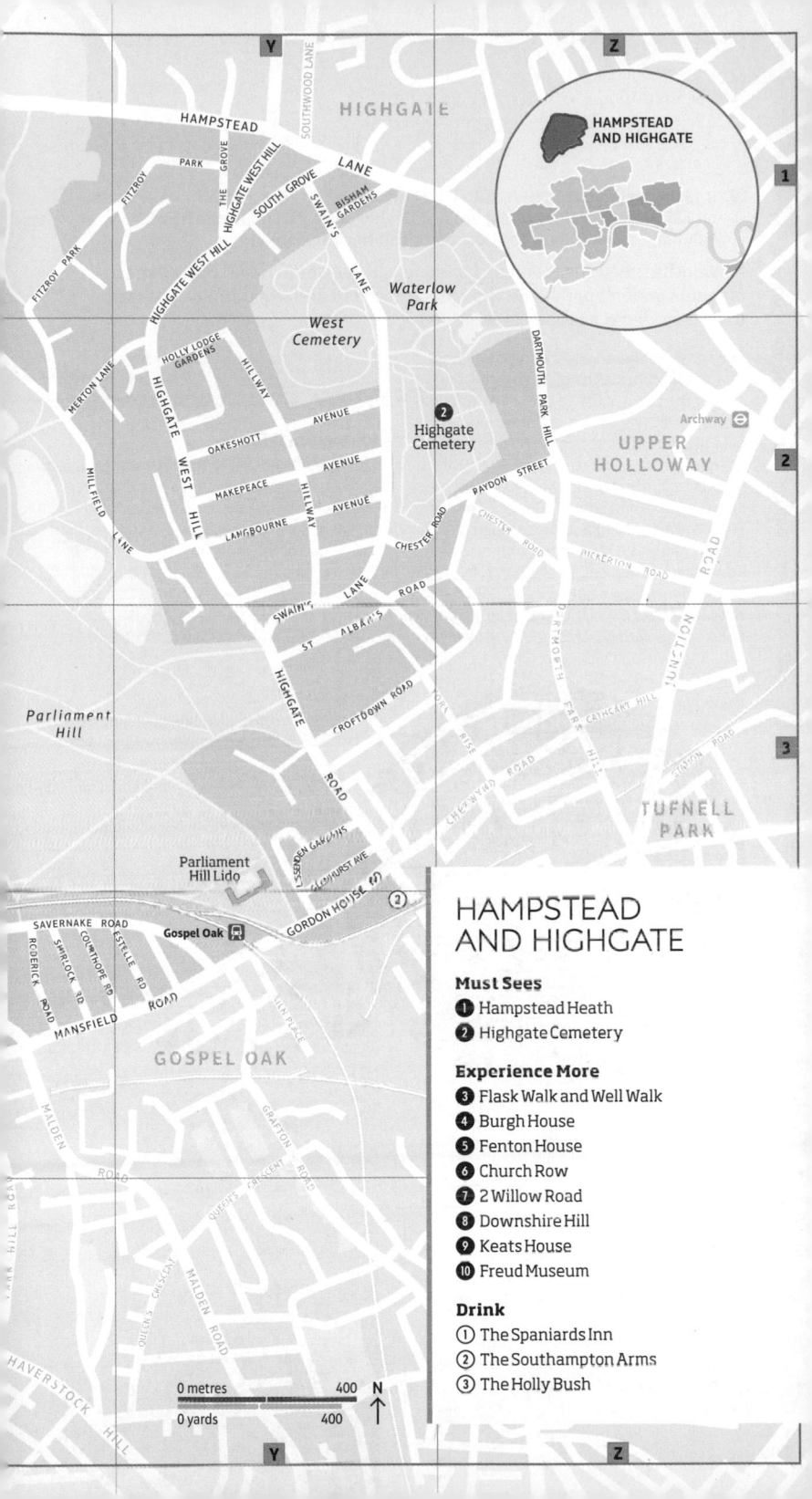

HIGHGATE

HAMPSTEAD AND HIGHGATE

Waterlow Park

West Cemetery

2 Highgate Cemetery

UPPER HOLLOWAY

Archway

Parliament Hill

Parliament Hill Lido

Gospel Oak

TUFNELL PARK

GOSPEL OAK

HAMPSTEAD AND HIGHGATE

Must Sees

1 Hampstead Heath
2 Highgate Cemetery

Experience More

3 Flask Walk and Well Walk
4 Burgh House
5 Fenton House
6 Church Row
7 2 Willow Road
8 Downshire Hill
9 Keats House
10 Freud Museum

Drink

① The Spaniards Inn
② The Southampton Arms
③ The Holly Bush

0 metres   400   N
0 yards   400

1

HAMPSTEAD HEATH

⊠X3 ⌂Hampstead NW3, NW5 ⊖Belsize Park, Hampstead, Kentish Town, Golders Green ⊞Hampstead Heath, Gospel Oak ⌚24 hrs daily ⓦHampstead Heath: cityoflondon.gov.uk; Kenwood House: english-heritage.org.uk

A favourite green space among Londoners, Hampstead Heath is the largest of inner London's parklands, though it is too wild and wonderfully unkempt to be considered a proper park.

The sprawling heath, separating the hilltop villages of Hampstead and Highgate, brings a slice of the countryside to the city, with large tracts of wild woodlands and meadows rolling over hills and around ponds and lakes. Covering an area of 3 sq miles (8 sq km), its natural habitats attract a wealth of wildlife, including bats and some 180 species of birds. There are also all kinds of landscaped areas, most notably The Hill Garden, a charming Edwardian garden once the grounds to Lord Leverhulme's house but now its raised pergola walkway, flowering plants and beautiful formal pond are open to all. Among the many other features of the heath is Vale of Heath, an isolated village tucked inside the southern boundary, and the picturesque Viaduct Pond.

Kenwood House

This magnificent white Neo-Classical mansion, its walls hung with paintings by old masters, overlooks splendidly landscaped grounds high on the edge of the north side of the heath. This is one of the most picturesque parts of the whole heath, with two large and lovely ponds, sweeping lawns and trails through the woodlands. There has been a house here since 1616 but the present villa was remodelled by

→

View over London from the green environs of Hampstead Heath

↑ Taking a dip in the men's bathing pond (there are women's and mixed ponds too)

GREAT VIEW
Hillside Heights

Parliament Hill, in the southeast corner of the heath, provides one of the most spectacular views over the capital, taking in The Shard, the skyscrapers of The City, the dome of St Paul's Cathedral and the Houses of Parliament.

Statue by Henry Moore in the grounds of Kenwood House ↓

↑ Grand Kenwood House, on the edge of Hampstead Heath

Robert Adam in 1764 for the Earl of Mansfield. Adam transformed the interior and most of his work has survived, including the highlight, the resplendent library, with its ceiling paintings, opposing apses and Corinthian columns. Some of the most precious paintings are hung here including works by Vermeer, Turner, Van Dyck, Hals, Reynolds and Rembrandt, whose self-portrait is the star attraction of the collection. The house features a tearoom and restaurant with a lovely garden seating area. In summer there are ticketed, open-air concerts in the grounds of Kenwood House, though many people pack a picnic and sit nearby to listen.

↑ Elegant rooms filled with old master paintings

HIGHGATE CEMETERY

Z2 **Swain's Lane N6** **Archway** **Check website for opening hours** **highgatecemetery.org**

Opened in 1839, this is London's best-known cemetery, most famous for epitomizing the Victorian obsession with death and the afterlife.

The two leafy sections of Highgate Cemetery, divided by a country lane, are full of flowerbeds, statues, elaborate tombs and overgrown gravestones, bathed in a light suitably subdued by the shade from the small forests of trees. For Victorians, preoccupied with death and insistent on burial rather than cremation, this was the graveyard of choice, where you could lie shoulder to shoulder with poets, artists and intellectuals. Both sections contain the graves of numerous iconic figures but it is the West Cemetery which is the more atmospheric and architecturally interesting. Its showpiece is the restored Egyptian Avenue, a street of family vaults styled on ancient Egyptian tombs, leading to the Circle of Lebanon, a ring of vaults topped by a cedar tree.

↑ Statue of an angel, one of many found among the tombs and trees

Did You Know?

The cemetery contains over 53,000 graves and more than 170,000 people have been buried here.

Karl Marx's tomb in its tranquil surroundings in Highgate Cemetery ↑

Must See

↑ Fenton House, whose treasures can be explored in the summer months

EXPERIENCE MORE

3
Flask Walk and Well Walk

📍 W3 🏠 NW3
🚇 Hampstead

Flask Walk is named after the Flask pub. Here, in the 18th century, the area's therapeutic spa water was put into flasks and sold to visitors or sent to London. The water, rich in iron salts, came from nearby Well Walk, where a disused fountain now marks the site of the well. There have been many notable residents of Well Walk: artist John Constable, novelists D H Lawrence and J B Priestley, and the poet John Keats. At the High Street end, Flask Walk is narrow and lined with old shops. Beyond the Flask pub it broadens into a row of fine Regency houses.

4
Burgh House

📍 W3 🏠 New End Sq NW3
🚇 Hampstead 🕐 Noon–5pm Wed–Fri & Sun ❌ Christmas week 🌐 burghhouse.org.uk

Since 1979, an independent trust has run Burgh House as the Hampstead Museum, which illustrates the history of the area and some of its notable residents. The museum owns a significant art collection, including works by the Bloomsbury Group painter Duncan Grant, along with furniture and archive material on the area. There is a display about Hampstead as a spa in the 18th and 19th centuries. In the 1720s, Dr William Gibbons, chief physician to the spa, lived at this address.

5
Fenton House

📍 V3 🏠 20 Hampstead Grove NW3 🚇 Hampstead 🕐 Mar–Oct: 11am–5pm Wed–Sun & public hols 🌐 nationaltrust.org.uk

Built in 1686, this splendid William and Mary house is the oldest mansion in Hampstead. It contains several specialist exhibitions: the Benton-Fletcher collection of early keyboard instruments – a harpsichord dating from 1612 is said to have been played by Handel – and a fine collection of porcelain. The instruments are kept in full working order and concerts are given in the house. The porcelain was largely accumulated by Lady Binning who, in 1952, left the house and its contents to the National Trust.

The buildings of Church Row, Hampstead, a perfect slice of Georgian history

6 Church Row

◉ V4 ⬛ NW3 ⊜ Hampstead

Church Row is one of the most complete Georgian streets in London. Much of its original detail has survived, notably the ironwork. At the west end is St John's, Hampstead's parish church, built in 1745. The iron gates are earlier and come from Canons Park in Edgware, Middlesex. Inside the church is a bust of poet John Keats. Artist John Constable's grave is in the churchyard, and a long list of other Hampstead luminaries are buried in the adjoining cemetery.

7 2 Willow Road

◉ W3 ⬛ NW3 ⊜ Hampstead ⬛ Hampstead Heath ◷ Mar–Oct: 11am–5pm Wed–Sun (tours only before 3pm) ⬛ nationaltrust.org.uk

The striking modernist 1930s home of Hungarian architect Ernö Goldfinger – designer of a number of Brutalist London tower blocks – is preserved almost exactly as he designed and lived in it, complete with many of his beguiling possessions. The relatively plain, unremarkable façade makes the sleek, stylish yet warm interior all the more memorable. Steps from the ground floor delicately fan out in a spiral leading up to the open-plan, beautifully efficient living space. Bathed in a natural light perfect for

↑ The Regency façade of St John's Downshire Hill, completed in 1823

viewing Goldfinger's precious 20th-century art collection, the geometrically designed rooms are full of innovative touches – removable walls, for example, that allow interior spaces to be reconfigured.

8 Downshire Hill

◉ W4 ⬛ NW3 ⊜ Hampstead

A beautiful street of mainly Regency houses, Downshire Hill lent its name to a group of artists, including Stanley Spencer and Mark Gertler, who would gather at No 47 between the two World Wars. The same house had been the meeting place of Pre-Raphaelite artists, among them Dante Gabriel Rossetti and Edward Burne-Jones. A more recent resident, at No 5, was the late Jim Henson, the creator of The Muppets.

The church on the corner (the second Hampstead church to be called St John's) was built in 1823 to serve the Hill's residents. Inside, it still has its original box pews.

Keats House

📍 W4 🏠 Keats Grove NW3
🚇 Hampstead, Belsize Park
🚆 Hampstead Heath
🕐 11am-5pm Wed-Sun
🚫 25 & 26 Dec 🌐 cityof
london.gov.uk/keats

Originally two semi-detached houses built in 1816, the smaller one became Keats's home in 1818, when a friend persuaded him to move in. Keats spent two productive years here: perhaps his most celebrated poem *Ode to a Nightingale* was said to have been written under a plum tree in the garden. The Brawne family moved into the larger house a year later and Keats became engaged to their daughter, Fanny. However, the marriage never took place: Keats died of consumption in Rome before two years had passed. He was only 25 years old.

A copy of one of Keats' love letters to Fanny, the engagement ring he offered her and a lock of her hair are among the mementos that are exhibited at the house, which was first opened to the public in 1925. Visitors are also able to see facsimiles of some of Keats' manuscripts, part of a collection that serves as an evocative and memorable tribute to his life and work. A 30 minute tour begins at 3pm.

Freud Museum

📍 V5 🏠 20 Maresfield Gdns NW3 🚇 Finchley Rd
🕐 Noon-5pm Wed-Sun (also Mon in Aug & Sep) 🚫 1 Jan, 25-26 Dec 🌐 freud.org.uk

In 1938, Sigmund Freud, the founder of psychoanalysis, fled from Nazi persecution in Vienna to this Hampstead house. Making use of the possessions he brought with him, his family recreated the atmosphere of his Vienna consulting rooms.

After Freud died in 1939 his daughter Anna (who was a pioneer of child psycho-analysis) kept the house as it was and in 1986 it was opened as a museum dedicated to her father. On display is the couch on which patients lay for analysis. A series of 1930s home movies shows moments with his dog as well as more distressing footage of Nazi attacks on his apartment. The bookshop has a large collection of his works.

In 2016 Anna Freud was commemorated with her own blue plaque on the front of the house, joining that of her father. This was only the 19th building in London to have been awarded the rare "double blue" accolade. Other properties with two blue plaques include 29 Fitzroy Square *(p156)* and the Handel and Hendrix house *(p99)*.

DRINK

The Spaniards Inn
Dickensian pub on Hampstead Heath with a colourful 500-year history, a beer garden for summer and an open fire in winter.

📍 W1 🏠 Spaniards Rd NW3 🌐 thespaniards hampstead.co.uk

The Southampton Arms
A relaxed traditional pub with a dinky beer garden, offering a superior range of ales from independent breweries.

📍 Y3 🏠 139 Highgate Rd NW5 🌐 thesouthampton arms.co.uk

The Holly Bush
A cosy 18th-century pub with low ceilings on a charming backstreet in Hampstead. Great pub grub too.

📍 V3 🏠 22 Holly Mount NW3 🌐 hollybush hampstead.co.uk

← A stained-glass skylight illuminating the library of Keats House

A SHORT WALK
HAMPSTEAD

Distance 1.5 km (1 mile) **Nearest tube** Hampstead
Time 20 minutes

Perched awkwardly on a hilltop, with its broad heath to the north, Hampstead has kept its village atmosphere and sense of being outside the city. This has attracted artists and writers since Georgian times and has made it one of London's most desirable residential areas. Its mansions and town houses are perfectly maintained and a stroll through Hampstead's narrow streets is one of London's quieter pleasures.

Did You Know?

Admiral's House was the inspiration for the home of Admiral Boom in PL Travers' *Mary Poppins*.

A welcome retreat from the city, Hampstead Heath's broad open spaces include bathing ponds, meadows and lakes (p290).

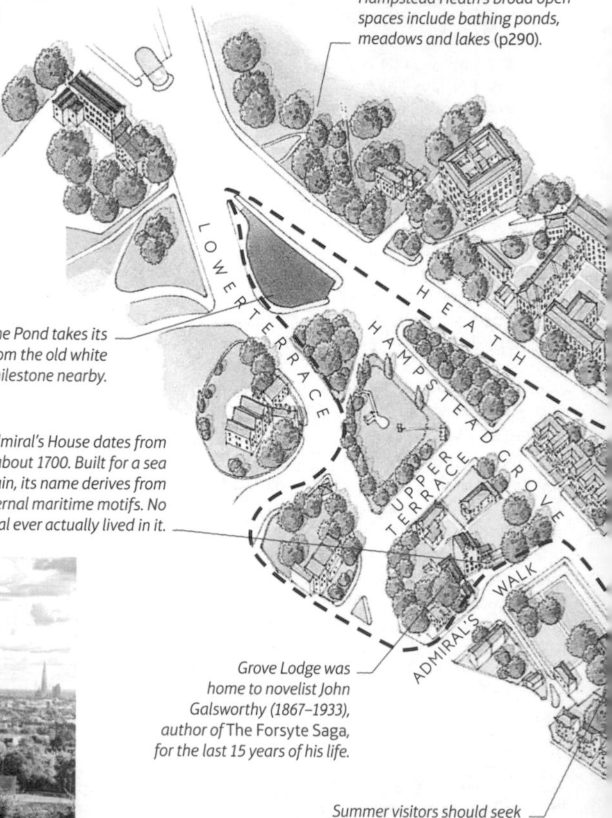

Whitestone Pond takes its name from the old white milestone nearby.

Admiral's House dates from about 1700. Built for a sea captain, its name derives from its external maritime motifs. No admiral ever actually lived in it.

Grove Lodge was home to novelist John Galsworthy (1867–1933), author of The Forsyte Saga, for the last 15 years of his life.

Summer visitors should seek out the late 17th-century Fenton House and its exquisite walled garden, which are well hidden in the jumble of streets near the heath (p293).

LOWER TERRACE

HEATH

HAMPSTEAD GROVE

UPPER TERRACE

ADMIRAL'S WALK

← Stunning views of the city from a hillside on Hampstead Heath

0 metres		100
0 yards		100

N

JOULE
designer jewellers
JOULE

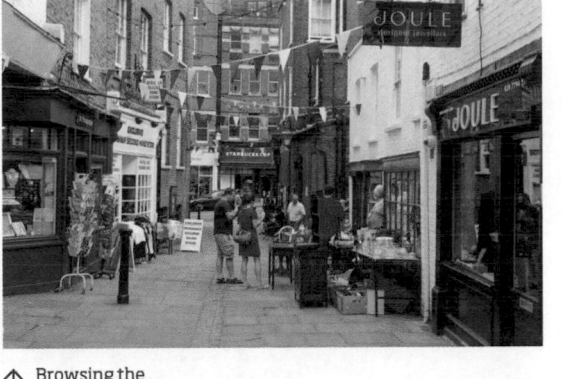

↑ Browsing the characterful shops on Flask Walk

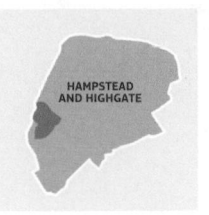

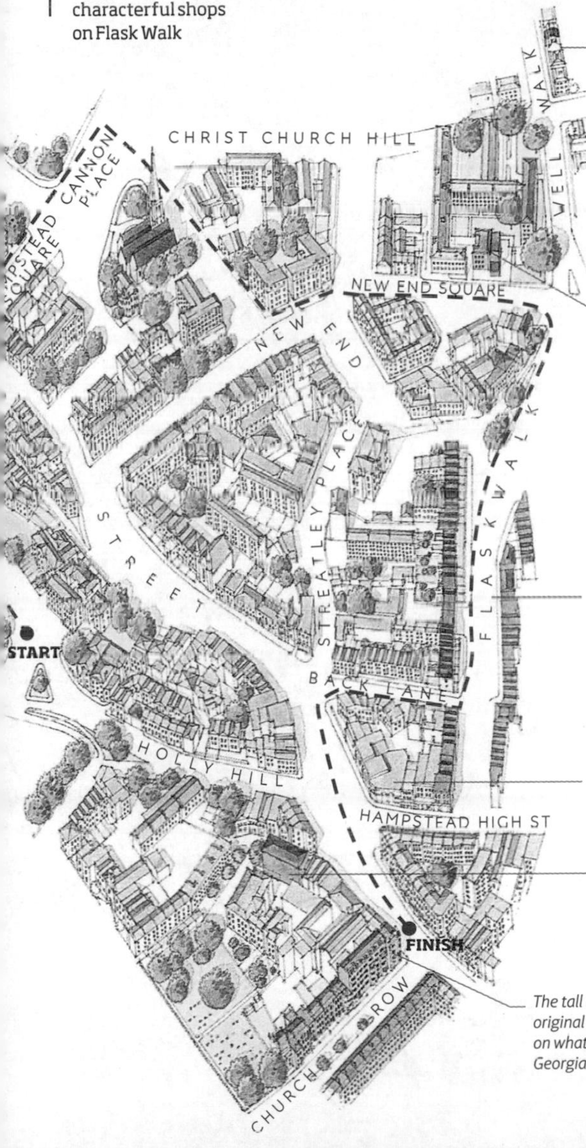

HAMPSTEAD
AND HIGHGATE

Locator Map
For more detail see p288

CHRIST CHURCH HILL
CANNON PLACE
HAMPSTEAD SQUARE
NEW END SQUARE
NEW END
WELL WALK
FLASK WALK
STREATLEY PLACE
STREET
BACK LANE
START
HOLLY HILL
HAMPSTEAD HIGH ST
FINISH
CHURCH ROW

No 40 Well Walk is where artist John Constable lived while working on his many Hampstead pictures (p293).

Built in 1702 but much altered since, Burgh House contains an intriguing local history museum and a café overlooking the small garden (p293).

Flask Walk is an alley of charming specialist shops that broadens into a residential village street (p293).

Hampstead station

The Everyman Cinema has been an arthouse cinema since 1933.

The tall houses on Church Row are rich in original detail. Notice the superb ironwork on what is probably London's finest Georgian street (p294).

GREENWICH AND CANARY WHARF

It was Henry IV's son, Humphrey, Duke of Gloucester and the brother of Henry V, who first established the royal foothold in Greenwich, in the mid-15th century, when he built himself the Palace of Placentia, originally known as Bella Court. Henry VIII was born in the palace, as were his daughters, Mary and Elizabeth. The palace was demolished at the end of the 17th century and the land where it stood is now occupied by the Old Royal Naval College; the royal hunting grounds are now gorgeous Greenwich Park. The buildings of the Naval College, the centrepiece of the UNESCO World Heritage Site referred to as Maritime Greenwich, started life as Greenwich Hospital, a home for wounded and retired sailors, opened in 1692. The conversion to a Royal Navy college in 1873 cemented an already well-established maritime heritage in Greenwich, one shared by Canary Wharf over the river, the site of the historic docklands since the early 19th century.

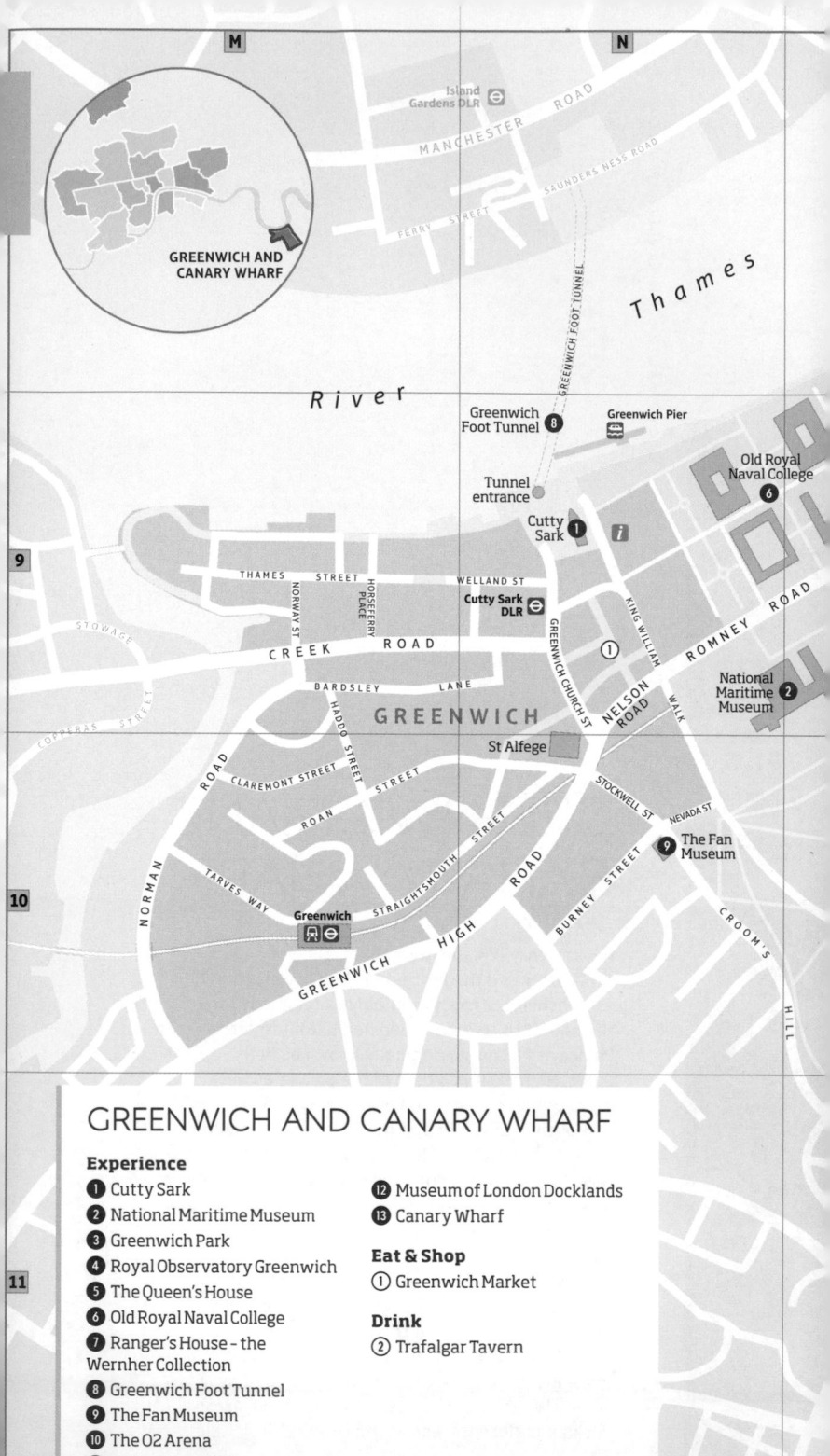

GREENWICH AND CANARY WHARF

Experience
1. Cutty Sark
2. National Maritime Museum
3. Greenwich Park
4. Royal Observatory Greenwich
5. The Queen's House
6. Old Royal Naval College
7. Ranger's House – the Wernher Collection
8. Greenwich Foot Tunnel
9. The Fan Museum
10. The O2 Arena
11. Emirates Air Line
12. Museum of London Docklands
13. Canary Wharf

Eat & Shop
1. Greenwich Market

Drink
2. Trafalgar Tavern

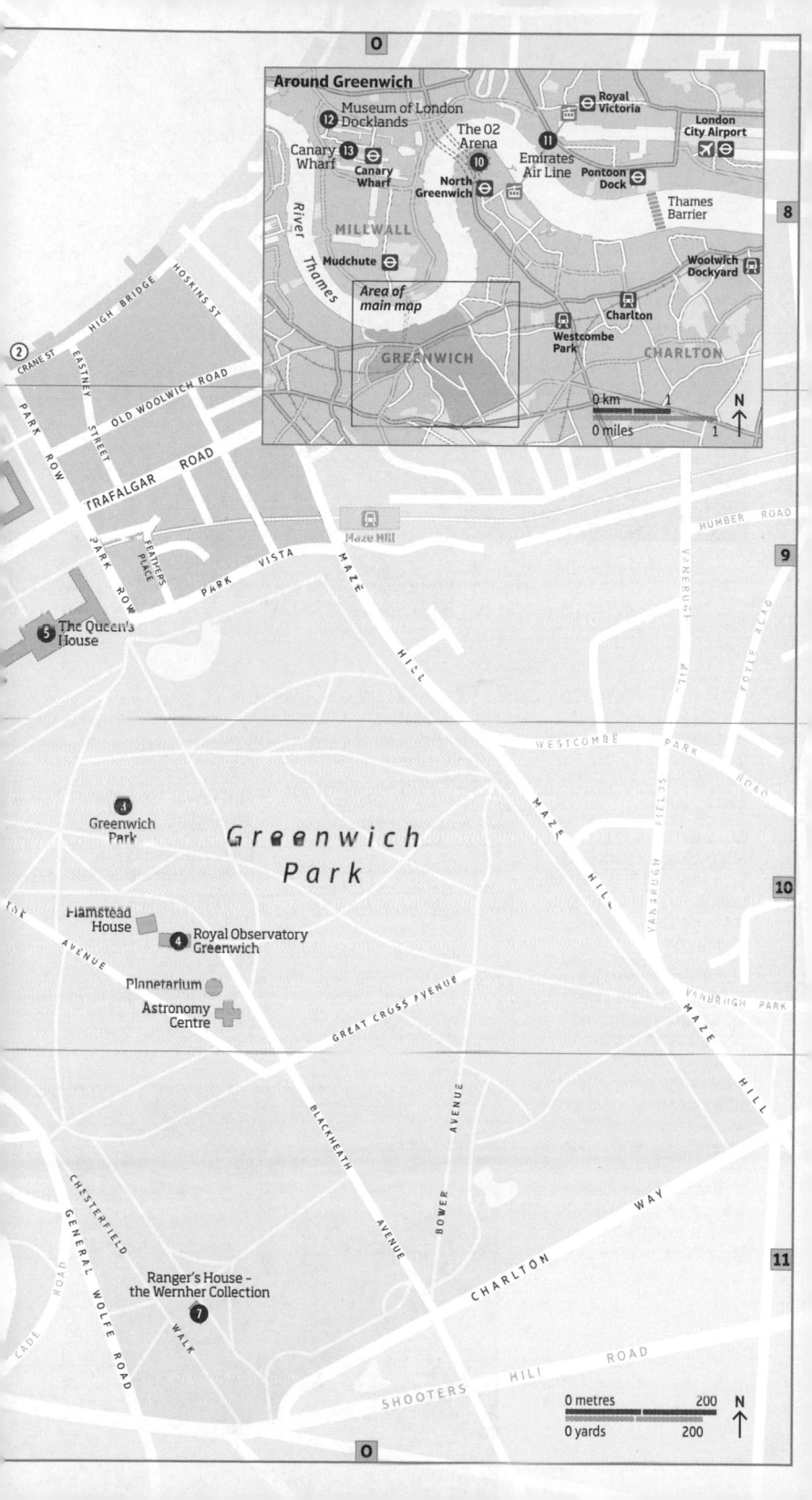

The structure holding the hull of the impressive *Cutty Sark* ↑

EXPERIENCE

❶ 🖼️ 💻 🏛️

Cutty Sark

📍N9 🏠King William Walk SE10 🚇Cutty Sark DLR ⛴️Greenwich Pier ⏰10am-5pm daily (last adm: 4:15pm) 📅24-26 Dec 🌐rmg.co.uk

This majestic vessel is a survivor of the clippers that crossed the Atlantic and Pacific oceans in the 19th century. Launched in 1869 as a tea carrier, it was something of a speed machine in its day, winning the annual clippers' race from China to London in 1871 in just 107 days. It made its final voyage in 1938 and was put on display here in 1957. In 2006 the *Cutty Sark* was closed to visitors for renovation work, which

suffered a major setback in May 2007 when the ship was severely damaged by fire. It was reopened by the Queen in spring 2012, fully restored and slightly raised in a glass enclosure. Visitors can explore the cargo decks and sleeping quarters below deck, take the ships wheel, and be entertained by tales from the costumed "crew". There are interactive displays on navigation and life on board.

❷ 🖼️ 💻 🏛️

National Maritime Museum

📍N9 🏠Romney Rd SE10 🚇Cutty Sark DLR ⛴️Greenwich ⏰10am-5pm daily (ground floor till 6pm Jul-Aug) 📅24-26 Dec 🌐rmg.co.uk

This museum – built in the 19th century as a school for sailors' children – celebrates

→ Portrait of a young Nelson, National Maritime Museum

Britain's seafaring heritage, from early British trade and empire to the expeditions of Captain Cook, and from the Napoleonic Wars through to the modern day. The Sammy Ofer wing, the biggest development in the museum's history, boasts "the Wave", a 20-m (65-ft) audiovisual installation in which images and films from the museum's vast archives unfurl in dramatic, thematic journeys.

The Nelson gallery looks at the course of British maritime history over the tumultuous 18th century, a period when seafaring heroes were considered national celebrities. A star exhibit is the uniform that Lord Horatio Nelson was wearing when he was shot at the Battle of Trafalgar in October 1805.

Rather more spectacular is the royal barge built for Prince Frederick in 1732, decorated with gilded mermaids and his Prince of Wales feathers on the stern. Throughout the museum there are numerous activities for children, such as navigating a ship around the world on a huge floor map.

③ 🖵
Greenwich Park

📍010 🏠SE10 🚇Cutty Sark DLR, Greenwich DLR 🚆Greenwich, Maze Hill, Blackheath ⏰6am until dusk 🌐royalparks.org.uk

Originally the grounds of a royal palace and still a Royal Park, Greenwich Park was enclosed in 1433 and its brick wall built in the reign of James I. Later, in the 17th century, the French royal landscape gardener André Le Nôtre was invited to redesign the park. The broad avenue, rising south up the hill, was part of his plan. It's a steep climb up the hilltop but one well-rewarded by sweeping views across London and more green space to explore.

---

④ 🍴🖵🏛
Royal Observatory Greenwich

📍010 🏠Greenwich Park SE10 🚇Cutty Sark DLR 🚆Greenwich ⏰10am-5pm daily (to 6pm late Jul-Aug) ❌24-26 Dec 🌐rmg.co.uk

The meridian (0° longitude) that divides Earth's eastern and western hemispheres passes through here, and millions of visitors come to be photographed standing with a foot on either side of it. In 1884, Greenwich Mean Time became the basis of time measurement for most of the world. Here you can journey through the history of time, explore how scientists first mapped the stars and see world-changing inventions, including the UK's largest refracting telescope. Visitors can even touch a 4.5 billion-year-old asteroid.

→

The onion dome of the Royal Observatory Greenwich, housing a colossal telescope

EAT & SHOP

Greenwich Market
A historic covered market with over 100 stalls. It's particularly strong on arts and crafts, vintage and antique items, but kooky clothes and accessories and food stalls feature too.

📍N9 🏠Greenwich Church St SE10 🌐greenwich market.london

The original building, Flamsteed House, was designed by Christopher Wren for the first Astronomer Royal, John Flamsteed, and it contains original instruments belonging to his successors, including Edmond Halley. This was the official State observatory from 1675 until 1948, when the astronomers moved to Sussex to escape London's bright lights. There is also a state-of-the-art planetarium here, the only one in London. There is an entry charge for Flamsteed House and the planetarium shows; the Astronomy Centre is free.

⑤

The Queen's House

📍09 🏠Romney Rd SE10
🚉Cutty Sark DLR 🚆Greenwich ⏰10am–5pm daily
🚫24–26 Dec 🌐rmg.co.uk

The Queen's House was designed by Inigo Jones and completed in 1637. It was originally intended to be the home of Anne of Denmark, wife of James I, but she died while it was still being built and it was finished for Charles I's queen consort, Henrietta Maria. After the English Civil War it was briefly occupied by Henrietta as dowager queen, but was not much used by the royal family after that. From 1821 to 1933 the Royal Hospital School was housed here.

Period highlights include the square Great Hall, the King's and Queen's Presence Chambers and the spiral cantilevered "tulip staircase", which curves sinuously upwards without a central support. The house focuses on the art collection of the National Maritime Museum. Following refurbishment in 2016, the Queen's House features Turner Prize-winner Richard Wright's gold leaf art installation on the ceiling of the Great Hall.

> **These ambitious buildings by Christopher Wren were built on the site of the old 15th-century royal palace, where Henry VIII, Mary I and Elizabeth I were born.**

⑥

Old Royal Naval College

📍N9 🏠King William Walk SE10 🚉Cutty Sark DLR, Greenwich DLR 🚆Greenwich, Maze Hill ⏰10am–5pm daily (until 6pm Aug & early Sep); grounds: 8am–11pm daily 🚫24–26 Dec & some Sat 🌐ornc.org

A landmark of Greenwich, these ambitious buildings by Christopher Wren were built on the site of the old 15th-century royal palace, where Tudors Henry VIII, Mary I and Elizabeth I were born, to house naval pensioners. At its peak, the then hospital was home to some 2,700 veterans.

The Painted Hall, which was intended as a dining room for the retired seamen, was opulently decorated by Sir James Thornhill in the early 18th century. The huge ceiling painting is the largest figurative painting in the country. In 1805, the hall was the location of a lavish lying-in-state ceremony for Lord Horatio Nelson, who was killed at the Battle of Trafalgar.

The hall is currently being restored, and while this project continues visitors have the opportunity to ascend the scaffolding and see the painstaking work close-up. Places can be booked on the website. There are also free guided walking tours of the site several times a day, for which no booking is required. They start from the visitor centre and last about 45 minutes.

↓ One of Wren's twin buildings that form the Old Royal Naval College

→

Statue by Bergonzoli and Chinese-themed tapestries at the Ranger's House

In 1873, the hospital was acquired by the Naval College in Portsmouth and it remained a training post for officers until 1997. During its heyday, the college was considered one of the best of its kind in Europe. It also trained thousands of Wrens during World War II.

There is a relaxed pub next to the visitor centre with a huge terrace overlooking the *Cutty Sark*, but visitors are also welcome to picnic in the grounds – provided that they dispose of litter thoughtfully.

Ranger's House – the Wernher Collection

📍 O11 🏠 Chesterfield Walk, Greenwich Park SE10 🚉 Cutty Sark DLR 🚉 Blackheath 🕐 Apr–Sep, for guided tours only 🌐 english-heritage.org.uk

The Wernher Collection is located in the Ranger's House (1688), an elegant building southeast of Greenwich Park *(p303)*. It is an enchanting array of over 650 pieces accumulated by South African mine owner Sir Julius Wernher in the late 19th century. The collection is displayed in 12 rooms and includes paintings, jewellery, furniture and porcelain. Highlights include Renaissance masterworks by Hans Memling and Filippo Lippi, over 100 Renaissance jewels, and an opal-set lizard pendant jewel. The tour ends with the magnificent sculpture of a woman and angel by 19th-century artist Giulio Bergonzoli. Tours are offered twice a day, Sunday to Wednesday and it is advisable to book ahead – check the website for details.

⑧ Greenwich Foot Tunnel

📍 N9 🏠 Between Greenwich Pier SE10 and Isle of Dogs E14 🚉 Island Gardens, Cutty Sark DLR 🚉 Greenwich Pier 🕐 24hrs daily

This 370-m- (1,200-ft-) long tunnel was opened in 1902 to allow south London labourers to walk to work in Millwall Docks. It is well worth crossing from Greenwich for the wonderful views, back across the river, of Christopher Wren's Royal Naval College and of Inigo Jones's Queen's House.

Matching round red-brick terminals, with glass domes, mark the top of the lift shafts on either side of the river.

DRINK

Trafalgar Tavern
A Victorian pub where visitors flock in their hundreds. Images of the area's maritime heritage, including Horatio Nelson, are scattered about.

📍 O8 🏠 Park Row SE10 🌐 trafalgartavern.co.uk

200,000

White glazed tiles were needed to line the Greenwich Foot Tunnel.

Both ends of the tunnel are close to stations on the Docklands Light Railway (DLR). Although there are security cameras, the tunnel can be eerie at night.

⑨ The Fan Museum

📍 N10 🏠 12 Croom's Hill SE10 🚉 Greenwich 🕐 11am–5pm Tue–Sat, noon–5pm Sun 🕐 1 Jan, 24–26 Dec 🌐 thefanmuseum.org.uk

One of London's most unusual museums owes its existence and appeal to the enthusiasm of Helene Alexander, whose personal collection of about 4,000 fans from the 17th century onwards has been augmented by donations. A small permanent exhibition looks at types of fans and fan-making, while the collection is rotated in temporary displays. On some days, afternoon tea is served in the pretty orangery at the back.

10
The O2 Arena

9 O8 **A** North Greenwich SE10 **⊖** North Greenwich **⏰** 9am-late **w** theo2.co.uk

The former Millennium Dome was the focal point of Britain's celebration of the year 2000. Controversial from its earliest days, it is nonetheless an amazing feat of engineering. Its canopy is made from 100,000 sq m (109,000 sq yards) of Teflon-coated spun glass-fibre, and is supported by over 70 km (43 miles) of steel cable rigged to 12 100-m (328-ft) masts. Now one of London's largest concert venues, the O2 also has bars, restaurants, a cinema and IndigO2, a smaller venue. You can also don climbing gear and ascend the outside along a long, bouncy walkway to the very top.

11
Emirates Air Line

9 O8 **A** Western Gateway E16/Edmund Halley Way SE10 **⊖** Royal Victoria DLR, North Greenwich **⏰** 7am-11pm Mon-Fri, 8am-11pm Sat, 9am-11pm Sun (to 9pm Oct-Mar) **w** emirates airline.co.uk

This cable car, crossing the Thames between the Royal Victoria Dock and the O2, provides spectacular views

Did You Know?

Sponsored by airline Emirates, the construction of the cable car cost a whopping £60 million.

during the five-minute trip. It's a magnificent way to cross the river. Travel-cards can be used as it is operated by London Transport. In the evenings the "flights" slow down, giving you more time to enjoy the panorama of city lights.

12
Museum of London Docklands

9 O8 **A** No 1 Warehouse, West India Quay E14 **⊖** Canary Wharf, Westferry **⏰** 10am-6pm daily **w** museumoflondon.org. uk/museum-london-docklands

Occupying a late Georgian warehouse, this museum tells the story of London's docks and their links from Roman times to the present. A highlight is the recreation

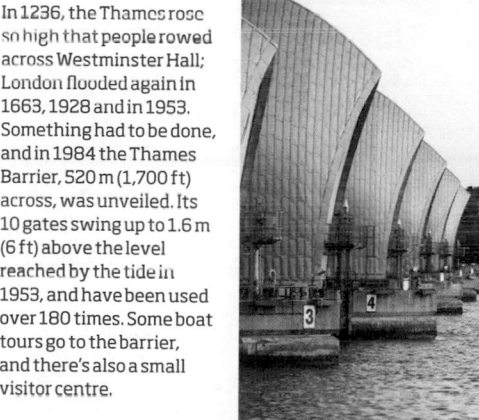

of the dark and dangerous "Sailortown" of Wapping in the 1850s.

🔟 Ⓨ 🖵 🛍

Canary Wharf

⊙ O8 ⌂ E14 Ⓔ Canary Wharf, West India Quay DLR

London's most ambitious commercial development opened in 1991, when the first tenants moved into the 50-storey One Canada Square. At 250 m (800 ft), it continues to dominate the city's eastern skyline with its distinctive pyramid-shaped top. The tower stands on what was the West India Dock, closed, like all the London docks, between the 1960s and the 1980s, when trade moved to Tilbury. Today, Canary Wharf is thriving, with a major shopping complex, cafés and restaurants.

↑ The Emirates cable car and the O2 Arena – the roof of which can be climbed *(inset)*

THE THAMES BARRIER

In 1236, the Thames rose so high that people rowed across Westminster Hall; London flooded again in 1663, 1928 and in 1953. Something had to be done, and in 1984 the Thames Barrier, 520 m (1,700 ft) across, was unveiled. Its 10 gates swing up to 1.6 m (6 ft) above the level reached by the tide in 1953, and have been used over 180 times. Some boat tours go to the barrier, and there's also a small visitor centre.

A SHORT WALK
GREENWICH

Distance 1.5 km (1 mile) **Nearest Tube** Cutty
Sark DLR **Time** 20 minutes

This historic town, with illustrious royal and naval
connections, is a UNESCO World Heritage Site. In Tudor
times it was the site of a palace much enjoyed by Henry
VIII, near a fine hunting ground. The old palace is gone,
but your walk will take you past Inigo Jones's exquisite
Queen's House, built for James I's wife. The route also
takes in museums, shops, cafés and markets, Wren's
architecture and the magnificent Royal Park, making
this an enjoyable short stroll.

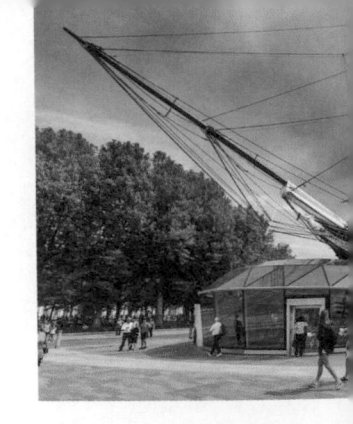

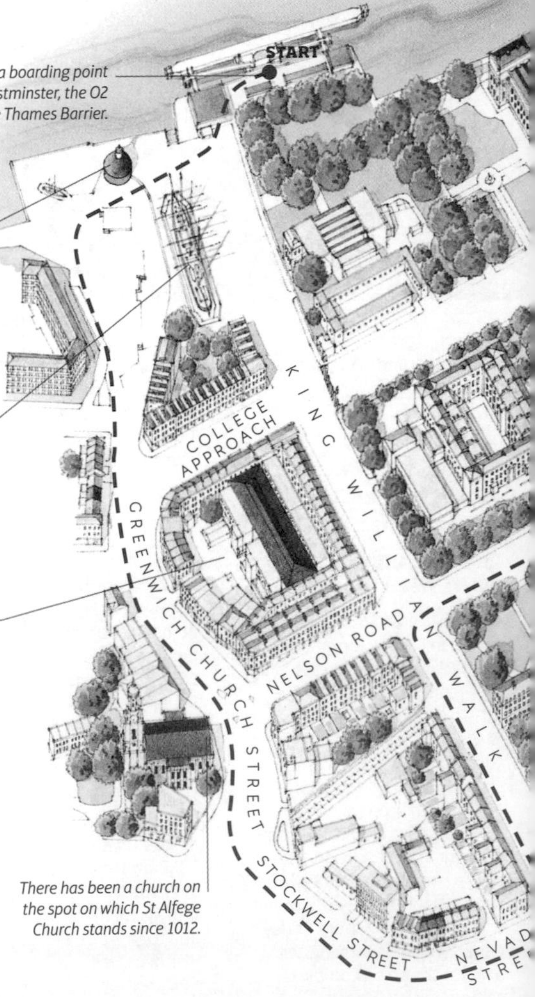

START

Greenwich Pier is a boarding point
for boats to Westminster, the O2
and the Thames Barrier.

Greenwich Foot Tunnel (p305),
leading to the Isle of Dogs under
the Thames, is one of two tunnels
built solely for pedestrians.

Clipper ships such as the
Cutty Sark (p302) once
traded across the oceans.

Greenwich Market, in the heart
of Greenwich, sells crafts,
antiques and books (p303).

KING WILLIAM
COLLEGE APPROACH
GREENWICH CHURCH STREET
NELSON ROAD
WALK
STOCKWELL STREET
NEVAD
STRE

Did You Know?

The Old Royal Naval
College had a starring
role in Marvel's *Thor:
The Dark World*.

There has been a church on
the spot on which St Alfege
Church stands since 1012.

← Cutty Sark, impressively restored and raised to allow visitors to explore above and below deck

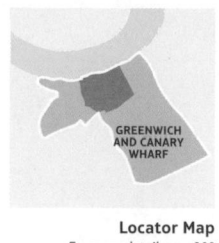

Locator Map
For more detail see p300

GREENWICH
AND CANARY
WHARF

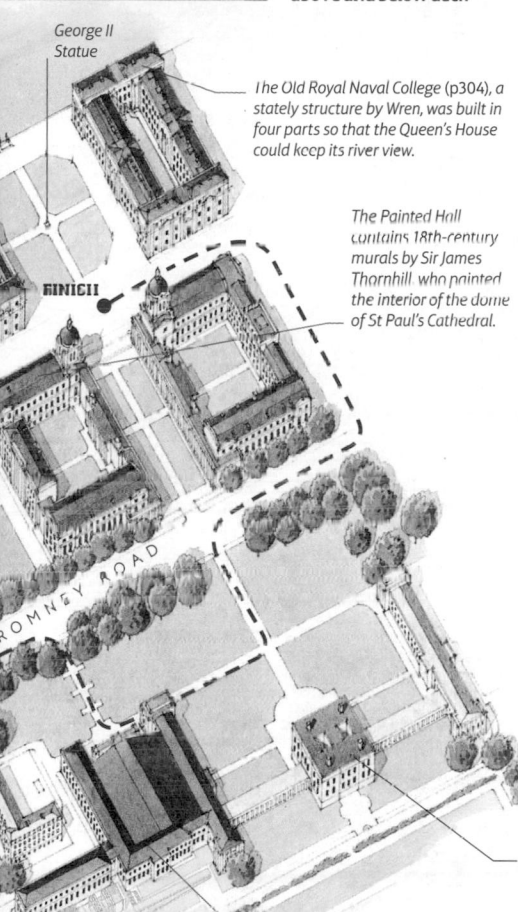

George II Statue

The Old Royal Naval College (p304), a stately structure by Wren, was built in four parts so that the Queen's House could keep its river view.

The Painted Hall contains 18th-century murals by Sir James Thornhill, who painted the interior of the dome of St Paul's Cathedral.

FINISH

ROMNEY ROAD

↑ John Rysbrack's George II statue (1735), depicting the king as a Roman emperor

On his return from Italy, the Queen's House (p304) was the first building Inigo Jones designed in the Palladian style.

Real and model boats, paintings and instruments such as an 18th-century compass illustrate naval history at the National Maritime Museum (p302).

0 metres   100
0 yards   100

N ↑

A deer in Richmond Park

BEYOND
THE CENTRE

London's high and mighty once sought refuge
from the city in their country manor houses,
located a short distance away from the centre.
Consumed by the rapid expansion of the Victorian
era, these stately homes and royal estates became
intertwined with sprawling suburbs, leading
to the boroughs of today. Post-war immigration
contributed to the identity of each of London's
neighbourhoods – from the West Indian
population in Brixton to the Hindu community
in Neasden – and their local characters continue
to evolve as regeneration of the city and
gentrification pushes ever further outward.

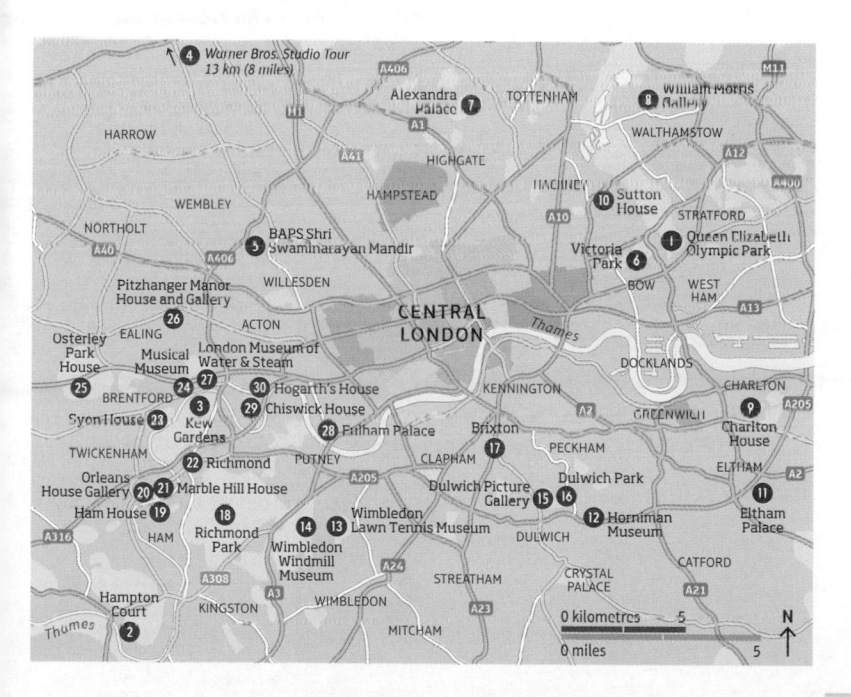

1 🏃 🖥

QUEEN ELIZABETH OLYMPIC PARK

🏠 E20 🚇 Hackney Wick 🚌 308, 339, 388, D8 🚆 Stratford, Pudding Lane 🕐 24 hrs daily; information point 10am–3pm daily
🌐 queenelizabetholympicpark.co.uk

Home of thet 2012 London Olympic Games, this East London site was transformed from an area of industrial wasteland into a world-class sporting hub with top-quality sporting venues.

As the only city to have hosted the Olympic Games three times – in 1908, 1948 and 2012 – London is justifiably proud of its place in Olympic history. The main site for the 2012 Olympics and Paralympics was a 225-hectare (560-acre) area of land stretching along the River Lea in east London, which was a fairly bleak former industrial area. The main attractions today are immediately familiar to anyone who watched the events: a series of large, functional but striking venues dotted amid meandering waterways and surrounded by quintessentially English wildflower gardens. Renamed Queen Elizabeth Olympic Park to commemorate the Queen's Diamond Jubilee in 2012, the site has been transformed into a permanent leisure attraction. Renovation continues around the periphery, but there is plenty to see and do, particularly if you catch one of the numerous events hosted here, including big sporting occasions and live music, or go equipped to try out some sports.

① The 6,000-seat velodrome is an iconic building in the Olympic Park and contains the fastest cycling track in the world.

② The pools at the London Aquatics Centre lie beneath the curving roof of this attractive building.

③ Visible from all over the Olympic Park, the ArcelorMittal Orbit tower gives visitors great views.

① 🏃 🖥

Lee Valley VeloPark

🕐 9am–10pm Mon-Fri, 8am–10pm Sat, 8am–8pm Sun. Book taster sessions online in advance
🌐 visitleevalley.org.uk

The Velodrome is the hub of a large cycling activity centre, with BMX and road tracks, and mountain-bike trails. Visitors can book taster sessions.

② 🏃 🖥

London Aquatics Centre

🕐 6am–10:30pm daily; check online for swim sessions and events
🌐 londonaquatics centre.org

Architect Zaha Hadid was inspired by the flow of water for her sweeping design for the Aquatics Centre. Everyone can swim in the competition and training pools here.

③ 🏃

ArcelorMittal Orbit

🕐 Apr-Sep: 10am-6pm daily; Oct-Mar: 10am-4pm daily
🌐 arcelormittalorbit.com

Designed by artist Anish Kapoor, the twisting steel tower is part sculpture, part viewing platform, with a thrilling 178-m (580-ft) slide.

The centrepiece stadium, set amid lush meadow land and waterways

INSIDER TIP
From the Water

To see the best of the park, take a 45-minute guided boat tour. Check leeandstortboats.co.uk for details.

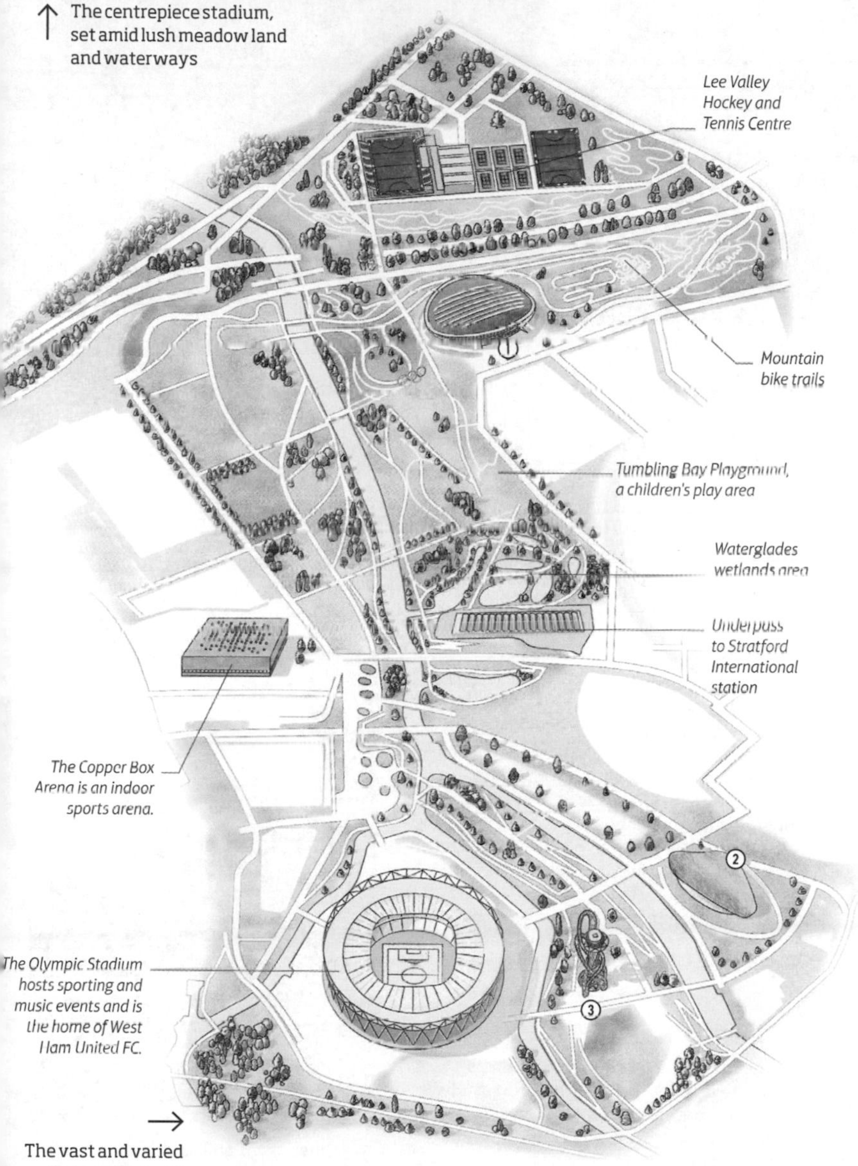

Lee Valley Hockey and Tennis Centre

Mountain bike trails

Tumbling Bay Playground, a children's play area

Waterglades wetlands area

Underpass to Stratford International station

The Copper Box Arena is an indoor sports arena.

The Olympic Stadium hosts sporting and music events and is the home of West Ham United FC.

The vast and varied Queen Elizabeth Olympic Park

HAMPTON COURT

📍 Surrey KT8 9AU 🚇 Hampton Court 🚢 Hampton Court pier (summer only) 🕐 Check website for opening hours 🌐 hrp.org.uk

With its impressively preserved palace, beautifully manicured gardens and location on the River Thames, the former stomping ground of Tudor king Henry VIII makes for an irresistible attraction.

Glorious Hampton Court began life in 1514 as the riverside country house of Cardinal Wolsey, Henry VIII's Archbishop of York. Later, in 1528, in the hope of retaining royal favour, Wolsey offered it to the king. Hampton Court was twice rebuilt and extended, first by Henry himself and then, in the 1690s, by King William and Queen Mary, who employed Christopher Wren as architect. There is a striking contrast between Wren's Classical royal apartments and the Tudor turrets, gables and chimneys elsewhere. The inspiration for the gardens comes largely from the time of William and Mary, who created a vast, formal Baroque landscape, with avenues and exotic plants.

FLOWER SHOW

The world's biggest flower show takes place every year at Hampton Court in July. Displays are on either side of Long Water and focus on growing your own food. Book tickets online.

↑ The sunken Pond Garden, once a pond that stored fish for Henry VIII's table

↑ Spectacular Hampton Court, seen from the Privy Garden

← An example of the formal and ordered style of the palace gardens

→ Fresh produce from the Kitchen Garden, sold to visitors once a week

Timeline

1528
△ Wolsey gives the palace to Henry VIII to try to keep favour with the king

1647
△ Charles I imprisoned by Oliver Cromwell

1734
△ William Kent decorates the Queen's Staircase

1992
△ State apartments damaged by a fire in 1986 are reopened

Exploring the Palace

As a historic royal palace, Hampton Court bears traces of many of the kings and queens of England from Henry VIII to the present day. The building itself is a harmonious blend of Tudor and English Baroque architecture. Inside, visitors can see the Great Hall, built by Henry VIII, as well as the state apartments of the Tudor court. Many of the Baroque state apartments, including those above Fountain Court, are decorated with furniture, tapestries and old masters from the Royal Collection.

Did You Know?

The Tudor kitchen prepared up to 1,000 meals a day for the court, including game, pies, lamb, venison and swan.

The Tudor Royal Chapel, refitted by Wren, except for the guilded vaulted ceiling

Queen's Guard Chamber

Haunted Gallery

Hung with tapestries beneath a hammer-beam roof, the Tudor Great Hall is sumptuously decorated.

1 The Tudor kitchen prepared a variety of dishes for the royal court, using ingredients such as Mediterranean almonds and Indian spices. Fresh meat was available at court too – at that time most people only ever ate stored or preserved meat.

2 The King's Staircase has wall paintings by William Kent, recreating the court of George I with real people of the time.

3 The Great Hall was used as a banqueting room and a theatre – William Shakespeare's King's Men performed here for James I over Christmas and New Year in 1603–4.

→

The vast Hampton Court with its mix of Tudor and English Baroque architecture

CARDINAL WOLSEY

Thomas Wolsey (c 1475–1530), who was simultaneously a cardinal, Archbishop of York and chancellor, was, after the king, the most powerful man in England. However, when he was unable to persuade the pope to allow Henry VIII to divorce his first wife, Catherine of Aragon, Wolsey fell from royal favour. He died while making his way to face trial for treason.

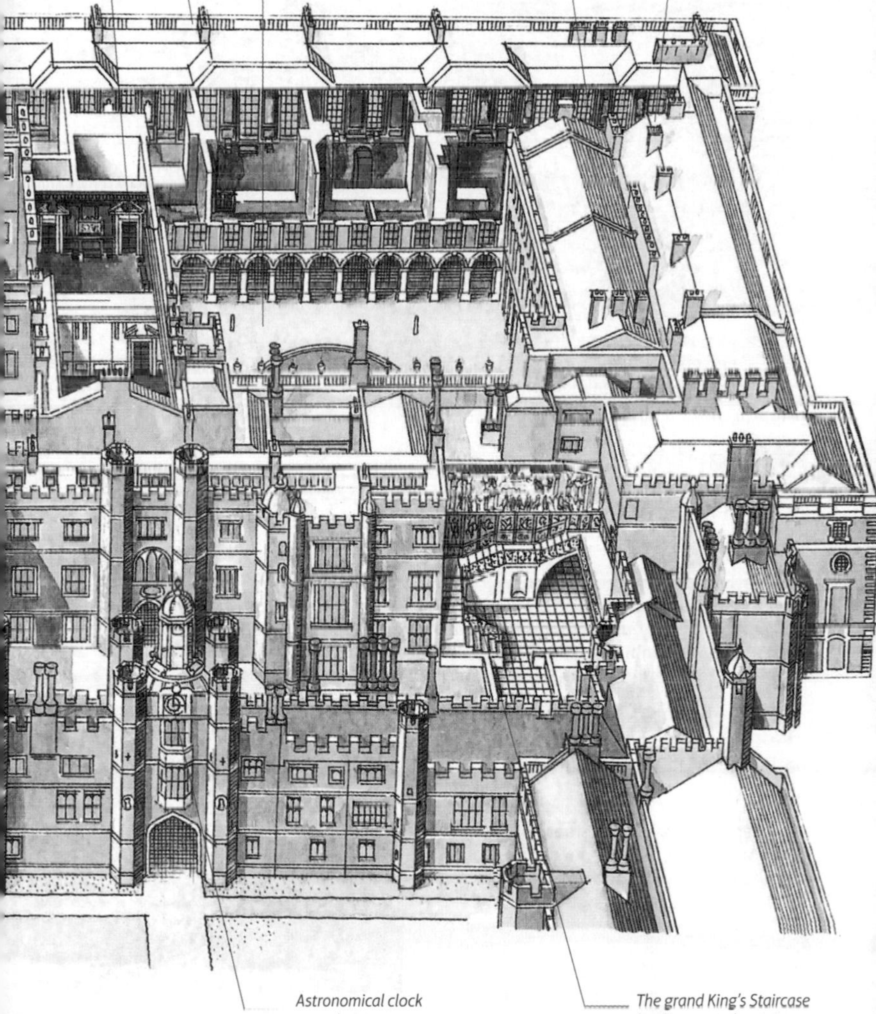

Queen's Presence Chamber

Wren's east façade

Fountain Court overlooked by the state apartments

Queen's Gallery with a marble chimneypiece

King's Great Bedchamber

Astronomical clock atop the entrance to Clock Court

The grand King's Staircase leading up to the state apartments

Immaculately manicured
flowerbeds in front of the
iconic Palm House ↑

③ 🔷🔶🍴🖥🛍

KEW GARDENS

🏠 Royal Botanic Gardens, Richmond TW9 3AB 🚇🚉 Kew Gardens
🕐 Mid-Feb–Mar: 10am–5:30pm daily; Apr–Aug: 10am–6:30pm Mon–Fri, 7:30pm Sat,
Sun & public hols; Sep–Oct: 10am–6pm daily; Nov–mid-Feb: 10am–4:15pm daily;
glasshouses & exhibitions close 30 mins before closing. Queen Charlotte's Cottage:
Apr–Sep: 11am–4pm Sat, Sun & public hols 🚫 24–25 Dec 🌐 kew.org

The Royal Botanic Gardens, Kew, are
a World Heritage Site. Given to the
nation in 1841, they display about
30,000 plants.

Kew's reputation was first established by
the British naturalist and plant hunter, Sir
Joseph Banks, who worked here in the late
18th century. The former royal gardens were
created by Princess Augusta, the mother of
George III, on the 3.6 ha (9-acre) site in 1759.
The Palm House was designed by Decimus
Burton in the 1840s and this famous jewel
of Victorian engineering houses exotic plants
in tropical conditions.

↑ Fine views from up among the tree
canopy on the Treetop Walkway

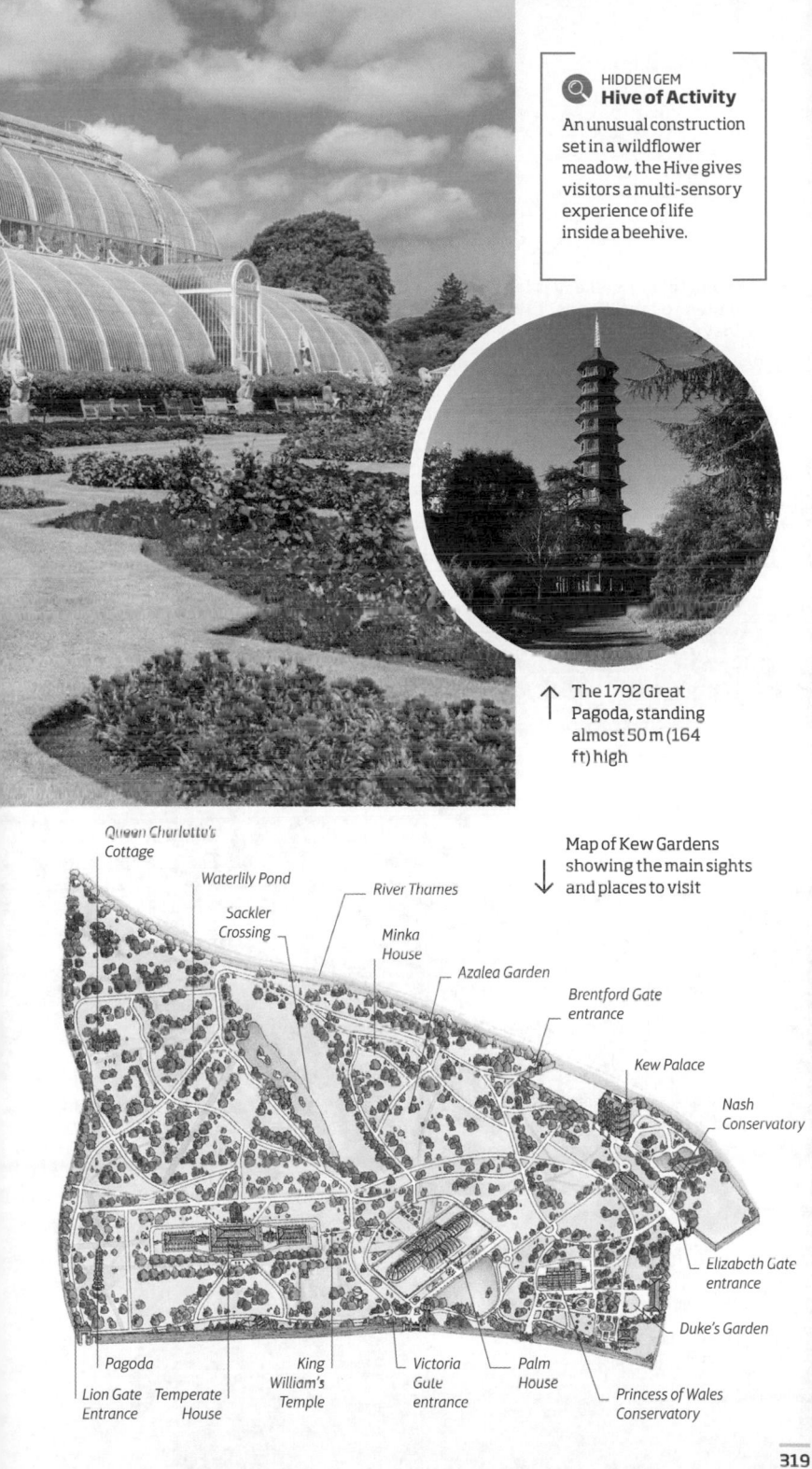

↑ The 1792 Great Pagoda, standing almost 50 m (164 ft) high

Map of Kew Gardens showing the main sights and places to visit ↓

Queen Charlotte's Cottage

Waterlily Pond

Sackler Crossing

River Thames

Minka House

Azalea Garden

Brentford Gate entrance

Kew Palace

Nash Conservatory

Elizabeth Gate entrance

Duke's Garden

Pagoda

Lion Gate Entrance

Temperate House

King William's Temple

Victoria Gate entrance

Palm House

Princess of Wales Conservatory

4

WARNER BROS. STUDIO TOUR: THE MAKING OF HARRY POTTER

Studio Tour Drive, Leavesden WD25 7LR Watford Junction (shuttle buses run from the station every 20 mins) 9.30am-10pm Mon-Fri, from 8:30am Sat, Sun & school holidays (final tour begins 6.45pm) wbstudiotour.co.uk

Walk the streets of Diagon Alley, enjoy a frothing glass of Butterbeer and admire the animatronics behind your favourite characters – this behind-the-scenes and in-the-scenes tour is an absolute must for budding wizards and witches.

Housed in a building adjacent to the studios where all eight of the Harry Potter films were created, The Making of Harry Potter tour brings you up close to the original sets, props, models and costumes used in the world-famous films. Visitors can wander into the imposing Great Hall at Hogwarts, walk up Diagon Alley, sneak into Dumbledore's office,

←

The front entrance of the Warner Bros. Studio Tour: The Making of Harry Potter

The iconic set of Platform 9¾, departure point for the Hogwarts Express ↓

Did You Know?

The Harry Potter series has sold more than 500 million copies, in 80 languages.

← Diagon Alley, home to the wand shop Ollivanders and Weasley's Wizard Wheezes

explore the Forbidden Forest and admire the Hogwarts Express locomotive at Platform 9¾. Just as impressive as the real-life sets is the huge, jaw-droppingly detailed scale model of Hogwarts School, used for the exterior shots in the films.

There's much more to marvel at throughout the tour, from costumes for the students at Beauxbatons Academy and the Yule Ball to Harry's broomstick and Hagrid's motorcycle as well as animatronic creatures including Buckbeak, a 6-m (20-ft) wide Aragog and a full-size Basilisk head. Secrets of the special and visual effects departments reveal how the Invisibility Cloak works and what role the green screen played. As you might expect, the three shops on site offer a huge range of take-home souvenirs.

↑ The office of Albus Dumbledore, first created for *Harry Potter and the Chamber of Secrets*

EAT

The Studio Café
Enjoy classic British fare at this quite basic canteen. Breakfast is well catered for with the Full English setting you up for the day. At lunch, tuck into hot or cold meals – soups, salads, sandwiches and the like.

£££

Backlot Café
This is the place to stop for Butterbeer, whether as a drink or an ice cream. There is basic hot food available here too.

£££

EXPERIENCE MORE

BAPS Shri Swaminarayan Mandir

🏠 105-119 Brentfield Rd, Neasden NW10 ⊜ Harlesden then bus 224 (or Stonebridge Park and bus 112) 🕐 Daily; Mandir and Haveli: 9am-6pm; Deities: 9am-12.15pm & 4-6pm (to 5pm Sat) 🌐 londonmandir.baps.org

Right out in northwest London, not far from Wembley Stadium, stands one of the most incongruous – and beautiful – religious buildings in the city, often known simply as the Neasden Temple. The intricately carved Hindu temple was completed in 1995, after a small army of volunteers from the local community banded together to raise funds and build it. Thousands of tonnes of Bulgarian limestone and Italian Carrara marble were shipped to India to be carved, then assembled on site like a giant jigsaw. The result is a staggeringly detailed, intricately carved temple. When the Great Hall is not closed for prayer, you can inspect some of the shrines to the deities close-up. The Haveli, the cultural education centre, features yet more beautiful carving, this time in Burmese teak and English oak.

Leave any large bags at the security desk across the road, dress modestly (with your shoulders, upper arms and knees covered) and remove your shoes when you enter the main building (cloakrooms are provided).

Victoria Park

🏠 Grove Rd E3 ⊜ Bethnal Green 🚆 Hackney Wick, Cambridge Heath 🚌 277, 425 🕐 7am-dusk

Victoria Park opened in 1845 as London's first public park. The venue for many political rallies in the 19th century and beyond, it became known as the "People's Park" and remains hugely popular. There are boats for hire on one of its two lakes; gardens, cafés, playgrounds, splash pools, tennis courts and a skate park. It's part of the largest belt of green space in the East End. Footpaths along Regent's Canal and the Hertford Union Canal hug two of its borders, linking up with the River Lee, a short distance away, on its journey around the Olympic Park.

Alexandra Palace

🏠 Alexandra Palace Way N22 🚆 Alexandra Palace ⊜ Wood Green then bus W3 🕐 Daily 🌐 alexandrapalace.com

Built as the People's Palace in 1873, Alexandra Palace has a slightly chequered history – it has burned down twice, once just 16 days after it opened, and again in 1980. From 1936 until 1956 the BBC's television studios were housed at Alexandra Palace, and in 1936 the first television transmission took place from here. Affectionately known as Ally Pally, the large, ornate Victorian halls now host a wide variety of events, from

DRINK

Crate Brewery
This canalside brewery is the place to go to sample the east London hipster scene: post-industrial styling and great craft beer.

🏠 Queens Yard, Hackney Wick
🌐 cratebrewery.com

trade and antiques fairs to large-scale concerts. Set in parkland, the building sits majestically exposed on a hill, so the views are spectacular, and it's a good spot for fireworks and funfairs (the website has details of events). There's a permanent ice rink and the grounds have a pitch-and-putt golf course, boating lake and playgrounds.

8 🖥️ 🏛️

William Morris Gallery

🏠 Lloyd Park, Forest Rd E17
🚇 Walthamstow Central
🕐 10am-5pm Wed-Sun
🗓️ 25 & 26 Dec, 1 Jan
🌐 wmgallery.org.uk

The most influential designer of the Victorian era, born in 1834, lived in this 18th-century house as a young man. It is now a beguiling and well-presented museum giving a full account of William Morris the artist, designer, writer, craftsman and socialist. It has examples of his work and that of other members of the Arts and Crafts movement – tiles

←

Victoria Park, part of a 3 km (1.5-mile) band of green space that opens up East London

by William de Morgan and paintings by members of the Pre-Raphaelite Brotherhood.

Interactive exhibits introduce visitors to techniques such as hand-printing and dyeing. There are regular special exhibitions, workshops and lectures.

9 🖥️

Charlton House

🏠 Charlton Rd SE7
🚌 Charlton House
🕐 9am-10pm Mon-Fri, 9am-5pm Sat 🗓️ Public hols
🌐 greenwichheritage.org/visit/charlton-house

Completed in 1612 for Adam Newton, tutor to Prince Henry, Charlton House is the best-preserved Jacobean mansion in London, for enthusiasts of that period. It is now used as a community centre, but many of the original ceilings and fireplaces survive, as does the carved main staircase and parts of the wood panelling. Other ceilings have been restored using the original moulds. The grounds contain a summer house reputedly designed by architect Inigo Jones, and a mulberry tree said to have been planted by James I in 1608.

↑ The exquisite, and intricately detailed *(inset)*, BAPS Shri Swaminarayan Mandir

10 🖥️ 🏛️ 🏛️ 🖥️ 🏛️ NT

Sutton House

🏠 2-4 Homerton High St E9
🚇 Bethnal Green then bus 253 🕐 Noon-5pm Wed-Sun (daily in Aug) 🗓️ Christmas, Jan (check website)
🌐 nationaltrust.org.uk

One of the very few Tudor merchants' houses in London to have survived in something like its original form, Sutton House was built in 1535 for Ralph Sadleir, a courtier to Henry VIII. It was owned by several wealthy families before becoming a girls' school in the 17th century. In the 18th century, the front was altered, but the Tudor fabric remains surprisingly intact, including original brickwork, fireplaces and wood panelling.

The clock tower of the Horniman Museum, designed in Arts and Crafts style ↑

conservatory, a bandstand, nature trails and a formal sunken garden as well as a Butterfly House and Animal Walk, a small petting zoo.

13 Wimbledon Lawn Tennis Museum

🏠 Church Rd SW19
🚇 Southfields 🕐 10am-5pm daily 🔒 1 Jan, 24-26 Dec 🌐 wimbledon.com

Even those with only a passing interest in the sport will find plenty to enjoy here. The museum explores tennis's development from its invention in the 1860s as a diversion for country house parties to the sport it is today. Equipment and tennis fashion from the Victorian era are on display and visitors can watch clips and recent matches in the video theatre. It's advisable to book ahead to take one of the tours, which include a visit to Centre Court.

11 Eltham Palace

🏠 Court Yard SE9 🚆 Eltham then a 15-minute walk
🕐 Feb-Mar: 10am-4pm Sun-Fri; Apr-Sep: 10am-6pm Sun-Fri 🔒 Oct-Jan
🌐 english-heritage.org.uk

This unique property lets visitors relive the grand life of two very different eras. In the 14th century, English kings spent Christmas in a splendid palace here. The Tudors used it as a base for deer-hunting but it fell into ruin after the English Civil War (1642–8). In 1935 Stephen Courtauld, of the wealthy textile family, restored the Great Hall and, next to it, he built a house described as "a wonderful combination of Hollywood glamour and Art Deco design". The palace has been superbly restored – especially the circular glass-domed entrance hall. Visitors are transported to a 1930s party and even

given the identity of a real guest. Note the carp-filled moat and the 1930s garden.

12 Horniman Museum

🏠 100 London Rd SE23 🚆 Forest Hill 🕐 10am-5:30pm daily; animal walk: 12:30-4pm daily; gardens: 7:15am-sunset Mon-Sat, 8am-sunset Sun and public hols 🔒 24-26 Dec 🌐 horniman.ac.uk

Frederick Horniman, a tea merchant, had this museum built in 1901 to house the curios he had collected on his travels in the 1860s. It features a music gallery, aquarium and world culture displays, but the highlight is a natural history gallery that contains a remarkable collection of taxidermy and skeletons, including the famous Horniman Walrus. The gardens have a Victorian

---

14 Wimbledon Windmill Museum

🏠 Windmill Rd SW19 🚇🚆 Wimbledon then a 30-minute walk 🕐 Apr-Oct: 2-5pm Sat, 11am-5pm Sun & public hols 🌐 wimbledonwindmill.org.uk

Built in 1817, the mill on Wimbledon Common now houses a museum exploring windmills, rural life and local history. Boy Scout founder Robert Baden-Powell wrote

Did You Know?

In 2018 the *New York Times* named the Horniman one of the "10 coolest museums in the world".

part of *Scouting for Boys* here in 1908, and there are display cases of early memorabilia from the scouting and Girl Guide movements.

The mill came out of service in 1864, but you can see some of the original workings on the upper floors, as well as try your hand at grinding grain on old mortars and querns, an activity popular with young children. There are also some beautifully crafted cutaway models of this and other mills.

15

Dulwich Picture Gallery

⌂ Gallery Rd SE21 🚉 West Dulwich, North Dulwich ⏰ 10am–5pm Tue–Sun & bank hol Mon 🚫 1 Jan, 24–26 Dec 🌐 dulwichpicture gallery.org.uk

England's oldest public art gallery, which opened in 1817, was designed by Sir John Soane (*p138*). Its imaginative use of skylights made it the prototype of most galleries created since. It was built to house the royal collection of the King of Poland when he was forced to abdicate in 1795. The superb collection has works by Rembrandt (his *Jacob III de Gheyn* has been stolen from here four times), Canaletto, Poussin, Watteau, Raphael and Gainsborough. The building houses Soane's mausoleum to Desenfans and Bourgeois, the art dealers who built the collection.

16 🖼️

Dulwich Park

⌂ College Road SE21 🚉 West Dulwich 🚌 176, 185, 197, P4, P13 ⏰ 7.30am–dusk

Just across the road from Dulwich Picture Gallery, this park was opened in 1890 on land previously owned by Dulwich College, the public school whose buildings lie to the south of the park. This is one of the prettiest of the borough parks, with paths weaving around colourful flowerbeds, sports courts and pitches, the bowling green, and central boating lake and duck pond. Dog walkers are confined to the perimeter, making the central lawns pleasant for play and picnicking. At weekends the outer loop fills with kids and adults messing around on the novelty bikes rented out by the park's resident cycle hire firm, London Recumbents.

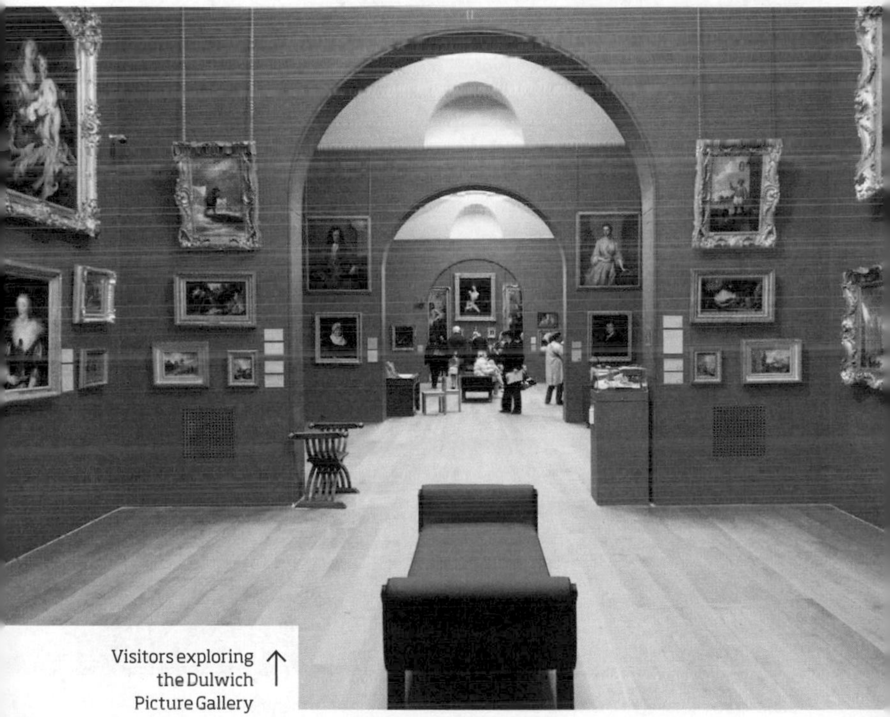

↑ Visitors exploring the Dulwich Picture Gallery

Relaxing on the riverside next to the 18th-century stone arch Richmond Bridge

Multinational flags in Brixton Village, one of a pair of colourful covered market arcades ↑

⑰ Brixton

 SW2, SW9 ⊖≋ Brixton

The unofficial capital of south London, Brixton has been characterized since the 1950s by one of the city's largest West Indian communities. Brixton Market loops around the centre along Electric Avenue, Pope's Road and Station Road, and is full of stalls selling Caribbean produce alongside arts, crafts, clothing and the usual market bric-a-brac. Brixton Village and Market Row, neighbouring market arcades, are filled with independent traders and an eclectic mix of food hotspots, including Mexican, Japanese, Korean and Spanish. Despite the march of gentrification, Brixton fiercely protects its roots and remains a brilliantly energetic part of the city.

⑱ Richmond Park

Kingston Vale SW15 ⊖≋ Richmond then bus 65 or 71 ⏰ 24 hours daily (7:30am-8pm Nov & Feb ☑ royalparks.org.uk

In 1637, Charles I built a 13-km (8-mile) wall round Richmond Park to enclose the royal park

as a hunting ground. Today the vast park is a national nature reserve and deer still graze warily among the chestnuts, birches and oaks. They have learned to coexist with the human visitors who stroll here on fine weekends.

In late spring, the highlight is the Isabella Plantation with its spectacular azaleas, while the Pen Ponds are popular with optimistic anglers. (Adam's Pond is for model boats.) The rest of the park is covered with heath, bracken and trees (some hundreds of years old). Richmond Gate, in the northwest corner, was designed by the landscape

gardener Capability Brown in 1798. Nearby is Henry VIII Mound, where in 1536 the king, staying in Richmond Palace, awaited the signal that his former wife, Anne Boleyn, had been executed. The Palladian White Lodge, built in 1729, is home to the Royal Ballet School.

⑲     Ham House

Ham St, Richmond ⊖≋ Richmond then bus 65 or 371 ⏰ Mar-early Oct: noon-4pm daily; mid-Oct-Feb: for prearranged tours only; gardens: 10am-5pm daily ⏰ 1 Jan, 24 & 25 Dec ☑ nationaltrust.org.uk

This magnificent house by the Thames was built in 1610, but its heyday came when the Countess of Dysart inherited it from her father, who had been Charles I's "whipping boy" (in his boyhood he took the punishment for the future king's misdemeanours). From 1672, she and her husband, a confidant of Charles II, modernized the

→

Syon House, built as a square around a central courtyard

house, and it was regarded as one of Britain's finest. The garden has been restored to its 17th-century form.

On some days in summer, a foot passenger ferry runs from here to Marble Hill House and Orleans House at Twickenham.

Pleasure boats plying the Thames at Richmond ↑

20  Orleans House Gallery

🏠 Orleans Rd, Twickenham
🚇🚉 St Margaret's or Richmond then bus 33, 90, 290, R68 or R70
🕐 10am–5pm Tue–Sun; gardens: 9am–dusk daily
🚫 1 Jan, Good Fri, 24–26 Dec
🌐 orleanshousegallery.org

This gallery occupies what remains of Orleans House, named after Louis Philippe, Duke of Orleans, who lived there from 1815–17. The beautifully restored Octagon Room was designed by James Gibbs for James Johnson in 1720. The gallery displays the Richmond Borough art collection, and there is also a community arts centre.

21  Marble Hill House

🏠 Richmond Rd, Twickenham 🚉 St Margaret's
🕐 Apr–Oct: Sat & Sun, for guided tours only; park and café: daily year-round
🚫 Public hols 🌐 english-heritage.org.uk

Built in 1729 for George II's mistress, Henrietta Howard,

the house and its grounds have been open to the public since 1903. Fully restored to its Georgian appearance, the house has a collection of paintings by William Hogarth and a view of the river and house in 1762 by Richard Wilson, who is widely regarded as the father of English landscape painting. The café is especially good.

22  Richmond

🏠 SW15 🚇🚉 Richmond

This attractive London suburb took its name from the palace that Henry VII built here in 1500. Many early 18th-century houses survive near the Thames and off Richmond Hill, notably Maids of Honour Row, built in 1724. The beautiful view of the river from the top of the hill has been captured by many artists, and is largely unspoiled.

23 Syon House

🏠 London Rd, Brentford
🚇 Gunnersbury then bus 237 or 267 🕐 Mid-Mar–Oct: 11am–5pm Wed–Thu, Sun & public hols; gardens: mid-Mar–Oct: 10:30am–5pm daily 🌐 syonpark.co.uk

The Earls and Dukes of Northumberland have lived here for 400 years – it is the only large mansion in the London area still in hereditary ownership. The interior was remodelled in 1761 by Robert Adam and is considered one of his masterpieces. The five Adam rooms house original furnishings and a collection of old master paintings.

The 200-acre (80-ha) park, landscaped by Capability Brown, includes a lovely 40-acre (16-ha) garden with more than 200 species of rare trees. The park's Great Conservatory inspired Joseph Paxton's designs for the Crystal Palace.

24

Musical Museum

🏠 399 High St, Brentford
🚇 Kew Bridge 🚇 Gunnersbury, South Ealing then bus 237 or 267 🕐 11am–5pm Tue, Fri–Sun & bank hol Mon
🌐 musicalmuseum.co.uk

The collection, arranged over three floors, chiefly comprises large self-playing instruments, including player (automatic) pianos and organs, miniature and cinema pianos, and what is apparently the only surviving self-playing Wurlitzer organ in Europe.

25

Osterley Park House

🏠 Jersey Rd, Isleworth
🚇 Osterley 🕐 Mar–Oct: 11am–5pm daily; first two weeks Dec: 11am–4pm Sat & Sun; garden: 10am–5pm daily; park: 7am–7:30pm (later in summer)
🌐 nationaltrust.org.uk

Osterley is ranked among Robert Adam's finest works, and its colonnaded portico and elegant library ceiling show why. Much of the

furniture is by Adam; the garden and temple are by William Chambers, architect of Somerset House.

26

Pitzhanger Manor House and Gallery

🏠 Mattock Lane W5
🚇 Ealing Broadway
🕐 House: closed for refurbishment; park: 7:30am–dusk daily 🕐 Public hols 🌐 pitzhanger.org.uk

Sir John Soane, architect of the Bank of England, rebuilt this manor house in 1804 as his own country residence. There are clear echoes of his elaborately constructed town house in Lincoln's Inn Fields *(p138)*. Soane retained two of the principal formal rooms: the drawing room and the dining room, designed in 1768 by George Dance the Younger, with whom Soane had worked.

While the house is closed for restoration, events continue to be held in the grounds, a public park since 1901 (see the website for details). The garden behind the house has been restored to how it would have looked in Soane's time.

27

London Museum of Water & Steam

🏠 Green Dragon Lane, Brentford 🚇 Kew Bridge, Gunnersbury then bus 65, 237 or 267 🕐 10am–3pm Wed–Fri, 10am–4pm Sat & Sun
🌐 waterandsteam.org.uk

This 19th-century water pumping station near the north end of Kew Bridge is now a museum of steam power and water. Its main exhibits are five giant Cornish beam engines that pumped water here from the river, to be distributed across London. The earliest engines, dating from 1820, are similar to those built to pump water out of Cornish mines. Visitors can see them working at weekends and on public holidays (times are posted on the website). The Waterworks gallery tells the story of

←

Gobelins tapestry from the "Loves of the Gods" series at Osterley Park House

↑ Part of the Knot Garden at Fulham Palace *(inset)*, originally created by Bishop Blomfield in 1831

London's water supply, in lots of interactive detail, and there's a fun outdoor area where younger children can play with the water features.

28

Fulham Palace

🏠 Bishops Ave SW6
🚇 Putney Bridge
🕐 Summer: 12:30–4:30pm Mon–Thu, noon–5pm Sun & bank hol Mon; winter: 12:30–3:30pm Mon–Thu, noon–4pm Sun; park: daylight hours daily 🚫 Good Fri, 25 & 26 Dec 🌐 fulhampalace.org

The home of the Bishops of London from the 8th century until 1973, the oldest surviving parts of Fulham Palace date from the 15th century. The palace stands in its own landscaped gardens, which comprise a delightful walled garden and a botanical garden. A restoration project of the house, completed in 2007, revealed a grand, long-hidden Rococo ceiling. Plans are in place to redevelop the site further. Tours are given 2–3 times each month; check the website for days and times, and also for details of talks and concerts held here.

29

Chiswick House

🏠 Burlington Lane W4
🚇 Chiswick 🕐 Apr–Oct: 10am–5pm Wed–Mon & bank hols; gardens: 7am–dusk daily 🌐 chiswickhouseandgardens.org.uk

Completed in 1729 to the design of its owner, the third Earl of Burlington, this is a fine example of a Palladian villa. Burlington revered Palladio and his disciple Inigo Jones, and statues of both stand outside. Built around a central octagonal room, the house is packed with references to ancient Rome and Renaissance Italy.

Chiswick was Burlington's country residence and this house was built as an annexe to a larger, older house (since demolished). It was designed for recreation and entertaining – Lord Hervey, Burlington's enemy, dismissed it as "too little to live in and too big to hang on a watch chain". Some of the ceiling paintings are by William Kent, who also contributed to the garden design.

The house was an asylum from 1892 until 1928, when lengthy restoration began. The layout of the garden, now a public park, is much as Burlington designed it.

Tours are offered to groups only, by prior arrangement – check website for details.

DRINK

The Bell and Crown
Lots of riverside outdoor seating and a rustic interior are found here.
🏠 72 Strand-on-the-Green, Chiswick W4

The City Barge
Great food and beer is available here daily and the Saturday brunch is legendary.
🏠 27 Strand-on-the-Green, Chiswick W4

Bull's Head
Cosy pub with good Sunday roasts and riverside picnic benches.
🏠 15 Strand-on-the-Green, Chiswick W4

30

Hogarth's House

🏠 Hogarth Lane W4
🚇 Turnham Green 🕐 Noon–5pm Tue–Sun & bank hol Mon 🚫 1 Jan, Good Fri, Easter Sun, 24–26 Dec 🌐 hounslow.info/arts/hogarthshouse

When the painter William Hogarth lived here from 1749 until his death in 1764, he called it "a little country box by the Thames" and painted bucolic views from its windows – he had moved here from Leicester Square *(p115)*. It has now been turned into a small museum and gallery, filled with engraved copies of the moralistic cartoon-style pictures with which Hogarth made his name. Salutary tales such as *Marriage à la Mode*, *An Election Entertainment* and many others can all be seen here.

NEED TO KNOW

Transport in London city centre

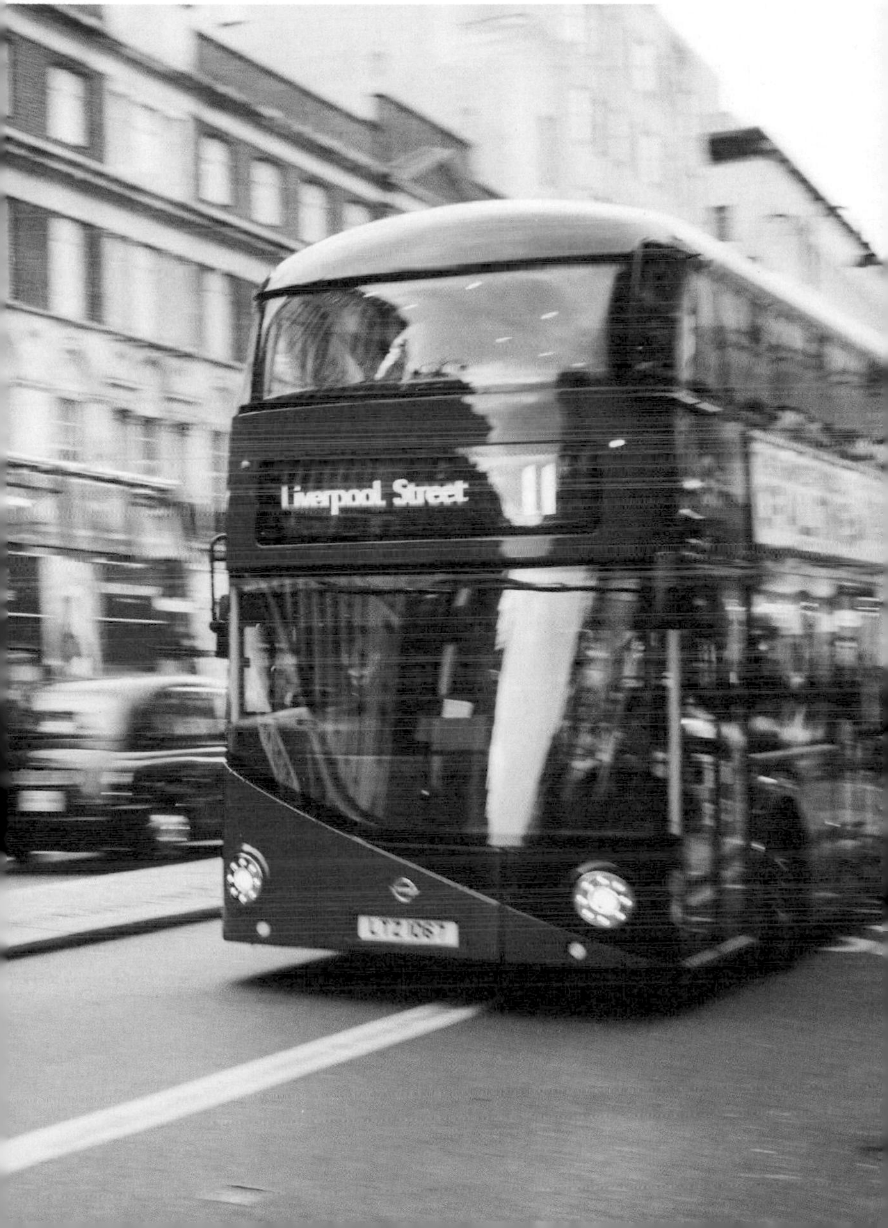
Liverpool Street
11

BEFORE YOU GO

Forward planning is essential to any successful trip. Be prepared for all eventualities by considering the following points before you travel.

AT A GLANCE

CURRENCY
Pound Sterling
(GBP)

AVERAGE DAILY SPEND

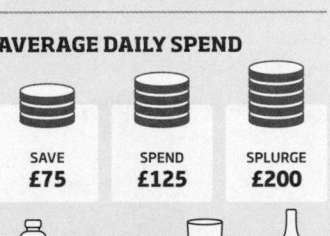

SAVE	SPEND	SPLURGE
£75	£125	£200

BOTTLED WATER	COFFEE	BEER	DINNER FOR TWO
£1	£2.50	€3.50	£70

CLIMATE

 The longest days occur May–Aug, while Oct–Feb sees the shortest daylight hours.

 Temperatures average 22°C (75°F) in summer. Winter can be very cold and icy.

 The heaviest rainfall is in October and November, but showers occur all year round.

ELECTRICITY SUPPLY
Power sockets are type G, fitting three-pronged plugs. Standard voltage is 230 volts.

Passports and Visas

For a stay of up to three months for the purpose of tourism, EU nationals and citizens of the US, Canada, Australia and New Zealand do not need a visa to enter the country, however this may change once the UK has left the EU. Consult your nearest British embassy or check the **UK Government** website for up-to-date visa information specific to your home country.
UK Government
🅦 gov.uk

Travel Safety Advice

Visitors can get up-to-date travel safety information from the UK Foreign and Commonwealth Office, the US State Department, and the Department of Foreign Affairs and Trade in Australia.
Australia
🅦 smartraveller.gov.au
UK
🅦 gov.uk/foreign-travel-advice
US
🅦 travel.state.gov

Customs Information

An individual is permitted to carry the following within the EU for personal use:
   Tobacco products: 800 cigarettes, 400 cigarillos, 200 cigars or 1 kg of smoking tobacco.
   Alcohol: 10 litres of alcoholic beverages above 22% strength, 20 litres of alcoholic beverages below 22% strength, 90 litres of wine (60 litres of which can be sparkling wine) and 110 litres of beer.
   Cash: If you plan to enter or leave the EU with €10,000 or more in cash (or the equivalent in other currencies) you must declare it to the customs authorities.
   These regulations may be subject to change once the UK leaves the EU, so consult the **UK Government** website for the most up-to-date customs information. If travelling outside the EU limits vary so check restrictions before you set off.

Insurance

It is wise to take out an insurance policy covering theft, loss of belongings, medical problems, cancellation and delays.

Emergency treatment is usually free from the National Health Service, and there are reciprocal arrangements with other EEA countries, Australia, New Zealand and some others (check the **NHS** website for details).

Specialist care, drugs and repatriation are costly. Residents of EEA countries should carry a European Health Insurance Card (**EHIC**), which allows treatment for free or at a reduced cost.

It is advisable for visitors from outside the EEA, Australia and New Zealand to arrange their own comprehensive medical insurance.

EHIC
W gov.uk/european-health-insurance-card
NHS
W nhs.uk

Vaccinations

No inoculations are needed for the UK.

Money

Major credit and debit cards are accepted in most shops and restaurants, while prepaid currency cards are accepted in some. Contactless payments are widely accepted in London, including on public transport. However, it is always worth carrying some cash, as many smaller businesses and markets still operate a cash-only policy. Cash machines are conveniently located at banks, train stations, shopping areas and main streets.

Booking Accommodation

London offers a huge variety of accommodation to suit any budget, including luxury five-star hotels, family run B&Bs and budget hostels.

Lodgings can fill up and prices become inflated during during the summer, so it's worth booking well in advance.

A comprehensive list of accommodation to suit all needs can be found on **Visit London**, London's official tourist information website.

Visit London
W visitlondon.com

Travellers with Specific Needs

Accessibility information for public transport is available from the TFL website *(p337)*.

In the City, Westminster, Camden and Kensington and Chelsea, a disabled driver badge allows you to park in blue-badge bays only.

Disability Rights UK publishes a guide listing recommended accommodation in the city.

Museums and galleries offer audio tours, which are useful to those with impaired vision. **Action on Hearing Loss** and **The Royal National Institute for the Blind** can also offer useful information and advice. Call theatres and cinemas to ask about wheelchair accessibility.

Action on Hearing Loss
W actionhearingloss.org.uk
Disability Rights UK
W disabilityrightsuk.org
The Royal National Institute for the Blind
W rnib.org.uk

Language

London is a multicultural city, in which you will hear many languages spoken. Many attractions and tour companies offer foreign language tours.

Closures

Mondays Some museums and tourist attractions are closed for the day.
Sundays Most shops close early or for the day.
Public holidays Schools and public services are closed for the day; shops, museums and attractions either close early or for the day.

PUBLIC HOLIDAYS 2019

1 Jan	New Year's Day
19 Apr	Good Friday
22 Apr	Easter Monday
6 May	May Day
27 May	Bank Holiday
26 Aug	Bank Holiday
25 Dec	Christmas Day
26 Dec	St Stephen's Day

GETTING
AROUND

London has one of the busiest public transport systems in Europe; understanding how it works will help you make the most of your trip.

PUBLIC TRANSPORT COSTS

SINGLE BUS JOURNEY

£1.50

Zone 1-9
(flat fare)

SINGLE TUBE JOURNEY

£2.40

Zone 1-2
(off peak)

DAILY TRAVELCARD

£12

Zone 1-6
(off peak)

SPEED LIMIT

MOTORWAY

70 mph
(112 kmph)

DUAL CARRIAGEWAYS

70 mph
(112 kmph)

SINGLE CARRIAGEWAYS

60 mph
(96 kmph)

URBAN AREAS

30 mph
(48 kmph)

Arriving by Air

Five airports serve London: Heathrow, Gatwick, Stansted, Luton and London City. With the exception of London City Airport, all are situated a significant distance from central London, with good transport connections to the city centre. For the best rates, book tickets in advance. For a list of transport options, approximate journey times and travel costs for transport to and from London's airports, see the table opposite.

Train Travel

International Train Travel

St Pancras International is the London terminus for Eurostar, the highspeed train linking the UK with the Continent.

You can buy tickets and passes for multiple international journeys via **Eurail** or **Interrail**, however you may still need to pay an additional reservation fee for certain trains. Always check that your pass is valid on the service on which you wish to travel before boarding.

Eurostar run a regular service from Paris, Brussels and Amsterdam to London via the Channel Tunnel.

Eurotunnel operates a drive-on-drive-off train service between Calais and Folkestone, in the south of England.

Eurail
w eurail.com
Eurostar
w eurostar.com
Eurotunnel
w eurotunnel.com
Interrail
w interrail.eu

Domestic Train Travel

The UK's railway system is complicated and can be confusing. Lines are run by several different companies, but they are coordinated by **National Rail**, which operates a joint information service.

London has eight main railway termini serving different parts of Britain (Charing Cross, Euston, King's Cross, London Bridge, St Pancras,

GETTING TO AND FROM THE AIRPORT

Airport	Transport to London	Journey Time	Price
London City	DLR	30 mins	from £2.80
	Taxi	20 mins	from £25
London Heathrow	Heathrow Express	15 mins	from £22
	London Underground	50 mins	from £3.10
	National Express Coach	1 hr	from £5
	Taxi	1 hr	from £50
London Stansted	Stansted Express	50 mins	from £10
	National Express Coach	1 hr 40 mins	from £5
	Taxi	1 hr 10 mins	from £75
London Gatwick	Gatwick Express	30 mins	£19.90
	London Thameslink	40 mins	from £10.70
	National Express Coach	1 hr 30 mins	from £5
	Taxi	1 hr 10 mins	from £60
London Luton	London Thameslink	40 mins	from £10.70
	National Express Coach	1hr 20 mins	from £5
	Taxi	1hr 10 mins	from £70

Paddington, Waterloo and Victoria). There are also over one hundred smaller London stations. Each main terminus is the starting-point for local and suburban lines that cover the whole of southeast England.

London's local and suburban train lines are used by hundreds of thousands of commuters every day. For visitors, rail services are most useful for trips to the outskirts of London and areas of the city without nearby Underground connections (especially in south London). If you are planning to travel outside of the capital, always try to book rail tickets in advance.

National Rail

W nationalrail.co.uk

Long-Distance Bus Travel

Coaches from European and UK destinations arrive at Victoria Coach Station. The biggest operator in the UK is **National Express. Eurolines** is its European arm, offering a variety of coach routes to London from other European cities. Fares start from around £20, and vary depending on distance. Book in advance.

Eurolines

W eurolines.eu

National Express

W nationalexpress.com

Public Transport

Most public transport in London is coordinated by Transport for London (**TFL**), London's main public transport authority.

Timetables, ticket information, transport maps and more can be found on their website.

TFL

W tfl.gov.uk

Fare Zones

TFL divides the city into six charging zones for Underground, Overground and National Rail services, radiating out from Zone 1 in the centre. On buses, there is a flat fare for each trip, no matter how far you travel.

Tickets

Tube and rail fares are expensive, especially individual tickets. If you expect to make multiple trips around the city in a short space of time, you can buy a one-day off-peak Travelcard, which gives unlimited travel on all systems after 9:30am on weekdays (or any time on Saturday and Sunday) within zones 1–4 or 1–6 for a flat fee.

If you wish to travel more freely, purchase a pay-as-you-go Oyster card or Visitor Oyster Card (valid for all London zones), which you can preload and top-up with credit (note that a £5 deposit is required when buying an Oyster card and you will need one card per person). You can also use contactless credit or debit cards in the same way as the Oyster card. It is cheaper to pay as you go using contactless or Oyster as fares are subject to daily and weekly caps.

When using public transport, you "touch in" with your card on a yellow card reader, and the corresponding amount is deducted. On Underground, DLR and Overground trains, you must also remember to "touch out" where you finish your journey, or you will be charged a maximum fare. Prices are higher during peak times: 6:30–9:30am and 4–7pm Mon–Fri.

Buy Travelcards and Oyster cards at Underground and local rail stations, or any shop that has the TFL "Ticket Stop" sticker in the window. You can also buy them from TFL before arriving; delivery is available to over 60 countries.

The Underground and DLR

The London Underground (commonly referred to as "the Tube") has 12 lines, all named and colour-coded, which intersect at various stations. The construction of an additional line, the Elizabeth line, is currently underway. Due to the phasing of the project, certain sections of the route will be in operation before the full railway is complete in December 2019.

Some lines, like the Jubilee, have a single branch; others, like the Northern, have more than one, so it is important to check the digital boards on the platform and the destination on the front of the train.

Trains run every few minutes 7:30–9:30am and 4–7pm; and every 5–10 minutes at all other times. The Central, Jubilee, Northern, Victoria and Piccadilly lines offer a 24-hour service on Fridays and Saturdays. All other lines operate 5am–12:40am Mon–Sat; 7am–11:40pm Sun.

The DLR (Docklands Light Railway) is an Overground network of driverless trains that run towards East London to Greenwich, Excel, Docklands, the O2, and London City Airport. It operates 5:30–12:30am Mon–Sat; 7am–11:30pm Sun, with trains departing every 3 minutes.

Stations with disabled access are marked on Tube maps, which are located on all trains and at every underground station.

The Overground

Marked on Tube maps by an orange line, the Overground connects with the Underground and main railway stations at various points across the city. It operates in much the same way as the Underground, and covers most areas of the city without nearby Underground connections.

Many smaller stations do not have staffed ticket counters, just self-service machines.

Bus

Slower but cheaper than the Tube, buses are also a good way of seeing the city as you travel.

Bus routes are displayed on the TFL website and on maps at bus stops. The destination and route number is indicated on the front of the bus and the stops are announced onboard.

Buses do not accept cash so a ticket, Oyster card or contactless payment is required.

A single fare costs £1.50, while unlimited bus travel caps out at £4.50 – just use the same card each time you use the bus to reach the daily cap.

The hopper fare allows you to make a second bus journey for free within an hour of travel. Travel is free on buses for under-16s as long as they carry a Zip Oyster card. Apply for one on the TFL website at least four weeks before you are due to arrive.

The Night buses (indicated by the letter "N" added before the route number) run on many popular routes from 11pm until 6am, generally 3–4 times per hour up to 2 or 3am. They cost slightly more than regular buses.

Taxis

London's iconic black cabs can be hailed on the street, booked online or over the phone, or picked up at taxi ranks throughout the city. The yellow "Taxi" sign is lit up when the taxi is free. The driver's cab licence number should be displayed in the back of the taxi.

All taxis are metered, and fares will start from around £2.60. Taxi apps such as UBER also operate in London.

The following services can be booked by phone or online:

Dial-a-Cab
w dialacab.co.uk
Gett Taxis
w gett.com/uk/
Licensed London Taxi
w licensedlondontaxi.co.uk

Driving

EU driving licences issued by any of the EU member states are valid throughout the European Union. This situation may change following the UK's departure from the EU. If visiting from outside the EU, you may need to apply for an International Driving Permit. Check with your local automobile association before you travel, or consult the UK Driver and Vehicle Licensing Agency (**DVLA**).

DVLA

Ⓦ dvlaregistrations.direct.gov.uk

Driving in London

Driving in London is not recommended. Traffic is slow moving, parking is scarce and expensive, and in central London there is the added cost of the **Congestion Charge** – an £11.50 daily charge for driving in central London 7am–6pm Mon–Fri.

In the event of an accident, contact the **AA** for roadside assistance.

AA

Ⓦ theaa.com

Congestion Charge

Ⓦ tfl.gov.uk/modes/driving/congestion-charge

Parking

Parking is prohibited at all times wherever the street is marked with double yellow or red lines by the kerb.

If there is a single yellow line, parking is normally allowed from 6:30pm–8am Monday to Saturday and all day Sunday, but exact hours vary, so always check the signs along each street before leaving your vehicle. Where there is no line at all, parking is free at all times, but this is rare in central London. Rental car drivers are still liable for parking fines.

Car Rental

To rent a car in the UK you must be 21 or over (or in some cases, 25) and have held a valid driver's licence for at least a year.

Driving out of central London will take about an hour in any direction, more during rush hours; if you want to tour the countryside, it can be easier to take a train to a town or city outside London and rent a car from there.

Rules of the Road

Drive on the left. Seat belts must be worn at all times by the driver and all passengers. Children up to 135 cm tall or the age 12 or under must travel with the correct child restraint for their weight and size.

Mobile telephones may not be used while driving except with a "handsfree" system, and third party insurance is required by law.

Overtake on the outside or right-hand lane, and when approaching a roundabout, give priority to traffic approaching from the right, unless indicated otherwise. All vehicles must give way to emergency services vehicles.

It is illegal to drive in bus lanes during restricted hours. See signs by the side of the road for restrictions.

The drink-drive limit *(p340)* is strictly enforced.

Cycling

You need a strong nerve to cycle in London's traffic, but it can be a great way to see the city. **Santander Cycles**, London's self-service cycle hire, has docking stations in central London. Bikes can also be rented from the **London Bicycle Tour Company** and other rental companies throughout the city.

Be aware that drink-drive limits *(p340)* also apply to cyclists.

Santander Cycles

Ⓦ tfl.gov.uk/modes/cycling/santander-cycles

London Bicycle Tour Company

Ⓦ londonbicycle.com

Walking

Walking is a rewarding way to get around in London. The centre is not large, and you will be surprised at how short the distance is between places that seem far apart on the Tube.

Boats and Ferries

Car ferries from Calais arrive in Dover, around 1 hour 50 minutes' drive from London.

Passenger and car-ferry services also sail from other ports in northern France to the south of England, as well as from Bilbao and Santander in Spain to Portsmouth or Plymouth.

Ferry services also run to other ports around the country from the Netherlands and the Republic of Ireland.

London by Boat

Some of London's most spectacular views can be seen from the River Thames.

MBNA Thames Clippers runs river services every 20 minutes on catamarans between Westminster and North Greenwich or Woolwich in both directions, via the London Eye, Bankside and Tower Bridge.

The Tate Boat, or RB2, is also operated by MBNA Thames Clippers and runs between the Tate Britain and Tate Modern museums. Oyster cards can be used on board, and Travelcard holders get discounted tickets. The Tate Members discount is available when buying tickets from the Tate, or at a self-service kiosk on a pier. It is not available when using an oyster or contactless credit or debit card.

A number of providers offer river tours and experiences on the Thames. Hop-on-hop-off services, themed cruises, dining experiences and sightseeing tours with commentaries are just a few of the options available.

MBNA Thames Clippers

Ⓦ thamesclippers.com

River Tours

Ⓦ tfl.gov.uk/modes/river/about-river-tours

PRACTICAL
INFORMATION

A little local know-how goes a long way in London. Here you will find all the essential advice and information you will need during your stay.

Personal Security

Pickpockets work crowded tourist areas. Use your common sense and be alert to your surroundings. If you are unfortunate enough to have anything stolen, report the crime as soon as possible to the nearest police station. Get a copy of the crime report in order to claim on your insurance.

Contact your embassy if you have your passport stolen, or in the event of a serious crime or accident.

Health

For minor ailments go to a pharmacy or chemist. These are plentiful throughout the city; chains such as Boots and Superdrug have branches in almost every shopping district or in the city.

If you have an accident or medical problem requiring non-urgent medical attention, you can find details of your nearest non-emergency medical service on the NHS website (p335). Alternatively, you can call the NHS 24 helpline number at any hour on 111, or go to your nearest Accident and Emergency (A&E) department.

You may need a doctor's prescription to obtain certain pharmaceuticals; the pharmacist can inform you of the closest doctor's surgery or medical centre where you can be seen by a GP (General Practitioner).

EU citizens can receive emergency medical treatment in the UK free of charge (p335), however this situation may change following the UK's departure from the European Union.

Visitors from outside the EU may have to pay upfront for medical treatment and reclaim on insurance at a later date.

Smoking, Alcohol and Drugs

The UK has a smoking ban in all public places, including bars, cafés, restaurants, public transport, train stations and hotels.

The UK legal limit for drivers is 80 mg of alcohol per 100 ml of blood, or 0.08 per cent BAC (blood alcohol content). This is roughly equivalent to one small glass of wine or a pint

of regular strength lager, however it is best to avoid drinking altogether if you plan to drive.

The possession of illegal drugs is prohibited and could result in a prison sentence.

ID

There is no requirement for visitors to carry ID, but in the case of a routine check you may be asked to show your passport and visa documentation. It is always useful to carry a photocopy of your passport ID page.

Local Customs

Always stand to the right on escalators or stairwells. Allow passengers to exit before you board public transport. On the Tube, it is customary to offer your seat to passengers who are less able-bodied, pregnant or elderly.

Visiting Churches and Cathedrals

Dress respectfully: cover your torso and upper arms. Ensure shorts and skirts cover your knees.

Mobile Phones and Wi-Fi

Free Wi-Fi hotspots are widely available in the city centre. Cafés and restaurants will give you their Wi-Fi password on the condition that you make a purchase.

Visitors travelling to the UK with EU tariffs are able to use their devices abroad without being affected by data roaming charges. Users will be charged the same rates for data, SMS services and voice calls as they would pay at home. This situation may change once the UK has left the EU.

Post

Standard post in the UK is handled by the Royal Mail. There are Royal Mail post office branches located throughout London, which are generally open from 9am–5:30pm Monday to Friday and until 12:30pm on Saturday.

You can buy 1st class, 2nd class and international stamps in post offices, shops and supermarkets. Distinctive red post boxes are located on main streets throughout the city.

Taxes and Refunds

VAT (Value Added Tax) is charged at 20% and almost always included in the marked price. Stores offering tax-free shopping display a distinctive sign and (for non-EU residents) will provide you with a VAT 407 form to validate when you leave the country.

Discount Cards

London can be a very expensive city, but there a number of ways in which sightseeing costs can be reduced. Students and under-18s pay lower admission to many exhibitions, and holders of an ISIC (International Student Identity Card) or IYTC (International Youth Travel Card) are eligible for a range of other discounts.

A number of visitor passes and discount cards are available online and from participating tourist offices. These cards are not free, so consider carefully how many of the offers you are likely to take advantage of before purch-asing. For a full list of the options available, consult the **Visit London** website.

One such card is the **London City Pass**, which offers free entry to more than 80 of the city's top attractions in the city, money-off selected tours and discounts in participating shops and restaurants, with the option of adding unlimited travel to the package.

The London City Pass
W londonpass.com
Visit London
W visitlondon.com

INDEX

Page numbers in **bold** refer
to main entries

ACKNOWLEDGMENTS

DK Travel would like to thank the following people whose help and assistance contributed to the preparation of this book

Karissa Adams, Adam Brackenbury, Elizabeth Byrne, James Davis, Sarah Dennis, Matt Dobbin, Bridget Fuller, Pauline Giacomelli-Harris, Meryl Halls, George Hamilton-Jones, Catherine Hetherington, Debbie James, Tom Morse, Chris Rushby, Mike Sansbury

Cartographic Data ERA-Maptec Ltd (Dublin) adapted with permission from original survey and mapping by Shobunsha (Japan)

Photographic Reference The London Aerial Photo Library, and P and P F James

PICTURE CREDITS

Front flap: **123RF.com:** Christian Mueller bl;
4Corners: Alessandro Saffo cb; **Alamy Stock
Photo:** Chris Lawrence cla, Enrico Della Pietra t;
Dreamstime.com: Michal Bednarek br; **Getty
Images:** oversnap cra;

Sheet map cover
Dreamstime.com: Michal Bednarek.

Cover images:
Front and Spine: **Dreamstime.com:** Michal Bednarek.
Back: **Alamy Stock Photo:** Jansos cl; **AWL Images:**
Nadia Isakova c, Alex Robinson tr; **Dreamstime.
com:** Michal Bednarek b.

For further information see: www.dkimages.com

DK | Penguin Random House

Main Contributers Matt Norman,
Michael Leapman, Alice Park

Senior Editor Ankita Awasthi Tröger

Senior Designer Owen Bennett

Project Editor Alice Fewery

Project Art Editors Dan Bailey, Toby Truphet,
Hansa Babra, Ankita Sharma, Priyanka Thakur

Design Assistant William Robinson

Factchecker Darren Longley

Editors Rebecca Flynn, Lucy Sienkowska,
Danielle Watt, Louise Abbott, Natalie Baker

Proofreader Debra Wolter

Indexer Helen Peters

Senior Picture Researcher Ellen Root

Picture Research
Harriet Whitaker, Marta Bescos

Illustrators Brian Delf, Trevor Hill,
Robbie Polley, Ann Child, Gary Cross,
Tim Hayward, Arghya Jyoti Hore,
Fiona M Macpherson, Janos Marffy,
David More, Chris Orr, Richard Phipps,
Rockit Design, Michelle Ross, John Woodcock.

Senior Cartographic Editor Casper Morris

Cartography Andrew Heritage,
Zafar ul Islam Khan, Suresh Kumar,
James Mills-Hicks, John Plumer,
Ashutosh Ranjan Bharti, Deshpal Singh Dabas

Jacket Designers
Maxine Pedliham, Bess Daly

Jacket Picture Research Susie Peachey

Senior DTP Designer Jason Little

DTP Coordinator George Nimmo

Senior Producer Stephanie McConnell

Managing Editor Hollie Teague

Art Director Maxine Pedliham

Publishing Director Georgina Dee

First published in Great Britain in 1993
by Dorling Kindersley Limited,
80 Strand, London, WC2R 0RL

Copyright © 1993, 2018 Dorling Kindersley Limited
A Penguin Random House Company
18 19 20 21 10 9 8 7 6 5 4 3 2 1

A CIP catalogue record for this book
is available from the British Library.
ISBN: 978-0-2413-1183-7

Printed and bound in China.

www.dk.com